African Histories and Modernities

Series Editors
Toyin Falola
The University of Texas at Austin
Austin, USA

Matthew M. Heaton
Virginia Tech
Blacksburg, USA

This book series serves as a scholarly forum on African contributions to and negotiations of diverse modernities over time and space, with a particular emphasis on historical developments. Specifically, it aims to refute the hegemonic conception of a singular modernity, Western in origin, spreading out to encompass the globe over the last several decades. Indeed, rather than reinforcing conceptual boundaries or parameters, the series instead looks to receive and respond to changing perspectives on an important but inherently nebulous idea, deliberately creating a space in which multiple modernities can interact, overlap, and conflict. While privileging works that emphasize historical change over time, the series will also feature scholarship that blurs the lines between the historical and the contemporary, recognizing the ways in which our changing understandings of modernity in the present have the capacity to affect the way we think about African and global histories.

Michel-Pierre Chelini
Philippe Adair • Eveline Baumann
Editors

Wage Dynamics in Africa

Achievements and Challenges

palgrave
macmillan

Editors
Michel-Pierre Chelini
Université d'Artois (Emeritus)
Arras, France

Philippe Adair
Université Paris Est Créteil
Val-de-Marne, France

Eveline Baumann
Université Paris Cité
Paris, France

ISSN 2634-5773 ISSN 2634-5781 (electronic)
African Histories and Modernities
ISBN 978-3-031-99799-0 ISBN 978-3-031-99800-3 (eBook)
https://doi.org/10.1007/978-3-031-99800-3

This Palgrave Macmillan imprint is published by the registered company Springer Nature Switzerland AG.
The registered company address is: Gewerbestrasse 11, 6330 Cham, Switzerland

Preface

Why a Book on African Wages?

The impetus for this book was derived from an observation of a marked divergence between the significance attributed to wages in socioeconomic contexts and the relative lack of attention afforded to research pertaining to African wages.

In today's world, wage earners make up just under half of the working population, and total wages and salaries account around 35% of global GDP. These proportions are not the same in all countries. In North America, Western Europe and Japan, wage earners account for more than 80% of the working population, and total wages and salaries account for about half of GDP. In Africa, wage earners represent a quarter of the working population with sharp contrasts between countries (e.g. less than 5% in Niger and more than 80% in Mauritius), and wages and salaries account for between 15% and 20% of GDP. However, this situation of inadequate wages does not appear to have been the subject of much scholarly attention, and wages do not seem to constitute a major issue in the available analyses of the African economy.

In general, we can see that the development of salaried employment is both effect and cause of economic growth. To some extent, the relative importance of salaried employment reflects the standard of living in a country's economy, even with the emergence of newer forms of so-called individual neo-entrepreneurship on platforms. In the context of Western Europe, it is evident that since the 2000s, wage growth has constituted approximately one-third of GDP growth, primarily through demand and consumption by salaried households. Once a certain level of savings has been attained, salaried households allocate the majority of their income to the consumption of goods and services. In Western countries, the final consumption of households, comprising both salaried and non-salaried individuals, constitutes approximately 50% of GDP. When examining the consumption of salaried households exclusively, the figure persists at a substantial 40% of GDP. This contributes positively to economic growth, which in turn serves as the source of their increasing remuneration. It is notable that these proportions are lower in Africa.

The contemporary socioeconomic landscape is characterised by two distinct terms for the concept of remuneration: “wage” and “salary”. These terms are employed in both advanced and emerging economies. Historically, in the United Kingdom and Europe, particularly during the Industrial Revolution in the nineteenth century, wages were typically disbursed on a daily, weekly or fortnightly basis to manual workers, whose numbers had increased in response to the expansion of factories and workshops. Conversely, the term “salary” was used to denote remuneration for those engaged in clerical or civil service roles, as well as for military personnel at all levels. The increased prevalence of the term “wage” can be attributed to the advent of industrialisation, which led to the emergence of the term “wage-owner” in English around 1870.

Subsequently, there was a decline in the population of manual workers from the 1960s and the 1970s, while the population of employees experienced a sharp increase, leading to the incorporation of office, service and commercial employees into the general category of “employees”. The monthly payment of wages to industrial workers served to mitigate these differences. The term “salary” has gradually encompassed all workers, employees, middle managers and senior managers, and more or less included “wages”. This development has occurred in different countries and across various socio-professional spheres. At this juncture, the two words have become largely interchangeable. However, this does not appear to be a universal phenomenon, which necessitates caution when employing both terms simultaneously.

The extant literature on the history, dynamics and future of wages remains, for the time being, limited in volume. It is noteworthy that two recent publications may be of relevance to the subject. One of these is an extensive study of labour in Africa in general, although it does not include a chapter on wages (Bellucci & Eckert, 2019), the other as a specific publication on wages in Africa (ILO, 2019). Otherwise, there are mainly a number of articles in specialised journals. The focus of these articles is geographically narrower, with examples including one or more countries, one or more sectors or a broader approach that includes Africa in a specific global issue such as the gender pay gap. The issue of salaries in Africa is still under investigation. Statistical data prior to 1990–2000 are incomplete and the literature on the subject remains limited.

The present volume does not profess to be exhaustive, as would be found in a complete catalogue or an encyclopaedia of African wages, nor is it a thematic handbook of applied African economics. The **objective of the present study** is to examine the salient characteristics of the African labour market, including the mean level and dispersion of wages, the predominant wage disparities (such as qualification, age, gender, region, company size and productivity of sectors) and the minimum wage policies.

The overarching objective of this study is to evaluate the significance of wages in the expansion trend of African economic growth, with a particular focus on their increasing role in the post-independence era.

The approach to wages is intended to be as comprehensive as possible from three main perspectives: the economics of wages, the sociology of wages and wage policies. The present book attempts to be the first historical, economic and sociological synthesis on the theme of wages in Africa from the 1960s on, supposing a better detailed knowledge of African historical statistics, especially wages and standard of living.

These perspectives are also to be considered in relation to the historical evolution of wages, which can then serve as a starting point for a prospective sketch of the future of wages in Africa and its role for growth. To be more precise, the issue under discussion is the divergence of the African labour market from the international evolution after the years 1960s–1980s: it did not exactly follow, e.g. the emerging model of the Asian countries, like the Four Dragons and then China, in the third phase of globalisation.

This choice of demonstration excludes some important components of the wage definition, thus maintaining an analysis centred on wages rather than on a more in-depth and detailed examination of the labour market (see Chap. 3, *Wages and Economic Development*). The chapter's principal focus is on theories and models; however, it is important to note that the text does not delve into an elaborate theoretical discussion of the supply of labour by the individual and family, labour demand, market equilibrium, human capital investment, etc. Conversely, the subject of labour supply, human capital and job mobility is addressed in Chap. 13, "Rising Labour

Market Segmentation in Egypt over 2012–2018: Youth Informal Employment is Prominent".

Similarly, the book cannot cover all the labour relations (See Jirjahn, 2025; Essen et al., 2024) and policies, with various models of dispute resolution, theories of labour movement and industrial strike actions, and political and institutional constraints to collective bargaining process. The question is addressed in several chapters of the publication, albeit in a scattered manner and via allusions (Chaps. 2, 5, and 9), and does not constitute the central subject of the publication as a whole. A similar approach would be required for any discussion of the novel trends observed in the African labour market, including but not limited to, contract work platforms such as Uber and the development of delivery activities.

Methodologically, the book consists of 16 chapters divided into four parts: "Overview of Wage Issues", "Wage Dispersion and Inequalities", "Wage Determinants" and "Wage Gaps". The study encompasses the entire continent, which will be divided into its five regions (Central, Northern, Western, Eastern and Southern Africa) according to the 1976 OAU definition. Nevertheless, it is not feasible to mention every region systematically in each of the analysed points, nor to cover all 55 African Union countries. The book will examine the main wage issues, such as the importance of informal work or the gender wage gap, by presenting some representative examples. Looking at labour issues in such a wide range of countries proved to be a valuable asset for the entire African continent and its sub-regions. Our coverage of African countries, is consistent, extended and diversified: from west to east, Senegal and Cameroon are covered twice and, together with Kenya, make up sub-Saharan Africa, while Egypt, Tunisia, Morocco and Mauritania belong to North Africa. Two chapters cite other countries, thereby increasing the geographical coverage of the analysis. Specifically, Chap. 2 ("Long-Term Wage Issues in Africa"), notably through the use of comparative tables, mentions also Seychelles, Rwanda, Burkina Faso, Mauritius, Botswana, Sudan, Ghana and Zambia. Chapter 5 ("Emerging Countries in Africa and Wage Dynamics") focuses explicitly on six other countries: South Africa, Kenya, Nigeria, Egypt, Ethiopia, and Morocco. Otherwise, it is worth noting that Johnson-Lans (2017) focuses only on four countries in East Africa (South Africa, Nigeria, Tanzania and Uganda) with regard to gender and racial wage differentials and the contribution of human capital (education and experience) to such differentials.

With the exception of some references to rentier states like Nigeria, e.g., analyses of such states have been partially eschewed because of their specificity. It is evident that a number of African countries are reliant on natural resources and consequently exhibit a rentier economy. Since the seminal work of Beblawi and Luciani (1987), the term "rentier state" has been utilised to denote a state that derives the bulk of its national income from rents paid by individuals, companies or foreign governments on the trade with natural resources. This is evident in the case of Algeria, Angola, Gabon, Ghana or Nigeria, which derive significant revenue from the export of oil. Additionally, iron ore from Mauritania and copper from Zambia are also notable examples of rentier situations, despite the minerals market's comparatively less volatile and significant nature compared to that of oil since the 1960s.

According to Ricardo (1817), rents differ from wages in that they are received without the necessity of labour and are regarded as "a reward for the ownership of a resource, the gift of nature". These rentier states have been observed to engage in the collection of income without concomitant enhancement of the productivity of the national economy or the political development of the state, through the imposition of taxes on citizens in order to develop public services, infrastructures and education institutions. This phenomenon is often referred to as the "curse of natural resources",[1] which occurs when a country's economic and political growth is stunted due to the focus on extracting and consuming these natural resources. Nevertheless, it is important to acknowledge the potential benefits of this phenomenon. For instance, Botswana's economy flourished following the discovery of diamond deposits in the 1980s,[2] a development that enabled the country to exit the list of less developed countries (LDCs).

[1] This phenomenon is frequently referred to as the "curse of raw materials" or "Dutch disease". The term "Dutch disease" was first coined to describe the unexpected surge in gas revenues experienced by the Netherlands during the 1960s and 1970s. This period was characterised by a tendency to reduce investment in domestic industry. The rise in export revenues led to the appreciation of the currency, while in other sectors, exports became less competitive compared to imports.

[2] Initially classified as a less developed country upon independence in 1966, it has since become one of the most prosperous countries on the continent, with a growth rate of 9% between 1970 and 2000. The country's mineral wealth, particularly diamonds (the third largest producer in the world), copper and nickel, has become a significant driver of this growth, but the prudent management of a stable, competent and corruption-free administration was just as important. Nevertheless, the risk of mining mono-industry persists. In 2023,

For the African continent, the **issue of statistical data** remains of significance. For further details, please refer to Sect. 2.1: "Collecting Salary Statistics" (Chap. 2). The International Labour Organization (ILO) website contains limited online data on African wages from 1995 to 2000, although the ILO is currently digitising and formatting its archives to include older data. The most reliable source of information on wages in various occupations is the ILO October survey, which has been conducted on an annual basis since 1924. However, it is important to note that the reliability of this data for African countries is limited before independence and even before the 1980s for some countries. The majority of African countries do not conduct independent wage surveys. Since 2017, the ILO has made significant efforts to collect data in approximately 25 African countries, covering around 84% of the continent's employees and 91% of total employee compensation on the continent from 2007 to 2017.

The collection of wage data is typically conducted through administrative records, such as social security forms and single treasury accounts, which often impede the extraction of detailed wage data. Wage documentation in advanced countries is specifically found in labour force surveys, household surveys, regular censuses and living standards measurement studies. However, African microdata are not widely available (see Chap. 6. "Top Expenditure Distribution in North Africa and Middle East Countries and the Inequality Puzzle" and in Tunisia, see Chap. 10). This is evidenced by the paucity of microdata in academic literature, with the exception of a few notable dissertations. A similar scarcity of microdata is observed in household surveys, with the ILO 2024 report highlighting the limited availability of such data sources. Egypt is a notable exception, with microdata being utilised in Chap. 13. While World Bank household surveys are considered convenient, their coverage remains uneven. For the continent as a whole, it is challenging to go beyond the ILO reports (ILO, 2024b).

From 1980 to 2023, the average annual inflation rate across the African continent was 7.5%, while the global average was 5.6% (World Bank database).[3] Nominal values, which represent the economy's current state,

it is estimated that diamond-related industries will account for approximately one-third of GDP.

[3] World Bank Database. Indeed, the initial dates of the chronology are not precisely congruent, and the subsets occasionally overlap. However, over a period of 50 years, these chronological and geographical disparities tend to diminish in significance. The African regions, namely the Eastern and Southern region (10.2%, 1974–2023), the Western and Central region (4.6%, 1981–2023), the Middle East and North Africa (5.3%, 1970–2023), and the Sub-Saharan Africa (8.1%, 1975–2023), are to be compared to the average world inflation rate (5.6%, 1981–2023).

and constant values, which provide a reference point to analyse the evolution of the real value, excluding inflation, are both important socioeconomic indicators. Both values are deemed significant and must be considered in conjunction with each other. Our work frequently cites both types of value; the most detailed presentation of the choice of wage values is in Sect. 3.1: "Average Gross Wage: Monthly or Annual? Current or Constant?" (Chap. 2). The same applies to GDP per capita at current prices and constant GDP per capita in 2011 international dollars[4] presented in Sect. 3.3: "A Little Rise in Wage Growth" (Chap. 2).

Concurrently, both values remain approximate. Since 1960, there have been substantial changes in the national consumer price indices of African countries. These changes have included shifts in weightings towards industrial products and services, and a transformation in product quality. To illustrate this point, consider the evolution from a fixed "telephone" in 1960 towards a mobile "smartphone" in 2020; the former is by no means equivalent to the latter. It is important to note that the correction by the price index does not solve all the problems related to the evolution of income and consumption. In the realm of wage-related developments, notable shifts have been observed, including the augmentation of the workforce since the 1960s, the emergence of novel sectors, the escalation in educational attainment and the development of trade unionism and collective bargaining.

The concept of "purchasing power" of wages is inherently complex and challenging to define with precision. The concept of evaluating the purchasing power of a wage in relation to a basket of goods and services is intriguing, as the equivalent of $100 in Johannesburg, South Africa, does not possess the same purchasing power as $100 in Nouakchott, Mauritania. The International Labour Organization has compiled a table of average

[4] The international dollar is not a genuine currency; rather, it is a unit of account that possesses equivalent purchasing power in a given country as the US dollar in the United States at a specified time. This concept is also referred to as the Geary-Khamis dollar, as it was initially developed in 1958 by Roy C. Geary, and subsequently refined between 1970 and 1972 by Salem Hanna Khamis. The University of Pennsylvania subsequently adopted the method to publish comparable statistics between countries on the gross domestic product and its components (Penn World Tables).The Geary-Khamis method employs two joint approaches: the construction of an "international price" for each material/commodity and a purchasing power parity for each country. When comparing living standards between countries, it is more reliable to compare gross domestic product per capita in Geary-Khamis dollars rather than exchange rates, which can vary significantly from year to year without affecting living standards.

gross monthly wages for approximately 30 African countries (ILO, 2024c) expressed in dollars on the one hand and in purchasing power parity (PPP) on the other. This data is utilised in an attempt to map average African wages in this Foreword. Associative or private organisations, such as Salary Explorer or the WageIndicator Foundation, offer more detailed wage statistics provided by employees, unions and companies themselves, with downstream consistency checking work.

What Are the Main Characteristics of African Wages?

While the African labour market shares similarities with other labour markets in the world, it also has some unique characteristics. For instance, only 27% of workers are employees, two-thirds of whom work in the informal economy.

According to the latest data collected and published by the ILO (ILO, 2024b, Excel file), the average annual growth in wages in Africa (out of 40 states) would be 2.4% between 2000 and 2022/2023. Eleven countries, constituting approximately one-quarter of the sample, exhibited negative growth rates ranging from −1% to −3% (like Algeria, Angola, Ghana, Kenya, Madagascar, Rwanda, Nigeria, Togo). In contrast, approximately 20 countries documented an average increase in wages between 0.5% and 3% (like Chad, Egypt, Ethiopia, Gabon, Mali, Mauritius, Morocco, Mozambique and South Africa) and approximately 10, another quarter, exceed 5% growth, though frequently with multi-year catch-up waves, which are then succeeded by periods of stagnation or even decline (like Benin, Burundi, Democratic Republic of Congo, Liberia, Zambia, Zimbabwe).

ILO notes (ILO, 2024b:17): "This is the region where wages performed the worst over the last decade, according to estimates based on available data. Since 2015, real wage growth in Africa has been either negative or very modest, and the most recent years are no exception". The ensuing tables, drawn from the most recent ILO *Global Wage Report* (2024b:14–17), encompass the period from 2006 to 2024. Africa exhibits the most deficient performance with regard to bi-decadal wage progression, with virtually zero annual growth, which aggregates to a 3% annual increase between 2006 and 2013 and a −3% annual decline between 2014 and 2024. In contrast, the other continents or geoeconomic areas defined by the UN have demonstrated comparatively superior performance, with North America and the European Union (between 1.5% and 2% per annum), the Arab States (2%), Latin America (2% to 2.5%), and two groups exhibiting a more rapid growth: the Asia-Pacific region (3% to 4%, excluding China) and Central and Western Asia (5%) (Figs. 0.1 and 0.2).

Wage growth in Africa has been slow since the 1990s, with the exception of countries such as Botswana or Mauritius, where it has been particularly rapid (mining, tourism). According to the ILO (2024a), over a decade (2013–2022), real wages have fallen or stagnated in several of the countries studied: Egypt (−49.1%), Tunisia (−1.2%), Morocco (0.0%) and Kenya (0.8%). This is due to inflation during the COVID-19 pandemic and a change in the relative share of formal and informal employment associated with an increase in wage inequality, as in Egypt, where informal employment increased over a decade.

Africa stands out as a region of extreme income inequality, with the top 10% having an income share of 55% and the bottom 50% less than 10% of the overall income (Chancel et al., 2023). Significant wage inequality persists due to a variety of factors, ranging from the dominance of the

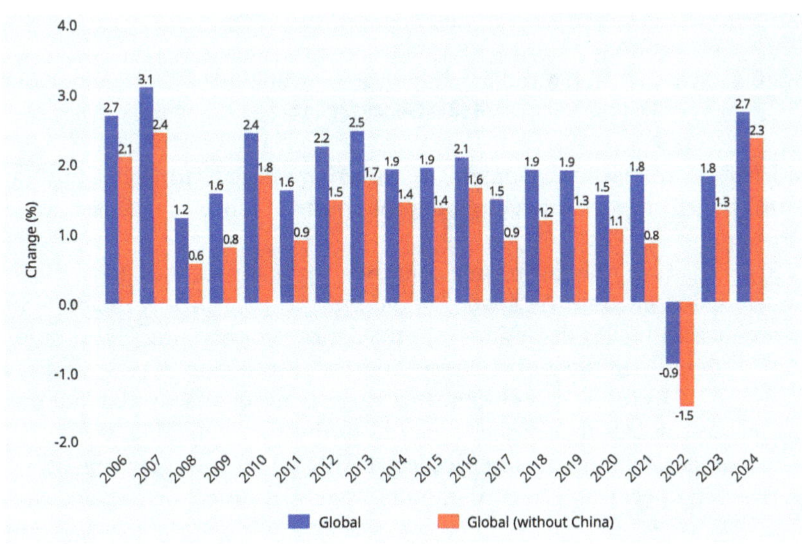

Fig. 0.1 Average global real monthly wage growth 2006–2024. Source: ILO (2024), *Global Wage Report, 2024–25*, Geneva, p. 14

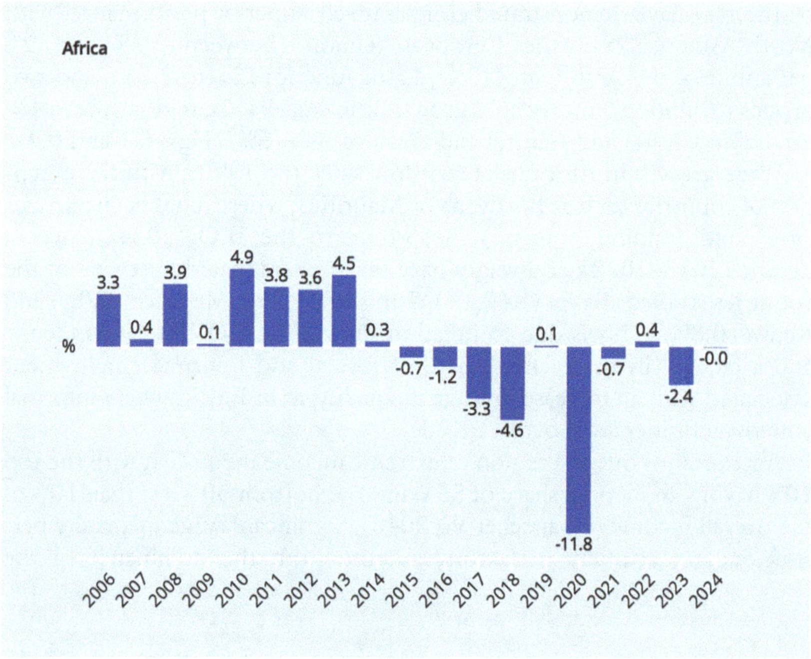

Fig. 0.2 Average African real monthly wage growth 2006–2024. Source: ILO (2024), *Global Wage Report, 2024–25*, Geneva, p. 15

informal sector, where women are overrepresented, to socio-cultural norms that foster discrimination, and often the absence of standard wage bargaining.

In comparison to high-income countries, inequality is, in general, much higher in low-income or lower-middle-income countries (categories in accordance with ILO definitions). In the African context, the Palma ratio[5] is situated between the global average indices (4 to 6) and the high indices (12 to 16). However, it is evident that there is an increase in the index as one moves towards the southern regions of the continent (Fig. 0.3).

In a similar manner, the interdecile gap D9/D1, that is, between higher salaries (engineer) and the minimum wage (labourer), is significantly

[5]The Palma ratio, as defined by Gabriel Palma, a Chilean economist, is a measure of inequality before tax. It is calculated by dividing the share received by the richest 10% by the share of the poorest 40%. Higher values indicate higher levels of inequality.

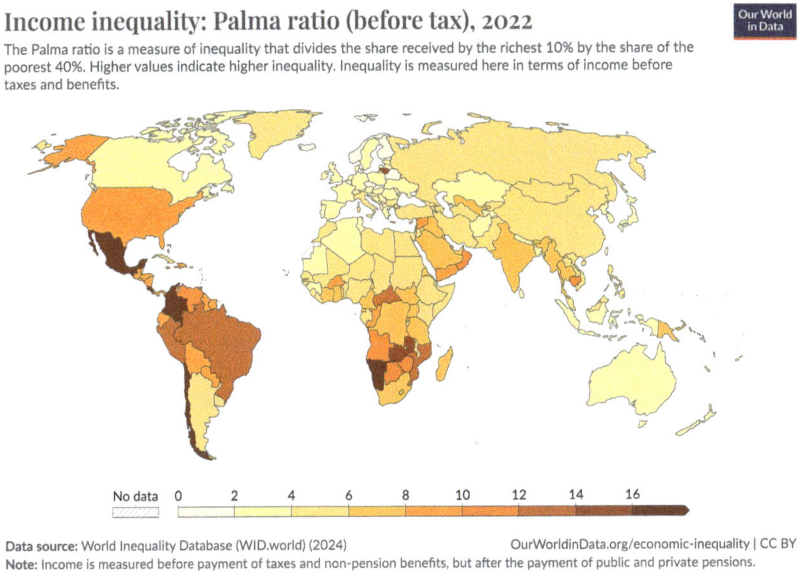

Fig. 0.3 Global Palma ratio in 2022, Africa above world average. Source: World Inequality Database, 2024

higher in Africa, where the majority of countries are in the low-income (D9/D1: 12.2) and lower-middle income countries (9.6), than in the high-income countries (3.4). In emerging countries, more or less new sectors such as IT and finance have given way to a pyramidal wage structure, characterised by a significant presence of low-income employees and a comparatively smaller number of average-income employees. In advanced countries, the wage structure assumes a more complex, spinning top-like shape, with a smaller proportion of high- and low-wage workers and a larger proportion of average wage earners, thereby reducing the overall wage gap. It is evident that as countries progress and prosper, the disparity between high and low salaries diminishes, despite variations observed between the American continent (4 to 5), Europe and Japan (3). In Africa, the figures are considerably higher, with Namibia (31), Tanzania (22), Kenya or Botswana (18), Nigeria (15), Madagascar (11) and a limited number of countries falling below the global average (7.5), such as the Republic of Congo (6) (Fig. 0.4).

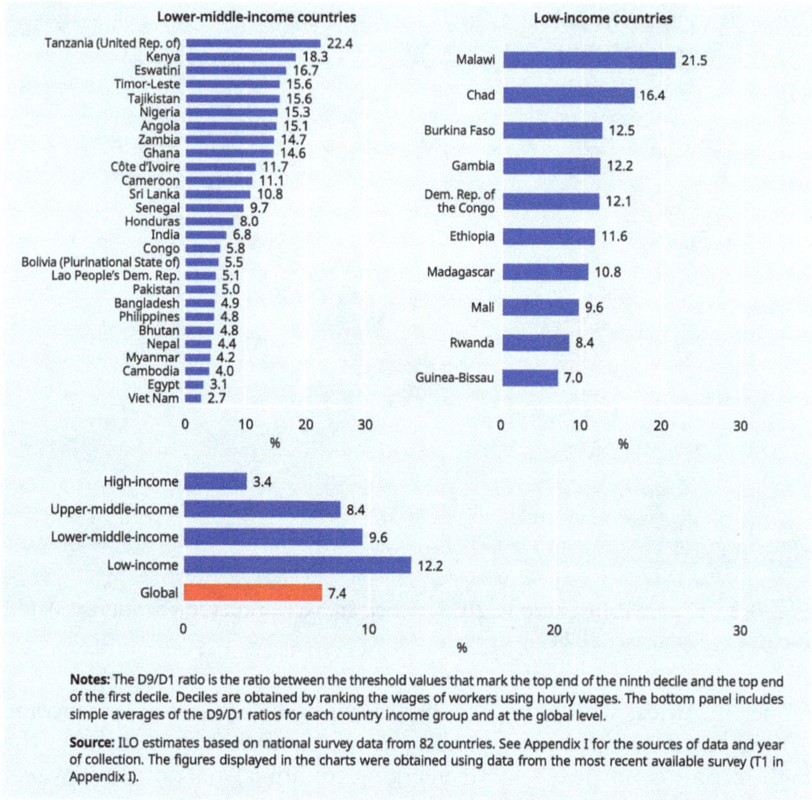

Fig. 0.4 Interdecile D9/D1 gap according to the global income countries classification (2022). Source: ILO (2024), *Global Wage Report, 2024–25*, Geneva, p. 41

In sub-Saharan Africa, the ILO reports that the median monthly income of men is more than twice that of women, and the income of female entrepreneurs is on average only two-thirds of that of male entrepreneurs (Diagana, 2022). The pay gap is higher in the informal and self-employed sectors. Much of the gap remains unexplained by worker and job characteristics, reflecting pervasive labour market discrimination against women. Sector, occupation and firm selection and human capital differences account for most of the explained wage gap (Abegaz & Nene, 2022).

The dominant employment status in low-income countries is that of non-wage workers, such as own-account and contributing family workers—the majority of whom are women—who earn little, while wage workers are mostly in the top half of the labour income distribution. Comparing formal and informal employment, the data show that formal wage employment is in the upper half of the labour income distribution. In contrast, own-account workers are overwhelmingly in informal employment and mostly in the lower half of the labour income distribution (ILO, 2024b).

How large is informal employment in Africa? As of year 2019, a sketchy comparison between five countries surveyed in the book (See Fig. 0.5) shows that informal employment affects over four out of five workers outside agriculture in Mauritania, Senegal and Kenya, whereas the share is almost three out of five workers in Egypt and almost one-third in Tunisia (ILOSTAT). Employment in agriculture being almost entirely informal is excluded, in accordance with the recommendation of the Delhi Group of experts (UN Statistical Commission, 2008). A sound basis for comparison is to use Labour Force Surveys (LFS), a standardised framework designed

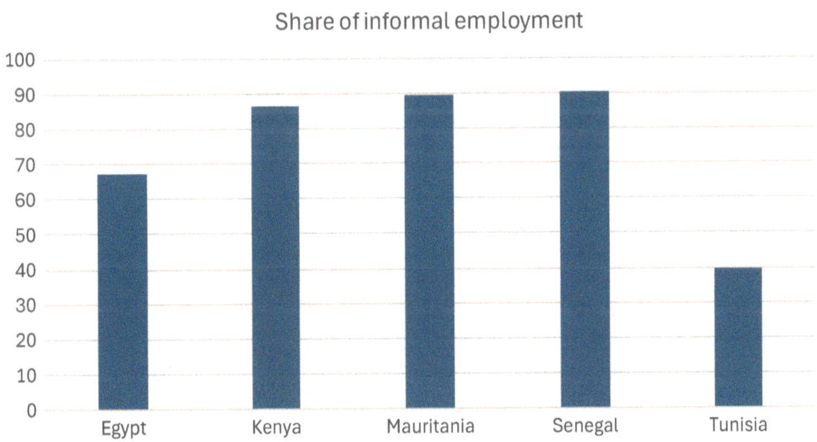

Fig. 0.5 The share of informal employment in total employment as of 2019: Several countries of interest. *Notes*: Non-agriculture employment. *Household Survey. **Labour Force Survey (LFS). No data for Cameroon in 2019. Morocco does not disclose LFS data to the ILO. *Source*: Sustainable Development Goal (SDG) indicator 8.3.1. dataset (ILOSTAT)

by the International Labour Office (ILO), whereas household surveys designed by the World Bank may focus on a larger definition of income.

It is acknowledged that, despite the persistence of significant global inequalities, particularly the perception of an increase among the affluent, the ILO observes a small decline in wage disparities between 2000 and 2022;[6] it attributes this decline to the average enrichment of households, which significantly increases the number of the middle-class households ("averaging effect"), and to the policies of decent work, which institutionalise the labour market in favour of the wage earner status ("salarisation effect").

Quantitative research on unions and collective bargaining with respect to sub-Saharan Africa, although quite sporadic, has been recently improving. Noteworthy is that extended informal employment is a serious challenge to workers' unionisation, which is also affected by ethnic divide undermining social cohesion. Hence, unionisation is limited to the small layer of formal employees in the private and public sectors. Unions exert some influence on wage determination. Within firms, according to modest evidence, unions play a protective role in enforcing labour regulations. A large literature survey documents that unions foster wage premium, which ranges from a weak share in Kenya to a substantial one in Ghana. However, a case study suggests that there is a wage penalty for union membership in Cameroon (Jirjahn, 2025).

The study yielded three primary conclusions. Firstly, a positive correlation was identified between the growth of wage employment and that of GDP: an increase in the number of wage earners corresponds to greater growth, and greater growth corresponds to an increase in the number of wage earners. Secondly, the boundary between formal and informal businesses and jobs appears to be shifting towards the future decline of the informal economy. This process of wage institutionalisation frequently coincides with periods of economic growth, the necessity to export, the payment of taxes, or the raising of capital; it is clearly advantageous for wage earners, as well as for society and the economy in general. Thirdly, the study identified that wage dispersion on the continent is relatively

[6] "Inequalities are found to be decreasing as the country income level increases, with all inequality measures being at their highest among low-income countries and at their lowest among high-income countries" (ILO, 2024b, p. 62). "The decrease in wage inequality, combined with an increase of about 36 per cent in the global real average wage over the last 20 years, is encouraging and also reflected in the significant progress that has been made in reducing working poverty since the beginning of the century" (ILO 2024b:99).

high, with significant disparities between deciles, a high Gini coefficient and important skill differentials within the workforce. It is noteworthy, however, that the gender wage gap aligns with the global average of approximately 15%. In Africa, the underrepresentation of women in the formal labour market is evident in the female labour force rate of 33%, compared to a global average of 40%. Although women hold qualifications comparable to those of their male counterparts, they are frequently overrepresented in the labour market prior to the age of 30, a period after which marriage and motherhood typically occur. Furthermore, they are concentrated in low-paid but stable sectors such as public administration and social services.

Epilogue: The Future of African Wages

The economic and demographic capacity of the African continent offers significant potential. The development of wage policies, frequently initiated from a minimum wage framework, is a notable and emergent trend towards the formalisation of specific sectors of the informal economy. It is anticipated that the subsequent generation of workers (2020–2060) will be both more numerous and better skilled, and will be entitled to a broader array of social benefits.

Whilst the target audience of the book is primarily academics, students (in economics, economic history, sociology or postcolonial studies) and practitioners such as human resources managers or Labour inspectors, it can also be directed towards other types of audiences interested in the role of wages as regards major income issues (distribution, negotiation, inequalities or dispersion of waged income). The fields of study are quite broad, given that wages are a multimodal reality linking many socioeconomic and sociopolitical subjects such as economic and social history, wage and social policies, changes in the standard of living, African international migration, the economics and sociology of work, and also the qualification of the workforce.

In addition, a prospective reflection on the long-term evolution until 2050 is provided, which lends credence to the hypothesis that the future for African salaried work may be positive. The study proffers an analysis of prospective developments in African wage history, encompassing a range of scenarios with variable potential outcomes. These include an increase in the importance and diversity of qualifications, the institutionalisation of the labour market and professional relations, a decline in the informal sector, a greater participation of women and young people in the workforce, and a higher regional or local economic growth.

The evolution of work in Africa in the future may be exemplified by platform capitalism and online gig work. Labour relations are currently undergoing far-reaching changes triggered by digital technology. Indeed, against a backdrop of accelerating connectivity, market economy has given rise to platform capitalism. Digital platforms play a pivot role in facilitating interactions, transactions and services between different user groups (Vallas & Schor, 2020). These platforms are either location based, which means that they allocate work that is tangible (e-commerce, retail platforms) and/or delivered (ride hailing, food delivery, domestic care), or they provide online gig[7] work, which refers to particular tasks such as data entry, image tagging, graphic design, and web development, each particular task being paid. Location-based platform work is visible and can be easily captured by statistics. In contrast, estimating online gig work raises considerable methodological problems. It comes therefore as no surprise that traditional labour market surveys do not capture (online) gig work, neither in terms of workers nor of pay.

According to estimates provided by the World Bank, between 4.4% and 12.5% of the global labour force is employed by approximately 550 online gig platforms worldwide (Datta et al., 2023). Whilst the platform capitalism is traditionally propelled by countries of the Global North, an increasing number of poor-income countries are currently setting up local platforms, the forerunners in Africa being Nigeria, South Africa, Kenya and Egypt. What is more, whereas between 2016 and 2020, job postings on one of the largest digital labour platforms increased by only 14% in North America, the growth rate was 130% in sub-Saharan Africa and 100% in the Middle East and North Africa (Datta et al., 2023: Chapter 3).

As regards the supply side, the abundant and flexible labour force in countries south of the Sahara is undoubtedly a valuable asset for online gig work: it provides numerous work opportunities for youth, women and relatively low-skilled workers, and it is appropriate for students. As to the demand side, online gig work is driven by small-scale companies which are widespread in the Global South. All in all, online gig work is expected to be a powerful leverage for income generation and contributes to decreasing the urban/rural divide and the job availability gap.

[7]The term "gig" is used in the music industry when a musician is paid for a particular performance. By extension, the term refers to an informal job.

However, as regards public policy, online gig work has to overcome competing goals, namely job creation on the one hand, and safeguarding job quality and workers' rights on the other. This is highly problematic insofar as unionisation is as good as inexistent and as, despite the idealisation of digital work (Anwar & Graham, 2021), online gig work resembles entrenched work arrangements characterised by high informality and low levels of social protection (Datta et al., 2023:27; Wood et al., 2023). In Nigeria, for instance, 75% of gig workers do not subscribe to a pension or retirement programme (Datta et al., 2023:3). Put in another way, given the high flexibility of workers and the ubiquity of other income opportunities, platform work—and its shortcomings in terms of labour legislation—is experienced differently in the Global South as compared to highly developed countries. Therefore, only regulations including all types of non-standard employment can be envisaged (Alzate, 2024).

Maps Appendix: Geography of African Wages and Salaries

This preliminary overview of the presentation concludes with a selection of five maps offering a convenient and improvable visualisation of African wages and salaries today, ranging from 2018 to 2024. The initial arrangement of the five maps in a condensed format is intended to provide a general overview of the cartographic demonstration (Fig. 0.6). Each map is then analysed in greater detail in an enlarged format.

These are:

- The initial figure (Fig. 0.7) provides an overview of the average gross monthly wages recorded and published by the ILO in 2021 for 39 states having provided reliable data. The ILO encourages readers to consider these figures with caution and acknowledges the possibility of retrospective revisions in the years to come. In all regions, the prevalence of the informal economy engenders difficulties in the collection of reliable data on real wage income. It is notable that the majority of northern Africa and a significant portion of the central and eastern regions of the continent are not represented. Morocco, Algeria, Nigeria and the Democratic Republic of Congo are not represented in the dataset.

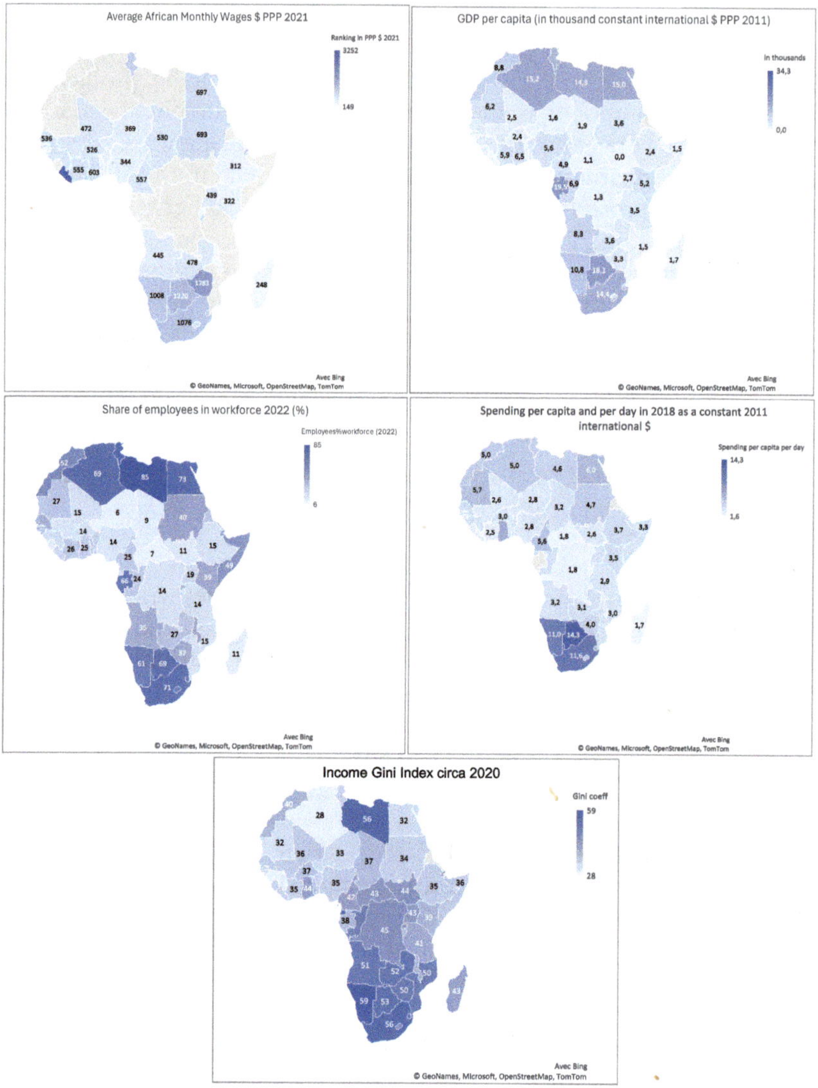

Fig. 0.6 Synopsis view of five continental maps

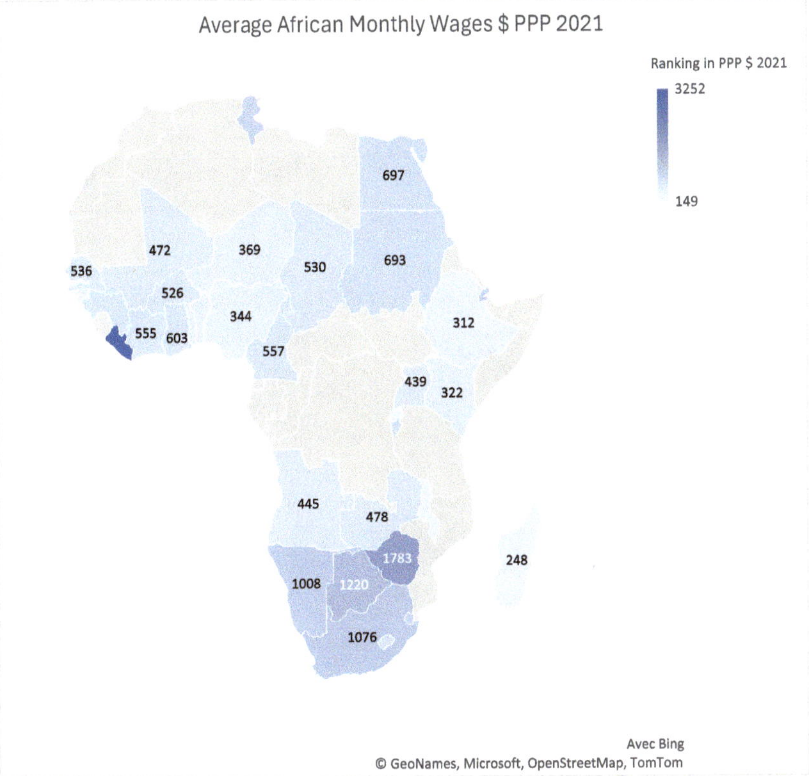

Fig. 0.7 Average African monthly wages $ PPP 2021 (by ILO, 39 states). Source: ILOSTAT, 2024, https://rplumber.ilo.org/data/indicator/?id=EAR_4MTH_SEX_CUR_NB_A&ref_area=AGO+BEN+BWA+BFA+BDI+CMR+CPV+TCD+COM+COG+COD+CIV+DJI+EGY+SWZ+ETH+GMB+GHA+GIN+GNB+KEN+LSO+LBR+MDG+MWI+MLI+MRT+MUS+NAM+NER+NGA+RWA+REU+SHN+SEN+SYC+SLE+ZAF+SDN+TZA+TGO+TUN+UGA+ZMB+ZWE&classif1=CUR_TYPE_PPP&latestyear=TRUE&type=label&format=.xlsx

The following four maps are conducive to enhancing the clarity of the wage situation through their varied and highly complementary approaches:

- The GDP per capita (Fig. 0.8) in constant international $ PPP 2011, which summarily translates the approximative standard of living of the population by taking into account the domestic purchasing power of national currencies. The source also comes from

Fig. 0.8 GDP per capita (in thousand constant international $ PPP 2011). Source: World Bank, series NY.GDP.PCAP.PP.KD, GDP per capita in constant international $ PPP 2011

the World Bank with regular updates. The foundation is anchored in constant value, and in 2011 international dollars, a methodological approach that renders it a robust reference point for the subject under discussion, in distance to the 2008 crisis and the subsequent turnaround in the African economy after 2015.

- The share of employees in the total working population (Fig. 0.9), which varies in Africa from 5% to 85% (!). The series is characterised by a relative good degree of homogeneity, and its currency is ensured by the ILO.
- As demonstrated in Fig. 0.10, the per capita and per day spending in constant 2011 international dollars (excluding non-wage

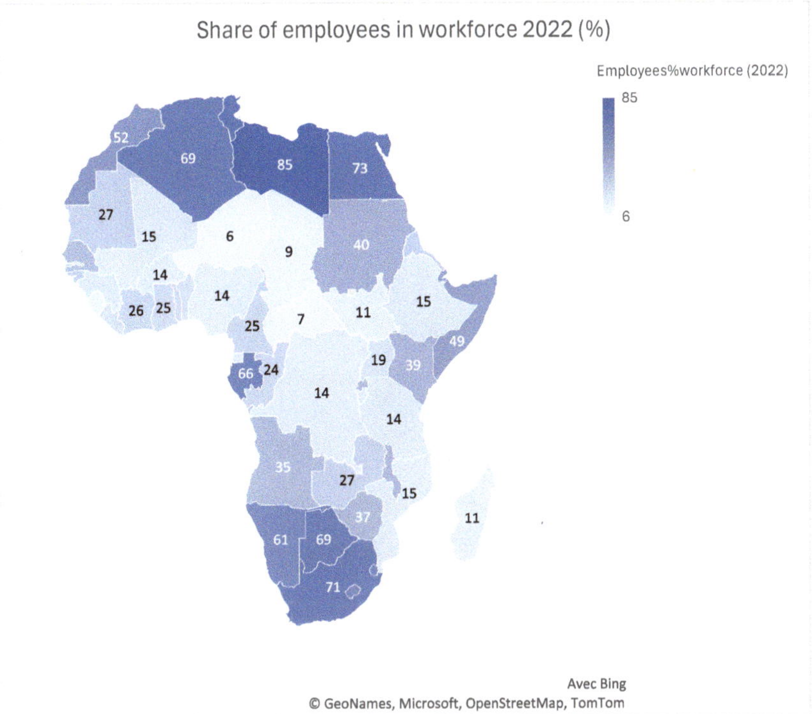

Fig. 0.9 Share of employees in the workforce 2022 (%). Source: ILOSTAT, Employment by status in employment - ILO modelled estimates, Nov. 2023 (%). https://rplumber.ilo.org/data/indicator/?id=EMP_2EMP_SEX_STE_NB_A&ref_area=DZA+AGO+BEN+BWA+BFA+BDI+CMR+CPV+CAF+TCD+COM+COG+COD+CIV+DJI+EGY+GNQ+ERI+SWZ+ETH+GAB+GMB+GHA+GIN+GNB+KEN+LSO+LBR+LBY+MDG+MWI+MLI+MRT+MUS+MAR+MOZ+NAM+NER+NGA+RWA+STP+SEN+SLE+SOM+ZAF+SSD+SDN+TZA+TGO+TUN+UGA+ESH+ZMB+ZWE&sex=SEX_T&classif1=STE_AGGREGATE_TOTAL+STE_AGGREGATE_EES&timeto=2012&type=label&format=.xlsx

income) is a more reliable indicator of economic dynamism, because it is based on observed household expenditure, as well as on secondary types of expenditure by companies, administrations and foreign economic actors (by sample surveys). The source is a private company (ATLAS.ti), initially a software company based in Berlin, founded in 1999 and then acquired in 2024 by Lumivero. The company's area of expertise lies in the development of analyti-

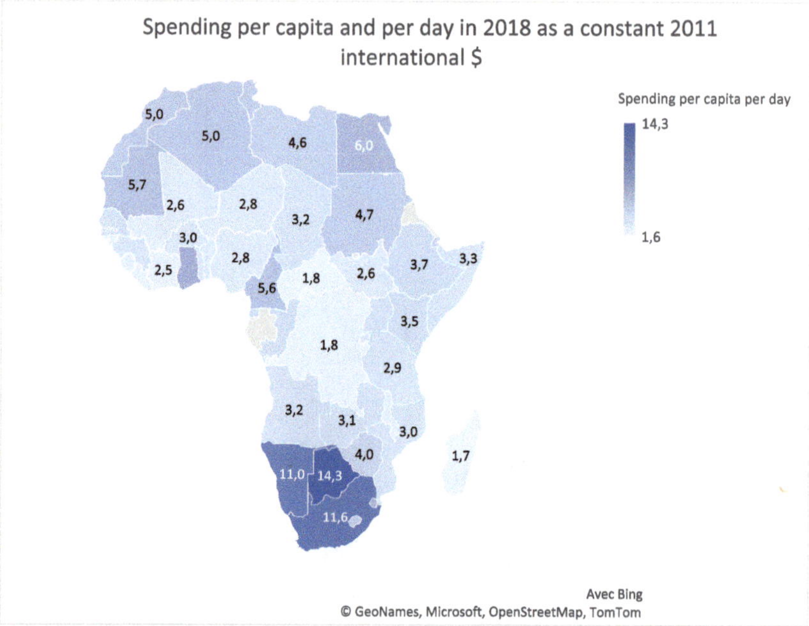

Fig. 0.10 Spending per capita and per day in 2018 as a constant 2011 international $. Source: Atlas AI (www.atlasai.co)

cal solutions that encompass qualitative, quantitative and mixed data types. Its clientele includes prominent entities such as Microsoft, the United Nations, the World Bank, Google, Boeing and numerous leading academic institutions worldwide. The primary sources of this consultancy appear to be household consumption surveys, which are less extensive and sometimes more reliable than salary surveys. The data underlying the map can be accessed online, with updated data available for a fee.

- The Gini index of incomes around 2020 (Fig. 0.11) frequently extends beyond wages alone, which account for only a quarter to a third of household income, with substantial variations in circum-

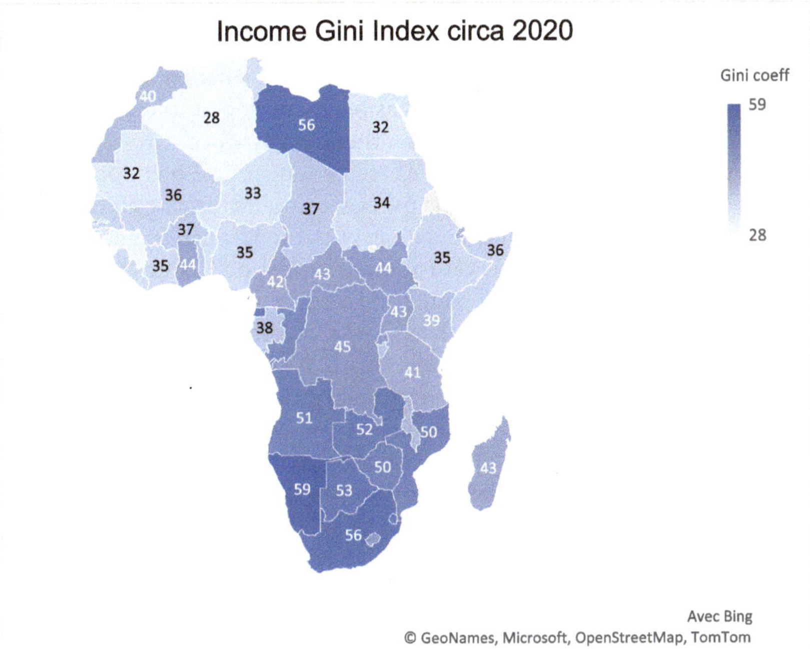

Fig. 0.11 Income Gini index circa 2020. Source: World Bank, series SI.POV. GINI, API_SI.POV.GINI_DS2_en_excel_v2_84027. The Gini coefficient has been calculated since 1960 for advanced countries and since 1990 for other states

stances by country. The index incorporates them within the definition of distribution inequalities, and its mapping is of considerable interest. The source also comes from the World Bank.

In addition, the Salary Explorer website was utilised as a resource. This online resource is designed to facilitate salary comparisons and provides a platform for career development, catering to the needs of both employees and employers. The site collects information provided by users, recruitment agencies, companies, employees, union members and potentially labour administrations. This enables the creation of a substantial database, which is then subjected to econometric analysis to ascertain the reliability, plausibility and consistency of the values. Companies utilise it for their investment projects, while employees can ascertain whether they are being remunerated appropriately. The site has been developed to offer country-by-country contextualisation, with synthetic analyses of the salary situation in each country. Almost all 55 African countries are mentioned.

The limitations of the site for the purposes of our work are at least three or four in number. Primarily, the data is presented in national currencies, with no provision for conversion to international dollars or PPP dollars. Secondly, the data is primarily communicated by users, which introduces the risk of overrepresentation of large- or medium-sized multinational companies and qualified employees. This is particularly evident, e.g., in the case of Morocco, where the average salary indicated by the site is three to four times higher than the actual figure. Furthermore, the site is intended for current events and does not present retrospective data. It is also noteworthy that some data is erroneous; for instance, at the end of January 2025, Niger and Nigeria have exactly the same values for average, low and high salaries. Nevertheless, it is imperative to recognise the long-term value of this "field" source in facilitating meaningful comparisons with more "institutional" data.

It is possible to expand the number of maps represented (e.g. gender pay gap, D9/D1 interdecile gap, minimum wage, etc.). However, the objective of this work is to provide a general approach as regards the salaried population and their wage income, rather than a comprehensive and exhaustive examination of all wage issues.

The reader will have observed the discrepancies regarding dates and the chronology for the five maps, and consequently, the series on which they are based. The African average monthly salary (Fig. 0.7) is expressed in 2021 PPP $, GDP per capita (Fig. 0.8) in constant 2011 international PPP $, the share of employees in the workforce as a percentage concerns 2022 (Fig. 0.9), expenditure per capita per day refers to 2018 (Fig. 0.10) in constant 2011 international dollars, the Gini index of income around 2020 (Fig. 0.11). To put it differently, the quantitative dispersion and chronological heterogeneity in the data may be a matter of concern.

We posit that this is not the case. The initial approach adopted was to utilise robust data, such as the constant international $ PPP of 2011. Subsequently, we determined that the interval spanning from 2011 to 2022, encompassing the five maps, exhibited sufficient temporal homogeneity to be considered as a unified entity. This period was chosen despite the African wage slowdown that commenced in 2015 and the economic downturn associated with the COVID-19 pandemic from 2020 to 2022. Finally, the "institutional" data itself is slightly heterogeneous in time; for example, the Gini index presented by the World Bank in its files concerns the last year available, i.e. in January 2025, from 2011 (Algeria) to 2022 (Zambia). As the set of five series and the five maps attached to them is voluntarily designed as a multi-perspective approach with flexible contours, to take into account the informal economy, uncertain data and other hidden variables, we can reasonably consider this statistical package as provisionally acceptable.

The main characteristics of wages and salaried employment that are evident in the maps are noteworthy. However, certain characteristics will be examined in further analyses, such as the role of oil, raw materials and minerals. Indeed, there is evidence that the correlation coefficients alone are not very convincing. The monthly wage PPP 2021 (incomplete, 39 states) presents low correlation coefficients with the other four series, ranging from 0.13 with the Gini to 0.32 with the GDP per capita. The coefficients of the five series are not significant at convincing levels (of around 0.85 to 0.90), but the most significant are the daily spending per capita/GDP per capita ratio (0.67), which is logical (consumer spending increases with the standard of living), on the one hand, and the share of employees in the workforce/spending day per capita ratio (0.61), on the other.

The map of GDP per capita and that of salaried employment overlap almost perfectly, implying that the growth of the standard of living mirrors the growth of salaried employment, and vice versa, as hypothesised in the initial research. Secondly, the north and the south of the continent demonstrate higher levels of development than intertropical Africa, without constraining the contrast between subtropical and tropical African regions exclusively to biogeographical criteria. This phenomenon is not homogeneous, as evidenced by the increasing inequalities measured by the Gini coefficient, which are more pronounced from north to south on the continent. Southern Africa, in particular, has the highest Gini coefficient.

This analysis suggests that wage employment is associated with rising living standards and the development of a more formalised labour market. It appears that both North and South Africa are currently experiencing a favourable progression in this regard.

Arras, France Michel-Pierre Chelini

REFERENCES

Abegaz, M., & Nene, G. (2022). Gender Wage and Employment Gaps in the Sub-Saharan Africa Economic Sectors. In E. F. Wamboye & B. Fayissa (Eds.), *The Palgrave Handbook of Africa's Economic Sectors* (pp. 919–941). Palgrave Macmillan, Springer Nature.

Alzate, D. (2024). *The Effect of Regulating Platform-Based Work on Employment Outcomes. A Review of the Empirical Evidence.* World Bank.

Anwar, M. A., & Graham, M. (2021). Between a Rock and a Hard Place: Freedom, Flexibility Precarity and Vulnerability in the Gig Economy in Africa. *Competition & Change*, *25*(2), 237–258. https://doi.org/10.1177/1024529420914473

Beblawi, H., & Luciani, G. (1987). *The Rentier State* (252 p.). Routledge.

Bellucci, S., & Eckert, A. (Eds.). (2019). *General Labour History of Africa. Workers, Employers and Governments, 20th–21st Centuries.* Woodbridge, James Currey in Association with the ILO Office for Africa, IISH and Rework.

Chancel, L., Cogneau, D., Gethin A., Myczkowski, A., & Robilliard, A.-S. (2023). Income Inequality in Africa, 1990–2019: Measurement, Patterns, Determinants. *World Development*, *163*, 106–162. https://doi.org/10.1016/j.worlddev.2022.106162

Datta, N., Rong, C., Singh, S., Stinshoff, C., Jacob, N., Simatchev Nigatu, N., Nxumalo, M., & Klimaviciute, L. (2023). *Working Without Borders: The Promise and Peril of Online Gig Work.* World Bank.

Delhi Group. (2008, February 26–29). Report of the Delhi Group on Informal Sector Statistics. UN Statistical Commission, Thirty-Ninth Session.

Diagana, O. (2022, March 7). Promoting Wage Equality in the Labor Market in Africa: A Moral Imperative. World Bank. https://blogs.worldbank.org/en/africacan/promoting-wage-equality-labor-market-africa-moral-imperative

Essen, G., Espi-Sanchis, M., Leibbrandt, V., & Ranchhod, V. (2024). Labour Regulation in Sub-Saharan Africa. Cape Town: Southern Africa Labour and Development Research Unit, University of Cape Town. SALDRU *Working Paper* 308.

ILO. (2019). *Wages in Africa. Recent Trends in Average Wages, in Gender Pay Gaps and in Wage Disparities* (32 p.). International Labour Organization, wcms_728363.WAGE.AFRICA.2019.pdf

ILO. (2024a). *Global Wage Report 2024–25.* International Labour Office.

ILO. (2024b). *Global Wage Report 2024–25 Executive summary.* ILO.

ILO. (2024c). https://ilostat.ilo.org/fr/blog/the-true-value-of-a-paycheck-understanding-ppp-adjusted-income-statistics/

ILOSTAT. *Sustainable Development Goal Indicator* 8.3.1. Informal employment dataset. International Labour Office.

Jirjahn, U. (2025). Unions and Collective Bargaining in Sub-Saharan Africa: Some Insights from Quantitative Studies. IZA *Discussion Paper* No. 17597. Institute of Labor Economics.

Johnson-Lans, S. (Ed.). (2017). *Wage Inequality in Africa* (V-84 p.). Palgrave Macmillan.

Ricardo, D. (1817). *On the Principles of Political Economy and Taxation* (3rd ed., 1821). John Murray. https://archive.org/details/onprinciplesofpo0000rica

Vallas, S., & Schor, J. B. (2020). What Do Platforms Do? Understanding the Gig Economy. *Annual Review of Sociology*, *46*, 273–295. https://doi.org/10.1146/annurev-soc-121919-054857

Wood, A., Graham, M., Lehdonvirta, V. & Hjorth, I. (2023). Networked but Commodified: The (Dis)Embeddedness of Digital Labour in the Gig Economy. *Sociology*, *53*(5), 931–950. https://doi.org/10.1177/0038038519828906

World Bank. (2024). Database, Inflation, Consumer Prices (annual % 1960–2023), excel file API_FP.CPI.TOTL.ZG_DS2_en_excel_v2_174.xls. The World Bank.

Contents

Notes on Contributors

Philippe Adair, PhD in Economics and PhD in Sociology, is Emeritus Professor of Economics and an ERUDITE research fellow at University Paris-Est Créteil, France. He specialises in Labour Economics (i.e., the informal economy) and Financial Economics (i.e., small business funding including microfinance) in developing and developed countries. He records over 100 publications. He is an Editorial Board member of *Mondes en Développement* (a ranked journal), a vice-president of *Association Tiers-Monde* and the Editor of the *Maghreb-Machrek* journal. References: Philippe Adair *at IDEAS* ideas.repec.org/e/pad118.html. Philippe Adair at *ResearchGate* www.researchgate.net/

Ghislaine Bamseck Famo completed her university studies in political science, specialising in diplomacy. An expert in cooperation and international relations, she completed in-depth studies in this field at the Hautes Études Internationales et Politiques. Currently a researcher at the Centre de Recherche et d'Études Histoire et Sociétés, she is continuing her research at the Université d'Artois, focusing on a thesis on the European Economic Community/European Union's development policy towards West Africa from 1975 to 2014. She approaches her research with a global vision of North-South relations.

Mahdi Barouni holds a PhD in Education Economics at the University of Burgundy in 2016 and is a co-author of "The Returns to Education in Africa: Some New Estimates" with Stijn Broecke, *The Journal of Development Studies*, 2014. Since 2017, Mahdi has been a senior economist in the Social Protection and Jobs Global Practice at the World Bank.

Eveline Baumann, PhD is a socioeconomist, honorary research fellow at CESSMA (Centre d'études en sciences sociales sur les mondes africains, américains et asiatiques, Université Paris Cité—IRD—Inalco). She has carried out field research in sub-Saharan Africa (Senegal, Mali, Cameroon) and the post-Soviet space (Georgia). Her main areas of interest concern labour, informal activities, small-scale fisheries, microfinance, and social protection. Her publications include *Sénégal. Le travail dans tous ses états* (Presses universitaires de Rennes, 2016) and, as a co-editor, *L'emploi à l'épreuve de ses marges, Revue française de socio-économie* (2016). https://www.cessma.org/BAUMANN-Eveline

Othmane Bourhaba holds a PhD in Economics from the Hassan II University Casablanca. He is an assistant professor at Université Moulay Ismail (Morocco). His research specialises in informal economy, inequalities and health economics.

Stéphane Callens is Professor of Economics at the University of Artois, in France. He is a researcher at the CNRS laboratory, LEM UMR 9221. He specialises in risks and has published numerous contributions and works in the areas of risk management (finance, health, environment, security).

Michel-Pierre Chelini Professor Emeritus of Contemporary Economic History at the University of Artois (Arras), and an associate professor at the Catholic Institute of Paris, specialises in the history of prices, inflation, wages, and the impact of household purchases on the French, European, and global economies since 1950.

He has recently published a history of wages in France from the 1940s to the 1960s, entitled *Histoire des salaires en France 1944–1967*, Berne, Peter Lang, 2021. He is currently leading an international informal research programme (WAGE: Wage Analysis in a Globalising Environment), initially supported by the National Research Agency (ANR), on wages and globalisation since the 1950s/60s. In particular, he is preparing the edition of a book on *Wages and Globalization, Initial findings* (Peter Lang, 2024–25) and occasionally contributes to the French newspaper *Le Monde* with opinion pieces on inflation and wages since 2022.

Jean Copans is retired Professor of Sociology and Anthropology (Université Paris Descartes, today Paris Cité) (2000–2008). He has taught previously at the Ecole des Hautes Etudes en Sciences Sociales (1970–1990) and at the Université de Picardie Jules Verne (Amiens) (1990–2000). He has been a visiting assistant professor at the Johns Hopkins University (Md.) (1975–76) and at the Université Laval of Québec (1977). He is an Africanist scholar, specialist of Senegal. He has published several books and numerous papers on the Islamic Brotherhood of the *Mourides*, the African working classes, and development problematics. He has also published on the history of French Anthropology including four textbooks.

Mhammed Echkoundi is a lecturer-researcher, economist at Mohammed V University in Rabat, Morocco. He prepared a doctoral thesis in France on governance and territorial dynamics of development. He works on issues related to governance, migration and development in Africa, Afro-African cooperation and African policy of new and old powers. Among his publications on the themes are (1) African countries facing the health crisis: inequalities in the face of health risks and poor global governance, (2) reforming globalisation for a new beginning of the African continent.

Sabine Nadine Ekamena Ntsama holds a PhD in Economics and is a lecturer. Her current and past research focuses on labour market economics, gender, applied macroeconomics and development economics. She is currently Head of the Quantitative Methods Department in the Faculty of Economics and Management at the University of Maroua, Cameroon.

Adrien Frontenaud holds a master's degree in Economics from Université Gustave Eiffel, France. His topics include labour market economics, international economics and development economics, with an expertise on job quality. He has participated in several conferences (ILO and EU) where he presented his current research. He has published two papers in peer-reviewed journals.

Hicham Hafid is a professor-researcher, economist specialising in Africa. He works at the Mohammed V University in Rabat, Morocco. He is also vice-president of the Moroccan Association of Economic Sciences (AMSE). He obtained his PhD in 2010 at the University of Aix Marseille III. He is the co-author of Echkoundi M. & Hafid H. (2020). *L'Afrique mon continent. Le Maroc acteur majeur de la coopération afro-africaine.* Ed. la croisée des chemins. He has coordinated several books, including, *Good governance and the fight against poverty in Africa: the case of Morocco, Gabon, DRC, Botswana and Mauritius (2016).*

Mama Hamimida holds a PhD in Economics from Nanterre Paris X University. She is Professor of Economics at Hassan II University in

Casablanca (Morocco). She is also a researcher at the Africa Observatory (CAP-Afriques) at the University of Quebec in Montreal (Canada).

Vladimir Hlasny has served as an economic affairs officer at the UN Economic and Social Commission for Western Asia in Beirut and as Associate Professor of Economics at Ewha Womans University in Seoul. He presently conducts research in labour and welfare economics, particularly in relation to Asia and the Middle East. He holds a PhD in Economics from Michigan State University.

Badri Houda holds a PhD in Economics from the University of Artois in France and Sousse in Tunis. She is a lecturer at the University of Lille and a researcher at the CNRS LEM UMR 9221 laboratory, specialising in the fields of inequalities, political systems and econometric analysis.

Abou Kane is Full Professor of Economics at Cheikh Anta Diop University in Dakar (UCAD), Senegal. He specializes in development economics and has published extensively on topics such as employment, human capital, agriculture, climate change, money, and official development assistance. Since 2020, he has served as the vice-dean of the Faculty of Economics and Management (FASEG) at UCAD, and from 2015 to 2020, he was the head of the Economics Department. Additionally, he heads the Public Economics Laboratory (LEP).

Oksana Nezhyvenko holds a PhD in Economics from University Paris-Est Créteil, France. She is an associate professor at the National University of Kyiv-Mohyla Academy, Ukraine. She works at the CNAM-Centre d'Etudes de l'Emploi et du Travail, France. She specializes in labour economics and records over twenty publications. Her main research topic is informal employment/undeclared work. Her areas of expertise include Ukraine (as a consultant for labour market issues at the ILO and UNDP), the European Union and Algeria. References: https://www.researchgate.net/profile/Oksana_Nezhyvenko2

Everlyne Ngare is a development and economics professional with over 10 years' experience in economic development, resource mobilisation, institute building, change management, and eco-system development with government, non-profit, corporate, and foundations. She is currently, a Business Development and Partnerships Head (Africa) at CAP-YEI and a lecturer at Moi University. Everlyne holds a master's degree in Finance, and she has served on many professional, national, governmental, and international working groups and forums, connected with economic development, youth and children services, poverty alleviation, informal sector employment, safe migration, skills training, and corporate social responsibility.

Gwenaëlle Otando holds a PhD in Development Economics. She prepared a PhD on the role of institutions in development at the University of Artois, France. She is president of the association AVECS. She has published several articles on the subject of institutions in Africa and worked for several years as a temporary attaché at the University of Artois. She worked in the Kif-Kif association as a project manager in the fight against discrimination. She currently teaches microeconomics, banking economics and business behaviour at the University of Artois.

Mamaye Thiongane, PhD in Economics, is a lecturer and researcher at the Faculty of Economics and Management at Cheikh Anta Diop University (UCAD), Senegal. His research interests include gender and social inclusion issues in education, health, and the labour market (both paid and unpaid). He is a member of the Public Economics Laboratory (LEP).

Ousmane Wague is Accredited Professor of Sociology of Development at the University of Nouakchott. Author of over thirty publications, he has coordinated and directed more than twenty projects, the last of which credited by the National Agency for Scientific Research as the winner of the 2024 prize for best research project. He is a member of the Technical Support Committee for the Optimal Development of the National Agricultural Land Heritage, of the Gender Equality Observatory at the University of Nouakchott, and Head of Mission in Mauritania of the research project "Gendered" and transformative social policy in post-COVID-19 Africa.

Emna Zamel holds a PhD in Economics at Toulouse School of Economics and Faculté des Sciences Économiques et de Gestion de Sfax (Tunisie), is a lecturer at the University of Carthage—Faculté des Sciences Économiques et de Gestion de Nabeul (Tunisie) and is a co-author of *Ni trop, ni pas assez mais pas … la bonne éducation?... Économique de l'inadéquation horizontale entre formation et emploi* with Professor Jean-Michel Plassard (Toulouse, 2022).

Abbreviations

AKNEEM	South Africa, Kenya, Nigeria, Egypt, Ethiopia, and Morocco
ALMP	Active Labour Market Program (Tunisia)
AMAL	Programme de recherche active d'emploi (Tunisia)
ANETI	National Employment Agency and Self Employment (Tunisia)
AOF	French West Africa
ARDL	Autoregressive Distributed Lag Model
BEST	Basic Employability Skills Training (Kenya)
BRICS	Brazil, Russia, India, China, South Africa
CAP-YEI	CAP-Youth Empowerment Institute
CEPE	Certificate of Elementary Education (Cameroon)
CFA franc	Franc de la Communauté Financière Africaine
CNPT	Standard National Occupational Classification (Cameroon)
CNSS	Social Security National Fund (Tunisia)
ECAM	Cameroon Household Surveys
EHESS	Ecole des Hautes Etudes en Sciences Sociales (France)
ENEU	Mexican Employment Survey
ENIGH	Mexican Income and Expenditure Survey
ERF	Economic Research Forum
GDP	Gross Domestic Product
GNI	Gross National Income
HDI	Human Development Index
HIECS	Egyptian Household Income, Expenditure and Consumption Survey
HIES	Household Income and Expenditure Surveys
ILO	International Labour Organization
IMF	International Monetary Fund
IT	Information Technology

IUT	University Institutes of Technology
KEPSA	Kenya Private Sector Alliance
LDCs	Less Developed Countries
LMPS	Labor Market Panel Survey
MENA	Middle East and North Africa
MEP	Ministère de l'Economie et du Plan (Cameroon)
MESR	Ministry of Higher Education (Tunisia)
MFI	Microfinance Institution
MFPE	Ministry of Vocational Training and Employment (Tunisia)
MINEFI	Ministère de l'Economie et des Finances (Cameroon)
NEET	Not in Education, Employment or Training
NGO	Non-governmental Organisation
NSI	National Institute of Statistics (Cameroon)
OLS	Ordinary Least Squares
ONCAD	Office National de Coopération et d'Assistance pour le Développement (Senegal)
PPP	Purchasing Power Parity
RIF	Recentered Influence Function
SAPs	Structural Adjustment Programmes
SDGs	Sustainable Development Goals
SME	Small and Medium Enterprise
SMIG	Interprofessional minimum wage
SNEEG	National Strategy for Gender Equity and Equality
SNIM	Société Nationale d'Industrie Minière (Mauritania)
SSE	Social and Solidarity Economy
SWIID	Standardized World Income Inequality Database
UNDP	United Nations Development Programme
VSE	Very Small Enterprise
VTCs	Vocational Training Centres (Kenya)
WAGE	Wage Analysis in a Globalising Environment
WIEGO	Women in Informal Employment: Globalizing and Organizing
YEDF	Youth Enterprise Development Fund (Kenya)

List of Figures

List of Tables

List of Boxes

CHAPTER 1

Introduction: A Journey into Theories and Stylised Facts About Wages in Africa

Philippe Adair

1 Introduction

History is a retrospective exercise whose merit is to express both the cumulative and the chronological evolution of theories and to show the recurrence of different, if not opposing, approaches rather than the emergence of an unbeatable synthesis. Against this backdrop, Hegel (1830: 332) rightly asserts that history repeats itself, but he is mistaken about the enduring character of synthesis. Facts, such as observations or statistical analyses of data, are clouded by neither idealism nor empiricism. They provide some designed but relevant content for interpreting (i.e., testing) theories. This articulation of facts and theories is at the heart of this book.

P. Adair (✉)
Université Paris Est Créteil, Val-de-Marne, France
e-mail: adair@u-pec.fr

M.-P. Chelini et al. (eds.), *Wage Dynamics in Africa*, African Histories and Modernities,
https://doi.org/10.1007/978-3-031-99800-3_1

2 An Overview of Macro Versus Micro Wage Theories Throughout Capitalist Development

2.1 Serfdom Versus Freedom

The beginning of modern wage theory in Britain and throughout Western Europe coincides with the end of the Middle Ages in the sixteenth century. Wages become a contemporary issue regarding the workforce that is set free from slavery and serfdom. It is worth noting that this was not the case in Africa, where colonisation and serfdom continued until the twentieth century.

In the late seventeenth century, the British liberal philosopher John Locke (1690 Chapter 1, Section 27) argued that labour could be considered a contractual arrangement because workers supposedly had ownership of their bodies and minds. In this respect, Locke was a precursor of the labour theory of value, paving the way for Smith (1776) and classical political economy.

2.2 A Classical Macro Theory of Wages: Wage Fund, Subsistence and Distributional Issues

In the late eighteenth century, a macro theory of wages emerged in which wages were first considered as an advance payment borne by capitalists and landlords (Quesnay, 1758; Smith, 1776); this later became the wage fund theory. Wages became the price, or rather the cost, of labour (or labour force) according to classical political economy (including Marx himself as a critic of this school of thought), whose approach was based on the supply side. Wages (as opposed to profits) were now seen as a matter of distribution between labour and capital, as noted by Ricardo (1817) and Malthus (1821), then Andrews (1892) and Marx (1867) had noted.

The wage fund theory held that wages depended on the relative amounts of capital available to pay workers and on the size of the labour force. Wages increase only when there is an increase in capital or a decrease in the number of workers.

This doctrine is rooted in Quesnay's *Tableau économique* (1758), in which landowners provide capital to peasants in the form of land leases. The amount of land and the rents derived from it are fixed, and the capital needed for farming supplies and food for the labourers in any one year is derived directly from the profits of the previous year's production.

Adam Smith (1776) assumed that workers were paid from a predetermined fund of wealth. This wage fund was created by savings from the accumulation of capital. The demand for labour and the wage rate depended on the size of the wage fund.

In line with the wage fund theory, subsistence theory was put forward by Ricardo (1817) who stated that: "The laborers are paid to enable them to subsist and perpetuate the race without increase or diminution." This payment was also known as "subsistence wages". If workers were paid less than subsistence wages, the number of workers would decrease as a result of starvation, death, malnutrition, disease, etc., and many would not marry. Wage rates would then rise to subsistence levels. Since the wage rate tends to be at subsistence level in all cases, this theory is also known as the "iron law of wages".

Although consistent with population theory (Malthus, 1803), which states that demography should adjust to resources, Ricardo's subsistence theory emphasised the supply side of the labour market and neglected the demand side. Any change in labour supply is the main determinant of the minimum real wages required to meet basic needs (such as food and shelter).

Similarly, Mill (1848) presented a definitive account of the wage fund theory, positing that the solution to increasing the wage rate above the subsistence level is to control population growth. If population grows faster than capital, wages fall.

The labour theory of value and the related theory of exploitation are key to Marx's contribution. Marx (1867), departed from the wage fund theory by arguing that workers work for part of each day, adding the value required to cover their wages, while the rest of their labour is performed for the enrichment of the capitalist. However, this is still a distribution issue, the adjustment of which depends on class struggle (i.e., bargaining power).

In contrast, Jevons (1871), although claiming to be inspired by Ricardo, rejected the wage fund theory as "purely delusional", thus decisively departing from the macroeconomic approach.

2.3 *The Shift to Microeconomics: A Focus on the Labour Market*

The marginalist revolution was initiated in the early 1870s by Jevons, Menger and Walras, triggering a shift towards demand. This new turn was driven by Jevons (1871), who linked wages as income to labour productivity within a theory of individual choice. He paved half the way to neoclassical partial equilibrium in the labour market, which Marshall (1890) based on both supply (diminishing marginal utility) and demand (increasing costs), although the determination of wages remained unachieved.

The full neoclassical theory of wages was presented by Hicks (1932) as a labour market equilibrium between supply and demand, with wages assumed to be flexible enough to adjust the level of employment.

2.4 Back and Forth Between Microeconomics and Macroeconomics: From Mutual Ignorance to Microfoundations

Keynesian theory shifts back to macroeconomics, emphasising the level of employment as the result of adjustment on the market for goods and services rather than on the labour market (Keynes 1936). To understand the dynamic role that wages play in the macroeconomic cycle, one may recall the suggestive aphorism proposed by Kalecki (1937, 79): "Workers spend what they earn; capitalists earn what they spend."

However, interdependence within the cycle does not provide a bridge to the theoretical issue of wages. Microeconomic theory holds that wages are a cost to employers and are ultimately determined through a bargaining process, while macroeconomic theory sees wages as income for employees who increase expected profits through spending. In the absence of a consensus, both theories developed in mutual ignorance.

In the late 1950s and early 1960s, a major development in microeconomic wage theory came to the fore: human capital theory, coined by Mincer (1958), Schultz (1961), and Becker (1964). The theory states that education (which provides knowledge) and experience (from skills and know-how) are embodied capital, and that investment in human capital has high economic returns, increasing both output and earnings for workers. Again, the focus is on labour supply.

In the 1970s and 1980s, New Keynesian theory introduced wages as a microfoundation for macroeconomics. Stiglitz argues that wages are an incentive device that increases the productivity and efficiency of workers. The positive effect of wages on productivity explains why employers refrain from lowering wages to avoid turnover (Stiglitz, 1974) and worker shirking (Shapiro & Stiglitz, 1984).

Another contribution to New Keynesian labour economics is the *insider-outsider* theory developed by Lindbeck and Snower (1988) in 1984. It explains persistent unemployment as a result of wage negotiations in a given firm driven by the power of insiders, a group of better-off employees. These employees are involved in a wage-bargaining process with the employer. The insiders aim to maximise their own wages and fight against the expansion of employment by keeping wages down and preventing outsiders from being hired. This contribution fuels both bargaining theory and segmentation theory in relation to the barriers to entry experienced by informal workers (Fields, 2023).

3 Mind the Gaps: Segmented Labour Markets and the Gender Divide

Several questions arise in relation to the wage issue(s). Is there a single labour market populated by representative agents who are similar in terms of their similar maximising behaviour? Does this explain wage differentials, even when human capital endowments are taken into account? Are wages the only price of labour? What is the price of unpaid care and chores? If the answer is negative according to strong empirical observations, it is time to bid farewell to the fictitious labour market and representative agents and to address segmented jobs and wage gaps, including the gender pay gap.

3.1 *Dualism and Labour Market Segmentation: The Prominence of Informal Employment*

Labour market segmentation theory (Doeringer & Piore, 1971; Reich et al., 1973) developed in the United States as a combination of internal labour market theory and dual labour market theory. It became a serious challenge to neoclassical labour market theory, contending that wages do not adjust to equilibrium in the informal segment.

3.1.1 *The Precursors of Dualism: From Macro- to Micropatterns Again*

Simultaneously, dual labour market theory developed its roots in less developed countries, especially in the early 1970s.

Actually, dualism was first introduced in the mid-1950s by Lewis (1954), who developed a theory of labour turnover from farming ("traditional sector") to the manufacturing industry ("modern sector"). Lewis's inspiration was classical macroeconomics rather than neoclassical microeconomics. Lewis's rather optimistic prediction was as follows: Disguised unemployment ("Unlimited labour supply") among farmers drives occupational mobility into manufacturing; when the latter rises to a tipping point, manufacturing wages begin to rise above farming wages, paving the way for growth and modernisation. However, Fields (2006) points out that wages may not converge across industries, leaving room for a more pessimistic interpretation of the Lewis model: A persistence of informal employment in manufacturing and services despite "modernisation".

Harris and Todaro (1970) then developed a probabilistic model of labour turnover, based on job search behaviour with a microeconomic foundation. The workforce flows from the agricultural sector A (rural area) to the non-agricultural sector B (urban area), despite the existence of urban unemployment. This flow is triggered by the gap between expected urban wages and agricultural wages. When the former equals the latter (equilibrium condition), which depends on the rate of urban unemployment, there is no longer any incentive for workers' geographic mobility.

Interestingly, the so-called informal sector emerged simultaneously in West and East Africa in the early 1970s. In relation to migrants in Ghana, an anthropologist (Hart, 1973) first introduced the term "informal sector" in 1971, based on observations dating back to the mid-1960s. He classified both legitimate and illegitimate informal income opportunities, and questioned whether informal economic activities had any autonomous capacity to generate income growth for the urban (and rural) poor (i.e., the "reserve army of urban unemployed and underemployed").

In 1972, Singer and Jolly (1973) also used the term "informal sector" in their report on disguised unemployment and poverty in Kenya, an ILO mission within the framework of the World Employment Programme. It is noteworthy that half of their sample consisted of employees and self-employed workers in the informal sector. The report described the rationale underlying employment policy strategies and proposed a set of interrelated policy measures capable of extending the benefits of economic growth to low-income groups, redistributing income more equitably and developing the informal sector in both urban and rural areas. The real issue was the political feasibility of the proposed redistribution strategy.

Fields (1975) takes a step forward by extending the job search model of Harris and Todaro to include the urban informal sector. His model comprises two sectors (formal and informal), while individual behaviour includes the option of employment or unemployment. Employment can therefore be in the formal or the informal sector, depending on the presence or absence of entry barriers. The probability of finding a job in the formal sector is lower for an informal worker than for an unemployed individual seeking full-time employment. Average wages are higher in the formal sector than in the informal sector. The formal sector is characterised by the existence of a minimum wage, the presence of trade unions and social security, and the use of incentives (efficiency wages), which are absent in the informal sector. However, not all incomes in the informal sector are necessarily lower than in the formal sector (especially non-wage income).

According to Fields (1990), the informal sector itself is heterogeneous and consists of two segments: the first segment (*lower tier*) is easily accessible because of low skill requirements and low wages, and the second segment (upper tier) has barriers to entry and average income is higher. The first segment is characterised by low employee turnover, and when turnover does occur, the flow is towards the formal sector. The second segment is characterised by a reverse flow of labour from formal wage employment to informal small businesses, which may be a second job related to a voluntary choice.

Beyond the simple dualism, the formal/informal divide is segmented into six categories according to work status and earnings: Formal self-employed, upper-tier informal self-employed, and lower-tier informal self-employed vs. formal wage employees, upper-tier informal wage employees and lower-tier informal wage employees (Fields, 2023). There is therefore segmentation in the labour market, but not a strict dualism if the concept is understood as a watertight division between formal and informal segments.

There are two opposing approaches to the distinction between upper-tier and lower-tier informal work. The first sees upper-tier informal employment as "voluntary", with workers choosing jobs that offer more independence and better earnings and working conditions than the formal sector. In contrast, lower-tier informal work is "involuntary" and a last resort option when individuals cannot find employment in either the formal or upper-tier informal sectors (Fields, 2023).

There are two competing explanations for why people work informally. The free choice approach view is that all workers can choose to work formally, depending on comparative advantage, preferences for independent work, and avoidance of payroll taxes and regulations. The segmented labour approach contends that the number of wage jobs is rationed relative to the size of the labour force.

3.1.2 Informality: From an Enterprise-Based to a Job-Based Definition: Extended Criteria

The ILO coined the following definition of the informal sector in 1993. The informal sector consists of a group of economic units, so-called unincorporated businesses, which are included in the household sector as defined by the United Nations System of National Accounts (one to nine employees, including the self-employed). These unincorporated businesses are not recorded because of tax evasion or because they do not keep proper accounts. The informal sector includes all family businesses that do not have an employee on a permanent contract basis, i.e., the self-employed category in the classification of occupations. Depending on the national context, the definition of the informal sector may be extended to include microenterprises with a few regular employees below a threshold of five or ten permanent employees. Last, for practical reasons, it may be useful to limit the scope of the informal sector to economic units that produce market goods and services, excluding agriculture, hunting, fishing and forestry.

In 2002, the ILO broadened the scope of the informal sector and changed the definition to capture informal employment, adopting a job-based concept of informality. Informal employment includes "all remunerative work (i.e., both self-employment and wage employment) that is not registered, regulated or protected by existing legal or regulatory frameworks (social insurance affiliation), as well as unpaid work undertaken in an income-generating enterprise" (ILO, 2013).

It is worth mentioning that the Expert Group on Informal Sector Statistics, known as the "Delhi Group", was set up in 1997 as one of the entities of the United Nations Statistical Division to address various methodological issues related to the treatment of the informal sector.

Also founded in 1997, Women in Informal Employment: Globalising and Organising (WIEGO) is a network focused on improving conditions for workers in the informal economy. Key contributions come from Chen (Chen & Carré, 2020) and Charmes (2019b). As its title suggests, WIEGO is dedicated to informal female workers who face vulnerability and inequality compared to their male counterparts. WIEGO links the issue of segmentation to the issue of gender, which we address below.

3.2 Labour Force Participation Versus Unpaid Care: Has the Gender Divide Narrowed?

Boserup (1970) was a pioneer in gender issues. In the 1980s and 1990s, so-called feminist economists systematically introduced gender issues. They challenged the neoclassical approach to gender inequality based on discrimination (Becker, 1957; Phelps, 1972) or task specialisation (Becker, 1981), discussed the mechanism and magnitude of the gender pay gap, developed female labour-supply decisions (labour force participation and employment as well as paid vs unpaid labour) and designed cross-country comparisons. Key contributions included Bergmann (1986), Goldin (1994), Jacobsen (1998) and Blau et al. (2001).

As an economic historian and labour economist, Goldin analysed the evolution of gender gaps in labour force and earnings (Goldin, 2014). She found that the distribution of earnings is characterised by a U-shape of female labour force participation relative to GDP per capita (Goldin, 1994).

Since the 2010s, the database has been growing. Since its first edition in 2013, the Gender Equality Index measures the position of women relative to men in terms of health status, household conditions, political representation and socio-economic resources.

4 Stylised Facts on Informality and Gender Issues in Africa

4.1 Africa: North Africa vs. Sub-Saharan Africa: A Different Picture of Informality

Three stylised facts are noteworthy regarding the macroeconomic picture of informal employment (Charmes, 2019a, p. 41). First, average (non-agricultural) informal employment is a persistent or structural phenomenon. Second, informal employment is negatively related to GDP per capita. Lastly, informal employment is countercyclical: It increased with slowing economic growth until the late 2000s and decreased with improving economic growth in the early 2010s. Trends and levels vary according to the impact of economic shocks and the employment policies designed to absorb them (Adair et al., 2023).

For instance, levels of informal employment vary, reaching an average of 50% in North Africa compared to 66% in sub-Saharan Africa in the decade of the 2010s (Charmes, 2019a). Simultaneously, the rate of informal employment appears to be loosely correlated with unemployment, suggesting that the former absorbs the latter to some extent. According to the ILO (2023a), the average unemployment rate in sub-Saharan Africa (5.7% in 2019) is almost half that of North Africa (10.9% in 2019).

Figure 1.1 shows that there are also distinct shares and trends for informal employment in North Africa. The overall trend is almost flat over the last decade (2010–2020), with an increase in Egypt and a decrease in both Morocco (highest share) and Algeria (lowest share).

4.2 *Gender: Contrasting North Africa with Sub-Saharan Africa*

The U-shaped pattern of female labour force participation relative to GDP per capita is questioned for 162 countries over the period 1990–2012. Using the World Bank's country income classification, low-income countries, a category that includes sub-Saharan Africa, do not fit this pattern

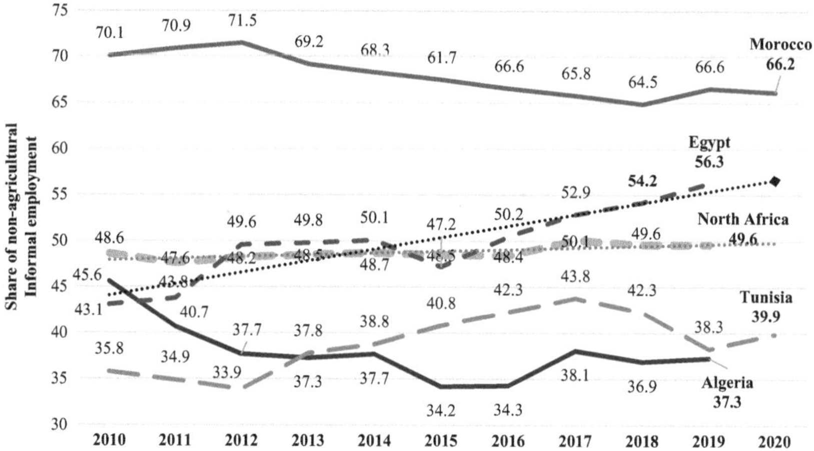

Fig. 1.1 Informal employment in North Africa: Shares and trends prior to the pandemic. *Notes*: Unweighted arithmetic mean. *Source*: Charmes and Adair (2022). Data on informal employment come from national employment surveys provided by the official statistical offices (Algeria, Morocco and Egypt) and estimates from the national employment survey and the five-year survey of microenterprises (Tunisia)

according to a quadratic prediction, although it does for lower middle-income countries, a category that includes North Africa (Lechman & Kaur, 2015).

Furthermore, the ILO (2023a) has developed a novel indicator that provides a more comprehensive view of labour underutilisation. The job gap includes in the numerator all those who would like to work but do not have a job, while the denominator includes all those who do not have a job and want one, plus total employment. This ratio is based on the same data sources as unemployment statistics, with the addition of labour force survey data to include all job seekers or other people not accounted for.

The job gap is also much higher among women than men. It is computed as follows:

$$\textit{Labour Income Gap} = \textit{Women's Total Labour Income} \,/\, \textit{Men's Total Labour Income}$$

The average job gap rate by country income group in 2019 shows a marked gender gap: 21.5% in low-income countries (including almost half of sub-Saharan African countries) compared with almost half (11.5%) in lower-middle income countries (including most North African countries and almost half of sub-Saharan African countries).

Combining the gender job gap with country income group, it is quite obvious that the gap is narrower when country income group is higher as reported in Fig. 1.2.

All countries surveyed in the book belong to the category of lower-middle income countries (1026–3995/$ Gross National Income—GNI per capita) according to the classification for country income in 2019. Tunisia is rather close to the ceiling of the category (3360$) and enjoys a narrower gender gap, Morocco (3190$) stands slightly below, whereas Egypt stands in the middle of the category (2690$) and all three countries are North African. All sub-Saharan countries, irrespective of their geographical setting, are rather located at the bottom of the category: Such is

Upper-middle-income countries 73
Middle-income countries 61
Lower-middle income countries 29
Low-income countries 33

Fig. 1.2 Relative labour income of women compared to men by country income group, 2019. *Note*: 100 = male level. *Source*: ILO modelled estimates database (ILO, 2023b) and GNI per capita, Atlas method, PPP (World Bank, 2019)

the case for Kenya (1750$), Mauritania (1660$), Cameroon (1500$) and Senegal (1450$).

Charmes (2019b) has compiled time use surveys from around the world since the 2000s, including 14 African countries, 3 of which are in North Africa. Notwithstanding personal time spent on sleep and leisure, total work is divided into unpaid care work (such as chores, childcare and care for other family members), which is mostly performed by women, and paid work (whether self-employed or wage-earning), which is mostly performed by men. He designed a ratio of women to men for unpaid care work, paid work and total work by region. Ranking the regions according to this gender ratio shows that the regions with the highest ratios are in the Middle East (also known as the Arab countries), North Africa and sub-Saharan Africa. Where women devote most of their time to unpaid activities, it is not surprising that they are less present in the labour market and therefore earn less. Inequality is then rooted in the patriarchal sexual division of labour (Becker, 1981).

According to Charmes (2022), the largest gender gaps in unpaid work are observed in North Africa, where women spend on average six times more time on this work than men, while in sub-Saharan Africa it is slightly less than three times more.

5 A Brief Presentation of the Structure and Content of the Book

This book gathers 16 chapters structured into four parts. It covers several countries from North Africa (Egypt, Morocco and Tunisia) and sub-Saharan Africa (Cameroon, Kenya, Mauritania and Senegal), among which Cameroon and Senegal are twice tackled. It is worth noticing that two chapters are dedicated respectively to overall Africa and to an emerging group of African countries. Wages issues are investigated according a large spectrum of social sciences, which include Anthropology and Sociology, Political Economy, Economic History and Economics. Distinct topics are addressed, such as stylised facts, with regard to the magnitude and dynamics of wages, and focus on differentials with respect to wage gaps due to labour market segmentation and gender.

5.1 An Overview on Wage Issues in Africa: Facts, Theories and Dynamics

Part I includes four chapters.

In Chap. 2, Michel-Pierre Chelini (University of Artois, France) provides an overview of stylised facts on wage distribution and growth in “Long-Term Wage Issues in Africa”.

In Chap. 3, Stéphane Callens (University of Artois, France) and Badri Houda (University of Lille) compare the contributions of pioneers such as Myrdal, Lewis and Hirschman in “Wages and Economic Development, Theories and Models”.

Chapter 4 is dedicated to the contribution of Jean Copans (University Paris Cité, France), who discusses wage employment from a historical perspective in “Labourers, Salaried Workers and Salary: Makings and Un-makings of the African Working Class”.

In Chap. 5, Gwenaëlle Otando (AVECs association, France), Mhammed Echkoundi (University Mohammed V, Rabat, Morocco) and Hicham Hafid (University Mohammed V, Rabat, Morocco) collect key data on wages and sketch a tentative new grouping of “Emerging Countries in Africa and Wage Dynamics”.

5.2 Income Inequalities, Wages and Causality

Part II comprises three chapters.

In Chap. 6, Vladimir Hlasny (EWHA Womans University, Seoul, South Korea) examines inequalities with Gini coefficients, especially throughout North Africa, in “Top Expenditure Distribution in North Africa and Middle East Countries and the Inequality Puzzle”.

Chapter 7 presents the contribution of Ghislaine Bamseck (University of Artois, France) with regard to gender gap and informality in “Labour Market and Wages in Cameroon Since Independence”.

In Chap. 8, Othmane Bourhaba (Moulay Ismail University, Meknès, Morocco) and Mama Hamimida (Hassan II University, Casablanca, Morocco) analyse long-term causal factors, including informality in “Income Inequalities and Informal Economy in Morocco”.

5.3 *Wage Determinants: Shocks, Representations and Earning Strategies*

Part III covers four chapters.

In Chap. 9, Eveline Baumann (University Paris Cité, France) tackles informality as an embedded strategy according to the approach of Karl Polanyi in "Labour in Senegal Under Structural Adjustment (1980s and 1990s): A Fictitious Market".

Emna Zamel (University of Jendouba, Tunisia) and Mahdi Barouni (University of Bourgogne, France) address the impact of education upon earnings in Chap. 10 dedicated to "The Effect of Higher Learning on Graduates' Salary in Tunisia".

In Chap. 11, Ousmane Wague (University of Nouakchott, Mauritania) analyses "The Perception of Wages in Contemporary Mauritania: Between Craze and Social Positioning".

Everlyne Ngare (Moi University and CAP Youth Empowerment Institute, Kenya) provides a focus on earning strategies and empowerment in Kenya in Chap. 12 dedicated to "Cultivating Youth Economic Resilience: Diverse Income Strategies".

5.4 *Wage Gaps: Youth, Informality and Gender*

Part IV gathers three chapters.

In Chap. 13, Adrien Frontenaud (France), Oksana Nezhyvenko (NaUKMA, Ukraine) and Philippe Adair (University Paris-Est Créteil, France) address the dynamics of labour market informality, from both the supply side and the demand side, in "Rising Labour Market Segmentation in Egypt over 2012–2018: Youth Informal Employment Is Prominent".

In Chap. 14, Mamaye Thiongane and Abou Kane (University Cheik Anta Diop, Senegal) discuss wage differentials, with regard to human capital and discrimination, in "Dynamics of Wage Disparities in Senegal: Differences in Productive Characteristics or Discrimination?".

In Chap. 15, Sabine Nadine Ekamena Ntsama (Maroua University, Cameroon) focuses on gender pay gap, with respect to discrimination according to a decomposition model, in "The evolution of the Gender Pay Gap in Cameroon".

In Chap. 16, Eveline Baumann (University Paris Cité, France) provides an assessment of the topics and sketches the challenges regarding wages in the "Conclusion: Labour, a Highly Political Issue with Manifold Research Challenges".

Conflicts of Interest The author has no conflicts of interest to declare that are relevant to the content of this chapter.

References

Adair, P., AlAzzawi, S., & Hlasny, V. (2023). Fostering Decent Jobs, Formalising Informal Employment and Spurring Job Mobility in MENA Countries. *Economic Notes, 53*(2), e12240. https://doi.org/10.1111/ecno.12240

Andrews, E. B. (1892). Rodbertus's Socialism. *Journal of Political Economy 1* (1): 50–67.

Becker, G. S. (1957). *The Economics of Discrimination* (2nd ed., 1971). The University of Chicago Press.

Becker, G. S. (1964). *Human Capital: A Theoretical and Empirical Analysis, with Special Reference to Education* (3rd ed., 1993). The University of Chicago Press. https://www.nber.org/books-and-chapters/human-capital-theoretical-and-empirical-analysis-special-reference-education-first-edition

Becker, G. S. (1981). *A Treatise on Family*. NBER Books, National Bureau of Economic Research. https://doi.org/10.2307/j.ctv322v4rc

Bergmann, B. (1986). *The Economic Emergence of Women*. Basic Books. www.scribd.com › document › 546004559

Blau, F., Ferber, M., & Winkler, A. (2001). *The Economics of Women, Men and Work*. Prentice-Hall.

Boserup, E. (1970). *Woman's Role in Economic Development*. St. Martin's Press.

Charmes, J. (2019a). *Dimensions of Resilience in Developing Countries: Informality, Solidarities and Carework*. Springer. www.academia.edu › 112414534 › Dimensions_of

Charmes, J. (2019b). *The Unpaid Care Work and the Labour Market. An Analysis of Time Use Data Based on the Latest World Compilation of Time-Use Surveys*. International Labour Office. www.ilo.org › publications › unpaid-care-work-and. wcms_732791.pdf

Charmes, J. (2022). Variety and Change of Patterns in the Gender Balance Between Unpaid Care-Work, Paid Work and Free Time Across the World and over Time: A Measure of Wellbeing? *Wellbeing, Space and Society, 3*. https://www.sciencedirect.com/journal/wellbeing-space-and-society/vol/3/suppl/C

Charmes, J., & Adair, P. (2022). Après un demi-siècle, l'économie informelle reste un concept heuristique et un ensemble flou [The Informal Economy is Fifty: A Heuristic Concept and a Fuzzy Set]. *Mondes en Développement, 50*(199–200) (3–4), 255–274. https://doi.org/10.3917/med.199.0259

Chen, M., & Carré, F. (2020). *The Informal Economy Revisited: Examining the Past, Envisioning the Future*. Routledge. www.wiego.org › research-library-publications

Doeringer, P., & Piore, M. (1971). *Internal Labor Markets and Manpower Analysis* (2nd ed., 1985). Heath. Sharpe New-York. https://doi.org/10.4324/9781003069720

Fields, G. S. (1975). Rural-Urban Migration, Urban Unemployment and Underemployment, and Job Search Activity in LDC's. *Journal of Development Economics, 2*, 165–188. https://doi.org/10.1016/0304-3878(75)90014-0

Fields, G. S. (1990). Labour Market Modelling and the Urban Informal Sector: Theory and Evidence. In D. Turnham, B. Salomé, & A. Schwartz (Eds.), *The Informal Sector Revisited* (pp. 49–69). OECD Development Centre Seminars. Fields52_Labour_market_modelling_and_the_urban_informal_sector.pdf

Fields, G. S. (2006). The Labor Market Dualism in the Lewis Model: Reply. *The Manchester School of Economic and Social Studies, 74*(3), 355–359. https://doi.org/10.1111/j.1467-9957.2006.00498.x

Fields, G. S. (2023). Informality and work status. In G. S. Fields, T. H. Gindling, K. Sen, M. Danquah, & S. Schotte (Eds.), *The Job Ladder. Transforming Informal Work and Livelihoods in Developing Countries*. Oxford University Press. United Nations University World Institute for Development Economics Research – UNU-WIDER (pp. 16–32).

Goldin, C. (1994). The U-Shaped Female Labor Force Function in Economic Development and Economic History. *NBER Working Papers* No 4707. National Bureau of Economic Research. In Schultz, T. P. (1995). *Investment in Women's Human Capital and Economic Development* (pp. 61–90). University of Chicago Press. https://doi.org/10.3386/w4707

Goldin, C. (2014). A Grand Gender Convergence: Its Last Chapter. *American Economic Review, 104*(4), 1091–1119. https://doi.org/10.1257/aer.104.4.1091

Harris, J. R., & Todaro, M. P. (1970). Migration, Unemployment and Development: A Two-Sector Analysis. *American Economic Review, 60*(1), 126–142. https://www.jstor.org/stable/1807860

Hart, K. (1973). Informal Income Opportunities and Urban Employment in Ghana. *The Journal of Modern African Studies, 11*(1), 61–89. https://www.jstor.org/stable/159873

Hegel, G. W. F. (1822–1830). *Lectures on the Philosophy of History* (J. Sibree, Ed. and Trans., 1956). Batoche Books. 2001. https://archive.org/details/lecturesonphilos00hegerich

Hicks, J. R. (1932). The Theory of Wages. London: Macmillan. 2nd ed., 1963.

ILO. (2013). *Measuring Informality: A Statistical Manual on the Informal Sector and Informal Employment*. International Labour Office. https://www.ilo.org/publications/measuring-informality-statistical-manual-informal-sector-and-informal

ILO. (2023a, May 31). *Monitor on the World of Work* (11th ed.). International Labour Office. https://www.ilo.org/resource/brief/ilo-monitor-world-work-11th-edition

ILO. (2023b). *Spotlight on Work Statistics n°12*, March. International Labour Office. https://www.ilo.org/sites/default/files/wcmsp5/groups/public/@dgreports/@stat/documents/publication/wcms_870519.pdf

Jacobsen, J. (1998). *The Economics of Gender.* Blackwell. https://archive.org/details/economicsofgende0000jaco_i4b5

Jevons, W. S. (1871). *The Theory of Political Economy.* Oxford University Press. https://archive.org/details/theoryofpolitica00jevouoft

Kalecki, M. (1937). A Theory of the Business Cycles. *Review of Economic Studies, 4*(2), 77–97. https://doi.org/10.2307/2967606

Keynes, J. M. (1936). The General Theory of Employment Interest and Money. https://archive.org/details/bmshri.generaltheoryofe0000john_f3y1

Lechman, E., & Kaur, H. (2015). Economic Growth and Female Labor Force Participation—Verifying the U-Feminization Hypothesis. New Evidence for 162 Countries over the Period 1990–2012. *Economics and Sociology, 8*(1), 246–257. https://doi.org/10.14254/2071-789X.2015/8-1/19

Lewis, W. A. (1954). Economic Development with Unlimited Supplies of Labour. *The Manchester School of Economic and Social Studies, 22*, 139–191. https://doi.org/10.1111/j.1467-9957.1954.tb00021.x

Lindbeck, A., & Snower, D. J. (1988). *The Insider-Outsider Theory of Employment and Unemployment.* MIT Press. https://archive.org/details/insideroutsidert0000lind

Locke, J. (1690). *Second Treatise of Government.* 2003. Project Gutenberg. https://www.gutenberg.org/ebooks/7370

Malthus, T. R. (1803). *An Essay on the Principle of Population* (4th ed.). J. Johnson. Google Books. https://archive.org/details/principleessayon00maltrich/page/n7/mode/2up

Malthus, T. R. (1821). Principles of political economy considered with a view to their practical application. https://archive.org/details/principlesofpoli01malt

Marshall, A. (1890). *Principles of Economics* (8th ed., 1920). Macmillan and Co. Online Library of Liberty. http://oll.libertyfund.org

Marx, K. (1867). Capital: A Critique of Political Economy, Volume 1. https://archive.org/details/owenlibrary_marx_capital-i-1.

Mill, J. S. (1848). In W. J. Ashley (Ed.), *Principles of Political Economy with Some of Their Applications to Social Philosophy* (7th ed., 1909). Longmans, Green and Co. Online Library of Liberty. https://oll.libertyfund.org/titles/mill-principles-of-political-economy-ashley-ed

Mincer, J. (1958). Investment in Human Capital and Personal Income Distribution. *Journal of Political Economy, 66*(4), 281–302. https://doi.org/10.1086/258055

Phelps, E. S. (1972). The Statistical Theory of Racism and Sexism. *American Economic Review, 62*(4), 659–661. https://www.jstor.org/stable/1806107
Quesnay, F. (1758). *Tableau oeconomique.* Macmillan 1894. Facsimile, British Economic Association. 2008. University of Toronto, Robarts Library. https://ia800902.us.archive.org/32/items/tableauoeconomiq00quesuoft/tableauoeconomiq00quesuoft.pdf
Reich, M., Gordon, D. M., & Edwards, R. C. (1973). A Theory of Labor Market Segmentation. *American Economic Review, 63*(2), 359–365. digitalcommons.unl.edu › econfacpub › 3.
Ricardo, D. (1817). *On the Principles of Political Economy and Taxation.* John Murray. 1821. https://archive.org/details/onprinciplesofpo0000rica
Schultz, T. W. (1961). Investment in Human Capital. *American Economic Review, 51*(1), 1–17. https://www.jstor.org/stable/i331528
Shapiro, C., & Stiglitz, J. E. (1984). Equilibrium Unemployment as a Worker Discipline Device. *American Economic Review, 74*(3), 433–444. https://www.jstor.org/stable/1804018
Singer, H. W., & Jolly, R. (1973). Unemployment in an African Setting: Lessons of the Employment Strategy Mission to Kenya. *International Labour Review, 107*(2), 103–115. https://link.springer.com/chapter/10.1057/9781137271631_9
Smith, A. (1776). *An Inquiry into the Nature and Causes of the Wealth of Nations* (2nd ed., 1778). W. Strahan; T. Cadell. Google Books. https://archive.org/details/inquiryintonatur01smit_0/page/n3/mode/2up
Stiglitz, J. E. (1974). Alternative Theories of Wage Determination and Unemployment in LDC's: The Labor Turnover Model. *The Quarterly Journal of Economics, 88*(2), 194–227. https://doi.org/10.2307/1883069
World Bank. (2019). *Gross National Income per Capita 2019.* The World Bank.

PART I

An Overview on Wage Issues in Africa: Facts, Theories and Dynamics

CHAPTER 2

Long-Term Wage Issues in Africa

Michel-Pierre Chelini

1 Introduction

Currently, half of the global workforce is employed, but this figure drops to a quarter in Africa, while it exceeds 80% in advanced countries. The global compensation of employees accounts for 40% of global GDP (World Bank), but only around 20% in Africa. Additionally, informal work, which ranges from 5% to 20% in advanced countries, affects two-thirds of African workers (ILOSTAT).

The characteristics of low wages and informal work are probably linked to insufficiently consolidated economic development. Currently, the continent remains the poorest in terms of GDP per capita and HDI (Human Development Index), with around 33 of the world's 45 Least Developed Countries (LDCs) in 2022–2024. The example of Botswana shows that LDC status is not inevitable. According to the International Monetary Fund, the nominal GDP per capita worldwide is projected to be $ 13,800 in 2024. In comparison, Africa's nominal GDP per capita represents $ 2000, with $ 4000 in North Africa and $ 1700 in sub-Saharan

M.-P. Chelini (✉)
Université d'Artois (Emeritus), Arras, France
e-mail: mpierre.chelini@univ-artois.fr

M.-P. Chelini et al. (eds.), *Wage Dynamics in Africa*, African Histories and Modernities,
https://doi.org/10.1007/978-3-031-99800-3_2

Africa. Advanced economies have a nominal GDP per capita of $ 58,000. In terms of Purchasing Power Parity (PPP), advanced countries have a nominal GDP per capita of $ 68,000, while Africa has $ 6500, with sub-Saharan Africa at $ 5000 and North Africa at $ 15,000.

The use of salaried employment reflects the concentration of companies with larger workforces, the institutionalisation of the labour market, the consolidation of taxation, and the socialisation of major social expenditures such as health and education. Wages are the result of various factors, including the stability of the country, respect for property rights, public and private capital investment, a business-friendly public attitude without corruption, the concentration of businesses, national effort in research and innovation, and a consistent level of qualifications among the population. There are also cultural and social factors at play, such as the desire to improve one's standard of living and domestic amenities, which is relatively high among the global middle class. Virtuous circles of development are difficult to establish in Africa, but Botswana, South Africa (Statistics South Africa, 2021) Mauritius or Morocco show that economic and wage expansion is achievable.

African wages exhibit several distinctive characteristics. Firstly, they are lower than the global average. Secondly, a smaller share of the population is employed. Thirdly, there are a fairly high proportion of informal employees. Finally, there is a greater degree of variance in wages across countries, sectors, age groups, gender, qualifications, and deciles compared to the global average.

This chapter analyses the insufficient and uneven state of the data and literature. It also discusses the slow evolution of continental average salaries since the 1980s and 1990s and presents the main situations of salary disparities.

2 Data and Literature on the African Labour Market

2.1 Collecting Salary Statistics

Data collection in Africa poses several challenges for researchers or decision-makers. While some data were collected by European administrations during the colonial period, they were often incomplete or not published in full. Although ILOSTAT provides wage series dating back to

1969, online data on African wages before 1995–2000 are limited. The ILO is currently digitising and formatting its archives and statistical directories to include older data.

The ILO's October survey, conducted annually since 1924, is the most reliable source of information on wages in various professions. However, it did not cover all areas until 1950. Since 1924, ILO member countries have been obliged to respond to the Organisation's annual surveys. Some of the world's countries were not members before the 1950s, some were colonies, and for a considerable period the data were provided in national currency only, without conversion to dollars. Nevertheless, these surveys provide objective data and should be used as the primary source of salary information from 1950 onwards. Some of these statistics have been published by the ILO in various publications, including the *Yearbook of Labour Statistics* (1950–1957), the *Statistical Supplement to the International Review of Labour* (1950–1963), and the *Bulletin of Labour Statistics*, which contains the results of the October survey (1964–2008).

With regard to the African continent, the ILO has made significant efforts to collect data since 2017 and has organised two statistical workshops in Africa to advance the subject of wages statistics (ILO, 2019a). Data on average nominal wages were collected in 28 countries, and data on real wages were collected in 24 countries using a specific questionnaire. This publication (ILO, 2019a) and the ILO 2018/19 *Global Wage Report* cover 84% of employees in Africa, representing approximately 91% of the total compensation of employees on the continent from 2007 to 2017.

This recent and specific ILO study on Africa (ILO, 2019a) was motivated by the continued interest in wage policies in Africa, in particular, the movements for policy review or minimum wage definition. While wage documentation can be found specifically in labour force surveys, then in household surveys, regular censuses, and living standard measurement studies, most African countries do not conduct independent salary surveys. Salary data are typically collected through administrative records, such as social security forms and Treasury single accounts. These records do not easily allow for the extraction of detailed salary data, including gender distinctions and only cover a portion of the target population.

Some surveys or general reports (IMF, 2000) occasionally provide wage data. The data collected generally refer to nominal wages, which are simply the amount of money paid to employees. Conversion into US dollars is always uncertain due to fluctuating exchange rates or different inflation rates, as well as the real domestic purchasing power of salary amounts.

These difficulties of documentation can be partly overcome through various means, such as using the scales of the civil service or public companies, despite their relatively low and irregularly increasing salaries, or by looking at the salaries of well-established private companies in the country. Additionally, GDP per capita or national income per capita can provide insight into the general economic evolution. The ILO also refers to national sources of microdata, which are sets of information available at the individual level, in ten African countries, such as the panel survey on the labour market in Egypt (OAMDI, 2018).

Additional sources, such as archives can be found with a variable range of data at the ILO in Geneva, in the African countries themselves, in United Kingdom or in France (Thioub, 1994)

2.2 *The Literature on Wages in Africa*

The literature on wages in Africa is limited. The African wage labour force is diverse, including employees, civil servants, soldiers, military personnel, mixed personnel, agricultural workers, semi-self-employed and semi-salaried workers, miners, railway workers, nurses, doctors, engineers, and lawyers. Their remuneration must be examined in the broader context of historiography, economics, and sociology of work. During the period of full colonisation (1880–1940), there was a greater emphasis on counting the working population and controlling it through measures such as displacement and the regulation of unionisation. In the 1950s, as independence approached, and in the early years of African independence in the 1960s, research shifted towards trade unionism and political action, rather than focusing on the income or status of African workers. The period marked by the Cold War and debates around Marxist ideologies raised questions about the emergence of an African "working class", the sociological impact of national economic policies, and the supposed "proletarianisation" of this group (Copans, 1987). However, research on labour in Africa was largely neglected in the 1990s after the end of the Cold War (Copans, 2014), with the exception of South Africa.

The renewed interest in Labour Studies in the 2000s is primarily linked to the deployment of global analyses, including post-colonialist perspectives. This has brought the issue of "exploitation" to the forefront, particularly in relation to global value chains. African employees may subsequently become vulnerable to exploitation by multinational corporations seeking to reduce their operational costs.

A recent major book on the history of labour in Africa since the end of the nineteenth century (Bellucci & Eckert, 2019) marks an important renewal of this approach in African studies. The ILO has also published several documents on wages in Africa (ILO, 2019a) and a prospective text on the future evolution of labour on the continent (ILO, 2019b), shortly after the IMF (IMF, 2018).

Between 10 and 20 topics are related to wages, such as collective bargaining or labour courts. Some texts define the status of "salary earner" for workers and employees (Copans, 1987, 2014). The economic history (Frankema & Van Waijenburg, 2012, 2018) of labour and growth, including wage information, can provide valuable context and distance from the current situation, even in national examples (IREMAM, De Chassey, Vergara, 1979).

Over the last 20 years, new themes have emerged regarding the breakdown of wages by gender and age (Hansen, 2008), as well as the analysis of migration (Girsberger et al., 2019) or minimum wage policies (Bhorat et al., 2017) and the question of qualifications and training. Several networks are currently conducting research on labour in Africa, such as the African Economic History Network (AEHN), the International Institute of Social History in Amsterdam, or the "Quantifying the Long Run History of Africa" project (University of Manchester).

2.3 *A Low Share of Wage Employment*

The African labour market has a low share of wage employment, in contrast to the majority of such employment in advanced countries (usually over 80%). This share has fluctuated since independence, ranging from 1% to 20% depending on the country in the 1960s. According to ILOSTAT, 27% of the continent's workers were employees in both 2012 and 2022). However, the absolute number of employees increased significantly over this period: 105 million out of 384 million active people and 135 million out of almost 500 million, respectively. Some 40 countries saw an increase in their share of the labour force, including Zimbabwe, Burkina Faso, and Ethiopia. Botswana remained at the same level, while about 15 countries experienced a decline, including Niger, Mauritania, and Nigeria (ILOSTAT).

More specifically, there are several categories of salaried employment rates in different countries. For example, Mauritius, Tunisia, and South Africa have high salaried employment rates of 82%, 74% and 71%

respectively of their total workforce. On the other hand, Côte d'Ivoire and Mauritania have average rates of 27%, while Chad, Central Africa, and Niger have very low rates of between 6% and 9%. The level of paid employment of the active population is linked to the economic, urban, industrial, and tertiary development of countries, as well as to the skills of the population.

3 Average Wage Increase in Africa: Low and Irregular

3.1 Average Gross Wage: Monthly or Annual? Current or Constant?

Tracking wage growth in Africa is challenging due to incomplete data sets for all countries since 1960. To improve accuracy, it is necessary to disaggregate questions and avoid bias. The average gross monthly wage is a starting point, but it has limitations as it does not reflect the real dispersion by occupation, gender, sector, and other factors. Researchers prefer net annual salaries to hourly salaries because of the irregularity of working hours. Gross values include applicable fringe benefits, but exclude significant benefits in kind. For longitudinal comparisons, such as between 1960 and 2020, it is best to use constant values in national currency or, preferably, in recent constant international dollars. Since 1990, the use of Purchasing Power Parity values has improved the accuracy of salary data by taking into account domestic purchasing power.

Inflation is an important consideration as it distorts data in current values. On the African continent, inflation in formal markets has averaged around 7% per annum since 1960 (IMF and World Bank databases). This represents an increase of just over 50 times in 60 years and is slightly higher than the global average annual inflation rate of 5%. The World Bank distinguishes between high-income countries (inflation of 2.5%), middle-income countries (7%), and LDCs (8%) as the main aggregates. For the United States and the European Union, the figures are lower, at around 3%. This results in a trend depreciation of African currencies against the dollar of about 3.5% per year, or eight times in 60 years, which complicates annual comparisons of African living standards from an international perspective.

Approximately 15 countries have an average inflation rate. For instance, South Africa has an inflation rate of 8.6%, Ethiopia 9.8%, Egypt 10.5%, and Algeria 11.1%. On the other hand, around ten countries have successfully controlled inflation, with rates below 4%. Cameroon, for example, has an inflation rate of 3.4%. Meanwhile, ten other countries are currently experiencing a significant increase in prices, with rates exceeding 20%. Uganda's inflation rate is at 24% and Zimbabwe's at 36%. The dispersion coefficient of inflation among African countries (9 out of a representative sample of 14 countries) is higher than that of advanced countries (0.5) due to their trade, economic, and political interrelations.

3.2 A Primary Source of Data

With regard to wages, the primary source of data is the ILO reports (*Global Wage Reports* since 2008–09 and ILO, 2019a) from 2008 onwards, which provide information for the period spanning 2000–2020. Between 2006 and 2017, the average real wages in Africa increased by approximately 20% due to gains in labour productivity. North Africa experienced a 22% increase, while sub-Saharan Africa experienced a 15% increase (ILO, 2019a, 2019b). According to the ILO, the average wages in Africa remained almost unchanged between 2006 and 2022, with a growth rate of only 0.1% per year. This is due to the decline in wages between 2015 and 2022 (−2.8%) after the growth between 2006 and 2014 (2.7% per year). By comparison, the global average salary increased by 1.8% per year over the same period. The country approach provides a more nuanced understanding of the stationary two-decade trend, while acknowledging that national data may be incomplete or discontinuous. For example, Algeria (0.4%), Botswana (−0.2%), and Ethiopia (0.1%) are within the average range, while several countries, such as Seychelles (4%), Togo (5.9%), and Benin (7.7%), experienced higher increases. Conversely, some countries are below the general trend, such as Angola (−3.1%), Tanzania (−3.3%), and Nigeria (−3.6%).

It is important to note that salary data can be distorted by national and regional currency exchange rates, which can lead to unexpected results. The year 2015 represents a pivotal juncture between the period of wage increases observed between 2006 and 2014 and the subsequent decrease observed between 2015 and 2022. In 2015, the estimated gross monthly salary ranged from $ 118 in Mali to $ 692 in Botswana, with countries such as Madagascar, Niger, Ivory Coast, and Ghana falling in between. This indicates a significant disparity of 1 to 10 between the most and least

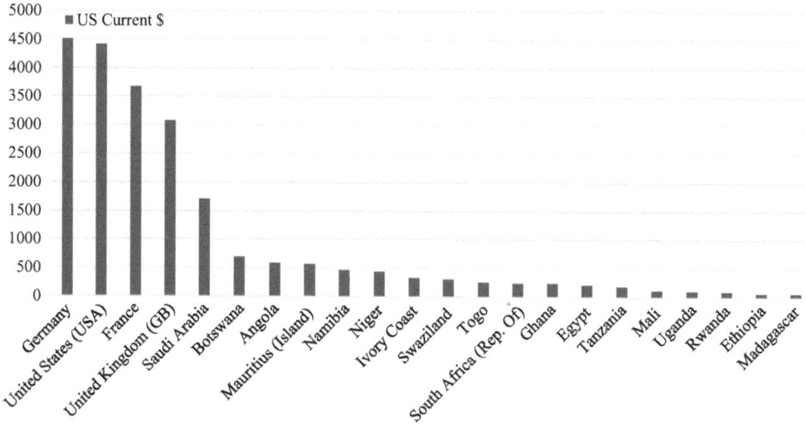

Fig. 2.1 Gross monthly wages in 2015 in US dollars. Source: ILO, ILOSTAT database

Table 2.1 African monthly average salary estimated in US $ for 2023

Country	*Average salary*	*Country*	*Average salary*	*Country*	*Average salary*
Morocco	1910	Gabon	925	Libya	482
South Africa	1712	Nigeria	729	Zambia	339
Seychelles	1517	Rwanda	628	Gambia	255
Kenya	1089	Zimbabwe	600	Ethiopia	165
Namibia	957	Burundi	568	Sudan	61

Source: salaryexplorer.com

advantaged countries, compared to the gap of 1 to 4 observed in Europe (Fig. 2.1).

In 2022, only eight countries provided consistent national data to the ILO. There appears to be a widening gap between Seychelles ($ 1048) and Rwanda ($ 29.57), which is an extreme case, as well as Egypt ($ 169), Burkina Faso (166), Mauritius (525), Botswana (492), Sudan (284), Ghana (203), and Zambia (203).

It is also possible to obtain recent data from **alternative sources** created with the aim of attracting foreign investment in Africa or helping consulting firms manage salary scales salary (Table 2.1).

Associative or collaborative sites, such as *Salary-Explorer* or LeJusteSalaire can provide data that is closer to the field, as it is provided by companies (HRD), unionists, or employees themselves. However, as with any collaborative construction, it is important to consider the representativeness of the data. In this case, there is a larger extreme gap between Morocco and Sudan, with a ratio of 1:30, while the gap between Ethiopia and Morocco is 1:12, which is more consistent with the other deviations.

Converting to PPP dollars can be a complex process, as the ILOSTAT data show. The exchange rate between the national currency and the dollar plays a significant role in this conversion. For example, the average monthly wage in Zimbabwe fell from $1500 in 2015 to $ 5 in 2021 due to inflation, which has exceeded 100% per year on occasion. Similarly, the average monthly salary in South Africa decreased from $1094 in 1996 to $556 in 2019, indicating a decline of 2.5% per year. In Kenya, the average monthly salary also decreased from $ 666 in 1990 to $ 316 in 2019. In contrast, the estimated monthly salary in the Seychelles increased steadily from $ 430 in 1990 to $ 1608 in 2019, which is almost quadruple and represents a real increase of 4.6% per year. The observed increase is driven by tourism (15% of GDP and 30% of employment), secondarily by financial activities and tuna fishing, and by a public sector that is both bloated (more than half of the workforce, the state budget represents a third of GDP) and honest. Similarly, Botswana experienced an annual increase of 3.4%, from $435 to $ 1187, driven by the country's rapid growth. At independence in 1966, Botswana was among the 25 least developed countries in the world. It exited the LDC group in 1994 and subsequently became one of the continent's most prosperous countries, with a 9% growth rate between 1970 and 2000. This growth was largely based on the presence of a stable, competent, and corruption-free administration, which ensured the prudent management of the country's mineral wealth, notably diamonds (the third largest producer in the world), copper, and nickel. The relatively small working population of the Seychelles (40,000 people) and Botswana (1.1 million) facilitate cooperation between public authorities, businesses, and social actors. On the other hand, the Egyptian Survey on Employment, Wages and Working Hours shows a tripling over 30 years (1990–2019), with an annual increase of 3.7%.

3.3 A Little Rise in Wage Growth

Wage growth has been relatively modest, not only over the last 20 years, but also in previous decades. Nevertheless, there is considerable variation across the continent, as evidenced by the contrasting situations in

Botswana, Kenya, and Egypt. The continent's real GDP, which is used as a control variable and expressed in constant 2015 US dollars, increased 6.4 times between 1960 and 2020. This growth occurred at an average rate of between 3% and 3.2% per year (World Bank). Over the same period, the resident population is estimated to have increased fivefold, from 280 million to 1.4 billion, with an annual growth rate of 2.7%. It is estimated that a significant portion of the wealth created in Africa is being absorbed by population growth, as evidenced by the slow increase in GDP per capita (0.6%) expressed in constant national currencies. A number of additional factors may contribute to the relatively slow growth in African wages. These include insufficient unionisation, the high proportion of rural workers who are less likely to be unionised, the size of the informal economy, and the prevalence of SMEs. Given the continent's average growth of approximately 3% per year, it is reasonable to posit that real wage growth would have been approximately 1.5% to 2% per year from the 1960s, with periods of increase (e.g., 1960–1975) and decrease (e.g., 2014–2022) alternating.

Nevertheless, at the individual level, there is a notable degree of long-term salary diversity. Each career evolves differently. Average workers are expected to receive a salary increase of between 25 and 50% over the course of their professional life duc to seniority and promotions, even if their career prospects are more limited than for an engineer. The limited career prospects in Africa since the 1960s have largely contributed to salaried pessimism, where executives represent only 10% of the active population. Furthermore, a significant proportion of workers reside in households and may receive a combination of income sources, including both income and capital income. The latter often exceeds the value of the average monthly wage.

It is evident that homogeneous salary series are still being developed in Africa. In their 2019 study, Frankema and Van Waijenburg (2019) constructed wage series for 34 African countries for six types of skilled workers, such as carpenters or electricians. However, they encountered significant difficulties in reconstructing these salaries from 1900–1920 to 2000–2020, with most of the data being incomplete over time. The data are typically in national or regional currencies, which makes conversion to dollars challenging.

As evidenced by several chapters in this book, the available data sets are limited to specific periods of approximately 10 or 20 years. For instance,

Bamseck's chapter on Cameroon in the 1970s and Wague's chapter on Mauritania in the 1990s represent such data sets.

4 African Wage Dispersion and Disparities

In Africa, diversity is prevalent across the continent and across regional subgroups. The ILO data distinguish five regions, namely West, East, North, South, and Central Africa, while the World Bank and the International Monetary Fund (IMF) generally limit themselves to North Africa, often combined with the Middle East (MENA), and sub-Saharan Africa.

4.1 No Significant Economic Take-Offs in Africa

Regarding economic development, there are industrialised states such as South Africa, several middle-income states including Egypt, Tunisia, Morocco, and Nigeria, and approximately 30 LDCs in the intertropical zone. Compared to Asian developments between 1960 and 2020, there are no significant economic take-offs similar to those of Singapore or South Korea, even in the case of countries such as the Seychelles or Botswana. It is true that the area was not at the heart of the Cold War with a contribution in Africa comparable to that of the United States and Japan to the economies of Southeast Asia.

The predominant development models in Africa after 1960 have been characterised by an initial focus on self-sufficiency, with the creation of local industrial sectors aimed at reducing external dependence and generating additional foreign exchange through the sale of national production. This has often resulted in the emergence of mono- or oligo-productions, as evidenced in the cases of Mauritanian iron, Zambian copper, or Botswana diamonds. The development of the domestic market has been impeded by low household living standards and inadequate infrastructure, which have precluded a dynamic internal expansion similar to that observed, for example, in the United States in the 1880s. Unlike Japan, Southeast Asia, and China, African countries have not experienced a significant increase in the export of processed products.

At the same time, the difference in size between states also plays a role. In 2020, the seven largest African countries had a combined population of 500 million, which is more than one-third of the total population. Their GDP was $ 1.5 trillion, and the average standard of living was $ 3000 per inhabitant (PPP $ 6000). Three major centres are emerging at the extremes of the continent. South Africa has a population of 58 million and a nominal per capita income of $ 6600. Egypt has a population of 104 million and a per capita income of $ 3700. Nigeria has a population of 200 million and a per capita income of $ 2300. Furthermore, four countries with a combined population of over 300 million have demonstrated regional influence: Algeria with a nominal per capita income of $4100, Morocco ($ 3400), the Democratic Republic of Congo ($ 1200) and Ethiopia ($ 850).

4.2 *Salaries Vary According to Determinants*

As in other continents, salaries vary depending on qualification, age (senior–junior), gender, sector of activity, and company size. It is important to note that these differences do not necessarily indicate inequality. For example, salaried doctors worldwide earn two to three times more than nurses due to differences in qualifications, responsibilities, and staffing levels. This study addresses three main areas of African wage dispersion: inter-decile gaps, the Gini index, and socio-professional qualifications. Other discrepancies are addressed in subsequent sections of this book, including the gender gap in the introduction (P. Adair).

The D9/D1 gap is a traditional measure that compares the approximate level of an unskilled worker (D1) with that of an engineer (D9). This gap varies between 3 (in Western Europe) and 5 (in the United States) in advanced countries. However, in Egypt and Tunisia, it reaches 3.9 and 5.4, respectively (ILO, 2019a, p. 18,). In Ethiopia and Madagascar, the gap is as high as 12 and 13, respectively, while in Tanzania and South Africa it reaches 18 and 22, respectively. In Namibia, the gap is as high as 28. The relationship between GDP per capita and the size of the gap is uncertain. However, it appears that poorer countries have a larger D9/D1 gap. In South Africa, the considerable inter-decile gap can be attributed to the disparity between the circumstances of black and white communities. The African D9/D1 gap is consistently larger than the P99/D1 gap, ranging from twice as large (Egypt 8.7) to four times as large (South Africa 95).

One factor contributing to the observed discrepancy is the disparity between the considerable proportion of unskilled individuals at the base of the active population and the relatively limited number of highly qualified roles. This results in a salary structure that resembles a pyramid rather than the more common "ace of spades" as in Western countries. This latter western shape is explained by a more central distribution of remuneration, with a significant but not considerable base around D1–D2 (unskilled workers), very strong polarisation around D4 (employees and workers), weaker around D7 (middle managers) and D9 (senior managers). The advent of new, well-remunerated professions (e.g., IT, finance, media) at the pinnacle of the hierarchy in Africa has served to exacerbate the existing disparities since the 1990s.

The usual Gini coefficient includes wages, although there is currently no global Gini coefficient specific for wages (World Bank database, Key Inequality Indicators). Therefore, for the purposes of this chapter, the Gini coefficient is used as a proxy for a Gini coefficient for wages. Africa is frequently portrayed on IMF or World Bank maps as an area of high inequality, similar to Latin America and the United States. The continent's Gini coefficient arithmetic average, unweighted by population or GDP, exceeds 0.40. According to the World Bank, the Gini coefficient decreased from 0.44 in 2000 to 0.41 in 2020. Notably, the Gini coefficient increases significantly towards the southern part of the continent. It varies across Africa, with values ranging from 0.27 in Algeria and 0.33 in Tunisia to 0.50 to 0.60 in southern Africa. South Africa has the highest Gini coefficient on the continent and in the world, at 0.63. Notably, six of the ten countries with the highest Gini coefficient are African states. The reasons for this phenomenon are still being debated. A number of studies have indicated a positive correlation between a country's standard of living and the reduction of inequalities. The United Nations Development Programme (UNDP) and Richard Wilkinson and Kate Pickett (Wilkinson & Pickett, 2010) have also highlighted this correlation. Nevertheless, this relationship is not always linear, as evidenced by the contrasting cases of Europe and the United States, where GDP per capita is similar and high but the Gini index is disparate (0.25 to 0.35 in Europe, 0.45 in the United States, then 0.37 after taxation).

Intuitively, the general view is that there is a fairly strong relationship between a low Gini coefficient, indicating lower social inequality, and a high gross domestic product (GDP per capita), but the relationship seems less clear in the case of Africa (see also UNPD, 2014). A number of countries show a correlation between rising standards of living and declining inequality. For instance, Seychelles, Tunisia, and Algeria are relatively affluent and egalitarian, while Mozambique is both poor and unequal. Uganda occupies a position somewhere between these two extremes. However, South Africa and Botswana are wealthy but highly unequal, and

Morocco ranks relatively well in terms of GDP per capita but is in the middle of the Gini index scale.

4.3 *The Challenge of Measuring the Wage Gap over Time*

Measuring the wage gap by qualification over time is challenging due to significant socio-professional dispersion. However, according to a series by Frankema and Van Waijenburg (2019) for 34 African countries and 6 types of skilled workers (1940–59 to 2000–2019), the wage gap between skilled workers and their labourer counterparts varies considerably across countries and time periods. Nevertheless, the premium skill range for electricians is consistently between 50% and 150%, while for clerks it is between 25% and 300%.

The salary differential between senior managers and workers varies considerably across Europe, with a ratio of 1 to 3, and in the United States, with a ratio of 1 to 5. In Cameroon, as studied by Bamseck in Chapter 7, the differential is similarly significant, with a ratio of 1 to 17. There is also a gap between senior managers and workers, with a ratio of 1 to 8.5, and between senior managers and specialised employees, with a ratio of 1 to 4.6.

In Africa, 40 million young people enter the job market each year, with 10 to 12 million of them holding diplomas that allow them to access management positions. However, due to the lack of suitable opportunities in their home countries, many are forced to emigrate. Apart from refugee migrations caused by war or drought, the majority of African migrants remain within the continent. For instance, Burkinabe migrate to the Ivory Coast, Malians to Morocco, and Mozambicans to South Africa. A recent study on an alternative website found that there is a 7-to-1 pay gap between agricultural managers or mining engineers and cashiers or merchandisers (Table 2.2).

5 Conclusion

The issue of wages in Africa continues to be an area of research. Although statistical data are available, they are incomplete prior to the 1990–2000 period and have to be collected from ILO registers, statistical bulletins, or government archives. There has been interest on the subject with research on the African "working class" dating back to the 1960s–1970s and the resurgence of labour studies from the 2000s to 2020s on global value chains. The African labour market is structured between regional, national,

Table 2.2 Some average monthly salaries by profession in 2023 (US $). Estimations

Occupation	*Average monthly salary (in USD)*
Agricultural manager	7500
Mining engineer	6074
Structural engineer	4600
Investment banker	3900
Chartered accountant	3800
Marketing manager	3500
Financial auditor	3500
Veterinarian	2000
Merchandiser	1667
Cashier	440

Source: africa.com

and continental dimensions, with networks of states such as the one that links Mozambique, Zimbabwe, South Africa and Botswana. This labour market is similar with some specificities, to other labour markets.

However, it is difficult to determine the evolution of the average African wage since 1960 due to the lack of solid data. Only 27% of African workers are employees and two-thirds work in the informal economy. Moreover, there are significant differences across countries. Since the 1990s, African wages have grown slowly, with the exception of countries such as Botswana and Mauritius, which have experienced rapid wage growth. Moreover, the period since 2014 has been characterised by a decline in African wages (ILO, 2022–23). Since the 2000s, there has been a significant increase in documentation on wages, particularly through targeted surveys by the ILO (2019a). Collaborative websites and consultancies also provide valuable insights into the wage landscape, despite potential inaccuracies due to their sources or target audiences (e.g., NGOs, wage marketing sites).

Wage dispersion in the region is relatively high compared to other parts of the world, with significant gaps between deciles and a high Gini coefficient, which includes both wage and skill disparities. The Gini coefficient has a unique feature in that it increases almost uniformly from the north to the south of the continent. The gender gap, however, is in line with the world average at around 15%. Women are underrepresented in the formal labour market, at only 33% of the total workforce compared to the global average of 40%. They appear to be as qualified as their male counterparts but are often under 30. Family responsibilities often prevent them from participating in formal employment after this age, and they are more concentrated in low-paid sectors such as public administration and social services. Across countries and sectors, women are often paid less than men, particularly in South Africa.

Africa has significant socio-economic potential due to its economic capacity in areas such as mining, agriculture, research, and services, and because of its demographic potential. Regulatory policies, such as the minimum wage in South Africa since 2018, can help support this potential. Workers may benefit from the increasing institutionalisation of some parts of the informal economy. Marketing websites promoting African outsourcing highlight the region's low cost of living, international multilingualism (including Arabic, French, English, and Portuguese), a young and educated population, and ongoing technological development, particularly in IT, data management, and call centres. The most business-friendly African countries for outsourcing currently include South Africa, Nigeria, Ghana, and Mauritius.

Conflicts of Interest The author has no conflicts of interest to declare that are relevant to the content of this chapter.

References

AEHN (Network). https://www.aehnetwork.org/data-research/africa-asia-occupational-wage-database/

Africa.com (media platform, since 2010). https://www.africa.com/

Bellucci, B., & Eckert, A. (Eds.). (2019). *General Labour History of Africa. Workers, Employers and Governments, 20th–21st Centuries* (pp. 637–717). James Currey; ILO Regional Office for Africa. ISBN: Print: 9789221331117.

Bhorat, H., Kanbur, R., & Stanwix, B. (2017). Minimum Wages in Sub-Saharan Africa: A Primer. *The World Bank Research Observer, 32*(1), 21–74. https://doi.org/10.1093/wbro/lkw007

Copans, J. (1987). Remarques sur la nature du salariat en Afrique noire. *Tiers-Monde, 28*(110), 315–332. https://www.jstor.org/stable/23590842

Copans, J. (2014). Pourquoi travail et travailleurs africains ne sont plus à la mode en 2014 dans les sciences sociales. Retour sur l'actualité d'une problématique du xxe siècle. *Politique Africaine, 133*, 25–43. https://doi.org/10.3917/polaf.133.0025

de Chassey, F. (1979). L'évolution des structures sociales en Mauritanie de la colonisation à nos jours. In *IREMAM* (pp. 235–277).

Frankema, E., & Van Waijenburg, M. (2012). Structural Impediments to African Growth? New Evidence from Real Wages in British Africa, 1880–1965. *Journal of Economic History, 72*(4), 895–926. https://doi.org/10.1017/S0022050712000630

Frankema, E., & Van Waijenburg, M. (2018). Africa Rising? A Historical Perspective. *African Affairs, 117*(469), 543–568. https://doi.org/10.1093/afraf/ady022

Frankema, E., & Van Waijenburg, M. (2019). The Great Convergence. Skill Accumulation and Mass Education in Africa and Asia, 1870–2010. *CEPR Discussion Paper* No. 14150. Africa-Asia Occupational Wage Database, 1870–2010, https://cepr.org/publications/dp14150

Girsberger, E. M., Méango, R., & Rapoport, H. (2019). Regional Migration and Wage Inequality in the West African Economic and Monetary Union. *AFD Research Papers Series*, No. 2019-97, February. https://www.uts.edu.au/sites/default/files/2019-06...0working%20paper.pdf

Hansen, K. (2008). *Youth and the City in the Global South*. Indiana University Press.

ILO. (2019a). *Wages in Africa, Recent Trends in Average Wages, Gender Pay Gaps and Wage Disparities*. International Labour Office. ISBN 978-92-2-134156-7.

ILO. (2019b). *Vers plus de justice sociale, Façonner l'avenir du travail en Afrique*. International Labour Office. ISBN 978-92-2-134131-4 (pdf Web).

ILO. (2022–23). *Global Wage Reports*, biannual since 2008–09, last edition 2022–23. https://www.ilo.org/resource/global-wage-report

IMF. (2000). https://www.imf.org/external/datamapper/NGDPDPC@WEO/OEMDC/ADVEC/WEOWORLD

IMF. (2018). *The Future of Work in Sub-Saharan Africa*. International Monetary Fund.

IREMAM. (1979). *Introduction à la Mauritanie*. Institut de recherches et d'études sur les mondes arabes et musulmans. Éditions du CNRS, Aix-en-Provence. https://books.openedition.org/iremam/1240?lang=en

LeJusteSalaire.Com. (2009, collaborative platform). https://www.lejustesalaire.com/en/salary-by-country/salary

OAMDI. (2018). *Panel Survey*. V. 1.4. Cairo: Economic Research Forum; Central Agency for Public Mobilisation and Statistics.

Statistics South Africa. (2021). Labour Market Dynamics in South Africa 2021. Pretoria. ISBN: 978-0-621-50789-8.

Thioub, I. (1994). Economie coloniale et rémunération de la force de travail: Le salaire du manœuvre à Dakar de 1930 à 1954. *Revue Française d'Histoire d'Outre-mer, 81*(305), 427–453. https://www.persee.fr/doc/outre_0300-9513_1994_num_81_305_3254

UNDP. (2014). *Human Development Report 2014. Sustaining Human Progress: Reducing Vulnerabilities and Building Resilience*. United Nations Development Programme. ISBN 978-92-1-126368-8.

Vergara, F. (1979). L'économie de la Mauritanie et son développement. In *IREMAM* (pp. 177–234).

Wilkinson, R., & Pickett, K. (2010). *The Spirit Level: Why Equality Is Better For Everyone*. Penguin. ISBN: 9780141921150.

World Bank database. Key inequality indicators https://pip.worldbank.org/key-inequality-indicators

CHAPTER 3

Wages and Economic Development, Theories and Models

Stéphane Callens and Badri Houda

1 Introduction

Today, wages are no longer a major topic of research on African economies (Bourel & Vadot, 2022). This theme was much more present in the early contributions to development economics. However, the question of wages was at the heart of the initial concerns of development economists, starting with the seminal contribution of the Arthur Lewis model. While the African continent now plays a key role in development economics studies, other continents have been key areas of study for the pioneers of development economics, such as Asia for Myrdal, the Caribbean for Arthur Lewis and Latin America for Hirschman.

Arthur Lewis's approach was commonly referred to as the Caribbean model. The pan-Africanism of African leaders in the second half of the twentieth century is often defined by the distance it seeks to mark from

S. Callens (✉)
University of Artois, Arras, France
e-mail: stephane.callens@univ-artois.fr

B. Houda
University of Lille, Lille, France

M.-P. Chelini et al. (eds.), *Wage Dynamics in Africa*, African Histories and Modernities,
https://doi.org/10.1007/978-3-031-99800-3_3

Caribbean models. The African leaders of the 1960s were those of an autonomous development of the African continent, unlike the approaches of African diasporas in the Americas, such as the one that led to the creation of the state of Liberia in the nineteenth century. Cheikh Anta Diop explicitly rejected the Arthur Lewis model, with its dynamic based on an indigenous industrial bourgeoisie.

Pan-Africanism is the optimism of a continental regionalism for Africa. Among the pioneers of development economics, the clearest position is that of Myrdal, who is pessimistic about all federated entities or those aspiring to them. He emphasises the fractures in North American societies. He is hostile to the construction of Europe, and diagnoses the impossibility of development for large Asian states, such as India.

Schematically, according to Myrdal, the wage societies of the world can be summed up in three situations: that of very high wages in North America and a civic fracture in that society, that of small Scandinavian-style "welfare states" that moderate migration to North America through social benefits, and situations of poverty traps, as in India, for example. It is only in Hirschman, with a recommendation to contextualise development approaches, that an opening is introduced for continental regionalism. For Hirschman, labour markets are less subject to exit decisions than the various economic approaches would suggest.

The theories and models of the situation of the wage society in Africa can be divided into three groups.

1. Those that call for a segmentation of the labour market. The founding contribution is that of Arthur Lewis, with a start of savings from the migration of a traditional and informal sector to a modern sector (Lewis, 1954). Gunnar Myrdal's contribution is also major in two respects, the impetus given to the civil rights movement by his 1944 book, and identification of poverty trap situations that complement and explain the limits of the initial Lewis model (Myrdal, 1944, 1968).
2. Structural macroeconomic approaches. A more precise understanding of the scope of short-term policies is made to better target the specific structures of the labour market in the analysis of wages.
3. Finally, syntheses call for an analysis of actors' games and industrial relations in the long term, such as studies on the history of labour in Africa (Cooper, 1996).

These three periods of the analysis of wages in Africa are indicated in the succession of Nobel Prizes in economics. A first era is that of the pioneers, with the major figures of Lewis (Nobel prize in 1979) and Myrdal (Nobel prize in 1974). There followed a period of withdrawal, in a general critique of all public action (e.g., Lucas Nobel in 1995). Finally, a renewal occurred bringing original approaches to the relations between civil and social rights, the analyses of the powers, with themes of governance and sustainable development, "capabilities", and the evaluation of public action, from Sen's Nobel in 1998 to that of Duflo-Kremer-Banerjee in 2019.

We propose a general framework to analyse the relevance of these different approaches. According to the World Development Indicators (World Bank), the percentage of wage workers is lower in sub-Saharan Africa (25%) than in the rest of the world (55%). However, the situation is very disparate, with less than 5% in Niger, but more than 81% in Mauritius.

We use the following outline: discussion of segmentation approaches, discussion of structural reforms, discussion of "industrial relations" approaches and, finally, a model analysis framework for a table of theories of wage in development.

2 The Pioneers: Hopes and Limits of Dual Models

2.1 *The Lewis Model*

Dual labour market models may exhibit a transitory state in a labour market, or a structural segmentation, for example, between a primary market offering higher social and wage status, and a secondary market with lower-quality jobs (Fig. 3.1).

The Lewis model proposed in 1954 is that of a transition based on a labour surplus (Lewis, 1954). In the original article, Lewis refers to an industrial "enclave" in an agricultural society. Wage formation is "conventional" in the original article, but the details are not specified. Agricultural society is characterised by an almost infinite resource of labour with exceptionally low incomes. Manufacturers can offer a salary that will maintain a rural exodus. This will eventually exhaust the surplus labour, in a moment since then known as the "Lewis turning point", from which wages begin to increase.

In the Lewis model, wages in a modern sector attract an infinite supply of labour from a traditional sector. There is an influx of wealth for

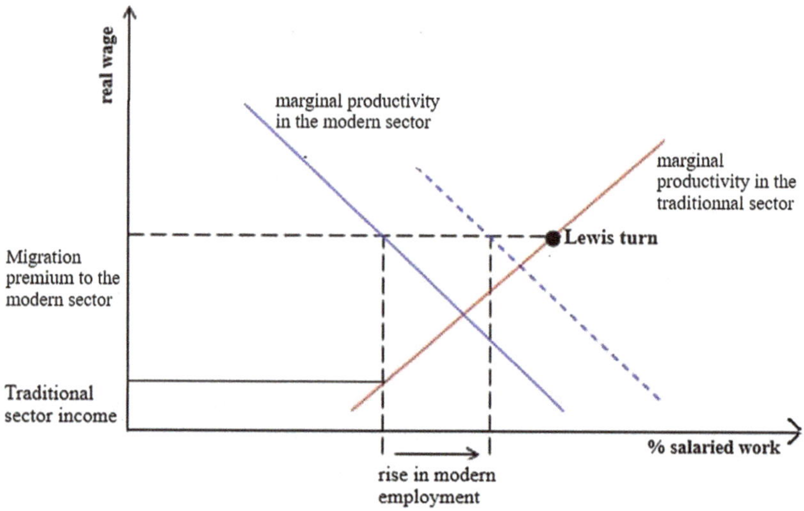

Fig. 3.1 Lewis Turn, depletion of demographic surplus. *Source*: Lewis (1954)

entrepreneurs and prosperity is installed. This model is sometimes referred to as the "Caribbean Model" because Lewis was originally from Saint Lucia, one of the islands of West Indies that moved from large banana plantations to a more diversified economy in services and agriculture. The "Lewis Turn" is the point where the economic system is left with a finite supply of labour. Wage earning is a "wealth trap" in this scenario.

In the Lewis model, land is a fixed factor, and capital is entirely mobile. For labour, Lewis's model requires the existence of a migration premium to mobilise labour from the first sector. This premium may not exist: either the income from the land is high, or the industrial prices are too low. Other aspects may come into play: restrictions on freedom of movement, the excessively isolated nature of industrial sites far from major communication routes and low-cost energy resources, or even different principles for setting wages than those underlying the reference to a labour market.

2.2 *The Need for a Social Safety Net: Gunnar Myrdal*

Gunnar Myrdal is Swedish and migrates to the United States to write his book on the American dilemma (Myrdal, 1944). He plays a pioneering role in the civil rights movement. Myrdal's dual model is not one of transition towards a prosperous wage society, but towards the structural persistence of segregation in the labour market.

His book on India (Myrdal, 1968) is very pessimistic about Asia, indicating that poverty traps prevent the Lewis scenario. The entrepreneur benefits from a surplus of labour at such low wages that it is useless to seek to improve his production processes, for example, by buying new machines. In this case, the migration premium is very low and encourages technological conservatism. Myrdal's conception of migration is that of a Swedish model of joint civil and social rights. This welfare state policy was developed to contain mass emigration from the Nordic countries to the United States. Joint civil and social rights moderate and regulate migration resulting from international wage differences.

2.3 *Diversity of Development Scenarios: Hirschman*

A third conception is expressed by Hirschman (1970), based on the observation of the quantitatively limited character of migratory phenomena, which would rather correspond to a situation where migration premiums would be extremely high. Hirschman insists on a contingent approach, downplaying the role of "Exit" (migration is an extreme behaviour, while mobility is supposed to be generalised in economic approaches), while "Voice" plays a very important role (Fig. 3.2).

A cross-analysis for the African continent does not give a linear relationship between Exit strategies, measured, for example, by the emigration of graduates, and a Voice strategy, measured by an indicator of freedom of trade union expression. One reading of this bimodality is that of migration due to the absence of Voice, and the functioning of a globalised labour market for part of the population with recognised skills.

2.4 *Return to Saint Lucia: Empirical Assessments of Pioneer Contributions*

The theoretical contributions of the pioneers were evaluated in their various dimensions. The island of Saint Lucia today has an economy based on a diversity of agricultural activities, services and products. The Caribbean model has not been generalised in the Caribbean, leaving large pockets of poverty and social violence in Central America. A body of literature indicates the counterproductive effects of investments in industrial enclaves in

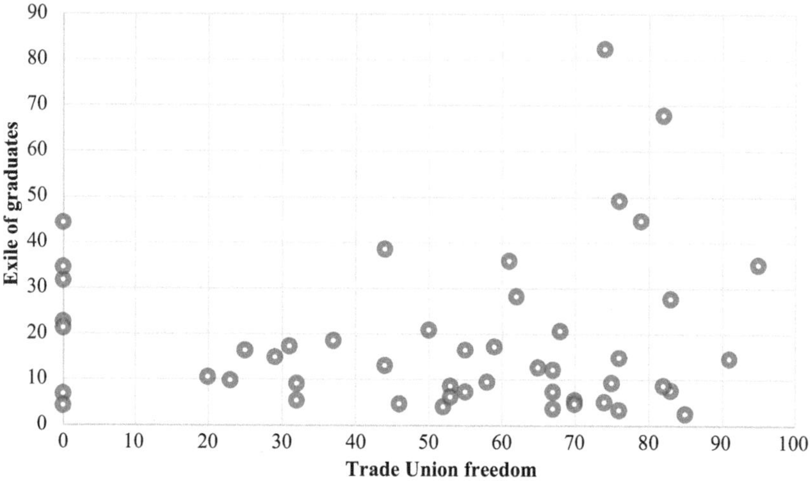

Fig. 3.2 Exit and Voice in Africa: exile of graduates and trade union freedom. *Source*: ILOSTAT

Africa, particularly due to an extractivist conception (Ongo Nkoa & Song, 2021). The most salient missing dimension in the pioneering conceptions is that of the variety economy, with a plural inscription in the flows of exchanges at different scales, from local to global—contemporary situation of the island of Saint Lucia, that of Arthur Lewis.

Changes in real wages are less volatile and follow productivity growth for African countries where wage labour is most frequent. This is consistent with a Lewis Turn type pattern, which cannot be ruled out in the case of Africa. A steady increase in real wages is associated with a majority of wage earners, while the average for the period 2006–2013 of real wages in countries where the wage earner is a minority experiences a downward trend (Fig. 3.3).

Contributions are made through poverty trap situations (the Todaro effect, the underinvestment of entrepreneurs in a situation of extreme labour abundance described by Myrdal) and contingency (an analysis of the context, not an application of a ready-made recipe).

Two underperformances are associated with the pioneers: Myrdal's prediction of a broken down Asia, and Lewis's prediction of an always beneficial rural exodus. Empirical analyses use and discuss the Lewis model in the Asian case, and provide explanations why this Lewis scenario works

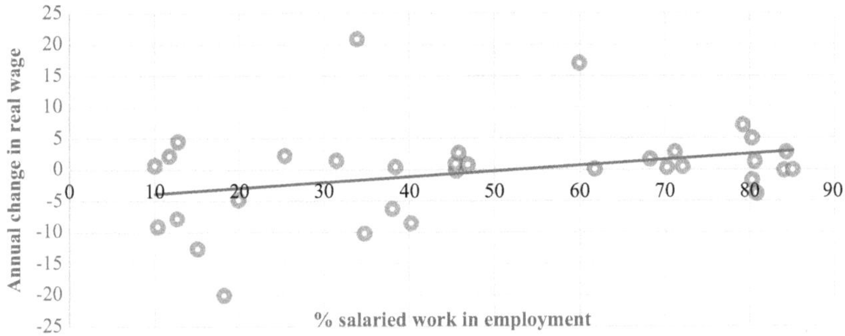

Fig. 3.3 Africa 2006–2013: annual change in real wage. *Source*: ILOSTAT

poorly in the African case (Gelb et al., 2016; Roubaud & de Vreyer, 2017; Rud & Trapeznikova, 2021). The Todaro effect is the formation of pockets of poverty and structural unemployment through rural-urban migration. One of the theoretical explanations put forward is behavioural: rural people value the benefits of urban employment, but overestimate their own ability to access it.

The collective work of Roubaud and De Vreyer (2017) proposes an evaluation of the relevance of the Lewis model for Africa. The book concludes that there is a lack of formalism in labour relations and that urban markets are extremely rigid. Based on a detailed analysis of urban labour markets, the book proposes to set priority on policies that address the various aspects of labour market approaches, and the adequacy of training.

The debate on the Lewis turning point focuses on Asia, with conjecture that this point was reached around 2010 with the value of 50% of wage earning in China (Zhang et al., 2011). As much as the literature encourages us to see globalisation as a very large-scale validation of Lewis's main theoretical intuitions for Asia, the analyses for the African continent discuss the factors that can explain the lesser empirical relevance of Lewis's model. For a panel of six sub-Saharan countries, Rud and Trapeznikova (2021) highlight the importance of labour market frictions in the face of transport and energy infrastructure problems. Gelb et al. (2016) focus on income conditions and show the difficulties specific to the formation of a premium for migration to employment in an African context. These two studies bring to the forefront for the African continent an unsolved factor that the methodological study by Manvoutouka Roth (2019:115) attempts to explain. In the labour market, "actors make choices between what is required of them, and what they themselves require of themselves" that is, based on arbitrations between the asceticism of the agent and that of an offer of a "conventional recalibration of norms". For this reason, the policies implemented can be structure-centred, or actor-centred. Structural approaches employ universal models for specific macroeconomic problems.

3 Structural Adjustments: Crisis and Theoretical Renewal

Structural adjustment policy in Africa can be traced back to the debt crisis of the 1980s. In theory (outside the field of development economics), radical proposals are made for zero debt (Buchanan & Wagner, 1977), and the inefficiency of any public action (Lucas Jr, 1976). Structural policies aim at better structuring macroeconomic policies over time. They have medium-term macroeconomic effects, and short-term social and redistributive effects.

Box 3.1 Examples of Structural Adjustment Policies in Africa in IMF Programme

IMF recommended reforms aimed at improving the efficiency of the tax system (e.g., Cameroon, Côte d'Ivoire, Ghana, Senegal); strict monetary policy to lower the inflation rate (e.g., Cape Verde, Ghana); privatisation of public enterprises for debt reduction and better governance, especially in the banking sector (e.g., Burkina Faso, Cameroon, Guinea-Bissau); reorganisation of the civil service, downsizing (e.g., Cameroon, Senegal, Guinea-Bissau); reform of the judicial system to create favourable conditions for investment (e.g., Burkina Faso); economic liberalisation (e.g., Burkina Faso, Cameroon, Cabo Verde, Côte d'Ivoire, Ghana); investment in education (e.g., Burkina Faso, Cameroon); investment in health (e.g., Burkina Faso, Cameroon); investment in infrastructure (e.g., Cameroon); reduction of public expenditure excluding education and health (e.g., Côte d'Ivoire), reduction of all public expenditure (e.g., Djibouti); policies to increase exports and extraction of natural resources; currency devaluation (e.g., Mauritania); trade liberalisation, removal of import restrictions (e.g., Ghana); abolition of price controls and state aids.

Source: Authors from IMF (1998)

A different formulation of this structuring of time horizons, that of sustainable development, was made at the time, by the Brundtland Report (1988). This reformulation serves as a reference for the United Nations general programme for the period 2015–2030, while the structural adjustment policies marked the last two decades of the previous millennium.

In economics, the term "structural" is polysemic. In the diversity of economic policy concepts, we need to distinguish more clearly between cyclical policies (e.g., fiscal stimulus at the bottom of the cycle), long-term consequences (e.g., structural unemployment) and intergenerational consequences (sustainable development). In addition, the term "structural" refers to the shift from fairly general modelling to specific approaches to structural reform, such as the introduction of a training policy.

The most salient effect of structural adjustment policies is the decline in public employment. With one exception (Capo Verde), this erosion of public employment did not lead to a rebound in private employment in the last two decades of the previous millennium. The most pronounced change in the progression of wage labour occurred in the cocoa zone (Côte d'Ivoire). The cultivation of cocoa led to the formation of a prosperous African capitalism from the 1940s and 1950s (Cooper, 2015:52).

A 1998 report is mixed: adjustment policies have indeed changed the operating conditions of the labour market, but "the modes of coordination based on hierarchy and proximity dominate over those of the market" (Hugon & Pagès, 1998:34–35). Structural issues persist, the weight of the public sector remains significant and new ones become more acute, such as the training-employment relationship, due to the deterioration of training systems and an increased gap between the aspirations of young people and market potential. For West Africa, the evaluations carried out by ILO conclude that there has been a reallocation towards the tradable goods sector and the private sector, a fall in the number of civil servants, the restructuring of public and semi-public services, the informalisation of employment, a fall in real wages and an improvement in rural employment (Hugon & Pagès, 1998:3). The development of an informal sector indicates that labour is regulated more at the households than at the level of organisations, firms or local authorities (Manvoutouka Roth, 2019).

4 Political Economy in Sustainable Development

A specialisation of economic policy is documented by the Millennium Goals (2000–2015) which address health and education issues, and the 17 Sustainable Development Goals (SDG 2015–2030) which cover most areas of public action. Goal 8 of the SDG focuses on decent work and inclusive growth.

Support for small businesses is formalised in point 8.3. Section 8.5 includes average salaries as an indicator. The achievement of the targets set in SDG 8, such as the elimination of child labour, is not on track. However, the issues of wage reappear as a simple variable observed in this SDG 8, whereas it was at the centre of debates and policies around the middle of the last century. SDG 8 indicators are used for a specific labour market policy, such as the NEET (Not in Education, Employment or Training) indicator. This type of indicator makes it possible to clearly characterise the measures to be taken for the labour market in question.

4.1 Sustainable Development, a Reformulation of Policies

The 2015 Paris Agreement on the objectives of the fight against climate change, as well as the 2015–2030 United Nations programme, has induced a general reformulation of policies. From the point of view of economic theories, structural approaches are situated in a so-called benevolent dictator perspective: the economist has a role of technician who determines the good policies that should be implemented by a "benevolent dictator". The pioneering models discussed the behaviours of agents, and the models differed according to a migration premium that could be of the "right size", that is, providing remuneration to the entrepreneur and the migrant (Lewis), or not: too low (Myrdal) or too high (Hirschman).

Naturally, Lewis's initial model leads to political economy considerations: if employees are in the majority, they have a potential majority electoral weight. The existence of a majority voting procedure reinforces their power. The evolution of Amartya Sen's work is that of a gradual emergence of a political economy approach. In a political economy approach, neither corporations, nor other organisations, nor public agencies are necessarily benevolent, contrary to the assumptions of structural macroeconomics. The first works of Amartya Sen are concerned with evaluating the relevance of a Lewis approach in the case of India (Sen, 1966). They relate to agricultural income. In 1978, Sen initiated studies on famines, by demarcating the Malthusian approach of a shortage of food supply in the world. The victims of famines depend on the insufficiencies of their rights of access to markets. In 1991, in their book on famines, Drèze and Sen (1991) say that once you have a free local press, you no longer have famine. The arrangement of organisations, public agencies and individual "capabilities" is decisive, in this political economy perspective.

The universal formulations of sustainable development are made within an institutional framework laid down by the SDG programme and the Paris Agreements. The diligence of companies and public agencies can be compared globally. In these innovative approaches, the African continent is best placed in the field of the fight against climate change, as it is the only continent that controls its greenhouse gas emissions.

Sustainable development is leading to a renewal of analytical tools. In the crisis of the cocoa zone, the sustainability approach is less superficial than the prescription alone of structural measures related to the limitation of public employment, as was the case in the period of structural adjustment.

A policy of emergence consists simply in filling a technological gap. Sustainable development entails the possibility of an error in the management of technological sectors, of a technological path that turns out to be flawed. Moreover, new developments can emerge from neglected technological sectors, such as sail-powered marine propulsion or the principles of bioclimatic construction.

4.2 SDG1: No Poverty, Equal Access

SDG1 starts from a minimum consensus on extreme situations: in the face of a famine, equal access and relief are necessary. The very pronounced worldwide decline in the most extreme forms of poverty lends credibility to a common goal of eliminating absolute poverty at the level of $1.25 a day. Because of progress made in Asia, these forms of poverty are now concentrated on the African continent.

In a macroeconomic model of the Wage Setting/Price Setting type, the structural dimension is supposed to have a rather negative contribution, maladjustment through an excess of labour regulations. The formulation of a social safety net in SDG 1 is extremely conservative, with an absolute poverty level of an extremely low numerical value. However, it marks a reversal from a basic structural model; here a social safety net is positively introduced. Structural policies combat over-regulation of the labour market. However, in the case of the African continent, the shared diagnosis of the African situation is that of labour market rigidities that do not stem from a regulatory approach (Roubaud & de Vreyer, 2017).

4.3 Political Economy of Wage Society

Approaches such as those of the historian Cooper problematise wage labour from a global and historical perspective (Cooper, 1996, 2015). The African continent has the maximum dispersion of the share of salaried work in employment in the world. Myrdal's pessimism stemmed from his country-specific approach to social policy and found that it was not ready to spread beyond northern Europe. Cooper's analysis shows the reluctance at the time of decolonisation to accept the expansion of the wage-earning society. Its intrinsically egalitarian character could be countered by segregationist regulations, as was the case in South Africa. In West Africa, wage labour is opposed by an idealisation of a rural Africa of landowners. Concerns about the management of social labour conflicts have been more decisive in East Africa. According to Cooper (1996, 2015), the fragmentation of the African continent into a political form of nation-state brings the disappearance of the simultaneity of political and social rights provided by the wage labour society.

5 Evaluate the Theoretical Contributions

The models can be evaluated on the side of the intrinsic performance of synthesis, and on the operational side: the ideal being that we get both a good understanding and an efficient operational means; but there are also intermediate situations and situations where operational resources are not implemented.

A better understanding of wage formation and the functioning of labour markets in Africa remains necessary, which is underlined by the literature, with the observation that the "wage" theme is under-explored in African studies (Bourel & Vadot, 2022). On the other hand, operational concerns are important; they are active policies in question. Approaches are becoming more specialised and contextualised. They move away from general models to studies of instruments such as minimum wage policies.

The intermediate situation of strong visions that facilitate coordination but encounter operational shortcomings is shared by the pioneer's era, albeit in a completely different context, and in a contemporary way. Long-term commitments are difficult to translate into operational terms.

5.1 *Long-Term Evolution of the Wage Society in Africa*

In African countries where the wage society is not in the majority, the average increase in the share of wage employment over the last 30 years since the end of apartheid in 1991 has been 0.2% per year (World Bank). This slow evolution means that only a few countries join the three regions of majority wage labour in contemporary Africa. The oldest is North Africa. New countries complete this region, such as Capo Verde and Morocco. Senegal is also experiencing rapid growth in its share of salaried employment. A new region, Southern Africa, was added in 1991, with the end of apartheid. It did not extend in the period 1991–2021. On the contrary, Zimbabwe, Malawi and Madagascar are among the few African countries where the share of salaried employment has decreased over the past 30 years. A third region is Equatorial Africa with three countries with a majority of wage earners: Seychelles, Gabon, Kenya. Rwanda is the country that has experienced the greatest progress in the wage-earning society and is located in this Equatorial Africa with majority wage earners.

Among the largest countries of the African continent in terms of their economic importance, two countries, South Africa and Egypt, are above the world average in the share of employees in total employment. The third, Nigeria, is close to the average for low-income African countries in sub-Saharan Africa (Fig. 3.4).

The foreseeable evolution is that of a probable expansion of the wage-majority zone in North Africa, with Mauritania, Senegal and possibly Sudan. This leaves the two Africas in the tropical climatic zones of the Northern and Southern Hemispheres for an Africa with a minority of wage earners. However, the projections for these two geographic regions differ. The situation in the tropical zone of the Southern Hemisphere is one of stagnation of the wage-earning society at an intermediate level. The UN's Inter-Agency Coordination Office speaks of "recurring situations" and not "complex" situations, which means that the role for local authorities is inappropriate. The need for coordination does not increase in internal administration of the United Nations. Interventions, for example, due

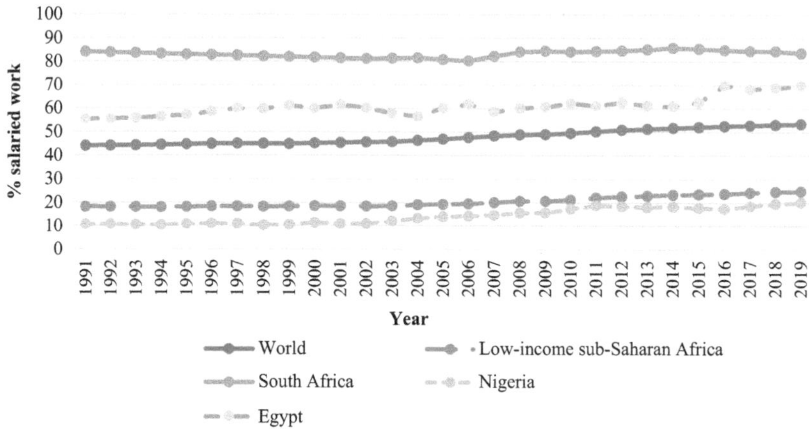

Fig. 3.4 Wage society (more than 50% salaried work) in Africa. *Source*: World Bank (1991–2019)

to a recurring situation of famine, are still managed by a single specialised agency of the United Nations (Fig. 3.5).

The reference situation for "complex" crises is that of the Republic of Haiti, where the coordination of international agencies dates back to an UN resolution adopted in 2004. This "remote control" of management delegated to UN inter-agency coordination has failed to stem the rise of social violence in Haitian society. The objectives and programming of operations are appropriate, but the level of achievement is disappointing, as in the case of the firearms collection programmes.

The United Nations Office for the Coordination of Humanitarian Affairs (OCHA) highlights the deteriorating situation in Africa in a triangle of "complex situations" that require coordination among major United Nations agencies. This triangle is located between Mali, DR Congo and Somalia. These "complex situations" affect a region where the minimum wage is below the absolute poverty value of $3.2 PPP per day, with a minority share of the wage-earning population which was around 10% since 1991.

5.2 *Three Trajectories of the Wage Society*

As far as the wage society is concerned, there are three Africas today:

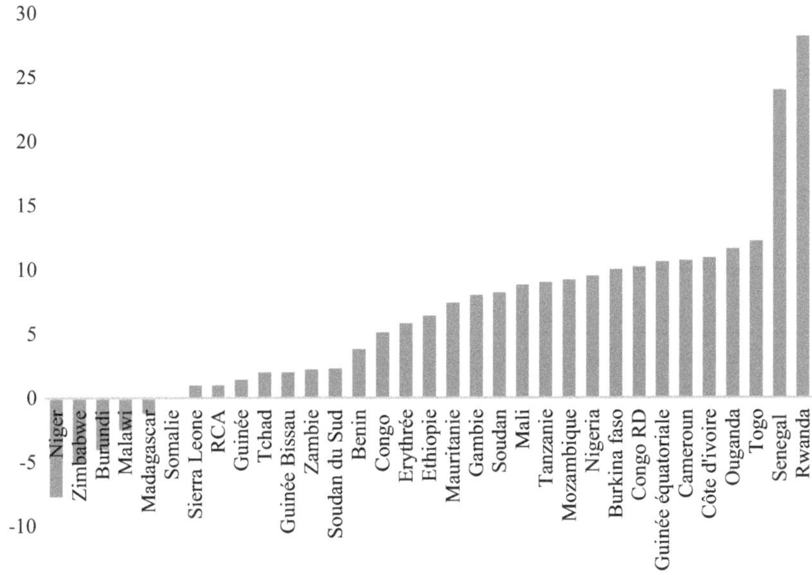

Fig. 3.5 Variation in the share of salaried labour where salaried workers are a minority. *Source*: World Bank (1991–2019)

1. a predominantly salaried Africa growing in the equatorial zone (e.g., Kenya above 50% since 2019) and is strengthening in North Africa. Mauritius has a wage employment rate comparable to that of Europe;
2. an Africa with a very low percentage of wage earners (e.g., Niger); and
3. a stagnating or fluctuating Africa (e.g., Malawi and Côte d'Ivoire).

For simplicity, we limit ourselves to three country trajectories: Niger, Mauritius, and Côte d'Ivoire (Fig. 3.6).

For the three countries compared:

- Niger has reduced absolute poverty, but with a decline in the wage society, while the minimum wage is at the absolute poverty line.
- In Côte d'Ivoire and Mauritius, the minimum wage is half the median wage. However, the fight against poverty has not been a priority in Côte d'Ivoire (Fig. 3.7).

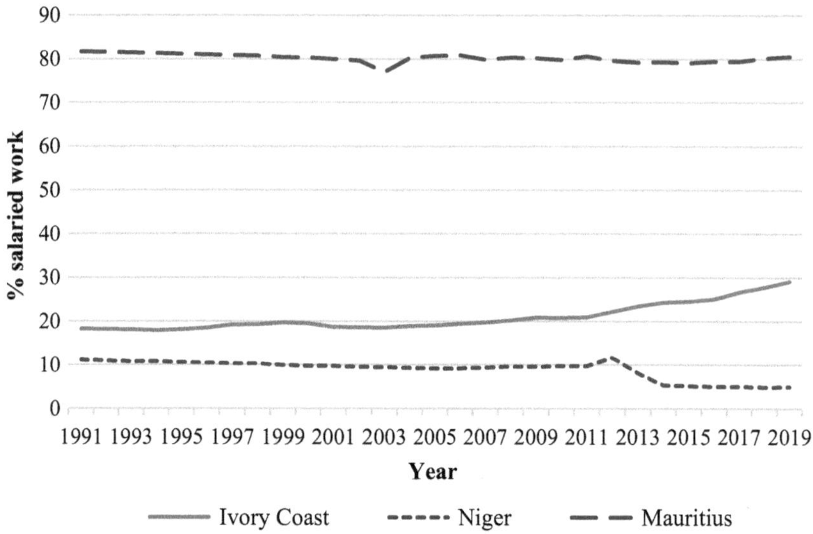

Fig. 3.6 Salaried work in Niger, Mauritius and Côte d'Ivoire (1985–2019). *Source*: World Bank (1991–2019)

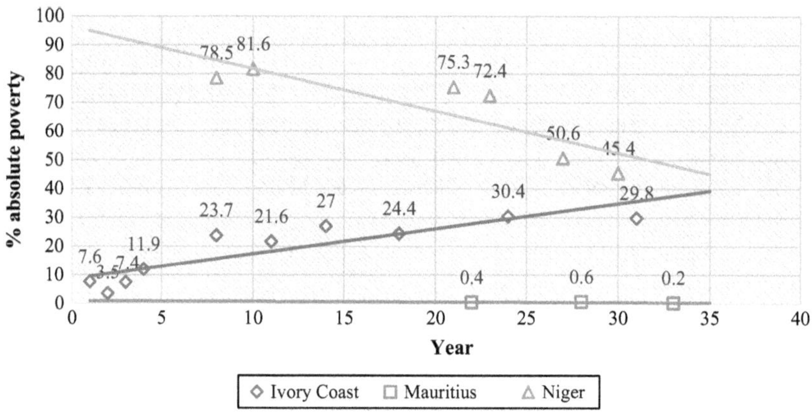

Fig. 3.7 Absolute poverty (below 1.9$ day) in Mauritius, Niger and Côte d'Ivoire. *Source*: World Bank (1985–2021)

Let us compare the trajectories of Côte d'Ivoire and Mauritius. What plays an important role for Côte d'Ivoire is agricultural unionism, in a corporatist conception associated with a single party with Houphouet-Boigny. The changes in the trajectory of the Côte d'Ivoire are the result of unsustainable choices of deforestation driven by agricultural unionism. Mauritius has a more complex relationship, with some union representation of employees, not just farmer operators.

6 Conclusion

The issues of wages in Africa today appear to be unjustly neglected. Theoretical approaches have been expanded, and their fields of relevance have been better defined. However, the models are unsatisfactory from an operational point of view, either because they have not been properly adapted to African situations or because of a lack of diligence in their implementation.

The lessons learned from the study of African labour markets are of great practical and theoretical importance for understanding the mechanisms of labour market formation and the political economy of wage labour.

Conflicts of Interest The authors have no conflicts of interest to declare that are relevant to the content of this chapter.

References

Bourel, É., & Vadot, G. (2022). Le salariat, un objet devenu (trop) discret en études africaines. *Cahiers d'études africaines, 39.* https://doi.org/10.4000/etudesafricaines.36030

Brundtland, G. H., & Khalid, M. (1988). *Notre avenir à tous.* Ed. du Fleuve.

Buchanan, J. M., & Wagner, R. E. (1977). *Democracy in Deficit: The Political Legacy of Lord Keynes.* Academic Press.

Cooper, F. (1996). *Decolonization and African Society. The Labor Question in French and British Africa.* CUP.

Cooper, F. (2015). *L'Afrique dans le monde. Capitalisme, Empire, État-Nation.* Payot-rivages.

Drèze, J., & Sen, A. (Eds.). (1991). *Political Economy of Hunger: Volume 1: Entitlement and Well-Being.* Clarendon Press.

Gelb, A., Meyer, C., & Ramachandran, V. (2016). Pays pauvres, pays bon marché? Regard comparatif sur le coût de la main-d'œuvre dans le secteur industriel en Afrique. *Revue d'économie du développement, 2,* 51–92. https://doi.org/10.3917/edd.302.0051

Hirschman, A. O. (1970). *Exit, Voice & Loyalty*. CUP.
Hugon, P., & Pagès, N. (1998). Ajustement structurel, emploi et rôle des partenaires sociaux en Afrique francophone. *Cahiers de l'emploi et de la formation du travail*, n°28. Genève, OIT.
ILO. ILOSTAT Data Base. International Labour Organisation. https://ilostat.ilo.org/
IMF. (1998). *Annual Report 1998*. International Monetary Fund.
Lewis, W. A. (1954). Economic Development with Unlimited Supplies of Labour. *The Manchester School, 22*(2), 139–191. https://doi.org/10.1111/j.1467-9957.1954.tb00021.x
Lucas Jr, R. E. (1976). Econometric Policy Evaluation: A Critique. In *Carnegie-Rochester Conference Series on Public Policy*, North-Holland, (1), 19–46. https://EconPapers.repec.org/RePEc:eee:crcspp:v:1:y:1976:i::p:19-46
Manvoutouka Roth, T. (2019). *Analyser le travail en Afrique*. Octarès.
Myrdal, G. (1944). *An American Dilemma* (2 vols.). Harper & Brothers.
Myrdal, G. (1968). *Asian Drama. An Inquiry into the Poverty of Nations* (3 vols.). Pantheon.
Ongo Nkoa, B., & Song, J. (2021). Les fragilités en Afrique: Une explication par les investissements directs étrangers? *Mondes en développement, 193*, 47–68. https://doi.org/10.3917/med.193.0051
Roubaud, F., & de Vreyer, P. (Eds.). (2017). *Les marchés urbains du travail en Afrique subsaharienne*. IRD Éditions.
Rud, J. P., & Trapeznikova, I. (2021). Job Creation and Wages in Least Developed Countries: Evidence from Sub-Saharan Africa. *The Economic Journal, 131*(635), 1331–1364. https://doi.org/10.1093/ej/ueaa110
Sen, A. K. (1966). Peasants and Dualism with or without Surplus Labor. *Journal of Political Economy, 74*(5), 425–450. https://doi.org/10.1086/259198
World Bank. (1985–2021). *World Development Indicators: SI.POV. DDAY*. Washington. https://data.worldbank.org/indicator/SI.POV.DDAY
World Bank. (1991–2019). *World Developments Indicators: SL.EMP.WORK. ZS*. Washington, The World Bank. https://data.worldbank.org/indicator/SL.EMP.WORK.ZS
Zhang, X., Yang, J., & Wang, S. (2011). China Has Reached the Lewis Turning Point. *China Economic Review, 22*(4), 542–554. https://doi.org/10.1016/j.chieco.2011.07.002

CHAPTER 4

Labourers, Salaried Workers, and Salary: Makings and Un-makings of the African Working Class

Jean Copans

1 Preliminary Considerations: The Structural Ambiguity of the Salary of Salaried Workers[1]

To study the African salaried working class as an anthropologist is, of course, to study salaried labour as such. But this also means studying at the same time un-salaried forms of labour in terms of complementary forms of revenue, as the general backdrop of any labour, and finally as an *internal part* of salaried labour itself. Study of salaried labour thus becomes that of the relationship between salaried labour and un-salaried labour, both during its genesis and in its present more or less stable state

[1] This section is made up of several excerpts from Copans (1987b).

J. Copans (✉)
Université Paris Cité, Paris, France
e-mail: copans.jean@orange.fr

M.-P. Chelini et al. (eds.), *Wage Dynamics in Africa*, African Histories and Modernities,
https://doi.org/10.1007/978-3-031-99800-3_4

(proletarianisation). Salaried labour is not an autonomous social relationship, but the basic questions remain: what kind of exploitative system and what type of labour force remuneration does it represent? To posit the problem in simple terms, what are the factors determining the cost of the labour force?

Why should we still mention today the conditions of the appearance of salaried labour? Because African societies can still be considered to be in a transitional situation, one of an articulation of modes of production and of productive transformations. Proletarianisation is still in the making, and many of its forms are, in a sense, the partial reproduction of older labour forms. In fact, the context is less that of a succession of distinct labour situations than that of an overlapping of multiple situations where one has to locate empirically its origins both in time and in social space.

The mobilisation of the labour force came into being without much economic calculation at the beginning other than for minimising the economic costs of its production and reproduction. The means utilised to give way to a specific labour mobilisation and then to organise it and reproduce it were neither those of the labour market nor those of a definite level of salary. One has to conclude that the major feature of this salaried position was that of the indecisiveness of the time duration of labour force employment. This duration is related to the type of mobilisation: pre- or un-capitalist forms of labour allocations, forced labour, or even a more limited implication regarding the sole payment of taxes. The labour force is thus submitted to a plural series of remunerations that are not at all determined by the cost of the labour force.

The social diversity of the population going through the proletarianisation process is not immediately transformed into a more homogeneous social setting—that of a pure proletariat based on the exclusive selling of its labour force. We must recall that the proletarianisation process is based on the transformation of the agriculturalist, the herdsman, or the artisan into a worker who no longer has any personal or self-sufficient means of production such as land, cattle, or tools. This traditional conception does not apply to all salaried workers since many are part-time migrants that still benefit from their original homestead. The change of social category and of residential location is long and problematic and may occur over several generations at least.

If the labour force is not yet a commodity, or if no equivalent can be worked out between the commodities produced by this specific labour force and those that are produced in order to 'produce' and 'reproduce' this labour force, this payment, or 'salary', cannot give birth to a salaried working force as such. One has to recall that, until the late 1940s, the colonial administration was very reluctant to facilitate such a transformation.

Proletarianisation does not lead to a salaried working class because the domination of commodities in the reproductive process does not concur with the domination of a salaried working class in the productive system. We should add that this situation is not at all exclusively African. How can such a class become the central mechanism of production if this transformation is blocked by the very group forcing this population to work within these new labour conditions? If we refer to Marx's distinction between the formal submission of labour to capital and true or real submission (and therefore in the capitalist market-oriented economy), we have to acknowledge that formal submission is not just a transitory economic phase, but also—and above all—a political objective of social control. The situation becomes an unstable one where salaried labour and un-salaried labour are reciprocally and unequally bound to each other. A strong administrative and political power (such as a colonial power) is thus necessary to keep a minimal form of cohesiveness within the labour force.

Let me give an example taken from my field experience in Senegalese factories in the early 1980s. I witnessed what I came to label an 'informal', or even a domestic, kind of salary management. In fact, salary is experienced as a concrete system of advances and restitutions, as is common in ordinary domestic social life. This is not a cultural interpretation for it benefits both the worker and his employer. The latter can thus 'hold' his employees very easily. Such a system is, in fact, quite costly since both partners have to elaborate a specific kind of accountancy to keep proof of their evolving situation. Some employers went as far as using a tontine type of contract, in which the enterprise participated as a specific contributor. One should note that this kind of remuneration dissolves any contractual or even ordinary arithmetical relation between the duration of labour and the level of remuneration. Salary is thus transformed into a clientelist relationship where bargaining and the balance of power are the dynamic means of exploitation. This relationship also concerns the state which is both an employer and a class mediator. Salaried and un-salaried relationships are thus kept in balance in an invisible way, for lack of anything better.

In the end, in the African context salary as such does not exist. Social determination (partly of precolonial or un-capitalist determination) and political determination (the colonial and then the postcolonial state) precede the role of capitalist productive determinations and therefore one witnesses no dominant class within the national relations of production as such. Exploitation must be mastered by other classes, either of another nature or of foreign origin. If a stabilised working class cannot be detected, it should be evident that the same processes apply also to dominant classes such as the bourgeoisie. Global society has to be built through some kind of social domination that is also embedded in a form of dominant political and economic structure. Unfortunately, the actual African version of society is yet too heterogeneous to be able to produce a salaried society in the long term.

2 A Historical Detour

Historical research into precolonial Africa is quite recent, going back to the early 1960s. But the uncovering of this history had to take into account contemporary analysis of the makings of modern Africa, first as a colonial situation, dependent on Western domination, and then as a specific new postcolonial world already in the making. Modernity was contrasted with tradition, although neither was very well defined when applied to the 1930–1960 period. Modernity was first understood as an effect of social and cultural changes produced by an external domination and then more carefully conceptualised as being proper to the internal structure of the new nation-states founded in the 1960s. Of course, the periods of colonial influence vary throughout the continent, following the agendas of European intrusion and international economic demands. Some African populations were submitted to the European slave trade back in the fifteenth century, whereas other populations underwent external economic and labour demands almost 400 years later at the turn of the twentieth century. The effects of the various slave trades (Arabic, Middle-Eastern, and European) produced deadly demographic results, but one is allowed to think that the mining economy—implemented in central and southern Africa in the late nineteenth century—brought about more drastic changes through an original capitalist exploitation system based on a racial and spatial segregation known as apartheid during the second half of the last century in South Africa. It is therefore obvious that the empirical observation and study of 'salaried' workers began in South Africa and in the two Rhodesia (today Zambia and Zimbabwe) in the 1930s and 1940s (Hunter, 1936; Wilson, 1941 and 1942; or Naville, 1952, in France).[2] The native labour question, as it was termed at that time, was an important concern for both political and religious authorities in Britain (Orde-Browne, 1933; Davis, 1933). But one has to wait for the end of the Second World War and the late 1940s, when forced labour was officially abolished in French colonies, to witness the beginnings of a French social science interest in 'modern' labour, salaried workers, unionisation, and labour conflicts. These new social categories were studied and described by the first French social anthropologists dealing with the colonial situation, Georges Balandier and Paul Mercier, in the early 1950s in the French Congo (Balandier, 1952, 1955) and in Senegal (Mercier, 1954).

The vigorous implementation of commercial agriculture (palm oil, groundnut, coffee, and cocoa) in the French African colonies encouraged geographers, ethnologists, and demographers to study first of all the numerous forms of agricultural labour caused by these colonial demands. This productive thrust continued throughout the first postcolonial decades of independence, which can be labelled very objectively as neo-colonial since this process reproduced the logics of an already old existing dynamic. This rural social science preoccupation has no urban and industrial equivalent withstanding the pioneering studies of G. Balandier and P. Mercier in the early 1950s. Therefore, a temporary dichotomy takes place between the British approaches (including the South African ones) and the French and Francophone ones, which were still very tentative over the following 20 years. On the other hand, the radical anti-colonial French views were based largely on the ancient communist, Marxist, and unionising tradition, a tradition that can be described as more or less dogmatic. This metropolitan conception of social classes and class struggle did not show much concern, unfortunately, for the sociological specificities of the local African societies (Barbé, 1964) and for a critical view (Cooper, 1996).

[2] One of the best social historic studies of that period can be found in *Chibaro* (Van Onselen, 1976).

The invention of genuine empirical researches devoted to the industrial and working classes took place in former British colonies such as Nigeria and Ghana, or even Kenya and Uganda. The English-speaking researchers, starting in the early 1970s, were influenced by their reading of Thompson's *The Making of the English Working Class* (Thompson, 1968) and also by debates concerning the dynamics of peasant struggles, on the one hand (Fanon, 1963), and those of urban, industrial, and mining classes on the other (Sandbrook, 1977a). A considerable series of studies dealt with understanding the complex makings of these new, or sometimes less new, African working classes: their emphasis was directed towards the various forms of class consciousness, unionisation, and union mobilisation through strikes and political—including nationalist—implications (Sandbrook & Cohen, 1975; Jeffries, 1978; Peace, 1979). A specific debate delved into the use of the notions of labour aristocracy (Arrighi, 1973; Jeffries, 1975) or lumpen-proletariat (Cohen & Michael, 1973; Sandbrook, 1977b). All these reflections were grounded in the various Marxist interpretations which, both on a theoretical and a political level, had been much debated since the early 1960s, especially those that dealt with the nature of colonial and imperial capitalist development, including their sociological class format. The central question was that of the possible birth of a specific salaried labour within pre-capitalist formations quite different from those pre-capitalist formations, such as slavery, feudalism, or even the tributary system, that had given birth to the first forms of capitalism in Western Europe (Hobsbawm, 1968; Gutkind et al., 1978). One can benefit from an up-to-date and global understanding and analysis of these phenomena and debates by consulting the very recent *Global History of African Labour History*, published by the International Labour Organization (ILO) for its hundredth anniversary (Bellucci & Eckert, 2020; Copans, 2021). One should also read the first synthesis on the African worker published by Freund (1988).

Hereunder are listed the endeavours of a French Africanist anthropologist to understand the nature of salaried labour, industrial working classes, and capitalist enterprise (1975–2000).

Box 4.1 A Bio-bibliographical Itinerary

1. Empirical evidence of plural forms of employment in the peripheral zone of Abidjan (C.E.G.I. mission Report 1965).
2. A Muslim Sufi Brotherhood (the *muriddiya*): from free agricultural labour towards urban, commercial, industrial, and then international strategies of income revenues (1966–2006) (Copans, 1977, 1980b, 2000, 2010a).
3. The transformations of Sahelian peasantry from colonial rule to the drought and famine crisis (1970–1980) (Copans, 1980a, 1981, 1983, 1987c).
4. From agricultural labourers to salaried workers: the makings of a working class in Dakar (1980–1990) (Copans, 1990a).
5. Migration workers, factory workers, industrial working classes: the makings of salaried labour throughout all Africa (1985–1997) and the role of indigenous entrepreneurs in Senegal (2000–2006) (Cabanes et al., 1995; Copans, 1977, 1981, 1985a, 1985b, 1987a, 1987b, 1988a, 1988b, 1990b, 1991, 1995a, 1995b, 1995c, 1996; Copans et al., 1987).
6. Isn't salaried labour rather an exception than the rule? (Copans & Bernier (Eds.), 1986, Copans, 1996, 1997, 2002, 2010b, 2020, 2021).

Source: See Copans in the list of references

The role of social anthropology, understood as a global comprehension of all social activities through the predominant use of oral documentation and in-situ eye-witnesses, is very important in African studies. I have no space to recollect this tradition here. One has to remember that French empirical social sciences, such as ethnology, anthropology, and sociology, appeared professionally only after the Second World War. There was a true generation gap lag compared with its British and American equivalents. This discrepancy was reinforced by the existence of a demand for applied research, for both administrative and socio-economic reasons, in the British Empire. The example of the Rhodes-Livingstone Institute, founded in 1939 in Lusaka (Northern Rhodesia, today Zambia), is a very telling one during the 1940–1950 period (Schumaker, 2001). A radical interpretation of social change and acculturation implied to study jointly the rising resistances and protest movements against colonial rule and industrial exploitation. Of course, such an empirical, theoretical, but also ideological, attitude facilitated the study of workers, mainly salaried, at the various levels of unionisation, in terms of their political but also their religious affiliations.

Functionalist and Marxist traditions have been, to some extent, obstacles (paradoxically in the latter case!) to the empirical approach of modern African working classes. The European-inspired models were almost a century old when social science researchers started to describe colonial social groups and classes. It is in fact sociologists and political scientists that explored this new field by concentrating their attention on spontaneous and union mobilisation, on the one hand, and on ideological and cultural forms of working-class identities, on the other. This domain began to be perceptible in the mid-1970s, but one has to add that this perspective was, from the start, international in spirit and not only Africanist or Latin Americanist. These were the new labour studies, as they were termed later (Cohen, 1980; Munck, 1988).

As an open-minded anthropologist, I was influenced by three different trends: the dynamic perspective of Balandier who had been the first to study an urban working-class group in the very early 1950s; the Marxist economic anthropology analysing modes of production and social classes in the 1960s and 1970s (Seddon, 1978); and lastly the politics conceptualised by J.-F. Bayart in the early 1980s in the journal *Politique africaine* as 'The politics from below'. Over two decades I have read, discussed, and publicised all this literature in my Ecole des Hautes Etudes en Sciences Sociales (EHESS) seminar, I have conducted empirical fieldwork on the Senegalese industrial workers of Dakar (as a member of an ORSTOM research team), and I have proposed a synthetic and specific view on the making of African salaried workers. One has to mention that this concern was explored at the same time by colleagues in non-Francophone African countries and in other 'southern' continents, especially in Latin America (Brazil, Colombia, Argentina) and in the Indian subcontinent (Bangladesh and India). All these researches were led from an anthropological perspective with an implicit concern for comparison. Social scientists should remember that, from the 1960s to the 1990s, the French sociology of labour tradition was unfortunately focused exclusively on French salaried workers, excluding all forms of un-salaried and foreign labour. Colonial economic history was seen as a copy of the genesis of European capitalism by way of a teleological kind of problematic. These working classes seemed to be atypical and therefore challenged traditional Marxist concepts and basic pro-proletarian ideology.

Colonial patterns of exploitation transformed themselves into the more global situations of what was still labelled underdevelopment. Salaried labour was viewed as the effect of internal migratory labour, which had to be stabilised and organised in the new production areas: mines, construction sites, commercial agricultural plantations, and harbour and transport infrastructures. Research focused firstly on forced and constrained labour and then on indentured, contract, and task forms of recruitment. It then took into account the effects of temporary or longer-term residential obligations within the labour sites and in specific urban quarters. Workers were progressively allowed to settle down with their families and remunerations soon had to include some kind of regular, though implicit, family or social allowance. Salary was thus very much constrained by its local histories, defined by the nature of specific productive demands, particular social groupings (defined by kinship ties, senior and junior hierarchies, so-called ethnic identities, etc.), and migratory experiences.

This anthropological problematic was thus based on a global conception of labour and labour workers, illustrated both by historical differentials and by complex anthropological structures. In fact, all forms of labour, *including* salaried mobilisation, had to be analysed by relating labour to their surrounding non-labour relationships, as mentioned previously by taking into account simultaneously all forms of labour (family, 'informal', unpaid). All these aspects are intertwined within the very process of the salaried 'contract' which was in fact a heterogeneous and unstable relationship and not simply a formal contractual one.

My intellectual exchanges—and then my editorial collaboration—with P. C. W. Gutkind started in 1975 and then extended through his own connections to an international community in Canada, Great Britain, the United States, Holland, and South Africa. This community consisted of social scientists concerned by what was then called the 'New international division of labour' in the late 1970s (Boyd et al., 1987). My first concerns dealt with agricultural labourers, which was quite normal in the 1960s in Ivory Coast and then in Senegal. I then read and commented on all the available literature in this domain, trying to elaborate a global conception of the African working classes by comparing the various case studies, both at a historical, economic, and anthropological level on the one hand and at a methodological and types-of-inquiries level on the other. This reflection led me to begin personal empirical researches on Senegalese industrial workers in the manufacturing and groundnut oil mill sectors. This experience led to various personal and collective publications. Unfortunately, my long sojourn in Kenya, which then ensued, did not allow me to initiate a new field of research because of the authoritarian political atmosphere of President Daniel arap Moi's regime which controlled and repressed all social movements and union mobilisation during the 1980s, thus effectively forbidding any field research on these topics.

In fact, the Structural Adjustment period (1980–1990) had a brutal effect on the rapid formation of a cohesive and active African working class, including employees and civil servants, with employment labour dynamic facing severe questions through generalised lay-offs and also a limited private investment strategy. By the mid-1980s, the 'informal sector' had become the centre of attention, and external migration overtook the interest in local industrial settings. This shifting situation led Western social sciences to put more emphasis on enhancing new enterprises, produced by private international investment. This level of reality had paradoxically been neglected by sociologists and anthropologists because of the domination of the state public sector and international development institutions. Aid ideologies also changed: national economic development programmes gave way to the fostering of anti-poverty and humanitarian policies (the refugee problem, e.g. related to migration) on the one hand and to the promotion of a local business class on the other. All these transformations resulted in the emphasis being put on a more world-market-oriented economy and on a set of values promoting individual self-advancement (see the role of A. Sen's ideas) rather than the values of a collective protection system institutionalised through a welfare state.

Unemployment, refugee camps, the weakening of the national state, and the disappearance of any kind of public economic strategy dissolved the small working communities: precariat replaced proletarianisation. At the same time some of these features came to the forefront in the Northern Hemisphere's forms of capitalism: the opposition between the heterogeneous peripheral forms of capitalism and the more homogeneous ones of the dominant Western Hemisphere became blurred. The former working-class strongholds became a changeable mixture of part-time labour, mini-jobs, 'uber' forms of contact, and massive unemployment. The making of the African working class became suddenly, in less than half-a-century, its un-making. The problematic in the 1980s and 1990s of the genuine elaboration of the workers through migration, the entrepreneurial process, and urban settlement has long-lived. At the turn of the twenty-first century it seems that we have to elaborate a brand-new hypothesis no longer based on the strengthening of class consciousness and on union mobilisation and organisation. Of course, workers are still workers, but their social and cultural identity is less visible than before. I don't think Africanist scholars can be consoled by the fact that such a condition is no longer only that of the former underdeveloped part of the world but of the whole global world. Back in 1997, I suggested the hypothesis that salaried labour was, in fact, a historical exception and that we should consider the latter not as a promise or a model but more commonly as the provisional nexus of a specific historical form of capitalist exploitation (Copans, 1997). Therefore there is no universal working class.

3 A Tentative Conclusion

The evolution of anthropological theories for the last 75 years has demonstrated a switch from a macro-structural or functional (including Marxism) understanding to a more agency-oriented and multi-dimensional theorisation. On the other hand, the dichotomic views of imperial exploitation have been submitted to more complex global and world dynamics. International migration became the central research topic, and the international division of labour of today has little to do with that of the 1980s. Although it had provoked a strong focus on salaried workers and on working classes, the 'new' division of labour of yesterday is now obsolete. That interest was also fundamentally related to an activist state of mind, whether Third-Worldist, communist, or simply internationalist. As I stated more than ten years ago, our vision of a permanent proletarianisation of workers around the world becoming progressively more and more salaried was both an activist ideological illusion and an ethnocentric theorisation (Copans, 2010b, 2014). Social classes and class-structured societies have been incorporated into a global domination system where all workers have increasingly had to deal more or less with a unique, though very heterogeneous, world labour market. Paradoxically, the globalisation of the various types of capital is not resulting in the class struggle becoming more and more international, and this globalisation is more symbolic than practical. In a sense, the working class is no longer a national class because of its great internal identity differentiations. The social status of the workers has seen them, first and foremost, become more and more submitted to the mobility of capital, to the relocation of factories, and to the transformation of their ordinary cultural and residential identities produced by the consumption society. The case of the detached European workers is a specific case of migratory workers, but nevertheless most people consider them as belonging to the social class system of their mother country and not to that of the host country, which may not be the case for the migrants of 'southern' origin who seem to belong provisionally to the host country.

A final comment is addressed to my colleagues in economics and in public policy studies. The Senegalese economist, N'Dongo Samba Sylla, a well-known specialist in monetary politics and a critic of the CFA system in French-speaking African countries, has suggested an alternative perspective to that based on the increasing role of salaried labour through the expansion of the world-market economy in African economies (Sylla, 2013). Following his analysis, economists and development specialists should rather direct their attention towards a new definition of public welfare management, including some kind of universal revenue. The domination of what we call 'informal' incomes (which ranges from overt generalised 'informal' activities to less visible petty and elite public and private corruption) has to be reformed and channelled towards a regular unsalaried form of income allocation. This proposition confirms that full salaried employment has also become a utopian image and can no longer be used as a slogan for a working-class political programme.

Conflicts of Interest The author has no conflicts of interest to declare that are relevant to the content of this chapter.

References

Arrighi, G. (1973). International Corporations, Labor Aristocraties and Economic Development in Tropical Africa. In G. Arrighi & J. Saul (Eds.), *Essays on The Political Economy of Africa* (pp. 105–151). Monthly Review Press.

Balandier, G. (1952). Le travailleur africain dans les 'Brazzavilles noires'. *Présence africaine, 13*, 315–330. https://www.jstor.org/stable/24346208

Balandier, G. (1955). *Sociologie des Brazzavilles noires.* Cahiers de la FNSP n°67 (2nd ed. 1985). Presses de la FNSP.

Barbé, R. (1964). *Les classes sociales en Afrique noire.* N° spécial *Economie et Politique.*

Bellucci, S., & Eckert, A. (Eds.). (2020). *General History of Labour in Africa. Workers, Employers and Governments, 20th–21st Centuries.* J. Currey in association with ILO Regional Office Africa.

Boyd, R., Cohen, R., & Gutkind, P. C. W. (Eds.) (1987). *International Labour and the Third World: The Makings of a New Working Class* (2nd ed. 2023, 'Routledge Revivals'). Gower Publication.

Cabanes, R., Copans, J., & Selim, M. (Eds.). (1995). *Salariés et entreprises dans les pays du Sud. Contributions à une anthropologie politique*. Karthala.

Cohen, R. (1980). *The 'New' International Labour Studies: A Definition*. McGill University, Center for Developing Area Studies (Working Paper 27).

Cohen, R., & Michael, D. (1973). The Revolutionary Potential of African Lumpenproletariat: A Skeptical View. *The Institute of Development Studies Bulletin (Brighton), 2–3*(5), 31–42. https://doi.org/10.1111/j.1759.5436.1973.mp52-3003.x

Cooper, F. (1996). *Decolonization and African Societies. The Labor Question in French and British Africa*. Cambridge University Press (African Studies Series n°89).

Copans, J. (1977). Politique et religion. D'une relation idéologique inter-individuelle à la domination impérialiste: Les Mourides du Sénégal. *Dialectiques, 21*, 23–40.

Copans, J. (1980a). From Senegambia to Senegal: The Evolution of Peasantries. In M. Klein (Ed.), *Peasants in Africa. Historical and Contemporary Perspectives* (Sage Series on Modernization and Development) (Vol. 4, pp. 76–105). Sage.

Copans, J. (1980b). *Les marabouts de l'arachide. La confrérie mouride et les paysans du Sénégal* (2nd ed. L'Harmattan, 1988), Le Sycomore.

Copans, J. (1981). Les classes ouvrières d'Afrique noire. Bibliographie sélectionnée, classée et commentée. *Cahiers d'Etudes africaines, XXI*(1–3), 81–83, 405–429.

Copans, J. (1983). The Sahelian Drought: Social Sciences and the Political Economy of Underdevelopment. In K. Hewitt (Ed.), *Interpretations of Calamity from the Viewpoint of Human Ecology* (pp. 83–97). George Allen and Unwin.

Copans, J. (1985a). The Marxist Conception of Class: Political and Theoretical Elaboration in the African and Africanist Context. *Review of African Political Economy, 32*, 25–38.

Copans, J. (1985b). The African Working Classes: Proletarianization, Informal Sector, Wage Labor and the Reproduction of Class Structure. *Bulletin de Liaison/Newsletter*, Nairobi, CREDU, *16*, 27–41.

Copans, J. (1987a). Des modes de production domestiques aux modes salariés : cycles de prolétarisation et proto-prolétarisation féminine. Réflexions à partir d'exemples africains. *Cahiers des Sciences Humaines, 23*(1), 75–87.

Copans, J. (1987b). Remarques sur la nature du salariat. *Revue Tiers Monde, 110*, 315–332.

Copans, J. (1987c) [1981]. The 'New' International Division of Labor and the Sahel of the 1970'. In R. Boyd, R. Cohen, & P. C. W. Gutkind (Eds.),

International Labour and the Third World: The Making of a New Working Class (pp. 179–199). Gower Publication.
Copans, J. (1988a). L'anthropologie des travailleurs du Tiers Monde. 'Les nouveaux enjeux de l'anthropologie. Autour de Georges Balandier'. *Revue de l'Institut de Sociologie, 3–4*, 275–283.
Copans, J. (1988b). The Making and the Unmaking of African Working Classes. In *African Futures* (pp. 141–183), 25th Anniversary Conference, Seminar Proceedings, 28, Center of African Studies, University of Edinburgh.
Copans, J. (Ed.) (1990a). Ouvriers, emploi et entreprises au Sénégal. *Pratiques sociales et travail en milieu urbain. Les Cahiers, 12*, ORSTOM.
Copans, J. (1990b). La formation et la déformation des classes ouvrières africaines : sur l'orientation de quelques recherches récentes. *Le Mouvement Social, 151*, 39–52.
Copans, J. (1991). De l'anthropologie des travailleurs à l'anthropologie de l'entreprise: Hypothèses africanistes. *Journal des Anthropologue, 43–44*, 29–37. https://doi.org/10.3406/jda.1991.158
Copans, J. (1995a). Le cercle des ouvriers disparus. Etat des lieux 1980. In R. Cabanes, J. Copans, & M. Selim (Eds.), *Salariés et entreprises dans les pays du Sud. Contributions à une anthropologie politique* (pp. 421–437). Karthala.
Copans, J. (1995b). Le débat Kenyan. In S. Ellis & Y.-A. Fauré (Eds.), *Entreprises et entrepreneurs africains* (pp. 421–437). Karthala.
Copans, J. (1995c). Entrepreneurs et entreprises dans l'anthropologie et la sociologie africanistes. In S. Ellis & Y.-A. Fauré (Eds.), *Entreprises et entrepreneurs africains* (pp. 127–139).
Copans, J. (1996). Recomposition ou décomposition de l'entreprise par les rapports sociaux? In R. Cabanes & B. Lautier (Eds.), *Profils d'entreprises au Sud. Les politiques de gestion face aux cultures et aux statuts* (pp. 63–99). Karthala.
Copans, J. (1997). Vers la fin de l'exception salariale. *Le Monde diplomatique, 1,* 2, [Republished in *Manières de voir, 35*, 36–37].
Copans, J. (2000). Mourides des champs, mourides des villes, mourides du téléphone portable et de l'internet. Les renouvellements de l'économie politique d'une confrérie. *Afrique contemporaine, 192*, 24–33.
Copans, J. (2002). L'anthropologie n'est-elle pas née, au fonds, des mines? In J.-C. Rabier (Ed.), *Formes de mobilisation dans les régions d'activités minières* (Actes du colloque international de Béthune, mai 2000) (pp. 67–86). IFRESI.
Copans, J. (2010a). Espaces mourides, territoires étatiques sénégalais et mondiaux. Comment l'appartenance confrérique interpelle l'espace national. *Islam et Sociétés au Sud du Sahara, 2*, 77–94.
Copans, J. (2010b). Mondialisation et salariat; une dynamique historique ou un ethnocentrisme analytique? *Les mondes du travail, 8*, 121–128.
Copans, J. (2014). Pourquoi travail et travailleurs africains ne sont plus à la mode en 2014 dans les sciences sociales? Retour sur l'actualité d'une problématique du XXe siècle, *Politique africaine, 133*, 25–43.

Copans, J. (2020). Have the Social Classes of Yesterday Vanished from Africanist Issues or is African Society Made Up of New Classes? A French Anthropologist's Perspective. *Review of African Political Economy, 163*, 10–26. https://doi.org/10.1080/03056244.2020.1753405

Copans, J. (2021). Review of S. Bellucci and A. Eckert (Eds.), *General Labour History of Africa. Workers, Employers and Government. 20th–21st Centuries, Africa* (Rome), *2*, 87–91.

Copans, J., & Bernier, B. (Eds.). (1986). Travail, industries et classes ouvrières. *Anthropologie et Sociétés, 10*(1).

Copans, J., Agier, M., & Morice, A. (Eds.). (1987). *Classes ouvrières d'Afrique noire*. Karthala-ORSTOM.

Davis, J. M. (Ed.). (1933). *Modern Industry and the Africans. An Inquiry into the Effects of the Copper Mines of Central Africa upon Native Society and the Work of Christian Missions*. Macmillan.

Fanon, F. (1963). *The Wretched of the Earth*. Grove Press.

Freund, B. (1988). *The African Worker*. Cambridge University Press.

Gutkind, P. C. W., Cohen, R., & Copans, J. (Eds.). (1978). *African Labor History*. Sage Series on Modernization and Development (Vol. 2, 2nd ed. 2025, Routledge Revivals). Sage.

Hobsbawm, E. (1968). *Labouring Men: Studies in the History of Labor*. Weidenfeld and Nicolson.

Hunter, M. (1936). *Reaction to Conquest: Effects of Contact with Europeans on the Pondo of South Africa*. Oxford University Press for the International African Institute.

Jeffries, R. (1975). The Labour Aristocracy? A Ghana Case Study. *Review of African Political Economy, 3*, 59–70. https://doi.org/10.1080/03056247508703257

Jeffries, R. (1978). *Class, Power and Ideology in Ghana. The Railwaymen of Sekondi*. Cambridge University Press, African Studies Series n° 22.

Mercier, P. (1954). Aspects des problèmes de la stratification sociale dans l'Ouest africain. *Cahiers Internationaux de Sociologie, XVII*, 47–65. https://www.jstor.org/stable/40688891

Munck, R. (1988). *The New International Labour Studies: An Introduction*. Zed Books.

Naville, P. (Ed.) (1952). Le travail en Afrique noire. *Présence africaine, 13*. https://www.jstor.org/stable/i24344847

Orde-Browne, M. G. S. J. (1933). *The African Labourer*. Oxford University Press, The International African Institute.

Peace, A. (1979). *Choice, Class and Conflict: A Study of Southern Nigeria Factory Workers*. Harvester Press.

Sandbrook, R. (1977a). The Political Potential of African Urban Workers. *Canadian Journal of African Studies/Revue canadienne des Etudes africaines, XI*(3), 411–433. https://doi.org/10.2307/483719

Sandbrook, R. (1977b). The Study of 'African Sub-Proletariat'. Review Article. *Manpower and Unemployment Research, X*(1), 91–105. https://www.jstor.org/stable/43391963

Sandbrook, R., & Cohen, R. (Eds.). (1975). *The Development of an African Working Class: Studies in Class Formation and Action.* Longmans.

Schumaker, L. (2001). *Africanizing Anthropology. Fieldwork, Networks and the Making of Cultural Knowledge in Central Africa.* Duke University Press.

Seddon, D. (Ed.). (1978). *Relations of Production: Marxist Approaches to Economic Anthropology.* F. Cass.

Sylla, N. S. (2013). Mesurer les difficultés d'absorption de la force de travail dans les pays en développement: Les limites du concept de taux de chômage. *Revue internationale du travail, 152*(1), 31–45. https://doi.org/10.1111/j.1564-9121.2013.00168.x

Thompson, E. P. (1968). *The Making of the English Working Class.* Penguin.

Van Onselen, C. (1976). *Chibaro. African Mine Labour in Southern Rhodesia, 1900–1933.* Pluto Press.

Wilson, G. (1941 and 1942). The Economics of Detribalization in Northern Rhodesia. Parts I and II, *Rhodes-Livingstone Papers* 5 (1941) and 6 (1942).

CHAPTER 5

Emerging Countries in Africa and Wage Dynamics

Gwenaëlle Otando, Mhammed Echkoundi, and Hicham Hafid

1 Introduction

The objective of this chapter is to analyse the economies of six African countries, which have been grouped together under the name AKNEEM to designate South Africa, Kenya, Nigeria, Egypt, Ethiopia and Morocco. These countries are notable in the African and global context for a number of reasons. Firstly, they are home to continent's some of the most populous countries, including Nigeria, Ethiopia and Egypt. Secondly, the countries in question have diversified economic structures. Egypt, Morocco and South Africa are all examples of countries that exhibit a high degree of economic diversification. Thirdly, they have demonstrated consistent and dynamic economic growth, with Kenya and Ethiopia being notable examples. Finally, the concept of emergence has gained

G. Otando (✉)
AVECs Association, Villeneuve d'ascq, France
e-mail: gwenaelleotando@gmail.com

M. Echkoundi • H. Hafid
University Mohammed V, Rabat, Morocco

M.-P. Chelini et al. (eds.), *Wage Dynamics in Africa*, African Histories and Modernities,
https://doi.org/10.1007/978-3-031-99800-3_5

prominence in recent years, superseding the concept of development. Following the conclusion of the Second World War, the focus of attention shifted to the field of development. At the conclusion of the Cold War, the focus shifted to emergence.

The objective is to situate the six countries in a global and continental context, comparing them with emerging countries and old industrial powers, and to understand their place in the African dynamic. The objective of this chapter is to identify the relationship between economic development and wage levels in these African countries. Each country represents a benchmark within its respective zone, namely, southern, western, northern or eastern Africa. In order to gain a comprehensive understanding of the economic situation in each of the six countries, a number of indicators have been employed. These include measures of economic growth, income per capita, exports, foreign direct investment flows, as well as the employment rate and the contribution of industries to employment. This necessitates an understanding of the relationship between gross domestic product (GDP), per capita income and the minimum wage. Furthermore, the impact of diversification of the productive structure on the evolution of wages is examined.

2 The Concept of Emergence: Genesis and Definitions

The term "emergence" is becoming increasingly prevalent in the academic literature to describe developing countries that have managed to emerge from situations of underdevelopment. This emergence is attributed to the implementation of certain economic policies and institutional configurations.

This emergence can be observed in their share of global wealth creation, their growing contribution to exports and their sophisticated industrial systems. Indeed, the remarkable success of countries such as South Korea, China, India, Brazil, Indonesia, Turkey and others has prompted the examination and study of their economic and institutional development models, which have become a source of inspiration for many developing countries. Consequently, the current phase of economic development represents a pivotal moment in its historical trajectory. The model is challenged in multiple ways. Firstly, it must be able to account for the major changes affecting some developing countries. Secondly, it must be able to accommodate the diversity of development models. "The North needs enough common sense and modesty to understand that it can learn something from the South" (Ki-Zerbo, 2006:181).

One of the main features of post-war development economics is that it has drawn from the analysis of the growth process in industrialised countries a number of lessons applicable to developing countries (Otando, 2011). From now on, this rise of the South through "South-South cooperation", without succumbing to imitation, represents a kind of "external economy" (Echkoundi & Hafid, 2020).

2.1 Definitions of the Concept of Emergence

Myrdal (1976:372) defines development as "a movement out of underdevelopment and poverty". Accordingly, the author posits that a country is underdeveloped in the absence of conducive conditions for work and life. These include low production, income and standard of living; unfavourable production methods, attitudes, and behaviours; and institutions that are unfavourable, both state structures and those governing economic and social relations in the family and neighbourhood.

In other words, according to Myrdal (1976), development signifies an upward movement of the entire system. Could emergence be this final stage of moving out of underdevelopment, but one that could be very slow? It is not coincidental that some authors have proposed the concept of "emerging countries", which are situated between two logics: that of emergence and that of development. These countries are unable to fully align themselves with either of these logics.

The dictionary defines emergence as "the state of that which is emerging". As Juignet (2015) notes, the concept of emergence can be defined as that of an economic and social system that is not static, but rather changing, in which new forms of existence can emerge. Van Agtmael (1981), a former economist at the World Bank, was the first to utilise the concept in an economic and financial context. Consequently, the term "emerging markets" was coined in the financial sector to refer to a distinct category of countries with significant investment potential. This implies that the concept of "emergence" should be regarded as an intermediate phenomenon between underdevelopment and development, rather than as an epiphenomenon.

The term "emerging economies" is defined by economic literature as "developing countries that are centres of attraction for foreign direct investment, that diversify and accelerate sustainable and harmonious economic growth, and that fit successfully into the global economy through their export capacity". According to Salama (2014:20), the term "emerging economies" is "a name that refers to countries whose total GDP is significant because of the size of the population (India and China) or whose per capita income is at least one-third of that of developed countries". Amin (2013:19) defines emergence as "largely involving sustained growth of industrial production in a country and an increase in the ability of its industries to compete globally". The author excludes extractive industries (mining and fuel) from the analysis, as these can generate strong growth without spillovers to other productive activities.

Overall, the emergence controversy is now alive and well in the way of redefining the role of the state in development policy. In fact, in their own definition of financial capitalism, represented by the financial agencies, emergence is the role of some countries in relation to the investment opportunities they have. It is assumed that all these countries, regardless of their differences, have followed a similar path of development, namely that of a market economy. The reality of emerging countries is quite different. The proponents of the regulatory school describe the best variant of the new capitalism.

In general terms, emergence refers to countries that are demonstrating economic dynamism, development and negotiation strategies that will enable them to be better integrated into the new global economy. It is evident that despite the ambiguity surrounding the concept of emergence, which is still in its infancy, it is opportune to characterise this new period, marked by the meteoric economic ascension of select countries, such as China, India, or secondarily Russia and Brazil, and the ripple effects of this new dynamism on other countries in the global South.

2.2 *The Emergence Criteria*

Overall, the concept of "emergence" is confusing and refers to several realities at a time. With its different meanings, it looked like the concept of "governance" when it first appeared in the early 1990s. Hence the need for a real work of analysis, precision and context so that the term can play the role of an analysis chart of some economic and institutional phenomena which are the characteristics of a set of countries of the South. Nevertheless, this concept is poised to become a pivotal element in the analysis of the developmental trajectories of select countries in the Global

South. Indeed, the economic emergence, unlike the dominant approach, can in no case be reduced to simple qualitative phenomena.

"Emergence refers to social and economic change paths closely centred on globalization" (Piveteau & Rougier, 2010). Similarly, for Amin (2013): "One can't speak of emergence in general, or even (Chinese, Indian, Brazilian, Korean) models in general. One must consider, for each case, the successive stages of the relevant emerging trends, identify their strengths and weaknesses, and analyse the dynamics of deployment of their contradictions".

It is clear that the criteria for classifying a country as "emerging" are so numerous and remain equivocal in the image of a concept in search of scientific legitimacy and theoretical thickness. However, a non-exhaustive list of criteria can be developed while taking the necessary scientific precautions so as not to mix up the concepts of "emerging countries", "pre-emerging countries", "emerging markets", "economic emergence", "political emergence" and "emerging power" (Table 5.1).

Three distinct approaches to emergence can be identified, namely the financial approach, the neo-institutional approach and the self-centred approach. The financial approach defines the emergence of the phenomenon of the convergence of the economies of the South with the model of the market economy (Anglo-Saxon capitalism). This approach is essentially modelled on the logic of financial markets, or "emerging markets" are those where investment opportunities (capital investment) are

Table 5.1 The different facets of emergence

Emerging markets	FDI attractiveness and quality of institutions
Emerging countries	Existence of a strong industrial system
Pre-emerging countries	Economic policies for emergence Institution building
Economic emergence	A very high rate on economic openness Upsurge in the global value chain Steady growth over several years
Political emergence	Assertion on the world stage Economic sovereignty Will to influence global governance
Emerging powers	Countries on the final stage of economic convergence with high population and substantial foreign currency reserves

Source: Authors

important. This is the approach of international financial institutions, rating agencies and investment banks. The other two approaches are derived from development economics.

The second approach is where emergence is associated with the development of the culture of capitalism in countries that were previously designated as "peripheries", through a process of integration into the world economy and closer adherence to the rules of globalisation. This approach may be described as "neo-institutional". The third approach posits that emergence is a unique phenomenon within the context of the world economy. It suggests that certain countries have managed to establish themselves on the global economic stage by pursuing distinct development paths, in which the state has played a pivotal role. This approach could be described as "self-centred development" (with a specific role for exports). This has resulted in the emergence of novel forms of capitalism.

According to Cohen (2013): "As Ulgen (2013:24) points out, with the spread of the concept of 'emergence', it is ultimately the analytical power of the concept of development in the face of ongoing change that is being challenged".

Table 5.2 shows the different emergence criteria selected by the international institutions (IMF and World Bank).

It is important to note that the economies of the AKNEEM countries exhibit significant differences in economic growth dynamics. With regard to the proportion of natural resources in GDP, two categories of countries can be identified: those with a high level of natural resources and those with a low level. For instance, Ethiopia, Nigeria and South Africa are experiencing economic growth driven by the exploitation of natural resources, energy and mining. In the case of Egypt and Kenya, natural resources account for 3% and 1% of GDP, respectively. In contrast, Morocco is categorised as a country without natural resources, as these account for less than 1% of GDP.

3 Emerging Countries: What Place for Africa?

3.1 The Major Emerging Countries

The emergence of new powers from developing countries highlights the failure of development policies advocated by international institutions. Indeed, it is the countries that have distinguished themselves from the shock therapy of international institutions that currently enjoy the status

Table 5.2 Determinants of emergence

Criteria according to the IMF and the World Bank	
Political and macro-economic stability	A political and social stability A healthy and vibrant public finance management
Economic dynamics and openness	Liberalisation of economic activities The opening to the outside through trade and investment The existence of a vibrant private sector, competitive, creative and visionary
A regulatory framework for quality	Streamlined administrative procedures A credible legal and judicial system
Long-term bases of appropriate development	The ability to absorb technology transfer The existence of good infrastructures A human capital in abundance
The quality of political leadership	The quality of institutions

Criteria for emergence according to CEPII
A level of wealth (income per capita in 1996 below 70% of the average level of OECD countries)
Increasing participation in international trade in manufactured goods (growth of exports of manufactured goods than 2% per year for the growth of world trade)
An attraction of international capital flows (the role of financial markets)

Source: Authors

of emerging powers. Development policies implemented by these countries gave pride of place to the State in the promotion, planning and coordination of development policies; hence the relevant qualification of "Strategist State" increasingly used to show the new role of the State in development. "In any case", writes Elie Cohen (2013), the principal economic phenomenon of the last forty years has been the tremendous rise of emerging countries".

The key factors driving the ascension of these four countries, collectively referred to as the BRICs despite their notable differences, include the role of institutions as one of the first (Goldstein & Lemoine, 2013). Indeed, these four countries have implemented a series of reforms in recent years with the objective of improving the quality of their institutions and creating local institutional configurations conducive to structural change. In the same dynamic, the distinguishing feature of the major emerging economies (China, India, Russia and Brazil) is also their capacity to develop robust companies that can rival Western counterparts. The pursuit of different national trajectories suggests the existence of a multitude of forms of capitalism. One might inquire as to whether these countries are in the process of transitioning to a standard market economy or whether they are attempting to develop new variants of capitalism (Goldstein & Lemoine, 2013).

Nevertheless, a number of other factors appear to be responsible for the remarkable and quite diverse ascension of these four countries. Firstly, it is evident that the significance of savings from these countries is on the rise. As demonstrated in the compilation edited by Lorenzi (2009: 38), emerging countries are distinguished by a surplus of savings. In 2006, the savings rate reached 57% of GDP in China, 28% in Russia and in emerging Asia excluding China. In 2023, the gross savings rate in India was 30%, while in Indonesia it was 37% (World Bank). This is a clear indication of the new global distribution of savings. The significance of capital goods and technology products in export structures is analogous to those of developed countries. The pattern of the South exchanging apparel for advanced machinery and equipment now appears to be obsolete (Lorenzi, 2009). Furthermore, globalisation has played an important role in the development of emerging markets. However, as Rodrik (2008) notes, "the beneficiaries of globalisation—China, India, Vietnam and other Asian countries—have not applied the rules of the Washington Consensus, and those who have tried to do so—most countries in South America and Africa—have only reaped limited benefits".

3.2 *The "Pre-emergent" African Countries*

In Africa, as in the major emerging markets, we are witnessing the rise of a number of countries that are clearly characterised by robust economic growth, significant institutional reforms, the introduction of new policies that diversify the upside of the global value chain, the importance of the middle class, the size of the population, as well as massive investment in infrastructure and the importance of financial centres. This is exemplified by countries such as South Africa, Kenya, Nigeria, Egypt, Ethiopia and Morocco, which can be grouped under the acronym AKNEEM. These countries are considered to be in a "pre-emerging" phase, although South Africa has already been designated as a member of the BRICS group. South Africa has experienced a period of subdued economic growth and social unrest in recent years, prompting questions about the suitability of its continued inclusion in this grouping (Table 5.3).

It is important to underscore the fact that in this block, some countries like Nigeria or South Africa are highly dependent on the export of raw materials, including mining, oil and gas, while others like Morocco, Kenya and Ethiopia followed a growth path based on the diversity of the production structure and better integration into regional and even global chains of value.

It is important to note that with a population of 592 millions in 2023 and the emergence of a large middle class, these countries have become attractive for investment in certain sectors such as the automotive industry, luxury goods, etc. In terms of demographics, Fig. 5.1 shows the position of Nigeria, Ethiopia and Egypt. In fact, these three countries will account together for 442 millions people in 2023. Nigeria is the most populous country in Africa, with a population of 213 millions, followed by Ethiopia (120 millions) and Egypt (109 millions). It is notable that, according to projections, Nigeria will be home to more than 440 millions people by 2050, making it an African and even global demographic power. A similar trend is observed in Ethiopia, where the population is projected to reach 220 millions by 2050, or 130 millions for the Maghreb countries.

Nigeria is the most significant contributor to this demographic dynamic, with a population comprising 35% of the total group. Ethiopia, Egypt, South Africa, Kenya and Morocco also play a significant role, with populations comprising 20%, 18%, 10%, 9% and 6% of the total group, respectively. Kenya, whose population has continued to grow since 1980, from 16 millions in 1980 to 53 millions in 2023, will be among the most populous African countries, with a total population of 97 millions in 2050. South Africa and Morocco are relatively less populous than the countries in this group, with 63 millions and 43 millions inhabitants respectively by 2050. The estimated total population of the AKNEEM group thus increases from 220 millions inhabitants in 1980 to nearly 600 millions in 2024, and demographic projections suggest nearly 950 millions in 2050, assuming that the growth trajectory remains unchanged. However, the simple fact of establishing projections can change the growth trajectory upstream.

As previously stated, one of the defining characteristics of emergence is the contribution to regional and global GDP. Figure 5.2 provides an overview of the contribution of the old and new powers, as well as African countries that are part of AKNEEM. In addition to the underlying trends

Table 5.3 Demography as a determinant of emergence

	Population in millions of inhabitants						*Share of world population*				
	1980	*1990*	*2000*	*2013*	*2025*		*1980*	*1990*	*2000*	*2013*	*2025*
Developed countries						*Developed countries*					
USA	233	258	289	324	354	USA	5%	5%	5%	5%	4%
Japan	116	122	126	127	123	Japan	3%	2%	2%	2%	2%
Germany		80	84	83	81	Germany		2%	1%	1%	1%
France	55	58	61	67	71	France	1%	1%	1%	1%	1%
UK	56	57	59	63	67	UK	1%	1%	1%	1%	1%
Italy	56	57	57	61	61	Italy	1%	1%	1%	1%	1%
Canada	25	28	31	35	39	Canada	1%	1%	1%	0.5%	0.5%
BRIC						**BRIC**					
Brazil	122	150	175	200	218	Brazil	3%	3%	3%	3%	3%
Russia			147	143	137	Russia			2%	2%	2%
India	699	869	1042	1252	1419	India	16%	16%	17%	17%	18%
China	984	1165	1280	1386	1449	China	22%	22%	21%	19%	18%
AKNEEM						**AKNEEM**					
South Africa	29	37	45	53	57	South Africa	1%	1%	1%	1%	1%
Kenya	16	23	31	44	59	Kenya		0.4%	1%	1%	1%
Nigeria	74	96	123	174	240	Nigeria	2%	2%	2%	2%	3%
Egypt	45	65	66	82	97	Egypt	1%	1%	1%	1%	1%
Ethiopia			66	94	125	Ethiopia			1%	1%	2%
Morocco	20	25	29	33	38	Morocco	0.4%	0.5%	0.5%	0.5%	0.5%

Source: UNCTAD, 2024, compiled by the authors

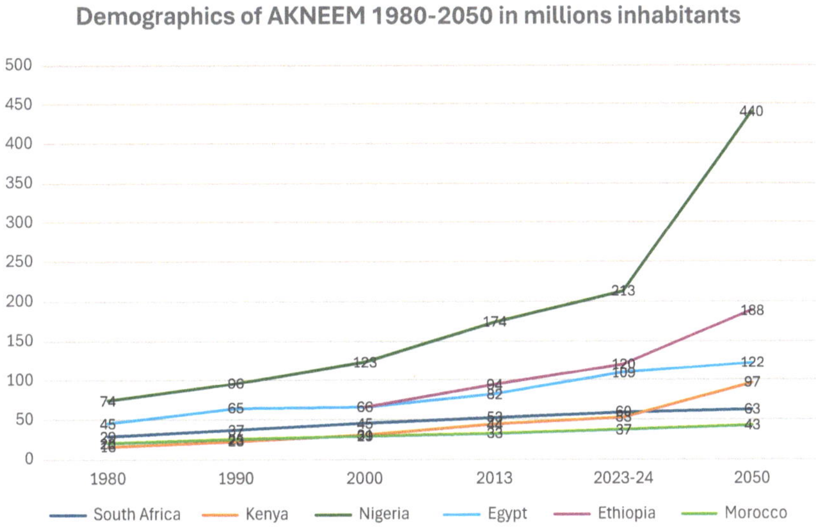

Fig. 5.1 Demographics of AKNEEM, past and future. Note: units in millions. Source: UNCTAD and World Bank data base, 2024 compiled by the authors

associated with the decline of shares in developed countries, which continue to contribute 43.7% of global GDP in 2022, we observe a significant shift from the BRICS, whose share has increased from 8% in 2000 to nearly 24% in 2022 and around 30% in 2024 (28% nominal, 32% PPP). This growth is largely driven by the growing contribution of China (17% of global GDP), India (4%) and Brazil (2%). With regard to the AKNEEM group, although its contribution to global GDP is relatively modest, it is nevertheless on an upward trajectory. Indeed, the proportion of global GDP contributed by the AKNEEM group increased from 1% in 2000 to 1.44% in 2013 and 1.6% in 2024. This contribution is insignificant in terms of the ability of these countries to influence the global economy, despite their role in the African regional economy. This is in contrast to the reality of the BRIC countries, which now exert a considerable influence on the global economy.

However, at the regional level, the influence of AKNEEM is considerable, with six countries accounting for 60 to 65% of the continental wealth, with a total of 1.700 billion in 2024 (Africa: 2.800 billion nominal, 10.800 billion PPA). In 2022, the total GDP of Nigeria reached 440 billion, South

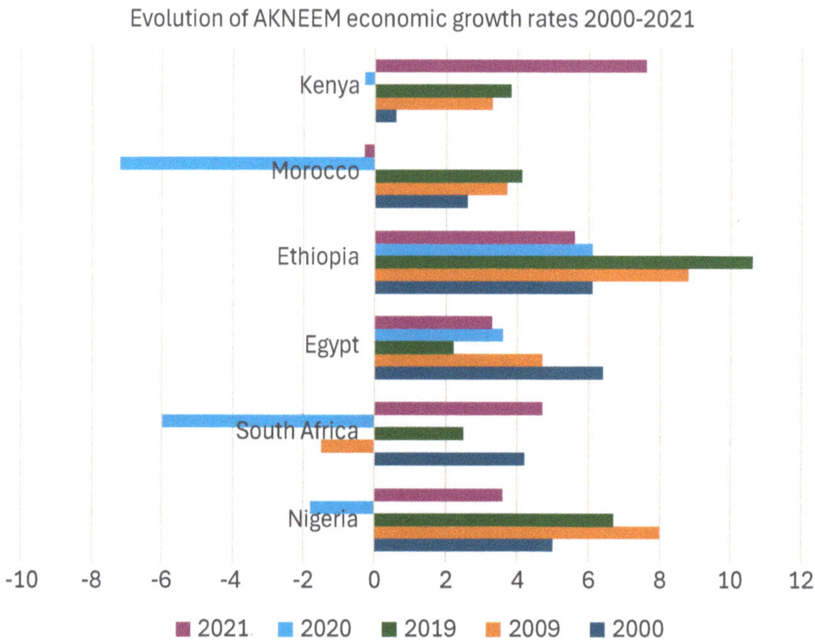

Fig. 5.2 Evolution of the economic growth rates of AKNEEM. Source: UNCTAD, 2024, compiled by the authors

Africa: 420, Egypt: 404, Morocco: 142, Ethiopia: 113, Kenya: 110. In terms of the AKNEEM group's GDP, Nigeria was the leading contributor, with a contribution of approximately 27%. South Africa, Egypt, Morocco, Ethiopia and Kenya, respectively, followed with contributions of 26%, 25%, 9%, 7% and 7%. As illustrated in Fig. 5.2, the majority of AKNEEM countries have demonstrated a consistent increase in growth over the 22-year period from 2000 to 2022, with an average growth rate of approximately 3%.

The 2019 crisis linked to the novel coronavirus (Covid-19) had a more pronounced impact on the economies of AKNEEM than that of 2008. This is due to the nature of this crisis and its consequences on global value chains, as well as the dynamics of supply and demand. Some countries, such as Morocco, Egypt and Nigeria, appear to have been more significantly impacted than others, with the growth rate experiencing a notable decline. The growth of some AKNEEM countries is largely driven by the export of oil and mining products. In Nigeria, 87% of total exports comprise oil, while in Egypt, the figure is 26%. In South Africa, 29% of exports are derived from mines and metals.

In comparison to the export concentration index, which allows for the assessment of the level of diversification, it is evident that there is a high concentration of exports in the cases of Nigeria and Ethiopia. Indeed, Nigeria exhibits the highest concentration index of the entire group, despite a decrease observed between 2000 and 2022, from 0.92 to 0.76. This can be attributed to the prevalence of energy resources in the composition of exports. Ethiopia is the second country in the group with a relatively high concentration index of 0.35 for 2022, in comparison to 0.48 in 2000. Kenya is the third country in the group in terms of export concentration, preceded by South Africa, Egypt and Morocco.

Globalisation has had a positive impact on the diversification of the productive structure of AKNEEM. While the number of products exported from South Africa decreased from 256 to 253 between 2000 and 2022, exports from other countries have been enriched with new products. This indicates a dynamic of industrialisation and tertiarisation. Consequently, the export structure of Nigeria was augmented by 15%, while that of Morocco, Kenya, Egypt and Ethiopia, respectively, by 13%, 14%, 7% and 60%. Despite the high concentration of exports from countries such as Nigeria and Ethiopia, their productive structure appears to be on the path to diversification.

4 The Wages Dynamic in the "Pre-emergent" African Countries

As illustrated in Fig. 5.3, labour income plays a significant role in the GDP of the AKNEEM countries. This is particularly evident in South Africa and Nigeria, where labour income accounts for 60.7% and 68.2% of GDP, respectively. This illustrates the significance of this mechanism in the redistribution of wealth at the national level. In the case of Egypt, Morocco and Kenya, the aforementioned share is reduced to 43.6%, 44.8% and 37.8% respectively.

Two African countries, South Africa and Nigeria, stand out for the proportion of labour income in their respective gross domestic products (GDPs). The average proportion of AKNEEM labour income in gross domestic product for the group is approximately 50%, a figure that is somewhat lower than that observed in Western advanced countries (50 to

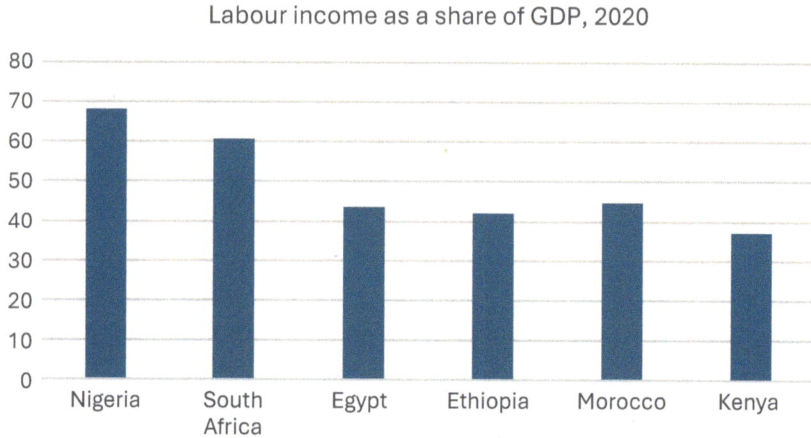

Fig. 5.3 Labour income as a share of GDP, 2020. Source: ILOSTAT, 2024

Table 5.4 GDP per capita and minimum wage

	Minimum wage, current $	*Nominal GDP per capita*
Nigeria	70	1700
South Africa	250	6700
Egypt	157	4300
Ethiopia	22	1000
Morocco	286	3400
Kenya	136	2100

Source: ILOSTAT, 2024

70%). This situation is primarily attributable to the lower proportion of wage labour and the duality of the economy, with a significant informal sector, despite the various policies implemented by the governments to integrate this sector into the formal economy.

The issue of minimum wages has been gaining in importance in the world of work since the 2000s, in part due to the influence of the International Labour Organization (ILO). Table 5.4 demonstrates that there is no correlation between national income per capita and the minimum wage. Indeed, in five countries in the group, the relationship between the two indicators is highly disparate. This is primarily attributable to the prevalence of the informal economy and the lack of dynamism in the

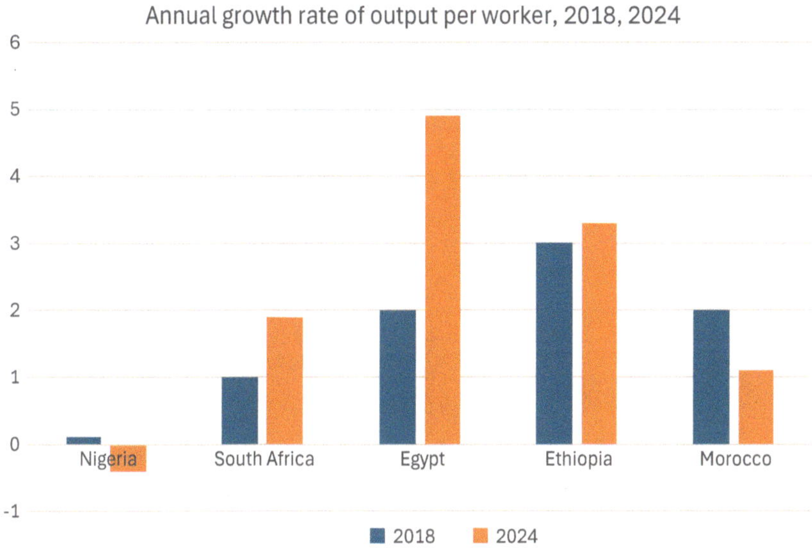

Fig. 5.4 Annual growth rate of output per worker, 2018, 2024. Source: ILOSTAT, 2024

labour market. On the one hand, the state plays a significant role in the field of employment. However, on the other hand, the question of unskilled work and its remuneration continues to occupy a peripheral place in the economic circuit (Fig. 5.4).

The annual growth rate of output per worker exhibited a decline in the majority of countries within the group over the period from 2018 to 2024. This provides information on the impact of the crises, in particular the Covid-19 pandemic and the Russia-Ukraine war, on production per worker. It is evident that the rise in the general price level resulting from disruptions in global value and supply chains, as well as the reconfiguration of the global energy market, has had a detrimental impact on workers' purchasing power, which has depreciated without being compensated by an increase in wages (Fig. 5.5).

The minimum wage level varies considerably from one country to another. It is evident that there are considerable discrepancies between the countries within the group. It is, however, paradoxical that in Nigeria, the most important economy in terms of GDP, the minimum wage is the

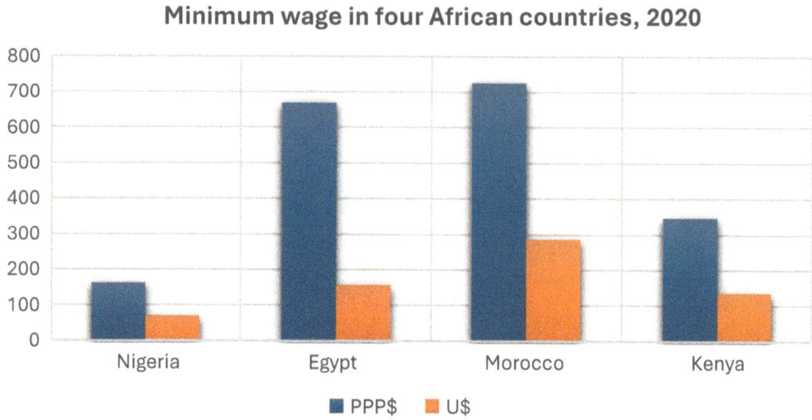

Fig. 5.5 Minimum wage in four African countries, 2020. Source: ILOSTAT, 2024

lowest. The minimum wage in US dollars is \$70, while in purchasing power parity (PPP) it is approximately \$163. In Kenya, the minimum wage is \$136, while in purchasing power parity (PPP) it rises to \$347. The circumstances in Egypt and Morocco diverge markedly from those of the other countries in the group. It is notable that the minimum wage is higher in Egypt and Morocco, at \$157 and \$286, respectively. In terms of purchasing power, the minimum wage is even higher in these two countries, reaching \$726 for Morocco and \$669 for Egypt.However, a correlation can be established between the minimum wage and the share of industry in the overall employment rate. Indeed, for countries like Ethiopia, the low minimum wage can be attributed to the substantial contribution of the agricultural sector to employment, which accounted for 62.8% in 2022, as illustrated in Fig. 5.6. This is in contrast to the weight of manufacturing, which barely exceeded 6.5%. Meanwhile, the service sector contributed 30.7% to employment. It is evident that the agricultural and service sectors are distinguished by the prevalence of the informal sector, family-based SMEs and VSEs. In contrast, the industrial sector is more structured and dominated by large companies and multinationals. This observation also applies to the case of Nigeria, where there appears to be a correlation between income per capita, population size and sectoral contribution to employment. The large population, in conjunction with the

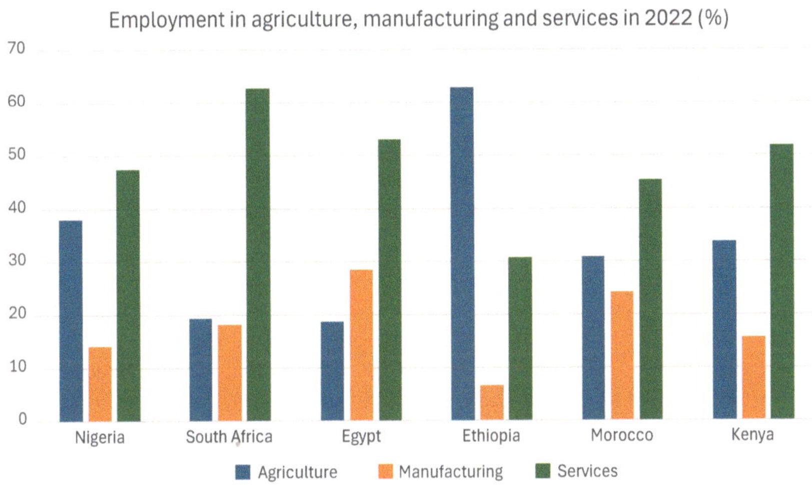

Fig. 5.6 Employment in agriculture, manufacturing and services in 2022 (% of total employment). Source: World Bank 2024

low level of industrialisation, has a negative impact on the minimum wage, particularly in a context where there is a significant unemployment rate among young people, who represent 80% of the Nigerian population.

A number of similarities can be observed in the situations in South Africa, Egypt and Morocco. Indeed, the three countries appear to possess a significant industrial base, with industry representing 28.4% of the total employment rate for Egypt, 24% for Morocco and 18.1% for South Africa. Furthermore, the contribution of services is noteworthy, with percentages of 53%, 45.3% and 62.7%, respectively.

A set of simple correlations between the estimated monthly salary and GDP, GDP per capita, population and the minimum wage does not give conclusive results, except in concordance with the minimum wage (R = 0.71), which itself depends same as the average salary and in inverse value with the total population (−0.70, fewer inhabitants = better salaries).

The subject of unemployment in Africa is complex due to the prevalence of informal and family economies, the relative importance of the agricultural and rural economy, and the lack of consistent statistical data for the entire continent. Despite these challenges, it is evident that the unemployment rate in South Africa is higher than in other AKNEEM countries. In 2022, it was 29.8%, a significant increase from 24.3% in

2020. This increase provides information on the deterioration of the labour market as well as the effects of the Covid-19 pandemic. Morocco ranks second in the list of countries with the highest unemployment rates. While the unemployment rate has been on a downward trajectory, it remains relatively high at 10.5% in 2022 compared to 11.1% in 2020. Egypt is in third place with an unemployment rate of 7% in 2022, compared to 7.9% in 2020. In contrast, East African countries appear to have relatively low official unemployment rates compared to North African and South African countries. Thus, for Kenya, the rate was 5.5% in 2022, compared to 5.6% in 2020. A similar trend can be observed in Ethiopia, where the unemployment rate decreased from 4.1% in 2020 to 4% in 2022.

As illustrated in Table 5.5, there are notable discrepancies between the six countries with regard to the unemployment rates for women and men. The unemployment rate is particularly high in South Africa, affecting both men and women. South Africa is followed by Morocco and Egypt, where women appear to be the most adversely affected by unemployment. Furthermore, East African countries such as Kenya and Ethiopia are less affected by unemployment, as evidenced by opinion polls conducted by the ILO. In conclusion, the disparities in unemployment between men and women in the six countries can be attributed to the characteristics of the labour market. It is evident that, despite the efforts made by countries such as Egypt and Morocco to modernise their family codes in order to enable women to enter the labour market, statistical unemployment remains a phenomenon that particularly affects women. It is important to note that the disparity is gradually diminishing in Morocco. The unemployment rate among women has been consistently declining as a result of the country's ongoing societal evolution, which is marked by a series of

Table 5.5 Share of unemployment in male and female labour force, 2020

	Unemployment, male (% of male labour force)	*Unemployment, female (% of female labour force)*
Nigeria	6%	5.5%
South Africa	28.4%	31.4%
Egypt	5%	15.9%
Ethiopia	2.9%	5.3%
Morocco	9.9%	12.3%
Kenya	5.2%	5.8%

Source: ILOSTAT, 2024

reforms aimed at promoting gender equality in various domains, especially in qualification policy.

5 Conclusion

The objective of this chapter was to identify the relationship between economic emergence and wage levels in six African countries, South Africa, Nigeria, Egypt, Ethiopia, Kenya and Morocco (AKNEEM). The six countries represent approximately 40% of the African continent's population and contribute 55% to 60% of its GDP; consequently, each state constitutes a reference economic centre within its zone (southern, western, northern, eastern Africa). Their average standard of living is slightly higher than that of the continent. In nominal terms, this is estimated at $3200, while in purchasing power parity (PPP) terms it is $9000. In contrast, the African continent's average standard of living is estimated at $2200 in nominal terms and $5800 in PPP terms.

A set of simple correlations between the estimated monthly salary and GDP, GDP per capita, population and the minimum wage does not yield conclusive results, except in concordance with the minimum wage (R = 0.71). This correlation depends on the average salary and in inverse value with the total population (−0.70, fewer inhabitants = better salaries). In more detail, the rankings can be explained by the presence of oil in Nigeria, raw materials and industry in South Africa, economic versatility in Morocco and a late take-off in the eastern part of the continent, including Kenya and Ethiopia.

Similarly, the relative importance of wage employment, the relationship between urban (services and industry) and rural (agriculture), and the role of the civil service or the public sector contribute to the ranking by decreasing place of labour income (which often includes those of sole proprietorships). Nigeria and South Africa exhibit a high rate of labour income, in contrast to Egypt, Morocco and Kenya, which exhibit lower rates.

The informal economy obscures the concept of "salaries", which in Africa are not typically presented as regular monthly salaries accompanied by pay stubs, tax filings, social insurance registration and social benefits. According to the Employers' Federation of Kenya, 99% of enterprises and 90% of the workforce are engaged in the informal economy. However, only 33% of GDP is attributed to this sector, with the remaining 67% being the responsibility of large companies, established SMEs, the public and parapublic sector.

This approach to salary dynamics sought to apply the concept of emergence in order to take into account economic, demographic and employment dynamics. The growth of AKNEEM since 1990–2000 has been considerable, with an average annual growth rate of between 5% and 10% across the countries concerned. However, the global financial crisis of 2008 and the subsequent impact of the Ukraine crisis in 2020–2022 have had a noticeable effect on the rate of growth, resulting in a sudden slowdown or even a downturn.

The six states in question are currently the beneficiaries of a series of reforms designed to strengthen the diversification of their economic structures through investments in infrastructure and integration into global value chains. The maintenance of high unemployment, the rapid increase in the debt rate, and the uncertainty surrounding the future of global value chains have a negative impact on their recent evolution. In addition to the aforementioned factors, there are several other key elements that are conducive to the long-term economic acceleration of these African countries. These include political stability or stabilisation, respect for property rights, the rejection of the mirage of raw materials and the intensive qualification of the active population, particularly women.

Conflicts of Interest The authors have no conflicts of interest to declare that are relevant to the content of this chapter.

References

Amin, S. (2013). Qu'est-ce que "l'émergence"? *Informations et commentaires, 163*, 19–22.

Cohen, E. (2013). *Crise ou changement de modèle?* La documentation française.

Echkoundi, M., & Hafid, H. (2020). *L'Afrique mon continent. Le Maroc acteur majeur de la coopération afro-africaine*. La croisée des chemins.

Goldstein, A., & Lemoine, F. (2013). *L'économie des BRIC. Brésil, Russie, Inde, Chine*. La Découverte.

Juignet, P. (2015). Le concept d'émergence, Philosophie, science et société [en ligne]. https://philosciences.com/le-concept-d-emergence

Ki-Zerbo, J. (2006). *À quand l'Afrique?* Presses universitaires d'Afrique.

Lorenzi, J. H. (2009). *La guerre des capitalismes aura lieu*. Le cercle des économistes. Perrin.

Myrdal, G. (1976). *Le drame de l'Asie, enquête sur la pauvreté des Nations*. Seuil.

Otando, G. (2011). *Le rôle des institutions dans le développement: Cas du Gabon.* Thèse de doctorat, sous la direction d'Uzunidis Dimitri, Université de Littoral Côte d'Opale, Dunkerque.

Piveteau, A., & Rougier, E. (2010). Émergence. L'économie du développement interpellée. *Revue de la régulation*, 1er Semester/Spring 2010. http://regulation.revues.org/7734

Rodrik, D. (2008). *Nations et mondialisation. Les stratégies nationales de développement dans un monde globalisé.* La Découverte.

Salama, P. (2014). *Des pays toujours émergents?* La documentation française.

Van Agtmael (Septembre 1981). Presentation at Salomon Brothers in New York.

Ulgen, F. (2013). Emergence économique et économies émergentes, in le développement en question. *Informations et commentaires, 163*, 23–27.

PART II

Income Inequalities, Wages and Causality

CHAPTER 6

Top Expenditure Distribution in North Africa and Middle East Countries and the Inequality Puzzle

Vladimir Hlasny

1 Introduction

A long-standing academic debate simmers regarding the true level and nature of inequality in the MENA region (Hlasny & AlAzzawi, 2019). The series of revolutions that shook the region in 2011 brought worldwide attention to this debate, and to the assertion that inequality played a central role in the stirring up of popular discontent. The extent to which different dimensions of inequality were responsible for regime falls in Egypt, Libya, Tunisia, and Yemen—and other significant political changes in Bahrain, Jordan, Morocco, and Syria—and the acuteness of the different dimensions of inequality in the first place are subjects of contention in the region.

Perceptions on the street and by the region's own commentators are that inequality and lack of access to career opportunities are grave problems that caused the uprisings. The foregone conclusions are in

V. Hlasny (✉)
Ewha Womans University, Seoul, South Korea
e-mail: vhlasny@gmail.com

M.-P. Chelini et al. (eds.), *Wage Dynamics in Africa*, African Histories and Modernities,
https://doi.org/10.1007/978-3-031-99800-3_6

contrast to objective measurements of inequality using household surveys, a phenomenon dubbed the MENA inequality puzzle (Ianchovichina, 2017). Bibi and Nabli (2010) and Ramadan et al. (2018) reviewed the available evidence of inequality in the region and concluded that MENA countries in particular fall within the range of countries with moderate inequality of household incomes and expenditures, compared to other regions such as East Asia, Latin America, South Asia, and Sub-Saharan Africa. Inequality measures based on both the Gini coefficient and the aggregate share of the top-to-bottom deciles have been relatively low and declining (Page, 2007). This does not appear to be due to poor data quality. While there are presently few parametric tests on the properties of income and expenditure distributions in the region, several recent studies have re-estimated inequality using parametric methods robust to various measurement issues pertaining to data quality, survey representation, and nonresponse (Hlasny et al., 2022).

First worth noting, a worldwide historic study using an assumption of lognormal income distributions anchored by national accounts statistics (Pinkovskiy & Sala-i-Martin, 2009) concluded that over the prior decades the MENA region had seen progress in reducing poverty rates as well as convergence towards the world average welfare level and contribution to a 'global middle class' (p. 29). Several studies have analysed the top ends of countries' income distributions using national accounts and tax microdata, or parametric values from other mostly developed countries (Alvaredo et al., 2017; Assouad, 2023). Using stylized parametric assumptions, or parameter values rather atypical of the region, they estimated higher degrees of national and cross-country inequality.

Alvaredo et al. (2017) estimated inequality using a mix of Pareto distributions for top incomes and lognormal distributions for the rest of incomes. In Egypt as well as in the rest of the MENA region, this approach yielded higher estimates of inequality, suggesting systematic underreporting of top incomes, but the new national estimates were still moderate. On the other hand, between-country gaps in income distributions gave rise to high estimates of inequality at the aggregate MENA region level. In Lebanon, Assouad (2023) found one of the highest income concentrations among all the countries included in the World Top Income Database due to the disproportional effect of profits and rents in the top quantiles.

Using within-survey information alone, Hlasny and Verme (2018) found that replacing actual top incomes or expenditures in the Egyptian Household Income, Expenditure and Consumption Survey (HIECS) sample with Pareto parametric estimates did not affect the computed Gini noticeably regardless how data were weighted, apparently on account of good sample properties of the data. The observed top 0.1% of incomes were found to be extreme or overstated (commanding a downward correction). However, the following 1% of incomes were found to follow the expected distributions more closely.

Our study adds to this literature by evaluating the dispersion of top expenditure observations in five countries in the region and commenting on the evidence of biases introduced by the potential mismeasurement of top expenditures. Our first contribution is to describe the top of the expenditure distributions in several MENA countries and provide parametric measures of the degree of dispersion of top expenditures. The second contribution is to deal with the suspected top expenditure issues by replacing actual top observations with values predicted under the Pareto distribution, which is commonly used as a good approximation to true population distributions across countries and years. By design, values drawn from this distribution are not subject to measurement errors or data censoring.

By comparing the fit of the Pareto distributions to the actual patterns of dispersion of top expenditures, the study provides evidence on the appropriate modelling of top tails of welfare aggregates in the MENA region, and by extension in developing economies worldwide. This second focus of our study thus contributes to the emerging literature on how precise the representation of the richest households is in MENA region surveys, and contributes to building a toolbox for MENA region scholars and policymakers for working with regional economic distributions.

In what follows, Sect. 2 briefly describes the data used and correction methods applied in our analysis. Section 3 presents the results. Section 4 discusses their implications in regard to the problem of assessing inequality in the MENA region.

2 Survey Data, Right-Tail Measurement Issues, and Correction Methods

2.1 *Available Data*

A number of MENA countries conduct household income and expenditure surveys (HIESs) periodically to collect evidence regarding the distribution and components of incomes and expenditures of their population. However, the surveys are not standardised in their definitions of expenditures, their sampling design, and their weighting schemes, and suffer from various potential statistical issues. This study relies on a set of HIESs harmonised by Economic Research Forum (ERF) in collaboration with national statistical agencies. All the HIESs available at the time of writing are used, including the surveys for Egypt 2008, 2010, and 2012; Jordan 2006 and 2010; Palestine 2007, 2010, and 2011; Sudan 2009; and Tunisia 2005 and 2010. These are high-quality, well-documented surveys that have been used successfully in prior studies. All household characteristics and flow variables such as expenditure components were standardised across the surveys according to their conceptual content, coding structure, and international standard definitions and classifications.

All HIES survey data are nationally representative and comparable across countries and years, but individual households cannot be tracked over time. In the following analysis, the surveys are used one by one as cross-sectional samples. Using multiple survey waves for four of the five countries allows us to follow the evolution of inequality over time and in the case of Egypt before and after the popular uprising. Replacing of top expenditures with smoother synthetic values allows us to comment on how robust inequality estimates and their trends are to measurement issues and sampling differences across survey waves.

While the five countries do not represent the entire MENA region, they show a mosaic of the economic conditions and survey practices across the region. The surveys differ in their sampling rate from the population and cover a heterogeneous block of countries in terms of their economic development, demography and labour force composition, inequality, and political climate.

The Egyptian surveys were administered during April 2008–March 2009, July 2010–June 2011, and July 2012–June 2013, that is, two years before the uprising, in its midst, and during the flux one year after the uprising when the Muslim Brotherhood was promoting a new national constitution.

The Jordanian surveys were collected in the 12 months following April 2006, and those following April 2010—for the most part before public protests in the country became widespread in the spring of 2011 and led to constitutional reforms. In Palestine, the surveys were collected throughout the years 2007, 2010, and 2011, at the time of relaxation of the Israeli security regime and prior to the September 2012 surge of major protests against domestic economic policy. In Sudan, the survey took place in the summer of 2009, three years prior to the start of Arab-Spring inspired protests against the government's austerity plans. Finally, the Tunisian surveys were administered during May 2005–May 2006, and June 2010–May 2011. Fieldwork for the second survey was thus at its height in January 2011 when major public protests erupted, motivated by people's economic and democratic concerns, and led to the toppling of the country's president. Seven years later, in January 2018, another wave of significant protests erupted in Tunisia lamenting the lack of economic progress since the regime change and the government's new austerity programme.

Summary statistics confirm that the three Palestinian waves appear comparable to one another, representative of the same population, and reflecting on socio-economic developments in the territory during 2007–2011. This helps to alleviate any concerns over the effect of the Israeli occupation and the 2006–2007 Gaza blockade on survey or sampling quality. Similarly, the results for Egypt 2010 versus 2012 and Tunisia 2005 versus 2010 appear to reflect on socio-economic conditions in the country rather than on deteriorating sampling quality amidst the popular uprisings.

HIESs include information on households' basic demographic and employment status, income and its sources, and expenditures on various commodities. This study uses only information on household size, total annual household expenditures per capita, and cross-sectional household sampling weights in the surveys. ERF adds up expenditure items according to the Classification of Individual Consumption According to Purpose rules. Expenditures cover food and beverages, alcoholic drinks and smokes, clothes, textiles and shoes, residence and its accessories, furniture, durables, health care and services, transportation, telecommunications, culture and entertainment, education, restaurants and hotels, various services, and commodities. The expenditure data are not subject to top-coding.

Expenditure per capita (in real year-2005 purchasing-power parity international dollars) is used as our welfare aggregate for a number of reasons. First, expenditures are typically used instead of incomes in emerging economies with significant rural sectors, where households earn incomes in kind and engage in household production. The corresponding streams of consumption are better captured through questions about implicit consumption expenditures than about incomes. Our usage of expenditures also facilitates comparison with other countries in the region as well as worldwide for whom income microdata are unavailable, mismeasured or yet non-analysed carefully. Second, expenditure data may be more precise given that income may be underreported and given that expenditure is smoother than income over time, especially in developing and rural areas. Third, expenditure data in the MENA region have been found to exhibit lower inequality than incomes (Bibi & Nabli, 2010), suggesting an even greater puzzle to observers of the recent economic and political developments in the region. This may suggest that the mismeasurement of top expenditures is more serious than that of top incomes, even if the rest of the expenditure distribution is reported accurately. Finally, the surveys for Tunisia and for Palestine 2007 do not report total or disposable income, so it is worthwhile comparing expenditures there to other expenditure distributions in neighbouring countries.

The eleven surveys differ significantly in the level and dispersion of the highest several expenditures. Among the highest twenty observations, the Egyptian data exhibit modest dispersion. The single highest expenditure exceeds the one ranked twentieth by merely 190% in 2008, 210% in 2010, and 120% in 2012. The Jordanian data show more substantial dispersion and include an influential outlying observation in the 2010 wave. In the 2006 wave, the highest observed expenditure per capita exceeds the second highest one by 64% and the twentieth highest one by 354%. In the 2010 wave, on the other hand, the highest expenditure per capita is more than seven times as high as the one in the second place and more than twelve times as high as the one ranked twentieth.

In Palestine 2010, the highest one or two expenditures appear extreme. In the 2007 and 2011 waves, the single highest expenditure is 29–43% higher than the second highest expenditure, and 189–262% higher than the one ranked twentieth. In 2010, however, an outlying top expenditure is 134% higher than the second highest one, and more than seven times as high as the twentieth highest one. It is likely that the small sample sizes in Jordan 2010 and Palestine 2010 are partially responsible for the presence of outliers.

In Sudan, the highest observed expenditure per capita exceeds the second highest one by 29%, and the twentieth by 189%, a medium degree of top expenditure gaps. In both waves of the Tunisian survey, the household with the highest expenditure per capita surpasses the expenditure of the second richest household by a mere 17–23%. Similarly, it surpasses the expenditure of the twentieth household by only 211–213%. Rather than having a single outlier, the Sudanese and Tunisian surveys have three to four outlying households—their expenditures are clustered nearby each other, while they exceed the following values by 50%. On the other hand, no further clustering of observations has been found lower down the expenditure distribution.

These patterns may represent the underlying national populations accurately or may arise from measurement or sampling issues. Jordanian and Palestinian data may suffer from bad quality or misreporting, making the dispersion appear greater than it is. Alternatively, Tunisian data may suffer from underreporting of the highest expenditures, making them appear concentrated within a narrower range than in reality. We can assess the share of aggregate expenditures controlled by the richest households—a common measure of economic inequality. These expenditure shares are higher in Jordan, Palestine, and Sudan and lower in Egypt and Tunisia. Since it is unclear whether the dispersion of top expenditures in one survey is too wide due to measurement issues, or the dispersion in another survey is too narrow due to underreporting, we take an agnostic view of the validity of each observation, and let parametric estimation on the distribution of top expenditures tell us which observations step out of the line relative to what would be predicted. Our method is not limited to the case of top-coding, but also allows for general mismeasurement, outliers, or nonresponse (Hlasny, 2020).

Looking at the share of aggregate expenditures accounted for by the top 0.1% of observations to as many as 20% of observations reveals a disproportionate concentration of wealth among the super-wealthy 0.2% of households in Jordan 2010 and in Sudan, where they command over 2.9–3.0% of aggregate expenditures. Tunisia 2005 is nearly at that level of concentration among the uppermost expenditure households. Regarding expenditure shares among the following 20% of households, Sudan and Tunisia 2005 exhibit disproportionate concentrations. The richest 1% (10% or 20%) of households control 7.6–7.8% (30.8–32.4 or 46.3–48.0%) of aggregate expenditures.

2.2 *Top Expenditure Measurement Issues*

One possibility is that the observations in the uppermost tail of expenditure distributions reflect true values of expenditures in the population, and should be included in measurement. Alternatively, extreme observations may arise from various errors and, if included, should be corrected for the identified errors.

It has been documented that the inclusion of extreme observations can significantly influence commonly used measures of inequality. To evaluate how sensitive inequality measurement is to extreme expenditure observations, without judgement on their authenticity, we would want to identify which observations are outliers and estimate our measures of inequality with and without them. In HIESs measurement errors may arise for several reasons, including intentional misreporting, errors in recollection, or data entry errors. Across survey waves, expenditure distributions may also exhibit different upper tails on account of sampling variability. Top expenditures may generally also be deliberately obscured by national statistical agencies to comply with privacy and national-security norms or correct for measurement problems, but this is not evident with the survey samples at hand. Due to the potential measurement problems and sampling differences across surveys, our estimation of inequality levels and trends may be biased.

To compare the actual distributions of top expenditures to distributions that may be predicted in the given countries, and study the presence of extreme values, we summarize the dispersion of economic outcomes by a parametric distribution, report properties of the estimated distribution, and use the estimates to correct top expenditures for suspected statistical problems. Parametric estimates for the top of the distribution could be combined with nonparametric statistics for the rest of the distribution to obtain more robust estimates.

2.3 *Replacement Using Pareto Distribution*

The Pareto distribution is one of several distributions used traditionally for evaluating potentially imprecise top incomes or expenditures vis-à-vis expected values. The Pareto distribution is highly skewed and heavy-tailed, and is thought to be suitable to model upper incomes, expenditures, wealth, or other welfare aggregates (Hlasny, 2019, 2021). As expenditures grow larger, the number of observations declines following a law dictated by a constant Pareto coefficient θ. The Pareto distribution can be described by its probability density function $f(x)=\frac{\theta}{x^{\theta+1}}, 1 \leq x \leq \infty$. Here x is the variable of interest, which in our case is real expenditure per capita. The Pareto coefficient θ can be estimated by maximum likelihood methods. A 'semiparametric' Gini coefficient is estimated by combining a 'nonparametric' Gini estimated among bottom incomes with the 'parametric' Gini computed under the smooth Pareto curve. This can be compared to an uncorrected nonparametric estimate.

The following empirical analysis relies on this method for re-estimating inequality. Top expenditure observations are replaced by random draws from the Pareto distributions estimated on them. The reason for estimating the distributions on the same observations as those that are being replaced (rather than, say, estimating right-truncated Pareto distributions only on lower expenditure values deemed reliable) is that this approach allows us to remain agnostic regarding the validity of any individual observation. The approach does not require us to decide which observations to use for estimation, and which observations to replace. Consequently, this approach can be viewed as addressing the problem when some expenditures are randomly under- or over-reported, or rank-proximity swapped. To the extent that different survey waves manage to cover different top-expenditure households through random sampling, this approach also mitigates the problem of overestimation of the variation in inequality across survey waves due to sampling errors.

Gini coefficient is used as the primary index of inequality, since it is well understood and easily estimable under both parametric and nonparametric distributions, and less sensitive to extreme observations than other indices. To the extent that the estimated Gini is affected by measurement issues, we may conclude that the consequences for other inequality measures would be more serious.

3 Results

Table 6.1 presents semiparametric estimates of Gini coefficients, obtained by replacing top expenditure observations with random values drawn from smooth Pareto distributions estimated among the top observations. Individual rows present the semiparametric estimates from the distributions of household expenditures per capita when the top 0.1–20.0% of values are replaced by random draws from the corresponding Pareto distributions.

The correction for potentially mismeasured top expenditures is shown to vary across surveys. In the three Egyptian surveys, replacing the top 0.1–5.0% of observations leads to a small but systematic increase in the Gini of 0.3–0.4 percentage points. This suggests that the reported expenditures are distributed slightly more narrowly compared to what one would expect under the Pareto law. Thus, we do not find evidence that the topmost 0.1% of expenditures are extreme or commanding a downward correction.

Table 6.1 Semiparametric estimates of Gini coefficients: Pareto distribution

	Egypt 2008			*Egypt 2010*			*Egypt 2012*			*Jordan 2006*			*Jordan 2010*		
Correction for extreme observations	*Observ. replaced [expend. share]*	*Pareto coef. θ (s.e.)*	*Gini (s.e.)*	*Observ. replaced [expend. share]*	*Pareto coef. θ (s.e.)*	*Gini (s.e.)*	*Observ. replaced [expend. share]*	*Pareto coef. θ (s.e.)*	*Gini (s.e.)*	*Observ. replaced [expend. share]*	*Pareto coef. θ (s.e.)*	*Gini (s.e.)*	*Observ. replaced [expend. share]*	*Pareto coef. θ (s.e.)*	*Gini (s.e.)*
Non-param.	0 out of		31.32	0 out of		31.42	0 out of		29.60	0 out of		35.81	0 out of		36.21
estimation	23,428		(0.28)	7719		(0.49)	7528		(0.42)	2897		(0.74)	2845		(1.31)
Semiparametr. estimation, top k% replaced															
$k = 0.1\% \times n$	43	3.258	31.31	12	3.377	31.45	12	3.964	29.62	8	3.429	35.78	8 [2.29%]	1.402	35.84
	[1.42%]	(0.637)	(0.28)	[1.42%]	(0.644)	(0.52)	[0.92%]	(0.867)	(0.43)	[1.44%]	(1.977)	(0.74)		(1.009)	(1.03)
$k = 0.2\% \times n$	82	3.071	31.34	27	2.749	31.47	27	4.290	29.62	9	5.258	35.76	19	2.188	35.63
	[2.28%]	(0.406)	(0.29)	[2.29%]	(0.503)	(0.54)	[1.70%]	(0.913)	(0.43)	[2.07%]	(3.616)	(0.76)	[2.88%]	(1.387)	(0.78)
$k = 0.5\% \times n$	207	2.819	31.38	59	3.061	31.46	59	3.962	29.60	34	2.431	35.92	35	3.324	35.49
	[4.24%]	(0.221)	(0.30)	[4.24%]	(0.439)	(0.54)	[3.39%]	(0.552)	(0.43)	[4.23%]	(0.463)	(0.92)	[4.43%]	(1.451)	(0.76)
$k = 1\% \times n$	393	2.701	31.41	123	2.531	31.51	116	3.312	29.69	67	2.981	35.73	44	4.940	35.43
	[6.68%]	(0.151)	(0.32)	[6.59%]	(0.248)	(0.56)	[5.72%]	(0.280)	(0.47)	[6.49%]	(0.531)	(0.70)	[6.47%]	(2.201)	(0.92)
$k = 2\% \times n$	790	2.563	31.48	245	2.550	31.53	232	3.047	29.71	132	2.721	35.78	89	3.859	35.40
	[10.34%]	(0.103)	(0.34)	[10.24%]	(0.186)	(0.57)	[9.26%]	(0.205)	(0.49)	[10.22%]	(0.311)	(0.75)	[10.44%]	(0.619)	(0.80)
$k = 5\% \times n$	1966	2.402	31.68	605	2.428	31.71	591	2.539	30.02	285	2.706	35.97	216	2.801	35.88
	[18.02%]	(0.061)	(0.37)	[17.87%]	(0.115)	(0.64)	[16.80%]	(0.110)	(0.60)	[18.57%]	(0.193)	(0.87)	[19.18%]	(0.217)	(0.99)
$k = 10\% \times n$	3744	2.401	31.59	1165	2.457	31.62	1150	2.511	30.03	482	2.664	35.95	417	2.599	36.49
	[27.14%]	(1.714)	(0.39)	[27.12%]	(0.085)	(0.67)	[25.86%]	(0.084)	(0.56)	[28.54%]	(0.149)	(0.90)	[29.41%]	(0.179)	(1.48)
$k = 20\% \times n$	6778	2.456	31.39	2173	2.472	31.53	2082	2.551	29.90	848	2.307	37.04	780	2.269	37.05
	[40.94%]	(0.034)	(0.36)	[41.07%]	(0.061)	(0.63)	[39.66%]	(0.065)	(0.56)	[43.97%]	(0.084)	(1.37)	[44.58%]	(0.102)	(1.41)
Mean (s.d.) if	–	2.962	31.36	–	2.930	31.47	–	3.882	29.63	–	3.525	35.80	–	2.964	35.60
$k \leq 1\% \times n$		(0.250)	(0.04)		(0.369)	(0.03)		(0.410)	(0.04)		(1.225)	(0.08)		(1.536)	(0.18)
Mean (s.d.) if	–	2.456	31.54	–	2.477	31.60	–	2.662	29.92	–	2.600	36.19	–	2.882	36.21
$k \geq 2\% \times n$		(0.076)	(0.13)		(0.052)	(0.09)		(0.257)	(0.15)		(0.196)	(0.58)		(0.687)	(0.72)

	Palestine 2007			Palestine 2010			Palestine 2011			Sudan 2009			Tunisia 2005			Tunisia 2010		
	Observ. replaced [expend. share]	*Pareto coef. θ (s.e.)*	*Gini (s.e.)*	*Observ. replaced [expend. share]*	*Pareto coef. θ (s.e.)*	*Gini (s.e.)*	*Observ. replaced [expend. share]*	*Pareto coef. θ (s.e.)*	*Gini (s.e.)*	*Observ. replaced [expend. share]*	*Pareto coef. θ (s.e.)*	*Gini (s.e.)*	*Observ. replaced [expend. share]*	*Pareto coef. θ (s.e.)*	*Gini (s.e.)*	*Observ. replaced [expend. share]*	*Pareto coef. θ (s.e.)*	*Gini (s.e.)*
Non-	0 out of		40.83	0 out of		39.18	0 out of		38.43	0 out of		39.88	0 out of		41.40	0 out of		38.49
par.	1231		(1.00)	3757		(0.57)	4317		(0.68)	7913		(0.74)	12,318		(0.55)	11,281		(0.42)
Semip. estim., top % replaced																		
0.1	2	4.247	40.86	12	3.300	39.16	8	3.081	38.49	7	2.429	39.92	10	2.948	41.39	11	4.051	38.49
	[1.14%]	(2.924)	(1.02)	[1.20%]	(1.011)	(0.59)	[1.26%]	(1.296)	(0.77)	[2.08%]	(0.697)	(0.79)	[1.81%]	(1.160)	(0.55)	[1.18%]	(1.041)	(0.43)
0.2	6	2.534	40.99	20	4.093	39.12	17	3.363	38.44	21	1.866	39.99	21	2.458	41.49	22	2.928	38.51
	[2.35%]	(1.061)	(1.17)	[2.17%]	(1.012)	(0.59)	[2.00%]	(1.338)	(0.65)	[3.02%]	(0.482)	(0.81)	[2.84%]	(0.598)	(0.58)	[1.99%]	(0.571)	(0.43)
0.5	13	3.665	40.87	35	3.684	39.10	37	3.807	38.40	51	2.322	39.82	69	2.470	41.47	64	3.081	38.57
	[4.33%]	(1.413)	(1.04)	[4.12%]	(0.738)	(0.63)	[4.11%]	(1.087)	(0.65)	[5.15%]	(0.561)	(0.76)	[5.06%]	(0.428)	(0.56)	[3.72%]	(0.506)	(0.45)
1	24	3.217	40.85	65	3.330	39.14	79	3.006	38.51	109	2.523	39.75	144	2.760	41.35	128	3.335	38.48
	[7.14%]	(0.731)	(1.14)	[6.74%]	(0.373)	(0.64)	[6.72%]	(0.449)	(0.71)	[7.59%]	(0.429)	(0.70)	[7.80%]	(0.362)	(0.48)	[6.07%]	(0.439)	(0.40)
2	47	2.733	40.99	125	2.979	39.18	136	2.815	38.63	205	2.731	39.69	280	2.610	41.52	258	3.234	38.55
	[10.96%]	(0.378)	(1.13)	[10.64%]	(0.267)	(0.67)	[10.69%]	(0.306)	(0.84)	[11.46%]	(0.326)	(0.66)	[12.05%]	(0.216)	(0.57)	[9.92%]	(0.275)	(0.42)
5	102	2.884	40.96	261	2.802	39.33	333	2.667	38.71	505	2.643	39.78	674	2.578	41.51	613	2.906	38.71
	[20.81%]	(0.298)	(1.23)	[19.65%]	(0.173)	(0.78)	[19.52%]	(0.185)	(0.80)	[20.13%]	(0.179)	(0.66)	[21.14%]	(0.126)	(0.58)	[18.53%]	(0.142)	(0.47)
10	184	2.303	41.67	489	2.539	39.77	618	2.572	38.88	985	2.423	40.06	1350	2.329	42.00	1174	2.759	38.90
	[31.85%]	(0.159)	(1.77)	[30.89%]	(0.116)	(0.95)	[30.15%]	(0.129)	(0.86)	[30.76%]	(0.105)	(0.86)	[32.36%]	(0.072)	(0.66)	[29.36%]	(0.094)	(0.54)
20	340	2.082	42.37	969	2.129	41.13	1141	2.210	39.95	1901	2.306	40.53	2662	2.088	42.96	2348	2.376	39.76
	[47.55%]	(0.104)	(2.00)	[46.70%]	(0.067)	(1.27)	[45.81%]	(0.074)	(1.36)	[46.27%]	(0.070)	(0.85)	[48.00%]	(0.043)	(0.75)	[45.35%]	(0.052)	(0.61)
Mean	–	3.416	40.89	–	3.602	39.13	–	3.314	38.46	–	2.285	39.87	–	2.659	41.43	–	3.349	38.51
if ≤1		(0.723)	(0.07)		(0.371)	(0.03)		(0.363)	(0.05)		(0.291)	(0.11)		(0.238)	(0.07)		(0.497)	(0.04)
Mean	–	2.501	41.50	–	2.612	39.85	–	2.566	39.04	–	2.526	40.02	–	2.401	42.00	–	2.819	38.98
if ≥2		(0.372)	(0.67)		(0.369)	(0.89)		(0.258)	(0.61)		(0.196)	(0.38)		(0.244)	(0.68)		(0.356)	(0.54)

Notes: For clarity, Gini coefficients and their standard errors are multiplied by 100. Pareto coefficients are estimated among the top *k* expenditure observations using maximum likelihood methods. Semiparametric Gini coefficients are computed using 100 random draws from the estimated respective Pareto distributions. Numbers in square brackets show aggregate expenditure shares of the replaced observations, considering household sampling weights

In Jordan 2006 and in all Palestinian, Sudanese, and Tunisian surveys, when 5% or fewer observations are replaced, the estimated semiparametric Gini coefficients are nearly identical to the nonparametric Gini coefficients (differing by −0.2 up to +0.3 pc.pt.). In Jordan 2010, replacing top expenditures leads to a drop in the Gini by 0.8 percentage points, presumably on account of the single outlying expenditure observation. Replacing this outlier and the following 34–88 expenditures (0.5–2% of the overall sample) decreases the estimated Gini from 36.2 to 35.4.

When 10–20% of observations are replaced with Pareto random draws, the estimated Gini coefficients consistently exceed the nonparametric values by up to 0.4 percentage points in Egypt, 1.2 in Jordan, 1.9 in Palestine, 0.6 in Sudan, and 1.6 in Tunisia. In this range of expenditures, observed expenditures per capita appear to be dispersed more narrowly than would be predicted under smooth Pareto distributions (relative to the dispersion of the topmost 0.1–5% of expenditures). This is most significant in Jordan 2006 and in all Palestinian and Tunisian surveys. Because this replacement of 10–20% of observations with random draws involves a large number of observations. This finding cannot be due to a few unlucky observations or a few unlucky draws but reflects a systematic departure of the observed distributions from the theoretically expected ones.

In all but the Egyptian surveys, the Gini corrections rise nearly monotonically as we replace more expenditures from only top 1% to as many as top 20%. In the three Egyptian surveys, by contrast, the corrections are systematically highest when 5% of expenditures are replaced. This suggests that in Egypt it is particularly the top ventile of expenditures (relative to the top 1%, or to the second ventile) that are dispersed too narrowly compared to what the Pareto law predicts, while in other countries it may be the second ventile and second decile where the actual dispersion is too narrow.

One measure of dispersion among top expenditures and a measure of the share of aggregate expenditures accounted for by them are the inverted Pareto-Lorenz coefficient, computed as $\beta = \theta/(\theta - 1)$. In all surveys except for Jordan 2010 and Sudan 2009, the inverted Pareto-Lorenz coefficient increases nearly monotonically as a greater percentage of top observations are used for the fitting and are replaced. This suggests that as more of lower expenditures are added to the analysis, the degree of dispersion at the top increases as does the expenditure share of the topmost observations. In Egypt and Tunisia, the increase in the inverted Pareto-Lorenz coefficient is modest as 1–20% of top expenditures are added (β

stagnates at 1.6–1.7 in Egypt 2008 and 2010), suggesting that a Pareto distribution with a single parameter may describe that entire range of top expenditures adequately. On the other hand, in Jordan 2010, the inverted Pareto-Lorenz coefficient falls drastically from 3.49 when only the top 0.5% of observations are evaluated to 1.25 when top 1% are evaluated. This is due to the one outlying observation.

We conclude that extreme observations are not problematic for inequality measurement in our sample of surveys (with the exception of a handful of observations in Jordan 2010 and Palestine 2010). Instead, it is the rather narrow dispersion of expenditures between the 80th and the 95th percentile that causes a divergence from what would be expected under the Pareto law.

The exact cut-off for expenditures used in the analysis is thus found to affect the estimated shape of the top-expenditure distribution. Different surveys display different sensitivity to the choice. The estimated Pareto coefficient varies by less than 0.4 points in Egypt 2008 and 2010 and in Sudan; up to 0.9 points in Egypt 2012, Jordan 2006, and Tunisia; up to 1.2 points in Palestine; and up to 2.7 points in Jordan 2010.

As can be seen, the estimated Gini coefficients are affected by the chosen cut-off for top expenditures. The correction for potentially imprecise top expenditures is −0.01–0.43 points of the Gini in Egypt; −0.81–1.23 points in Jordan; −0.08–1.95 points in Palestine; −0.19–0.65 points in Sudan; and −0.05–1.56 points in Tunisia. These differences in corrections are modest in size. Consequently, individual specifications of the top income distribution (nonparametric, or Pareto parametric estimated from different cut-off points) cannot be clearly rejected in favour of each other. Confidence intervals around the various Pareto estimates and the nonparametric estimates of the Gini coefficients overlap, implying that neither set of estimates can be clearly rejected regardless whether Pareto or nonparametric estimation is truly appropriate.

Table 6.1 shows that the Pareto distributions fitted to top expenditures vary across different delineations of the top expenditures. When the distributions are fitted only among the top 1% or fewer observations, the Pareto coefficients vary in the range 2.5–4.0 in Egypt, 1.4–5.3 in Jordan, 3.0–4.2 in Palestine, 1.9–2.5 in Sudan, and 2.5–4.1 in Tunisia. When the fitting is among top 2–20% of observations, the Pareto coefficients are notably lower and tighter, at 2.4–2.6 in Egypt, 2.3–3.9 in Jordan, 2.1–3.0 in Palestine, 2.3–2.7 in Sudan, and 2.1–3.2 in Tunisia. In all surveys but Sudan, the coefficients drift downward near monotonically as a greater share of expenditures are used for fitting. Coefficient standard errors indicate that there is more noise around the estimates when the sample sizes are small, particularly in the Jordanian samples. The estimates become precise only when at least 2% of top observations (47–790 observations or more in our samples) are used for estimation. These facts jointly suggest that the uppermost observations are not distributed as smoothly and widely as the Pareto law would predict, perhaps due to some underreporting or censoring at the top end. Using 95% confidence intervals, Pareto coefficients estimated on top 2% of expenditures are significantly higher than those estimated on top 20% of expenditures in Jordan 2010, Palestine 2010, and Tunisia 2005 and 2010.

One motivation for the replacement of actual top expenditures with synthetic values was to mitigate the sampling error in inequality measurement due to sampling variability across survey waves. Under the conjecture that the true Gini coefficient is stable across nearby years (Li et al., 1998), we could expect the semiparametric Gini to be more stable than the observable nonparametric Gini. Indeed, in most model specifications for Egypt and Jordan, and in one half of model specifications for Palestine and Tunisia (refer to Table 6.1), the semiparametric Gini coefficients exhibit less variation over time than the nonparametric ones. At the same time, the semiparametric Gini coefficients carry standard errors that are only 20% higher than the nonparametric standard errors, and are of the same size in Sudan 2009 and lower in Jordan 2010. This suggests that the method advanced in this study has distinct benefits over traditional nonparametric estimation of the Gini and its trend over time, particularly in datasets where there are clear outliers but also in other datasets where top income issues are merely suspected.

Finally worth noting, the Pareto and inverted Pareto-Lorenz coefficients and Gini coefficients can be compared to those in prior studies. Using estimates, the top expenditures in the five MENA countries considered here have lower inverted Pareto coefficients—and thus exhibit lower dispersion and lower aggregate expenditure shares—than incomes in Argentina, India, and even Singapore over the past two decades (Atkinson et al., 2011: figures). They are on par with the inverted Pareto coefficients for incomes in Mediterranean Europe (France, Italy, Portugal, Spain). Even restricting attention to prior estimates for expenditures, using Hlasny and Verme's (2018) estimates, our five countries exhibit an inverted Pareto coefficient below the median of emerging economies worldwide, or 1.7 (1.8 for income). Even the highest estimates of the inverted Pareto coefficients in our study, when estimated on fully 20% of top expenditures, range between 1.6 and 1.9, near the median for emerging countries worldwide.

4 Discussion

This study has attempted to evaluate the patterns of dispersion of top expenditures in eleven surveys from five MENA countries, and their implications for the measurement of inequality in the region and emerging countries worldwide. We have also attempted to correct the inequality estimates for potentially mismeasured top expenditures. Inspection of the eleven surveys indicates that the topmost expenditures in the Egyptian surveys are distributed fairly narrowly, followed by the Tunisian and Sudanese surveys, while in the Jordanian and Palestinian surveys they are quite dispersed. The 2010 waves of the Jordanian and Palestinian surveys contain clear outliers that affect the measurement of inequality. We thus attempted to correct for such values that are potentially non-representative of the underlying population using values drawn from the expected Pareto distribution.

In our study using only survey data on expenditures, the Gini coefficient is estimated consistently between 0.30 and 0.32 in Egypt, 0.35 to 0.37 in Jordan, and 0.38 to 0.43 in Palestine, Sudan, and Tunisia. Replacing observed top expenditures with synthetic values helped to refine the Gini coefficients systematically albeit modestly. Across all surveys, replacing of the top 20% of expenditures yielded higher Gini coefficients suggesting that in that range of expenditures actual values are dispersed more narrowly than predicted under smooth Pareto distributions (relative to the dispersion of the topmost 0.1–5% of expenditures).

We also found that different countries exhibit different sensitivity to the correction of potentially contaminated top expenditures. In Egypt, followed by Palestine and Tunisia, the estimated inverted Pareto-Lorenz coefficient is near invariant to the cut-off for the definition of top expenditures, suggesting that Pareto distributions may describe the top expenditures rather well in support of the Pareto law. In Jordan and Sudan the inverted Pareto-Lorenz coefficient fluctuates, suggesting that Pareto distributions do not track the upper tail too closely. Modelling of top expenditures in these countries may require a more complex parametric form.

Our estimates of the dispersion of top expenditures (using inverted Pareto coefficients), or all expenditures (using the Gini coefficients) are below or at the mean of the range put forward by Atkinson et al. (2011) for income and expenditure distributions in emerging countries. Particularly in Egypt, inequality is modest. Top expenditures in Egypt are distributed rather smoothly and can be approximated well as Pareto. The falling inequality is thus not due to the presence or absence of extreme observations in any year. The same can be said about the falling inequality in Palestine and Tunisia. Trend in Jordan, however, hinges on the inclusion of a few outliers.

Generally, whether the observed or the synthetically derived Gini coefficients are closer to the true degree of inequality in the five countries is unclear, as it depends on the source of the observed dispersion of top expenditures. Differences across the various Gini estimates are also modest in view of their differences across countries. Indeed, nonparametric Gini coefficients vary by as much as 11.8 percentage points across the five countries (29.6 in Egypt 2012 to 41.4 in Tunisia 2005). The width of confidence intervals around all estimates—shown in Table 6.1—implies that neither set of point-estimates can be clearly favoured over others.

These conclusions are based on the assumption that the expenditures on which parametric distributions were estimated are not systematically understated. The Pareto estimation and replacement could account for problems when some expenditures were randomly under- or over-reported, or rank-proximity swapped, but the method could not account for systematic underreporting of expenditures. With this potential problem, the parametric approximations would themselves lead to underestimation. To the extent that there is no clear evidence in existing literature regarding systematic underreporting of expenditures in MENA countries, this method appears appropriate. In fact, claims of underreporting of expenditures in regional household surveys are rare and based on suspicions rather than on information that underreporting takes place, how much underrepresentation there is, and through which channels it operates.

Alvaredo et al. (2017) used external data for the tops of income distributions in the region, and derived greater corrections and higher estimates of the Gini coefficients. In the MENA region, however, external data such as national accounts and tax records are not compatible with survey data on household expenditures, due to issues such as the size of the oil sector, unreported remittances from abroad, neighbourhood and family transfers across households, and tax avoidance. Whether household survey data alone or in combination with national accounts data can provide more relevant estimates of economic inequality is an open question. Moreover, economic inequality across households is also entangled with other dimensions of inequality, such as health inequality, inequality of opportunities, and inequality between countries. All these factors drive a wedge between people's perceptions and the reality of inequality.

That expenditures are distributed more equally than incomes or wealth has been observed around the world, due to households' propensity to save and borrow to smooth consumption, and households' different incentives for (mis-)reporting the alternative variables. In the MENA region, moreover, consumption tends to be funded by incomes of extended families. Finally, the relative equality of consumption expenditures may also paradoxically reflect the burden on the poorest households of an inadequate public provision of welfare, education and health services, and other infrastructure in MENA countries. Households in poor neighbourhoods must pay out of pocket to compensate for lacking public transportation, car damage on poorly maintained roads, lack of health insurance, or property theft, something that wealthy households do not allocate money to. Whether the observed incomes or expenditures are better proxies for households' achievements or welfare continues to attract debate.

We conclude that neither the uncorrected Gini coefficient nor the semiparametric Gini coefficients can be favoured over one another theoretically. Assuming that nonparametric estimates are consistent for latent true Gini coefficients but potentially inefficient due to a handful mismeasured cases, and that the semiparametric estimates may be more efficient but inconsistent due to misspecification, similarity of the two sets of estimates suggests that neither measurement errors nor specification errors are sufficiently grave to let us clearly reject either set of Gini coefficients. Whether the nonparametric or the Pareto parametric Gini coefficients are closest to the latent true Gini coefficients remains a question for future research. We should consider using multiple alternative estimates to construct plausible intervals for the countries' true levels of inequality.

Conflicts of Interest The author has no conflicts of interest to declare that are relevant to the content of this chapter.

References

Alvaredo, F., Assouad, L., & Piketty, T. (2017). *Measuring Inequality in the Middle East 1990–2016: The World's Most Unequal Region?* CEPR Discussion Paper No. DP12405, October 2017.

Assouad, L. (2023). Rethinking the Lebanese Economic Miracle: The Extreme Concentration of Income and Wealth in Lebanon, 2005–2014. *Journal of Development Economics, 161*, 103003.

Atkinson, A. B., Piketty, T., & Saez, E. (2011). Top Incomes in the Long Run of History. *Journal of Economic Literature, 49*, 3–71.

Bibi, S., & Nabli, M. K. (2010). *Equity and Inequality in the Arab Region*, ERF Policy Research Report No. 33, February.

Hlasny, V. (2019). Expenditure Distribution in Arab Countries and the Inequality Puzzle. *Journal of Economic and Social Measurement, 44*, 177–201.

Hlasny, V. (2020). Nonresponse Bias in Inequality Measurement: Cross-Country Analysis Using Luxembourg Income Study Surveys. *Social Science Quarterly, 101*(2), 712–731.

Hlasny, V. (2021). Parametric Representation of the Top of Income Distributions: Options, Historical Evidence, and Model Selection. *Journal of Economic Surveys, 35*(4), 1217–1256.

Hlasny, V., & AlAzzawi, S. (2019). Asset Inequality in MENA: The Missing Dimension? *Quarterly Review of Economics and Finance, 73*, 44–55.

Hlasny, V., & Verme, P. (2018). Top Incomes and the Measurement of Inequality in Egypt. *World Bank Economic Review, 32*(2), 428–455.

Hlasny, V., Ceriani, L., & Verme, P. (2022). Bottom Incomes and the Measurement of Poverty and Inequality. *Review of Income and Wealth, 68*(4), 970–1006.

Ianchovichina, E. (2017). *Eruptions of Popular Anger: The Economics of the Arab Spring and Its Aftermath.* MENA Development Report, Washington: World Bank.

Li, H., Squire, L., & Zou, H.-F. (1998). Explaining International and Intertemporal Variations in Income Inequality. *Economic Journal, 108*(446), 26–43.

Page, J. (2007). Boom, bust, and the poor: Poverty dynamics in the Middle East and North Africa, 1970–1999. *Quarterly Review of Economics and Finance, 46*(5), 832–851.

Pinkovskiy, M., & Sala-i-Martin, X. (2009). Parametric estimations of the world distribution of income. National Bureau of Economic Research Working Paper No. w15433.

Ramadan, R., Hlasny, V., & Intini, V. (2018). Inter-group Expenditure Gaps in the Arab Region and Their Determinants: Application to Egypt, Jordan, Palestine and Tunisia. *Review of Income and Wealth, 64*(s1), S145–S188.

CHAPTER 7

Labour Market and Wages in Cameroon Since Independence (1960/2022)

Ghislaine Bamseck Famo

1 Introduction

Cameroon is a country in Central Africa, which had a small population in 1960 (5 million), but has grown very rapidly, with a current population of 29 million, almost a six-fold increase in 62 years (2.8% per year). The net population density has risen from 10 inhabitants/km^2, the continental average at the time, to over 50 inhabitants/km^2, just above the current average (40 inhabitants/km^2). There are 309 ethnic languages (Barreteau & Hedinger, 1989), but the official languages, English (in the southwest) and French (80% of the population is French speaking), the legacy of the 1919–1960 colonial period, are creating a trend towards linguistic unification (Owona, 1996). Since gaining independence in 1960, the country has undergone significant economic and demographic changes. Economic growth has fluctuated over the years, with periods of growth and slowdown on either side of a very respectable average of 3.5% per annum over 60 years. On a constant basis, growth can be divided into two main phases,

G. Bamseck Famo (✉)
University of Artois, Arras, France
e-mail: gbamseck@gmail.com

M.-P. Chelini et al. (eds.), *Wage Dynamics in Africa*, African Histories and Modernities,
https://doi.org/10.1007/978-3-031-99800-3_7

around 5% per year between 1960 and 1986 (quadrupling) and a further 3.8% between 1994 and 2022 (tripling), separated by a sharp drop (−30%) followed by a decrease of −5% per year between 1987 and 1993 (World Bank data, n.d.). These developments have had an impact on the labour market, with sectoral losses or gains in employment. The evolution of the labour market in Cameroon has also been influenced by factors related to legislation and changes in working conditions, but also to the recognition of decent work and people's relationship with work. The post-independence period was marked by economic and social adjustments, and Cameroon became a member of the International Labour Organization in 1960 (Atangana-Mebara et al., 1984). Our study of employment and wages in Cameroon highlights the importance of these aspects for the socio-economic development of the country.

2 Cameroon's GDP, Overall Growth, and Economic Demography over 60 Years

The analysis began in the 1960s with the collection of solid empirical data on the labour market in Cameroon (Mveng, 1963). While the country's GDP in constant terms has been multiplied by eight in 60 years (1960–2020), its GDP per capita has increased by only 50%, i.e., by one and a half times, due to the aforementioned five-fold increase in the population. On average, GDP has been growing by 3.5% a year and GDP per capita by only 0.8%. There is a good chance that in the long run wage trends will be quite close to the latter figure.

Since the 1980s, Cameroon's economy has grown at an average annual rate of around 4% despite regional crises. These fluctuations in Cameroon's economic growth have been influenced by events such as the devaluation of the CFA franc in 1994, pressure from the Bretton Woods institutions, and disputed presidential elections, all of which have had an impact on the country's business and investment environment. As in most countries, investment remains a key factor in Cameroon's economic development, influencing both short-term cyclical fluctuations and long-term production capacity.

The demographic transition in Cameroon between 1960 and 1990 was marked by moderate population growth until the mid-1960s, mainly due to natural increase. Demographic change has been an important factor influencing economic and social policy, with significant implications for employment and the need for social infrastructure such as education and health.

In 1960, Cameroon's population was estimated at 2,600,000, with a slightly higher percentage of women (50.1%) than men (49. 9%), which is characteristic of a young country. In fact, half of the population is under 17.7 years old, and the proportion of children under 15 is 43.6%. People aged over 60 account for only 5.5% of the total population. Despite a steadily growing urban population, the majority of the population (55% to 65%) remains in rural areas.

The demographic boom highlights a predominantly young population, with two-thirds of Cameroonians aged under 25, or around 20% of the working population. Young men are generally employed in precarious jobs, while young women struggle to find their place in the labour market (Njike Njikam et al., 2005). After independence, the independent peasantry declined significantly and gradually disappeared in favour of a labour market based on wage employment in agriculture, mining, energy, and trade. According to ILO statistics, the active agricultural population will fall from 68% in 1990 to 43% in 2020. As a result of various laws, including the French Houphouet-Boigny law of 11 April 1946, forced labour was definitively abolished in favour of so-called free labour, with the recognition of trade union rights and the creation of a proper labour inspectorate. In 1952, this led to a specific labour code for the French colonies (CHATEFP, 2015). Salaried employment then became a genuine status, a source of social recognition and identity (Moulier-Boutang, 1998).

Growth in constant data can be divided into two main phases, around 5% per year between 1960 and 1986 (quadrupling) and a further 3.8% between 1994 and 2022 (tripling), separated by a period of crisis (−30%) between 1987 and 1993 and then −5% per year (World Bank). GDP per capita has been growing at a much slower rate due to strong demographic growth (2.8% per year) and inflation, resulting in a similar chronology except for the first phase: 0% per year between 1960 and 1973 (all economic growth absorbed by demographic growth), 5% between 1973 and 1986 (rise in oil export prices), then a sharp recession of −5% per year between 1987 and 1994 (oil counter-shock), and a return to very slow growth from 1995 to 2020 (1% per year). By 2022, with an annual GDP per capita of $1600 in nominal terms and $4400 in purchasing power parity terms, Cameroon ceased to be considered a miracle country, ranking around 150th in the world in terms of nominal or PPP GDP per capita, behind Angola, Bangladesh, and Côte d'Ivoire, on a par with Benin and ahead of Burkina Faso and Ethiopia.

In the 1960s, Cameroon's GDP in current dollars rose from 614 million in 1960 to 1.15 billion in 1970, but in constant 2010 dollars it rose from 4.8 billion to 5.9 billion, which reduces the apparent magnitude of the increase. The World Bank classified Cameroon as a middle-income country during this period. In 1964, for example, its GDP per capita in constant 2010 dollars was around $973, compared with $1142 for the African average or $14,000 for the Euro-North American average.

With the exploitation of oil in the 1970s, Cameroon saw its growth rate rise to an average of 7.5% until 1985 and based its development model on three key points: the development of large public and semi-public industrial production units, highly capital-intensive investment strategies, and the transfer of sophisticated equipment and technology, usually on a turn-key basis. This development programme led to the creation of large construction sites that generated a large number of jobs in the 1980s, even though an employment crisis emerged in the wake of the demographic boom. After a period of sustained growth between 1965 and 1985, the situation deteriorated from 1986 onwards. Despite an internal desire to readjust, the country plunged into economic recession and unemployment, both rural and urban, suffered greatly, requiring donor assistance to implement structural adjustment programmes in 1989. The devaluation of the CFA franc did not help matters. The years 1995–2000 saw a return to a better situation, with a high growth rate in the informal sector, which accounts for 85% of employment in Cameroon. In order to better understand the rest of our study, it is necessary to take a closer look at the different sectors of activity in Cameroon.

3 The Cameroonian Labour Market: Public and Private, Formal and Informal, Collective Agreements

Since independence, Cameroon's economy has gone through several successive phases of prosperity (1965–1984), economic recession (1985–1993), and an attempt at economic recovery (since 1994) (Mboudou, 1982). Commodity prices then plummeted with the oil counter-shock and the country plunged into a deep crisis, despite an impressive internal readjustment effort. To emerge from the crisis, the authorities had no choice but to appeal to international donors, and structural adjustment programmes (SAPs) were put in place. The aim of the SAPs was to correct the internal situation before any prospect of growth could be glimpsed, but they were accompanied by severe measures that had a profound impact on employment. We gradually moved from a situation where the state was the main provider of decent paid employment to one where the private sector had to take over. Faced with the inability of the formal private sector to absorb the flow of labour entering the market, we witnessed the development of the informal private sector, which increased the precariousness and instability of employment.

It was from the 1980s onwards, with structural adjustment, that the public sector labour market lost its efficiency, leaving the private sector with an equal share.[1] The wage share of the public sector is much higher than that of the private sector, with wages rising steadily until the economic and financial crisis. Employees in the private sector with the same qualifications as those in the public sector received lower salaries depending on their sector of activity. By accepting the principles of the SAP, the government reversed this upward trend by reducing the level of public salaries by 60 to 70% between 1987 and 1993, freezing salary increases, and laying off thousands of civil servants. The devaluation of the CFA franc on 11 January 1994 considerably reduced the gap between public and private sector wages, leading to poverty, rising unemployment, and, above all, the spread of corruption in Cameroon (Lachaud, 1994). Finally, informal subsistence activities began to proliferate, making the informal sector the main source of employment in urban areas.

If we look at the Table 7.1, we can see that employment in the public sector takes precedence over employment in the private sector, where the gap is significant at around 60%, with salaried employment dominating in urban areas. Under Cameroon's liberal labour code, minimum wages are set independently in the two sectors. Moreover, private sector employers are restricted in their decisions on recruitment, employment contracts, wages, dismissal, promotion, and trade union action. The public sector is more subject to decisions by public authorities, including the status of civil servants, collective labour agreements, and pay scales. In the modern sector, the main decline in employment has been due to downsizing in the administration, while in the modern private sector the situation has been

[1] In the private sector, there is no distinction between the formal and informal sectors, as in the public sector.

Table 7.1 Salaried workers and employment (private and public sectors) in Cameroon: 1970s and 1980s

Parameters	*Public sector*	*Private sector*
Standard deviation in thousands of CFA francs/week	47.1	29.6 (31.1)
25ᵉ percentile	(32.4)*	13
75ᵉ percentile	23.4	33
Median	62	21
	39.5	
Percentage difference (Public sector-private sector)/private sector	59.1	59.1
Structures (%)	6.1	7.9
Premiums, benefits	6.4	2.8
Benefits in kind		
Employment in the capital (percentage of the urban working population)	22.3	21.7
Total	188	105

Note: Including bonuses, allowances, gratuities, social benefits, and perks. Average value of contributions over each period

Sources: World Bank (March 1990) and Lachaud (1994)

more or less stable over the same period. However, there has been a drastic fall in the rate of salaried employment, from 63.9% in 1983 to 22.1% in 1993 in industry and from 20.6% to 12.6% in commerce. In the public sector, the poor results obtained after the implementation of the SAPs led to a double contraction of wages in January and November 1993, with rates reaching a total of 65% in extreme cases. As can be seen in Table 7.2, from the beginning of the implementation of the SAPs in 1989 until 1993, the number of employees fell in both the public and private sectors decreased, represented by undeclared employees (Mebara, 2001).

Furthermore, in 1987 the public sector had around 187 companies employing 100,000 people, i.e., three-fourths of the civil service workforce, with a wage bill of between 100 and 120 billion CFA francs; transfers and subsidies amounted to some 150 billion, i.e., 18% of public expenditure and 50% of annual oil revenues.

With the economic and financial crisis, the state found it difficult to manage its companies and opted to privatise them in order to stimulate the country's economy gently. At the time, the private sector was given a slight boost, although it remained very closed, as it was underdeveloped in

Table 7.2 Structure and evolution of employment in the informal sector 1989/90–1997/98

Informal sector	*1989/1990*	*1992/1993*	*1993/1994*	*1994/1995*	*1995/1996*	*1997/1998*	*1998/1999*
Bosses	25,000	25,000	25,000	25,000	30,000	30,000	35,000
Unpaid family workers	85,000	90,000	90,000	95,000	95,000	100,000	100,000
Undeclared employees	95,000	90,000	27,000	30,000	45,000	50,000	50,000
Self-employed entrepreneurs	195,000	210,000	215,000	220,000	225,000	230,000	235,000

Source: MINEFI/DSCN/SS (1999) *Les comptes nationaux du Cameroun selon la SCN93*, Volume 2

Cameroon. There are very few private sector companies, which is why development in Cameroon is slowing down. Young people leaving secondary school or university are better trained to enter the civil service, but ultimately lack the training to enter the private sector (commercial law, accounting, and marketing). Private rates of return to education in Cameroon are positive in the formal public and private sectors, but negative in the informal sector, which is more organised in the form of survival self-employment. Most of these people are forced to engage in trade (agriculture, textiles) in order to live or even survive in precarious and unproductive jobs. The size of the informal sector, the large number of working poor whose activities are not recognised, registered, protected, or regulated by the public authorities, and the demographic boom have led the country to a certain disorganisation of the labour market.

It should also be noted that the primary sector, dominated by agriculture, employs three-fourths of Cameroon's population, with export agriculture (cocoa, coffee, cotton, palm oil, rubber) making slow progress and food agriculture developing satisfactorily. Forestry is another sector in constant development, with millions of hectares of timber production (around 8.2 million in 1984, 7.4 million in 1990, and 8.5 million today, compared with 20 million hectares of forest, or 45% of the country's surface). Forestry officially contributes 7% of GDP and provides 45,000 jobs, but it also disturbs fauna and flora.

The secondary sector includes mining and energy, industry, construction, and public works. Before the economic crisis of 1985/87, the main industrial sectors in Cameroon were food processing; textiles and leather; wood; chemicals; metals (dominated by ALUCAM, the largest metallurgical plant in French-speaking Africa, and its subsidiary SOCATRAL), building materials (dominated by CIMENCAM), and electricity (underdeveloped).

The tertiary sector includes transport, hotels, tourism, trade, and financial institutions. Cameroon's financial system is linked to that of the CEMAC countries, whose currency is the Franc de la Communauté Financière Africaine (CFA). On the Cameroonian labour market, the procedures for matching labour supply and demand are governed by relatively rigid institutional rules. These rules establish correspondences between the educational characteristics of workers, the job categories they can occupy, and the resulting salary. These rules are set out in the Standard National Occupational Classification (CNPT) and in the collective agreements, which define the correspondences between different sectors of activity and wage zones. The CNPT, which dates back to 1970, was directly inspired by the equivalences between training and employment used in the French civil service between 1936 and 1950 (Saglio, 1986). It plays an extremely important role in adjustment in that it channels employers' strategies by maintaining a differential value for the different levels of education, while allowing very low wage levels for the majority of employees. This quantitative adjustment concerns only 10% of permanent employees, 78% of whom are self-employed in the informal sector, the majority of whom work in agriculture, which accounts for almost 30% of fiscal resources. The tertiary sector is the most important, accounting for almost half of GDP (48.5%) in the 1990s.

4 Average Pay and Socio-professional or Gender Differences

In the centre, the proportion of employees is 38%; in Douala, the economic capital, the proportion is even as high as 40%. The geographical mobility of employees remains high, and the reasons for this mobility are linked to several factors: insufficient pay, generally in the public and service sectors; difficult work in construction and transport, with complaints coming mostly from the youngest employees; the prospect of limited promotion, which generally concerns the over-50s; redundancy is a reason often affecting young, inexperienced employees, although it is sometimes voluntary and provoked by more experienced employees; company closures are generally due to a lack of financial resources to manage staff; and a fifth point is linked to personal reasons, particularly in the banking and insurance sectors. Motivation for mobility varies according to age, level of education and qualifications, and job function (Atangana-Mebara et al., 1984).

The private and semi-public sector is unusual in that its employment structure consists of 75.4% unskilled or low-skilled jobs, 23% skilled or supervisory jobs, and 1.5% senior management jobs (in France today, 20% of senior managers and 25% of middle staff). This generally low level of qualification of salaried jobs is the result of the evolution of the entire production system and of the entire workforce, with a primary sector that is highly labour-intensive, unskilled, cheap, and export-oriented, a commercial system that is focused on import-export, and a still very strong presence of expatriate managers. The only sector that has undergone radical change is public administration, which was fully nationalised after independence (Fig. 7.1).

We note here that agriculture was on the rise in the 1990s and constituted a significant part of the Cameroonian economy, compared to 2022,

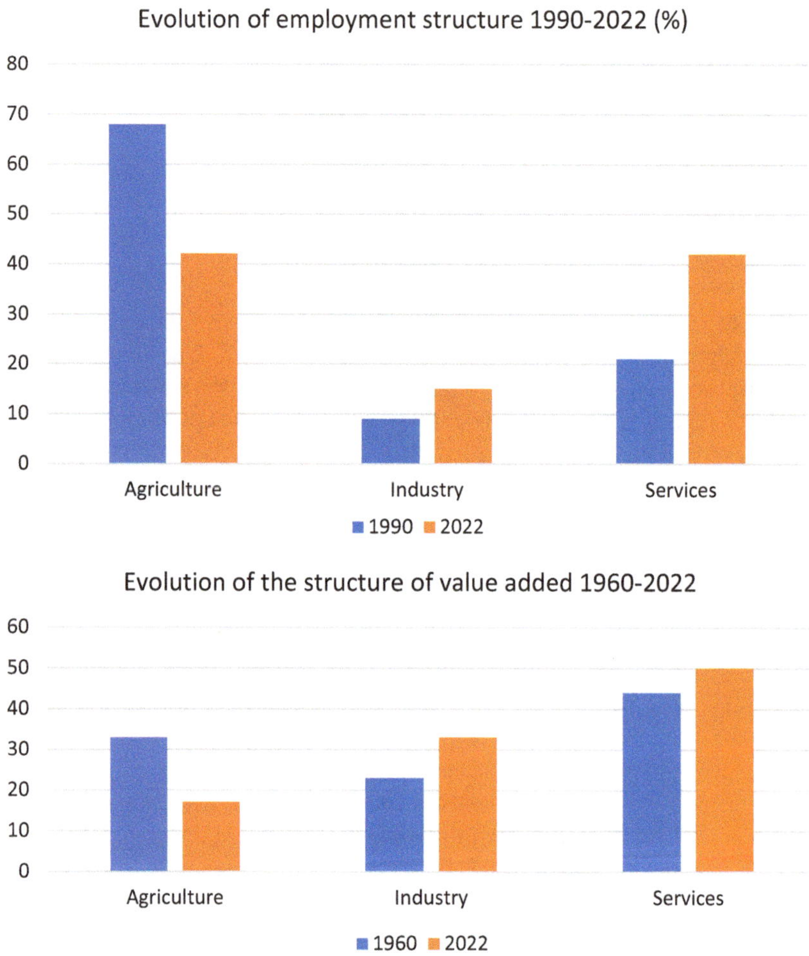

Fig. 7.1 (7.1.bis) Employment and sectoral value added in Cameroon (%), 1960–1990–2022. Source: World Bank, classified by https://perspective.usherbrooke.ca/

where the service sector dominated; industry has also developed strongly compared to the 1990s. The structure of employment is not identical in the three sectors of the economy, and in particular the average level of qualifications increases as one moves from primary to secondary and from secondary to tertiary education, with the primary sector remaining largely dominant in terms of number of employees. The integration of young people into the workforce has often been discussed in terms of their professional orientation. Indeed, some young people fresh from primary, secondary, and university education find it difficult to find their first job because of their rather general qualifications, which often prevent them from being recruited for so-called practical positions, i.e., those that lead directly to salaried employment. Some of them often need additional on-the-job training to adapt to certain sectors of activity, such as in the private sector.

In the public sector, which was the most developed in the 1960s, young people are trained to enter certain tertiary, primary, or secondary sectors and, for the most qualified, the civil service on leaving school, but they encounter difficulties in finding their first job, as this takes time depending on the diplomas obtained and the level of qualification. According to a 2005 survey, 45% of graduates found their first job in less than three months, 38% in about six months, and 15% in more than two years (Njike Njikam et al., 2005). Paradoxically, between 1966 and the early 1970s, it was the modern private and semi-public sector that recruited the majority of young people under the age of 35, accounting for 59 to 60% of employees, with an average age of 32.5 years and a standard deviation of around 10.34 (Amougou, 2018). Technical and higher education graduates are quick to find work, as their training enables them to enter the world of work quickly after their studies.

In Table 7.3, for the late 1980s, the activity rate recorded for 15–64-year-olds is 64% on average for the country as a whole, which is very reasonable (France 70%) given the youthfulness of the Cameroonian population, where more and more 15–20-years-olds are continuing their studies. The activity rate is high in the East (78%) because of the low percentage of housewives, and lower in the North (61%) because of the higher number of women outside the labour market. In the area of activities producing unprocessed materials, or the primary sector, the percentage of employees who are mainly young is 55%, with an average age of 30 or less. Experienced workers have more jobs in the secondary and tertiary sectors. The proportion of young workers aged 30 or under increases with professional

Table 7.3 Activity rates of the population aged 15 and above by province (1990)

Activity rates by province	*Working population*	*Population aged 15 and above*	*Activity rate*
Coastline	300,204	497,081	60.4
West	300,685	490,780	61.3
East	156,217	200,236	78
Centre-South	558,500	827,818	67.5
North	772,586	1,247,436	61.9
Southwest	209,132	306,053	68.3
Northwest	286,071	464,254	61.6
Total	2,583,395	4,033,658	64

Source: Mesple-Somps (1992)

qualifications, with an unexpected but logical increase in managerial positions (higher education). They account for 63% of manual workers, employees, 37% of employees or skilled workers, 15% of supervisors, and 24% of managers (Njike Njikam et al., 2005:38). It should also be noted that young people are employed in areas that do not necessarily require a high level of qualification, such as food processing, breweries, or textiles. Older skilled workers outnumber young people in occupations requiring a high level of qualification, such as supervisors, managers, or skilled workers.

Table 7.4, which cross-references skills and age, is extremely interesting. Age differences are not very significant in the wage and employment structure of these decades in Cameroon, but the internal differences between the best-paid employees in the group (such as blue-collar workers and skilled employees aged 30–34) are much greater, and the gaps between socio-professional categories by qualification (labourers, blue-collar workers, managers) are even wider. First of all, the age distribution is not entirely homogeneous across qualification levels. For example, young people aged 25–29 represent between 22% (manual workers, skilled workers and employees, senior managers) and 27% (middle managers) of the cohort. Similarly, in the 40–44 age group, manual workers make up 4.1% of the total population of manual workers, but the figure rises to 10% for skilled workers and senior managers and 12% for skilled workers and middle managers. Because of the youthfulness of the Cameroonian population, more than half of the workers in Table 7.5 are aged between 25 and

Table 7.4 Average monthly earnings of employees by occupation and age in the 1970s and 1980s

Job held by the company	*<20*	*20–24*	*25–29*	*30–34*	*35–39*	*40–44*	*45–49*	*50–54*	*>55*	*Package*
Labourer %	5.3	33	22.2	11.3	10.5	4.1	1.3	4.2	8.1	100
Average remuneration	15,524	14,655	16,322	21,322	15,518	15,430	15,766	18,029	11,390	15,960
Coefficient of variation	0.19	0.43	0.46	0.92	0.52	0.65	0.43	0.23	0.65	0.61
Labourer + employment %	1.2	12.8	24.8	23.7	10.4	12.7	6.6	4.5	3.3	100
Average remuneration	18,553	29,537	31,277	35,469	33,363	32,308	36,207	36,881	38,393	33,048
Coefficient of variation	0.51	0.37	0.39	0.75	0.42	0.42	0.57	0.37	0.49	0.54
Worker + Qual. employee %		9.2	22.1	22.7	21.5	10.3	6.3	6.5	1.3	100
Average remuneration		52,654	57,445	57,073	61,797	53,287	71,244	72,862	58,495	59,322
Coefficient of variation		0.35	0.36	0.45	0.35	0.42	0.31	0.51	0.36	0.40
Middle management %		3	27.3	15.7	15	12.3	6.5	5.9	4.2	100
Average remuneration		133,770	120,054	113,613	177,337	122,245	112,944	118,620	131,144	118,957
Coefficient of variation		0.21	0.30	0.40	0.44	0.42	0.34	0.46	0.27	0.36
Executives %		1.4	21.9	30.8	18.8	9.9	5.8	5.1	6.3	100
Average remuneration		158,000	228,274	268,417	332,113	330,881	282,184	322,294	218,413	276,570
Coefficient of variation		0.37	0.38	0.27	0.27	0.65	0.57	0.47	0.78	0.38

Note: the CFA franc is the currency unit

Source: Njike Njikam et al. (2005, p. 238, Table 112)

Table 7.5 Pay by job and gender: monthly wages in Cameroonian companies in the 1970s

Jobs	*Average salaries*	*Standard deviation*	*Coefficient of variation*	*Percentage of category*
Labourer	16,199	9959	0.6148	95.2
Men	11,572	3835	0.3314	4.8
Women				
Unskilled workers and	32,393	18.172	0.5535	95.6
employees	37,838	9.782	0.2585	8
Men				
Women				
Skilled workers and	59,393	24.171	0.4070	92
employees	58,517	25.021	0.4276	3.8
Men				
Women				
Middle management	282,366	105.301	0.3729	92.1
Men	208,579	127.375	0.6107	7.9
Women				
Senior executives	–	–	–	–
Men				
Women				

Source: MEP (1976, pp. 168 and 172). Pay in CFA francs

35. The population aged 15 and over exceeded four million in 1976. It consists mainly of self-employed workers (78%), with a very small proportion of salaried workers (14.9%) and an average unemployment rate of 5.9% (BIT, 1979).

Wage differentials by age, which can be high (50–80%) in advanced countries, were very moderate in Cameroon in the 1970–1980s. The differences within each category are much higher than the age differences or the same differences in advanced countries. On average, the dispersion is close to half a unit (around 0.45 for all categories), which means, for example, that for employees and skilled workers aged 30–34 earning an average of 57,000 CFA francs, the absolute standard deviation is 26,000 francs (i.e., 13,000 francs on either side of the average 57,000) and the maximum/minimum distribution varies between 44,000 and 70,000 francs. It should also be noted that the internal gap decreases with qualification: 0.61 for manual workers, 0.38 for senior managers; this may be due to the size of the companies and the definition of the jobs. Senior managers are generally graduates and tend to be concentrated in larger companies; manual workers work in all sectors and in all types of companies, and their situation is very different depending on the productivity of their sector and their company (SME). A final aspect of Table 7.5 is the sizeable gap between senior managers and manual workers, which indicates the scarcity of the former and the abundance of the latter. Whereas in the United States or Europe we find gaps ranging from 1 to 3 to 1 to 5, in Cameroon in the 1970s and 1980s we find a gap of 1–17 between senior managers and manual workers, 1–8.5 for manual and specialised workers, 1–4.6 for skilled workers, and 1–2.3 for middle managers.

Another element of segmentation between employees is the distinction between the formal and informal sectors. Informal employees are all those who are not registered under an employment contract, are not affiliated to the social security system, and do not benefit from paid annual leave. Employment in the informal sector was estimated at less than 50% in 1987 but increased significantly to over 90% in the late 1990s and early 2000s (Kouete, 2020). Female workers make up part of the informal sector.

Analysing the gender pay gap in Cameroon means discussing aspects of discrimination and gender in the labour market, as well as differences in pay depending on working conditions, education, and training. Traditionally, women's education has been organised by society for several generations with the aim of having them look after children and the home; they are therefore considered to be housewives or homemakers. Women's schooling gradually changed after independence and their entry into the labour market was not easy given their status. Their entry has been marked by inequalities and differences, and women are mainly found in the tertiary and informal sectors (services and commerce) rather than in the primary (except agriculture) and secondary sectors, and they have no real place in positions of responsibility (Ekamena Ntsama, 2014).

Back in the 1970s, women found it easier to get their first job than men (who were more likely to work in the formal sector), depending on their qualifications. For example, women with a Certificate of Elementary Education (CEPE) found their first job after seven months, while men waited at least 10 months.

However, there are far more male than female employees. Women's participation in companies in the private or modern sector is around 5%, because their social ambitions are more limited by the culture of society, which directs them towards a domestic destiny, and by their academic training. Paradoxically, it is the tertiary sector that pays better than other sectors, which is why it is difficult to find a job there quickly. However, in

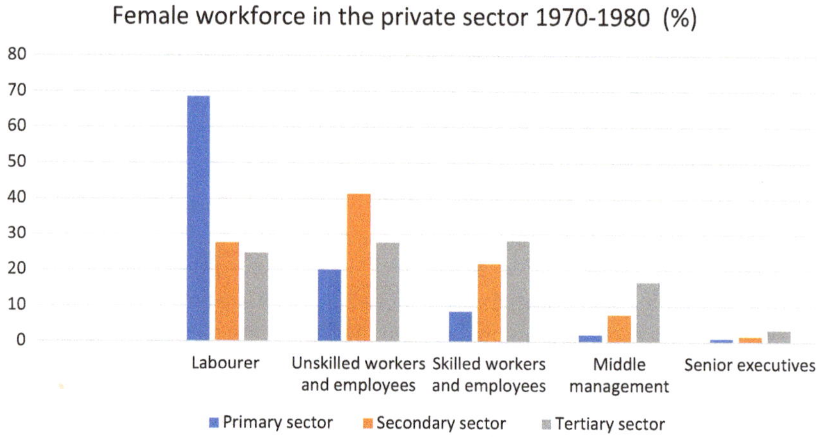

Fig. 7.2 Female workforce in the private sector in the 1970s. Source: MEP (1976)

the other sectors, where there are more men, lower pay, and more difficult work, jobs are found more quickly because there are fewer applicants. Women prefer less strenuous jobs with less risk of injury, accident, or death. We note that the position of women as employees in Cameroonian companies is low, and for those who manage to get positions in companies, they are treated similarly to some men, at least up to middle management level. Given the low number of women in companies, what can be said about the distribution of salaries? We will illustrate this with Fig. 7.2. In some areas, such as skilled jobs and senior management, women occupy a more important place than men in office jobs. In general, however, we see that men's salaries are higher than women's because of their field of activity and their professional qualifications (Fig. 7.2).

The position of women in the labour market has changed since 1990; the proportion of women in the workforce has risen, but still does not exceed that of men, as is the case in the vast majority of countries around the world. Female enrolment in schools has also improved (Castel, 1995). In the 2000s, 71.8% of women were enrolled in primary school, compared with 84.8% of men (Ekamena Ntsama, 2014). Schooling and better education have enabled them to acquire more skills and take up paid jobs that allow them to take charge of their own lives, thereby increasing the proportion of women in the labour market. The causes and consequences of these changes include a decline in fertility and an increase in divorce. Nevertheless, the number of women in the labour market continues to fall. The unemployment rate is higher for women (4.5%) than for men (3.1% in 2010). Companies generally prefer to recruit men, as women are seen as having domestic and reproductive tasks that are crucial to the upkeep of the home. Women are more likely to be looked after by their partner, husband, or a male family member. When it comes to educational qualifications, many women go on to study literature or humanities, while men prefer science or hard sciences, which means that the most highly qualified men are more likely to end up in positions of responsibility.

We note here that women's access to the labour market is much more complex than that of men, as they are concentrated in certain tertiary and primary sectors, and positions of responsibility are predominantly held by men. We can see from Table 7.5 that men earn more than women in the manual and middle management sectors, with a slight difference among skilled workers, and that women earn more among skilled workers. It should also be noted that these differences vary according to age, seniority in the company, and the sector in which they work.

Compared with Scandinavia, where the Gini coefficient at the time was 0.20, which is considered a very egalitarian threshold, the United States with 0.40 after taxes, which is a less egalitarian threshold, and Latin America (0.60), which is the least egalitarian, Cameroon is classically situated at a significant level of inequality for emerging countries, with a Gini coefficient of 0.45 in 1996, corresponding to large masses of poor households, wealthy elites, and a still small middle class. The downward trend that began reduced the coefficient to 0.42 in 2001, and despite an increase to 0.43 in 2007, the current index seems to be around 0.40, indicating a slight reduction in inequality, perhaps linked to the country's overall growth and the rise of the middle classes (Chetboun et al., 2021).

5 Conclusion

Our objective was to analyse the historical evolution of the salaried employment and the labour market in Cameroon in the post-independence period, in the context of the evolution of the dynamics of labour law and the labour market. Our results show that the structure of employment in Cameroon is more concentrated in the public sector. In the 1960s and 1970s, education was considered the best route to salaried employment, with 92.5% of skilled jobs and 7.5% of unskilled jobs. The primary sector dominated in terms of the number of employees compared to the labour-intensive secondary and tertiary sectors. Moreover, the secondary and tertiary sectors would have to become more important than the primary sector for the employment structure to expand.

In terms of qualifications, labourers and skilled workers are the most present in the employment structure, to the detriment of middle and senior managers, who are still in short supply. Pay and working conditions, especially in the primary sector, are such that it is often the employers who are looking for workers. Some companies are looking for a majority of unskilled workers, many of whom are found in under-educated regions, as most of them do not require any training to be recruited, which also explains the geographical displacements.

Our analysis shows that the negative aspect of the primary sector is the instability of a large number of unskilled workers who are unable to progress, in the general context of a relatively young workforce. There are some rather large differences in the range of wages paid to employees by sector of activity, age, gender, job title, and geographical area. Earnings are lowest in the primary sector, while those working in the tertiary and secondary sectors earn almost twice as much as those in the primary sector. It should be noted, however, that in rural areas food and accommodation are less expensive and are sometimes provided by the employer or landlord. In addition, the weak position of women in the labour market compared to men is significant, as they are concentrated in manual or unskilled occupations and very few are in managerial positions, with an average salary that is lower than that of men, with the exception of senior managers.

Conflicts of Interest The author has no conflicts of interest to declare that are relevant to the content of this chapter.

References

Amougou, G. (2018). *Esquisse d'histoire des politiques de développement au Cameroun: Un regard contextuel.* University of Yaoundé II, Working Paper Developmental State Strikes Back? 2/2018.

Atangana-Mebara, J. M., Martin, J-Y., & Ta Ngoc, C. (1984). *Education, Emploi et Salaire au Cameroun.* UNESCO, International Institute for Educational Planning.

Barreteau, D., & Hedinger, R. (1989). *Description de langues camerounaises.* ORSTOM-ACCT.

BIT. (1979). *Perspectives sectorielles, Rapport présenté au gouvernement du Cameroun, Programme des Emplois et des Compétences Techniques.* PECTA.

Castel, R. (1995). *Les métamorphoses de la question sociale, Une chronique du salariat.* Fayard.

CHATEFP. (2015). *Droit du travail dans les colonies XIX siècle aux années 60.* Proceedings of the conference-debate in Paris, organised by the Ile-de-France regional group of the Comité d'histoire des administrations chargées du travail, de l'emploi, et de la formation professionnelle and the Association pour l'étude de l'histoire de l'inspection du travail.

Chetboun, D., Zamo Akono, C., Bendzeme, T., Ebaa Ebaa, J. B., & Niekou, R. (2021). *Transformation structurelle et Inégalités de revenus au Cameroun: 2001–2014* (pp. 1–34). Research Papers.

Ekamena Ntsama, S. N. (2014). Les écarts salariaux de genre au Cameroun. *Revue multidisciplinaire sur l'emploi, le syndicalisme et le travail, 9*(2), 124–146. https://doi.org/10.7202/1036261ar

Kouete, V. (2020, January). *Cameroon: 90% of the Labour Force Trapped in the Informal Sector.* Blog Internet Private Sector Development. https://blog.private-sector-and-development.com/2020/01/23/cameroon-90-of-the-labor-force-trapped-in-the-informal-sector/

Lachaud, J.-P. (1994). Les écarts de salaires entre les secteurs public et privé en Afrique francophone: Analyse comparative. *Économie et prévision,* 1994/116/89–118.

Lachaud, J.-P., Nkwayeb, R., Inack, S., & Ndiffo, J. (1996). *Pauvreté et marché du travail au Cameroun, le cas de Yaoundé.* International Institute for Labour Studies, Discussion Papers, n°47.

Mboudou, A.-M. (1982). *Le financement du développement au Cameroun.* PhD in economics, University of Yaoundé.

Mebara, S. (2001, November). *Profil sociodémographique des ménages pauvres en milieu urbain: Le cas de Yaoundé,* PhD, Institut de formation et de recherches démographiques. Under the supervision of Aka Kouamé, Yaoundé.

MEP. (1976). *Quatrième Plan quinquennal de développement économique, social et culturel.* Ministère de l'Économie et du Plan.

Mesple-Somps, S. (1992). *Recueil de données statistiques. Le Cameroun.* Mission Française d'Étude de la Dépense Publique en Afrique subsaharienne, DIAL.

MINEFI/DSCN/SS. (1999). *Les comptes nationaux du Cameroun selon la SCN93* (Vol. 2). Yaoundé.

Moulier-Boutang, Y. (1998). *De l'esclavage au salariat, économie historique du salariat bridé.* Presses Universitaires de France.

Mveng, E. (1963). *Histoire du Cameroun.* Présence africaine.

Njike Njikam, G. B., Fotzeu Mwaffo, V., & Lontchi Tchoffo, R. M. (2005). *Caractéristiques et déterminants de l'emploi des jeunes au Cameroun*. International Labour Office.

Owona, A. (1996). *Naissance du Cameroun, 1884–1914*. L'Harmattan.

Saglio, J. (1986). Hiérarchies salariales et négociations de classification, France 1900–1950. *Travail et Emploi, 27*, 7–20.

World Bank data, classified by the Canadian site of the University of Sherbrooke. (n.d.). https://perspective.usherbrooke.ca

CHAPTER 8

Income Inequalities and Informal Economy in Morocco

Othmane Bourhaba and Mama Hamimida

1 Introduction

High levels of income inequality and the depth of poverty are two distinctive features of Morocco's socio-economic situation. Indeed, Oxfam (2018) reports that the three richest individuals in Morocco alone held more than 44 billion dirhams in 2018. The report estimates that the increase in the wealth of the "top" three richest in one year is comparable to the consumption of nearly 375,000 of the poorest Moroccans in 2018. Similarly, according to the World Bank database, 31.1% of the Moroccan population lives below $5.50 per day. Thus, according to the HCP (2017), subjective poverty in Morocco in 2014 was 45.1%.

At the same time, the expansion of the informal economy has clearly increased, infiltrating all fundamental aspects of socio-economic systems. The size of the informal economy in Morocco constitutes between 30%

O. Bourhaba (✉)
LEAM, Moulay Ismail University, Meknès, Morocco
e-mail: o.bourhaba@umi.ac.ma

M. Hamimida
Hassan II University, Casablanca, Morocco

M.-P. Chelini et al. (eds.), *Wage Dynamics in Africa*, African Histories and Modernities,
https://doi.org/10.1007/978-3-031-99800-3_8

and 40% of GDP (Bourhaba & Hamimida, 2016). On the one hand, the informal economy can contribute to development due to its role in reducing unemployment and promoting local economies; on the other hand, this economy is also seen as a sign of underdevelopment and non-sustainability, given the nature of poor working conditions and the precarious nature of informal employment.

The prevalence of informal economies across the world has received continued attention over the past decade. However, for both Morocco and other developing countries, the link between inequality and informality has received little attention in the literature because the direction of causality and the degree of feedback between the two phenomena are not clear. This chapter addresses this link, presents a review of empirical literature concerning the behaviour of these variables in Morocco and studies the relationship between variations in informality and inequality using econometric modelling.

2 The Informal Sector and Income Inequality: What Links?

At first glance, informal activity does not necessarily translate into greater inequality. This is because informal work promotes an increase in household income through the employment opportunities that it offers. Indeed, the main contribution of the informal economy to the most vulnerable individuals passes through the channel of employment. The lack of employment opportunities in the formal economy forces many people to seek employment in the informal economy to earn a living. Although their income remains low, the informal economy offers them an alternative source of income. However, certain elements suggest that a large informal economy leads to greater inequality.

Rosser et al. (2000, 2003) were the first to publish articles proposing an empirical assessment of the relationship between these two phenomena. They found a positive correlation between inequality and the size of the informal sector. Rosser et al. (2000) analysed 16 developing countries, between 1987 and 1989 and between 1993 and 1994. They observed a positive relationship between inequality and the size of the informal sector in developing economies. They explained their findings by arguing that the informal sector reduces the amount of tax revenue, which negatively impacts the effectiveness of a government's redistributive policies. They thus concluded that a growing informal economy leads to more inequality.

Eilat and Zinnes (2002) argue that the informal sector can affect income distribution negatively or positively, i.e., informal activity can increase inequality or decrease it. Regarding the negative correlation between the informal sector and income inequality, the authors state that if informal activities are associated with anti-competitive behaviours, they can transfer economic surplus from consumers to equity holders, increasing inequalities. On the other hand, if informal activities provide employment for people with low incomes, an informal activity can, in this case, have a positive effect on the distribution of income. The authors' empirical results show a non-statistically significant relationship between the size of the informal sector and the Gini coefficient in developing countries.

Bertoli and Farina (2007) advocate a more equal distribution of wages among formal economic activities than among informal ones, thus linking the increase in inequality to the increase in informal work. This study is consistent with the findings of Binelli and Attanasio (2010) who use two different data sources: the Mexican Employment Survey (ENEU) and the Mexican Income and Expenditure Survey (ENIGH) for the period from 1987 to 2002, in order to study the relationship between the informal economy and income inequality. The authors explain that wage inequality increased simultaneously with the increase in informal activity in Mexico. Indeed, Binelli and Attanasio (2010) observed the activity of Gini percentiles and hourly real wages among informal and formal workers over time, which allowed them to better observe the dispersion between formal and informal activities. They therefore found that inequality is always higher for informal workers than for formal workers at both the bottom and the top of the wage distribution. They also suggest that the rise in informality could be an important factor in explaining the evolution of wage inequality during the 1990s.

Similarly, using Italian data from 2000 to 2004, Elia and Di Porto (2011) suggest that the increase in informal work reduces formal wages, which increases inequality. They also explain that informal work can be dominated by low-skilled individuals and, therefore, the reduction of informal work can lead to fewer inequalities since workers can receive higher income by working in the formal economy. Krstić and Sanfey (2011) analyse the extent and evolution of informality and inequality in the Serbian labour market between 2002 and 2007 using data from the Living Standard Measurement Surveys. The authors show that informal workers earn significantly less than those in the formal sector and that informality plays an increasingly important role in explaining income inequality in Serbia. According to Meghir et al. (2012), the decline in informality leads to a decrease in income inequality. Based on a theoretical model simulated by empirical observation with Brazilian data from the period 2002 to 2007, the authors show that if the authorities increased the costs of informal activities by 10%, by increasing fines and detection and inspection, this would result in higher average wages and improved welfare.

Along the same lines, Filho and Estevão (2012) show that excessively institutionalised environments can also affect informal activity and inequalities. Analysing Brazilian data between 1981 and 2009, the authors affirm the existence of a causality between informal work and the rise of inequalities. More recently, Benjamin et al. (2014) have also provided evidence that greater informality means lower productivity. Therefore, lower productivity leads to lower average wages. Hence, the more unequal the distribution of enterprises between formal and informal activities, the more unequal the income distribution will be. Thus, according to these arguments, the more the informal companies, the greater the income inequality. Xue et al. (2014) also find a robust positive relationship between informal activity and rising income inequality in China using China Urban Labour Survey data from 2005 and 2010. The authors show that the wages of informal employees were 67% of those of formal sector employees, and this large income gap raised the Gini coefficient to 0.42 in 2005. Another study by Lukiyanova (2015), using data for Russia from 2000 to 2010, also shows that there is, in fact, a difference between earnings in the formal and informal labour markets. This analysis notably concludes that informal labour incomes are more prone to polarisation, which leads to greater inequality. The author finds that a 10% increase in informal activity leads to a 1–5% increase in inequality. Using Egyptian data, El-Haddad and Gadallah (2021) conclude that the private informal sector is the main contributor to the increase in inequality caused by the wage structure effect. For at least two reasons, (1) because this sector does not apply a minimum wage; and (2) the existence of strong wage competition on the informal labour market, particularly with the arrival of new entrants.

As the literature shows, most empirical studies analysing the link between income inequality and the informal sector have found that the informal sector has a positive impact on the increase in income inequality. Thanks to this overview, it is possible to conclude that the informal sector has an amplifying effect on income inequalities for at least three reasons. The first is the effect of the informal sector on increasing income inequality through the increase in the share of low-paid jobs. Indeed, all the studies undertaken on wages in the informal sector show that informal workers earn, on average, less than formal workers. Adding to this, the competition between the formal sector and the informal sector pulls wages down, given the non-existence of a minimum wage in the informal sector. The informal sector, therefore, harms the level of wages in the labour market, and this has an impact on the increase in income inequality.

The second mechanism is the fact that the informal sector is characterised by low taxation, which contributes to the amplification of inequalities for at least two reasons: first, because economic agents operating in the informal sector are taxed less, which disadvantages those who do not have access to the informal economy and creates wage inequality between employees in the two sectors. Then, because public expenditure is the channel through which a government can implement economic and social policies in order to improve the living conditions of the population, and the informal sector leads to low tax revenues, which will deprive the tax system of playing its role of secondary distribution.

The third mechanism is the absence of labour market regulation and social protection. Importantly, due to informal work, many workers fall outside the scope of labour market regulations and social protection, which weighs on rising inequality. Because workers have no protection against dismissal, in the majority are subjected to working conditions that endanger their physical and mental health, knowing that they have no social protection in the event of illness or a work accident. Moreover, the absence of a retirement pension widens the level of inequalities between formal and informal workers.

The direction of the causality between inequality and the size of the informal sector is difficult to predict, especially because the economists working on the subject hold widely differing views which may be explained by the specificities of each country or each region. Therefore, this reinforces the importance of assessing the causal link between the informal economy and income inequality for the case of Morocco.

3 Data and Methodology

The empirical application proposed in this section aims to contribute to existing findings. It focuses on a single-country study and seeks to extend the analysis by using the most recent available data. First, it will explore the direction of the causal link between informality and income inequality for Morocco, then provide a detailed analysis of the nature of this relationship. To do this, we will use Granger's causality test (1969) and an AutoRegressive Distributed Lag model (ARDL).

3.1 Data

The database consists of five representative variables: inequality, informality, urban planning, GDP per capita and education. The variables were collected between 1960 and 2007 (the choice of this period is mainly due to the availability of data for the case of Morocco, more details on the data will be provided below). The sample of the study consists of a single country, namely Morocco, for which the data of the dependent variable were obtained from the study undertaken by Solt (2016), who carried out comparable estimates for 174 countries. Forty-seven observations were used in the regression analysis, and the full data set was not used for this study as several observations of the independent variables were missing. The data sources and specific indices derived from these data sources are described below.

The dependent variable of this study is "inequality", taken from the database: the Standardised World Income Inequality Database (SWIID). The SWIID database provides comparable estimates of the Gini index. According to Solt (2016), SWIID uses a custom missing-data algorithm that minimises reliance on problematic assumptions by using as much information as possible from close years in the same country to estimate inequality statistics for missing years in "Luxembourg Income Study" using data from regional collections, national statistical offices and academic studies.

To measure the size of the informal economy, the database developed by Elgin and Oztunali (2012) was used. Based on a dynamic general equilibrium model, the authors succeeded in constructing a panel dataset of 161 countries over the period 1950 to 2009. The strength of this database is that it is the largest in the literature, and this allows for more robust estimates.

Data for the "urbanisation" variable was obtained from the World Bank database. This variable measures the urban population in a country as a percentage of the total population. It also refers, according to the World Bank, to people living in urban areas as defined by national statistical offices.

GDP per capita: This is the gross domestic product per capita, measured in current US dollars, and obtained from "World Development Indicators" published annually by the World Bank. It is a very useful indicator to observe the level of economic development in a country.

Education can have an impact on inequalities. A proxy variable was used for the "education" variable, i.e., the rate of enrolment in tertiary studies (raw rate % of the population). The data was obtained from the World Bank. According to the latter, the enrolment rate is calculated independent of age and expressed as a percentage of the total population of the group five years after graduation from secondary school.

3.2 *Empirical Methodology*

The econometric approach involved two main stages: First, a Granger test was carried out, then we attempted to simulate an ARDL model.

Granger test: The idea behind causality tests (Granger, 1969) is to assess whether certain economic series observed in the past affect others in the present. This method allows us to verify the existence of a causal relationship between the two variables and to determine the direction of the causality. The method corresponds to the estimation of the following equations:

$$\text{Informal}_t = \sum_{i=1}^{m} \alpha_1 \text{informal}_{t-1} + \sum_{i=1}^{m} \beta_j \text{Inequality}_{t-j} + \delta_1 t + u_{1t} \tag{8.1}$$

$$\text{Inequality}_t = \sum_{i=1}^{m} \lambda_1 \text{Inequality}_{t-1} + \sum_{i=1}^{m} \mu_j \text{Informal}_{t-j} + \delta_2 t + u_{2t} \tag{8.2}$$

Where *Inequality* refers to the magnitude of inequality, and *Informal* represents the size of the informal sector, *it* is both the time period and the error term.

In our study, causality in the sense of Granger (1969) makes it possible to draw conclusions on the causal link between the informal sector and income inequality. In other words, it enables us to identify whether more inequalities amplify the size of the informal sector, or, on the contrary, if a large size informal sector creates economic dysfunctions that amplify biases in the distribution of income.

The ARDL Model: To verify the mechanisms linking the informal sector and income inequality in Morocco, an empirical study was carried out using an autoregressive step lag (ARDL) model between 1960 and 2007. ARDL models can explain more complex dynamical features and also eliminate residual autocorrelation (by selecting appropriate lags). Also, modelling in ARDL can be applied regardless of whether the variables have a root unit or whether the covariance is stationary. Note that the ARDL model has limitations including stationarity assumption, sensitivity to lag length and inability to capture nonlinear relationships. Despite these, the ARDL model remains valuable for dynamic relationship analysis.

Following an empirical analysis of the literature on income inequality, a model was created showing the main factors affecting income inequality in Morocco. A simulation of the model is presented below:

$$\begin{aligned} \text{glog}(\text{Inequality}_t) = \alpha + \theta_1 \,\text{loglog}(\text{Inequality}_{t-2}) + \beta \,\text{loglog}(\text{Urbanisation} \\ + \beta_1 \text{loglog}(\text{Urbanisation}_{t-q}) + \gamma \,\text{loglog}(\text{Informal}_t) \\ + \gamma_1 \,\text{loglog}(\text{Informal}_{t-r}) + \delta \,\text{loglog}(\text{GDP\_capita}_t) \\ + \delta_1 \,\text{loglog}(\text{GDP\_capita}_{t-s}) + \varphi \,\text{loglog}(\text{Education}_t) \\ + \varphi_1 \text{loglog}(\text{Education}_{t-u}) + e_t \end{aligned} \tag{8.3}$$

Where *Inequality* refers to the magnitude of inequality, *Urbanisation* to the urban population, *Informal* to the size of the informal sector, *GDP_capita* to GDP per capita (current US$), and *Education* to the enrolment rate in tertiary education, and it is the error term; *q*, *r*, *s*, *u* represent the delay lengths to include, and *t* is the time period.

4 Results

4.1 Granger Test Estimates

Table 8.1 shows the results of the Granger (1969) test estimates with several lags. R-Studio software is used for the calculations.

It is deduced from the Granger causality test that there is a causal relationship between the two variables, meaning that the informal sector causes income inequalities. The relationship in both directions was tested

Table 8.1 Granger's test estimate of Eq. (8.2)

Number of lags	*F statistics*	*P-value*
1	8.5852	0.00697**
2	42.012	2.093–08***
3	31.981	7.925e–08***
4	24.597	7.02e–07***

Note: *** significance at 0.1%, ** significance at 1%, * significance at 5%

Source: Authors' calculations

Table 8.2 Estimation of an ARDL model

Variables	*Coefficient*	*Std. error*	*t-Statistic*	*P-value*
$Inequality_{t-1}$	–0.16377	0.07153	–2.289	0.038106**
$Urbanisation_t$	2.86331	0.43863	6.528	1.34e–05***
$Urbanisation_{t-q}$	*–0.70760*	0.32531	–2.175	0.047245*
GDP_capita_t	*–0.13773*	0.03752	–3.671	0.002518**
GDP_capita_{t-r}	*0.07177*	0.02552	2.812	0.013861*
$Informal_t$	*0.99037*	0.27697	3.576	0.003042**
$Informal_{t-s}$	*0.45196*	0.07442	6.073	2.87e–05***
$Education_t$	*–0.03699*	0.04842	–0.764	0.457516
$Education_{t-s}$	*–0.04576*	0.01710	–2.676	0.018099*
Constant	*–2.15815*	0.41402	–5.213	0.000131***

Note: R-squared: 0.9373. *** significance at 0.1%, ** significance at 1%, * significance at 5%

Source: Authors' calculations

as explained in Eqs. (8.1) and (8.2). Verification was done for both equations (both directions of causality). After verification, the estimation of Eq. (8.2), as shown in Table 8.1, provides robust results that confirm the causal link between the informal sector and income inequality.

4.2 *Estimation of the ARDL Model*

Table 8.2 shows the results of the log-estimated ARDL model.

The R-squared interpretation shows that education and all variables were significant at p-value <0.05. The model explained 93% of the variability of income inequality. Partial autocorrelation function (PACF) and autocorrelation function (ACF) tests were used to analyse the problem of endogeneity, and the result of both tests indicated the absence of endogeneity. R-Studio software was used for the calculations.

The impact of the informal sector on income inequality is significant in the short and long terms. From the results, it can be concluded that the informal sector has an amplifying impact on income inequality in Morocco, both in the short and long terms. The results also show that the level of economic growth makes it possible to reduce inequalities in the short term but that a growth in GDP per capita leads to greater inequality in the long term. This fact can be explained by the poor distribution of the wealth produced. Thus, the rise of the urban population has an immediate positive impact on the growth of inequalities. Moreover, an increase in the schooling rate in Morocco leads to a decrease in long-term income inequality according to the results of our model.

The estimation with an ARDL model made it possible to eliminate the autocorrelation of the residuals for all the series studied (verification with the ACF and PACF tests). Moreover, the model is of good quality for all countries as shown by the high R^2.

5 Conclusion

The econometric analysis allowed us to confirm the positive empirical link between the size of the informal sector and the level of income inequality. Informality is therefore one of the unnoticed causes of the amplification of income inequality in Morocco. The process of this amplifying effect may be described as follows: first, the presence of the informal economy is a signal of weak labour regulations and an inefficient legal system. Several formal companies do not hesitate to resort occasionally or on a more regular basis to additional undeclared labour. There are many undeclared micro-enterprises and small- and medium-sized enterprises acting informally as subcontractors for certain activities of large companies. This lack of regulation in the informal labour market increases the share of low-paid jobs compared to the formal economy, as employers tend to take advantage of this situation of informality to pay workers in this economy with a salary below the fixed hourly minimum wage. Thus, as explained by Günther and Launov (2006), in an informal labour market, workers are generally subject to lower remuneration than similar workers in the formal sector, where wages are set above clearing price market for institutional or efficiency reasons. Informal employment is therefore a generator of income inequalities between employees.

The truth of pay gaps, however, is not so straightforward, as the informal economy displays a more heterogeneous reality. Indeed, as Mejjati (2014) shows, the income of employers in the informal sector in Morocco is generally higher than the local minimum wage; this confirms the hypothesis of the legalist school which states that engaging in the informal economy is a conscious choice on the part of entrepreneurs who choose to avoid the costs of official registration and therefore take advantage of deregulation to increase their profits. Nevertheless, it should be noted that even if the remuneration of the heads of informal units is higher than the minimum wage and that of employees in the informal sector, it remains, on average, at a lower level than the remuneration of the heads of formal enterprises (Mejjati, 2014) because the level of qualification is lower and the marketing channels are, in general, less developed than in the formal economy. Thus, there is a large income gap even among the heads of informal units. According to the HCP (2007), the fifth quartile achieves an average turnover which is 138.1 times higher than that of the first quartile. The conclusion is that the informal sector amplifies income inequality because it fuels an income gap both between informal and formal workers, and between informal workers themselves.

A second argument identifies the provision of public goods and services financed by the collection of taxes and duties as a transmission channel from informality to inequality. The informal sector which is characterised by low taxation, and a greater participation in informal employment, further reduces the tax collected and, consequently, affects the quality and quantity of public goods and services, leading to modest redistribution. This behaviour ultimately triggers a spiral effect: theft.

The incentive for businesses and individuals to pay taxes decreases because paying taxes does not translate into better public goods and services. This increases participation in the informal sector, which tends to have more dispersed and lower wages than the formal sector.

The third form of influence of informality on levels of inequality may be explained by the absence of social protection. A high level of informality implies that a significant proportion of people have no social protection and therefore often lack protection in the event of non-payment of wages, layoffs with neither notice nor compensation, unsafe working conditions, and an absence of benefits such as pensions, sick pay, and health insurance. Indeed, in Morocco as in other developing countries, informal workers do not benefit from any protection against shocks such as accidents and illnesses, the compulsory stoppage of production and work due to natural disasters or epidemics such as the Covid-19 pandemic, and so on, resulting in persistent income inequalities in society.

The main conclusion from our analysis is that a policy formalising informal work, and a set of norms and institutional mechanisms to govern wage formation in the formal sector, could play an important role in the reduction of inequalities in Morocco.

Conflicts of Interest The authors have no conflicts of interest to declare that are relevant to the content of this chapter.

References

Benjamin, N., Beegle, K., Recanatini, F., & Santini, M. (2014). *Informal Economy and the World Bank*. World Bank.

Bertoli, S., & Farina, F. (2007). *The Functional Distribution of Income: A Review of the Theoretical Literature and of the Empirical Evidence Around Its Recent Pattern in European Countries*. University of Siena.

Binelli, C., & Attanasio, O. (2010). Mexico in the 1990s: The Main Cross-Sectional Facts. *Review of Economic Dynamics, 13*(1), 238–264. https://doi.org/10.1016/j.red.2009.10.003

Bourhaba, O., & Hamimida, M. (2016). An Estimation of the Informal Economy in Morocco. *International Journal of Economics and Finance, 8*(9), 140–147. https://EconPapers.repec.org/RePEc:ibn:ijefaa:v:8:y:2016:i:9:p:140-147

Eilat, Y., & Zinnes, C. (2002). The Shadow Economy in Transition Countries: Friend or Foe? A Policy Perspective. *World Development, 30*(7), 1233–1254. https://EconPapers.repec.org/RePEc:eee:wdevel:v:30:y:2002:i:7:p:1233-1254

Elgin, C., & Oztunali, O. (2012). Shadow Economies Around the World: Model Based Estimates. *Working Papers 2012/05*. Bogazici University.

El-Haddad, A., & Gadallah, M. M. (2021). The Informalisation of the Egyptian Economy (1998–2012): A Driver of Growing Wage Inequality. *Applied Economics, 53*(1), 115–144. https://doi.org/10.1080/00036846.2020.1796917

Elia, L., & Di Porto, E. (2011). Undeclared Work and Wage Inequality. *Working Papers, No 201108*, Università della Calabria.

Filho, C., & Estevão, M. (2012). Institutions, Informality, and Wage Flexibility. Evidence from Brazil. *IMF Working Papers 12/84*, International Monetary Fund.

Granger, C. (1969). Investigating Causal Relations by Econometric Models and Cross-Spectral Methods. *Econometrica, 37*(3), 424–438.

Günther, I., & Launov, A. (2006). Competitive and Segmented Informal Labour Markets. *IZA Discussion Papers No. 2349*.

HCP. (2007). *Enquête nationale sur le secteur informel (2006–2007)*. Direction de la Statistique. Rabat. Haut-Commissariat au Plan.

HCP. (2017). *Pauvreté et prospérité partagée au Maroc du troisième millénaire, 2001–2014*. Rabat. Haut-Commissariat au Plan & Banque Mondiale.

Krstić, G., & Sanfey, P. (2011). Earnings Inequality and the Informal Economy. *The Economics of Transition, 19*(1), 179–199. https://doi.org/10.1111/j.1468-0351.2010.00400.x

Lukiyanova, A. (2015). Earnings Inequality and Informal Employment in Russia. *The Economics of Transition, 23*(2), 469–516. https://doi.org/10.1111/ecot.12069

Meghir, C., Narita, R., & Robin, J. M. (2012). Wages and Informality in Developing Countries. *NBER Working Paper No. w18347*.

Mejjati Alami, R. (2014). *Le Secteur Informel au Maroc*. Editions PEM.

Oxfam. (2018). *Partager la richesse avec celles et ceux qui la créent*. Oxfam International.

Rosser, J. B., Rosser, M. V., & Ahmed, E. (2000). Income Inequality and the Informal Economy in Transitions Economies. *Journal of Comparative Economics, 28*(1), 156–171. https://doi.org/10.1006/jcec.2000.1645

Rosser, J. B., Rosser, M. V., & Ahmed, E. (2003). Multiple Unofficial Economy Equilibria and Income Distribution Dynamics in Systemic Transition. *Journal of Post Keynesian Economics, 25*(3), 425–447. https://www.jstor.org/stable/4538839

Solt, F. (2016). The Standardized World Income Inequality Database. *Social Science Quarterly, 97*(5), 1267–1281. https://doi.org/10.1111/ssqu.12295

Xue, J., Gao, W., & Guo, L. (2014). Informal Employment and Its Effect on the Income Distribution in Urban China. *China Economic Review, 31*(C), 84–93. https://doi.org/10.1016/j.chieco.2014.07.012

PART III

Wage Determinants: Shocks, Representations and Earning Strategies

CHAPTER 9

Labour in Senegal Under Structural Adjustment (1980s and 1990s): A Fictitious Market

Eveline Baumann

1 Introduction

Senegal in the early 1980s: the post-colonial "économie de traite", based on the export of primary goods and the import of processed devices, had led to a veritable disaster. Distortions were numerous in the highly subsidised rural sector, with its predominant groundnut production; the manufacturing industry was underperforming; the social state was inadequately designed; recurrent droughts and the deterioration of terms of trade had led towards everyday hardship, thus accelerating the rural exodus.

Unsurprisingly, Senegal became the object of considerable interest in the eyes of the World Bank and the International Monetary Fund. The donors' dogma was clear: only a market economy could help move forward towards what was considered as genuine development, the ultimate objective being a global project, i.e., spreading neoliberal ideas all over the

E. Baumann (✉)
Université Paris Cité, Paris, France
e-mail: eveline.baumann@ird.fr

M.-P. Chelini et al. (eds.), *Wage Dynamics in Africa*, African Histories and Modernities,
https://doi.org/10.1007/978-3-031-99800-3_9

world (Berg, 1990; Copans, 1988, 1990; Diop & Diouf, 1990; Duruflé, 1994; Fall, 2011). This needed in-depth adjustments.

As to labour, promoting a "labour market" in line with the market theory turned out to be a major challenge. However, work situations were highly heterogeneous and exposed to significant extra-economic constraints, with economic, social, political and religious aspects being closely intertwined. Put in another way, labour is not a basic run-to-the-mill commodity.

Karl Polanyi's vision of the market economy (1947, 2001) will guide the argumentation (Sect. 2). The Senegalese economy will be traced during the first two decades following the country's independence (Sect. 3), which will help understand the disastrous impact of Structural adjustment reforms and the decision–makers' response through employment programmes (Sect. 4). I will then highlight the findings from the theoretical point of view (Sect. 5) and, lastly, examine the labour landscape through a Polanyian lens (Sect. 6).

2 Labour and Economic Theory: Mainstream *Versus* Karl Polanyi

2.1 The World Bank and the "Hire and Fire" Attitude

In the 1980s, there was a firm belief that only a shock therapy could help eradicate the distortions of the economy. These distortions—due to subsidies, import restrictions, over-staffing in state-led companies and the public sector—and the state's over-indebtedness genuinely existed. Structural adjustment was deemed to be the solution, with economic growth being the sine qua non. Downsizing the state was viewed as of utmost importance. This meant privatisation of companies, severe restriction of state expenditure and strict control of the recruitment in the public sector, the country's biggest employer. In this regard, labour is considered a tradable commodity like any another, and its price is determined by the supply and demand curve; hiring workers must be as easy as possible, and so must their dismissal. From a purely economic point of view, the idea appeared to be coherent (World Bank, 1981).

However, reality is more complex by far. Whereas wage labour only concerns a minority of the workers, the spectrum of labour situations is extremely wide, comprising self-employed, family workers, interns and apprentices, non-free labour, etc. These manifold situations go hand in hand with historically constructed power relations and are viewed as part of the social contract. Therefore, making labour supply and demand meet requires much more than a balance between mutual expectations expressed in terms of money and in-kind benefits.

2.2 *Karl Polanyi: Another Approach Is Possible*

The writings of Karl Polanyi provide support for in-depth comprehension of labour as a multi-faceted field. Among his concepts, the *embeddedness* of the economy is particularly helpful (2001): the economy is immersed in social relations and cannot be viewed as an autonomous space. *Embeddedness* has given way to multiple enlargements referring also to the cultural, political and religious context (Granovetter, 1985; Servet et al., 1998). Polanyi argues that the amplification of the market economy leads to the risk of dis-*embedding* the productive system, thus separating it from its complex background, which might give way to social unrest. This challenge requests state-driven protective measures.

The idea of dis-*embedding* is closely linked to another concept, the double movement. The self-regulating market as a gradual process fosters the commodification of land, money and labour (Maertens, 2008; Munck, 2006). At the same time, spontaneous counter-movements may emerge to preserve the integrity of society and keep the economy *embedded* in society. Here again, state regulation may be the response to the people's wish to defend society (Polanyi, 2001:90–91).

The third element of interest refers to the concept of fictitious commodities (Polanyi, 1947; Paton, 2010): like land and money, labour is not a classical commodity but a fictitious one: "Labor is only another name for a human activity which goes with life itself, which in its turn is not produced for sale but for entirely different reasons" (Polanyi, 2001:75). This specificity may also hasten a counter-movement.

3 Senegal from Independence to Structural Adjustment

3.1 The Curse of a Groundnut-Centred Economy and Changing Labour Structures

On the eve of independence in 1960, Senegal was far more fortunate than its neighbours. The "jewel of French West Africa" had an extensive transportation system, the key prerequisite to the enhancement of trade. The groundnut production, vividly encouraged by Paris since the 1920s, had become the backbone of Senegal's economy. With the *Mouride* brotherhood being the main protagonist (Copans, 1988), it represented 60% of GDP and 80% of export earnings. The groundnut sector and the manufacturing industry, controlled by French and Lebanese entrepreneurs (Amin, 1969), were inextricably intertwined, with numerous oil mills and the production of farm equipment.

However, the groundnut production was potentially detrimental to subsistence and also responsible for dramatic soil erosion. Notwithstanding the imminent breakdown of the system, the authorities of independent Senegal continued the headlong pursuit of the groundnut strategy, hastening the so-called malaise of the peasantry.

In the 1960s, the primary sector provided work for eight to nine Senegalese out of ten, be it on small farms or on behalf of wealthy religious landowners. The manufacturing industry's salaried labour force accounted for 5% of the active population; 11% worked in the service sector, including civil service (World Bank, 1981:178). The private sector was the main contractual employer (83,000 employees, 79% of total wage labour), whereas the public sector—22,000 employees in 1961 (Fall, 1992:74)—was still limited.

It is noteworthy that during colonial times, the concentration of civil servants in Dakar was a significant feature regarding labour structures: seven out of ten French civil servants in French West Africa were posted to Senegal (Fall, 1992:69), and, unsurprisingly, they influenced the perception of work. On the one hand, traditionally, the Senegalese society places high value on labour: it is associated with physical strain and teamwork. On the other hand, wage work had become synonymous with prestige (Fall, 2011:72). Based on technical abilities or written language skills, it is characterised by regular income, and a minimum of social protection and legislation.

Regarding the fight for independence, the national bourgeoisie was a quintessential asset; students and young intellectuals were on the front line of this struggle. The authorities of independent Senegal had to reckon with this highly influential social stratum and provide subsequent jobs. The challenges were numerous: inequalities between expatriates and Senegalese workers were tremendous (Fall, 2011:159–160), exacerbating social discontent and fostering the organisation of workers in unions.

3.2 Senghor's "African Socialism" and a Plethora of Civil Servants

In line with Senghor's "African socialism", village-based cooperatives were supposed to become the new regime's cornerstone and squeeze exploitative intermediaries out of the market. In reality, local politicians and *marabouts*—i.e., Muslim leaders—took control of a large number of them. The groundnut sector was regulated by ONCAD (Office National de Cooperation et d'Assistance pour le Développement), which finally became an administrative monster with a plethora of employees of all kinds—6000 in 1981 (Fall, 1997:13). In fact, colonial exploitation had given way to "exploitation by the new state" (Mbodji, 1991:20). What is more, the withdrawal of French price subsidies, high competition on the world market, dreadful weather conditions and groundnut diseases had a negative impact (Diop & Diouf, 1990; Mbodji, 1991; Thioub et al., 1998): the share of groundnut exports in GDP was divided by two. Predictably, the purchasing power collapsed all over the country.[1]

Despite the pro-independence discourse, the manufacturing industry remained under the control of the French and Lebanese capital (Youm, 1991). The national capital was weak and limited to the trade sector. An openly pro-French bank network backed the predominance of foreign capital. The political independence of the neighbouring countries implied the shrinking of the market for industrial devices, which led to a tremendous over-capacity in the local manufacturing industry and a downward trend in private investment.

The creation of public enterprises was intended to outweigh this trend. Like other impoverished countries, Senegal benefited from the recycling

[1] In rural areas, the real revenue *p.c.* during the 1970s was 30% lower than during the 1960s. In towns, the decrease corresponded to 36%. Calculations based on Duruflé (1994:193).

of petrodollars under soft loan conditions, which inevitably led to a reversal of the respective shares of private and public work: public employment grew from 21% (1961) to 53% of entire wage work (1983), whereas private employment dropped from 83,300 to 59,000 (Fall, 1992:74).

Whilst the Senegalese decision-makers neglected the diversification of the groundnut-centred production system, the state-led and over-staffed enterprises pursued a policy of high salaries, which harmed the companies' competitiveness and triggered protective measures and subsidisation. In a vicious circle, Senegal had to increasingly rely on external sources of finance, thus precipitating the state's indebtedness.

3.3 Muslim Leaders, Traders and Political Stability

Senegal's political stability is intricately linked to the relationship between the state and the religious leaders, particularly those from the *Mouride* brotherhood. Thanks to their political intelligence, they succeeded in adapting to new situations, from colonisation to independence and later to the introduction of the market economy.

The roots of this specific relationship go back to colonial times when the French decided to control colonial subjects with the help of local dignitaries, thus pursuing political as well as economic objectives (Copans, 1988; Cruise O'Brien et al., 2002; Diop & Diouf, 1990; Fatton, 1986). The *marabouts* urged their *talibé* (disciples) to cultivate groundnuts on their lands. Being part of the relationship linking disciples and *marabouts* (Cruise O'Brien, 2008; Diop, 1984), the *talibé* workforce was as good as free.

The *marabouts* were provided wide support by the state. Indeed, religious dignitaries massively benefited from loans which were only partially paid back (Diop, 1984:49). Moreover, Touba, the spiritual centre of the *Mouride* brotherhood, was declared beyond government control. Lastly, the national decision-makers used to turn a blind eye on the *marabouts*' non-respect of fiscal obligations. The counterpart of these privileges consisted in guaranteeing social peace in rural areas and in the *marabouts*' injunctions (*ndigël*), especially as regards electoral support.

The close ties with their disciples, on the one hand, and the strong relationship with the state, on the other, contributed to the tremendous power of the *marabouts* during the Senghor period. The balance proved to be fragile, though: social inequalities between the mass of groundnut producers and the privileged minority close to the state apparatus were reinforced (Cruise O'Brien, 2008).[2] Moreover, bad meteorological conditions, soil erosion, decreasing prices for groundnuts, falling productivity and profitability for the producers, and disastrous living conditions, led the groundnut farmers to escape the official distribution chains and turn towards subsistence agriculture and contraband. The groundnut system had shown its limits.

To overcome the "malaise of the peasantry", the *marabouts* pronounced a *ndigël* encouraging their disciples to leave the hinterland for urban areas where the living conditions were unquestionably better. The rural exodus led to a dramatic increase in urbanisation and generated a plethora of informal activities,[3] particularly in Dakar.

Wholesale traders, too, played a vital role as concerns political stability (Thioub et al., 1998). Given that the groundnut export had been nationalised, the development of the local entrepreneurship appeared to be in jeopardy. Yet, President Senghor succeeded in satisfying those local businessmen who remained loyal to him: they were given access to lucrative export-import activities, got transport licences and were implicitly allowed to avoid taxation.

The turmoil in the groundnut sector and growing dissatisfaction with the unfulfilled promises of independence gave way to a crisis affecting society in its entirety (Fatton, 1986). To master the crisis, Senghor opted for a top-down response within the framework of a "profoundly elitist ideology of development" (Fatton, 1986:731). Intellectuals were supposed to re-establish the leadership of the ruling class and neutralise popular protest. Power was henceforth shifting to urban areas; religious leaders continued pulling the strings, albeit to a lesser degree.

[2] In 1973, "civil servants were not less than seven times, and very probably over ten times better off than peasant farmers" (Cruise O'Brien, 2008:131).

[3] Informal in the sense of non (or only partially) registered activities, the absence of labour contracts, the prevalence of family workers, the conflict between private and professional interests as regards financial management.

4 Labour and Structural Adjustment: Efficiency *Versus* Social Requests

4.1 Glaring Imbalances and Shock Therapy

After two decades of command economy, the Senegalese state was as good as bankrupt. Social discontent was palpable, particularly among the urban elites who had played a vital role during the struggle for independence. This predicament called for aid from the international community, led by the World Bank and the International Monetary Fund. Their response was unambiguous: in-depth reforms were to be implemented as a mandatory stage prior to the market economy. Senegal became a testing ground for Structural adjustment. Abdou Diouf, Senghor's "natural" successor, was expected to implement the reforms.

The donor-imposed conditionalities were expected to increase the economy's productivity, promote exports, limit public expenditures and orient public finance to propel growth. National decision-makers were prompted to foster entrepreneurship and encourage private initiatives. Subsidies of farm inputs were predicted to come to an end, which led to the dismantling of marketing and extension services, the privatisation of the distribution channels for agricultural devices and food, and the liberalisation of imports of rice, the staple food of the Senegalese population. The industrial production system was forecast to diversify and become cost-effective. The 90 state-owned and para-statal businesses were to shut down or accept privatisation.

As regards labour, priority was given to combat high labour costs, overstaffing, and an insufficiently flexible labour legislation. The public Employment agency had been prompted to close down, and the labour code was expected to be reformed, according to the donors' ideology.

4.2 Labour, the Adjustment Factor "par Excellence"

The adjustment efforts were to primarily affect the technical capital, which was a tremendous challenge: some companies were over-equipped, whereas others could ill afford to adapt their obsolete equipment to modern standards. Both types of companies were thus reluctant to invest in technical capital. The real problems were not necessarily those the international experts asserted but concerned the intermediate consumption costs on the one hand and labour costs on the other. As the entrepreneurs had no control over the prices of the intermediate factors, they prioritised workforce cuts and reducing labour costs.

In broad terms, the labour costs were high compared to those in other countries South of the Sahara, and productivity was low. A factory worker earned nine times the GDP p.c. in Senegal, against twice the GDP p.c. in non-CFA countries such as Zaire, Gambia, Guinea, Ghana, Mauritania, and Morocco. Salaries in public administration showed a similar imbalance. Between 1973/74 and 1981/82, the government's wage bill had increased by 16% per year, and the number of civil servants by 6% (Berg, 1990:9–15).

The reforms were to concern first of all public administration: retiring civil servants were not replaced, and recruitment was frozen. Graduates therefore could no longer benefit from job security, whereas hitherto they were automatically admitted to the civil service. Encouraging voluntary redundancy was a key element of the adjustment measures, and finally, many civil servants accepted to leave their job. That being said, given the tremendous challenge for the Senegalese intelligentsia, the advocated reforms were implemented only timidly.

In contrast, the reforms regarding industry had more rapid and far-reaching dire consequences. Indeed, during the 1980s, more than 21,000 industrial wage workers lost their job (Berg, 1990:10), which corresponded to 16% of the total salaried labour force.

One thing is certain: the salaried workers—and their families—were the "visible" losers in the Structural adjustment programmes, given the multiplier effect of their remuneration. No wonder, the disastrous outcome of the reforms brought about a swing in public opinion, and the public discourse as regards wage earners changed dramatically. Civil servants, especially, were about to lose their prestige because they were obliged to resort to loans on usurious terms (Baumann & Fall, 2013:272–273). The state, compelled to dismiss staff at the donor community's request, was no longer viewed as an economic player. Simultaneously, according to the slogan "Africa needs its entrepreneurs" (World Bank, 1989:135), private entrepreneurs, with little conventional schooling, became increasingly acknowledged.

However, wage earners and employers represented only a minority of the workforce, 16% as to the first, 1.3% as to the second.[4] Indeed, at the end of the 1970s, 39% of the active population were independent (i.e.,

[4] Calculations based on MEF (1982:tab.19).

self-employed); 44% were family workers or apprentices, but they attracted much less attention (Morice, 1987). Their remuneration depended on the goodwill of the head of the household or the business owner. None of them had a legal status. This was also the case of the disabled whose pittance as beggars is frequently the only income of their family (Fassin, 1990). Viewed as a threat to social order, their activity is undertaken in highly insecure conditions (Collignon, 1984). Primarily illiterate, these workers were visible but voiceless, because not organised in unions or any other pressure group. All things considered, education and vocational training turned out to be a discriminating—if not the most discriminating—factor as regards access to a decent job.

4.3 Employment Creation as a Powerful Political Instrument

In the early 1980s, the country's governing body was ageing and lacked well-trained white-collar workers. French assistance was still ubiquitous, comprising 1900 "coopérants", to a large extent teachers (Ndaw, 1984:16). In the private sector, the situation was similar: three white-collar workers in five were foreigners. The discrepancy in salaries between nationals and non-nationals was tremendous (Ndaw:57 and 120), which exacerbated the young intellectuals' wrath. Among them, the students of the one and only Senegalese University—Cheikh Anta Diop—undoubtedly embodied the best-organised group.

The decision-makers were increasingly concerned about the poor employment prospects of graduates (Conseil économique et social, 1968; Secrétariat à l'emploi, 1985). President Abdou Diouf's response consisted in launching the so-called Opération maîtrisards, a project addressing university graduates, mostly economists and jurists, which ran from 1981 to 1984.[5] It consisted in giving them the opportunity of embarking on a high-ranking civil servant career, thus rejuvenating the public administration. Simultaneously, young economists were offered internships in French-owned companies, which opened the perspective to a leadership position. This second component was particularly ambitious: 550

[5] A "maîtrisard" has achieved a "maîtrise", which roughly equals a bachelor's degree. Some 20 in-depth interviews with "Opération maîtrisards" beneficiaries were conducted between 1996 and 2005 (corpus Baumann Sénégal/DES/1996–2005). See Baumann (2016: 233–237) and Sarr (1989).

graduates were to create their businesses in bakery, artisanal fishing, urban transport by mini-bus, printing and market gardening.

It was a truly spectacular project given the enormous costs ... and the disastrous outcome, due to its approach disconnected from economic and social reality. The graduates having benefited from internships in private companies were far from embarking on the career of what the project leaders called the future "capitaines d'industrie" (industry tycoons) because the companies were unwilling to offer them regular employment. The creation of small businesses proved to be a failure. The 150 companies set up by the graduates generated at best 2200 jobs. A single of those graduates' job cost as much as ten million CFA francs (30,500 €), on top of the direct and indirect subsidies granted by the state. Not a single company had survived 15 years after the end of the project.

The "Opération maîtrisards", which has never been officially evaluated, appears as an emblematic example of the employment creation projects which were to follow. Indeed, one element remained constant—the projects are designed in haste, without any prior market survey, under pressure from the street, and frequently against all common sense. The paternalist attitude was a far cry from the idea of the innovative and risk-taking entrepreneur.

Undoubtedly, the project also represents a breaking point regarding labour in Senegal: the public image of intellectuals was henceforth discredited, while petty self-employment was no longer considered a problem but a second-best option. The idea was that informal activities could be "formalised" by measures such as training, awareness-raising of legal obligations, so-called financial education, etc. The "small is beautiful" approach was also in line with the neoliberal ideology of encouraging entrepreneurship, female to an increasing extent. The nascent microfinance movement was to complement this vision (Baumann et al., 2015). In addition, loans represented a means of satisfying the political clientele; all the more as paying them back was not necessarily the donors' priority.

5 Matching Labour Supply and Demand: Theory *Versus* Practice

5.1 A Fictitious Market

The neoclassical labour market theory is based on the idea that the balance between demand and supply can be achieved more or less spontaneously. As to the hypotheses of this model, information is of the utmost importance (Gazier, 1992:153–155). The "labour market" is thought to be transparent, and job seekers and employers can make informed decision. The individual jobseeker acts independently from others, considering only the material aspect of a job, without any social or moral pressure.

Reality does not confirm these hypotheses though. In the Global South, and particularly in Senegal, information is scarce, thus hampering conscious arbitration. As Pierre Bourdieu put it for Algeria in the 1960s, "in the majority of cases, it's not the worker who chooses the job but [...] the job chooses the worker, or the boss, or hazard" (Bourdieu, 1963:270, author's translation). Institutionalised mechanisms favouring the match of labour demand and supply are poor.[6] As a consequence, personal relations play a tremendous role. Moreover, cash income is not the only determining factor for accepting a job: prestige and rent-seeking, as well as social, political and religious motivations are elements to be accounted for.

The most salient characteristic of the Senegalese labour landscape was—and still is—high segmentation, with a glaring imbalance between different types of labour. Schematically, on the one hand, the state and so-called modern companies, unable to satisfy the abundant labour demand. Like nowadays, only for the small minority of wage workers, working hours, paid leave, health insurance, retirement, etc., made sense. On the other hand, the bulk of the active population, i.e., the self-employed (mostly in agriculture), family workers and apprentices, corresponded to 83% of the workforce (MEF, 1982:table 19). Rural exodus, explicitly encouraged by religious dignitaries, continued fostering self-employment and exacerbating these imbalances. There is evidence: the Senegalese labour world cannot be viewed as a market as the economic theory would have it.

[6] Private recruitment agencies appeared only in the 1990s, addressing primarily white-collar workers.

5.2 *Poor Data on Labour and Scarce Employment Policy Tools*

Effective public labour policy calls for coherent statistical coverage. In this respect, the young state had to face considerable shortcomings: information on labour was mostly collected as a by-product of the population censuses. Specific surveys were rare (MEF, 1982) and limited to the Dakar region (MEFP, 1993). The array of informal activities generally concerned only the "modern" segment (Ndiaye, 1990). At best, the surveys corresponded to snapshots, with categories evolving over time, thus hampering comparability (Baumann, 2016:65–104). In short, data on labour in Senegal was incoherent in the 1980s—and it remains essentially so 40 years later.

Some advances cannot be denied though. There was a sudden—and legitimate—interest in female work. The informal economy came increasingly under the spotlight, thanks to the interest of international agencies (Ndiaye, 1990; Van Dijk, 1986; Zarour, 1989). Statisticians also questioned working time, underlining the idea of under-employment.

Be it as it may, the root of the problem has not been solved until now: there is a profound unease about the categories used for data collection. Working-age population, economically occupied and active, unemployed, under-employed, retired, etc.: these categories had been developed by and for industrialised countries, but they are exogenous to the local realities.

Unemployment is undoubtedly the most problematic category: a jobless person does not have legal status. At the same time, bringing an end to joblessness is relatively easy: a simple supplier credit is enough to start itinerant trade, but isn't this a kind of disguised unemployment? Strong seasonal fluctuations, mainly in the primary sector, make the definition of unemployment even more complex. Are farmers or fishermen jobless or occupied during the offseason?

The different surveys and population censuses have used extremely heterogeneous categories, which prohibits the elaboration of times series. The latter are essential for coherent labour policy, though. No wonder getting access to reliable data on labour in Senegal is simply "a puzzle" (World Bank, 2007:26).

It is no coincidence, therefore, that labour policy consisted primarily in fostering self-employment, by injecting money, according to the belief that financial techniques can help overcome maldevelopment. This approach had another advantage: perpetuate cronyism in the run-up to the elections.

6 The Labour Landscape Through a Polanyian Lens

6.1 Embeddedness *and Market Economy*

In Senegal, religion, politics and the economy are closely intertwined. Whilst 90% of the population are Muslims, religion may be considered as *the* most important element regarding society (Villalón, 1994:416). Particularly the *Mourides* play a prominent role. According to the social contract, the *talibé* usually follow their *marabout*'s injunctions. Polanyi's *embeddedness* may help understand why the former accept working for free on their spiritual leaders' farms or why they leave the groundnut production and turn towards urban informal activities. They simply hope for material and symbolic protection, and reward in the hereafter.

The shift to a market economy has given a new impetus to *Mouride* entrepreneurship. Indeed, the dignitaries know how to encourage their disciples to occupy profitable niches.[7] However, increasingly market-driven ambitions have an impact on the articulation between religion, economy and power and may engender a trend towards *disembedding* economy from the social environment.

Labour relations can also be intertwined with ethnicity and kinship, for instance as regards apprentices and domestic workers—the *bindaan* (little maids). According to an unwritten contract, their "patron" is supposed to provide care in case of illness or hardship, hence the idea of an implicit wage. Therefore, in contrast to the more or less neutral relations in the market economy with its protection system, the "patrons" play the role of a tutor.

Embeddedness can finally be related to the caste system: certain activities are reserved for specific groups, such as woodworking, fishing, cattle breeding. Some professions are particularly protected against outsiders—such as crafts that need fire (blacksmiths, jewellers) or transmitting tradition (griots)—which is also a factor guaranteeing social cohesion.

Embeddedness of labour should not be idealised, though. Violence does exist, be it against apprentices, *bindaan* or *talibé*. New rules are emerging given higher awareness of injustice. The hitherto social contract has started

[7] Since the 1990s, the *Mouride* community can rely on a widespread network, reaching out as far as Marseille and New York, Djeddah, Hong Kong and Guangzhou, while influential figures continue pulling strings in the holy city of Touba and the Sandaga Market in Dakar.

eroding, and the *marabouts'* injunctions are followed with less respect than during the pre-neoliberal period. More and more young *Mourides* tend to distance themselves from their spiritual leaders who are far too attracted to earthly pleasures. When it comes to taking on workers, personal relations are less significant; domestic staff is less frequently chosen among the kinship and extended family (Leimdorfer & Marie, 2003), but according to socially neutral criteria. As to white-collar salaried workers, a growing number of recruitment agencies help keep personal pressure on the employer at bay.

6.2 *Postponing, a "Soft" Counter-Movement*

Regardless of the cultural context, the introduction of new, exogenous rules may be highly problematic: they risk undermining a balance that has been built up over the course of history. People only rarely refuse these rules straightforward, but may prefer strategies such as reinterpreting, avoiding or postponing.

The Senegalese decision-makers had no choice but consent to the introduction of market mechanisms and the downsizing of the state. However, the political context was not conducive to painful reforms. Fearing that the Structural adjustment might backfire on them, the high officials who were expected to implement reforms delayed their completion as much as possible. No wonder, ten years after having been launched, the reforms were considered as being "postponed" (Berg, 1990): there was "not much real adjustment" and "Senegal's economy [was] no more competitive than [it was] a decade ago"; "lack of implementation" was due to "the erosion of Senegalese political will" (Berg, 1990:iii). In other words, a counter-movement in a Polanyian perspective was at work.

These self-protective tendencies waned progressively, though. Indeed, market rules became increasingly widespread due to the marketisation of health and education, consultancy, legal counselling, labour market services, financial intermediation, etc., thus creating numerous job opportunities. As to the acceptance of market reform, the commodification of tertiary education is an outstanding example: the creation of private universities was to exceed the most optimistic projections made by World Bank experts (Baumann, 2016:89–90).

All things considered, the conversion to market economy has been successful for certain categories of actors, those having succeeded in adapting the rules of the game to their advantage. *Embeddedness* and the patronage system had not disappeared, thus limiting social malaise.

6.3 Limits to Commodification and Permanent Salaried Work

According to Karl Polanyi, the commodification of labour is a "vital organizing principle" of the market economy (Polanyi, 2001:76), but it may be thwarted for multiple reasons.

In the 1980s and 1990s, and still nowadays, Senegal's economy is structurally unable to massively recruit (permanent) contractual workers: it is essentially based on the primary sector, which stands for high seasonal fluctuations necessitating a flexible labour force. Therefore, small-scale farms mostly rely on unpaid family workers; food processing plants prefer temporary to permanent workers.

Whereas the number of prime employers—such as the banking sector—is limited, the bulk of the production units corresponds to micro-units and self-employment. The very existence of these units is linked to the low purchasing power of the population, but not only. Above all, self-employment represents a second choice for poorly qualified workers. Given their low level of vocational training, especially as regards management, they rarely succeed in expanding an existing business, which hampers hiring workers and vertical accumulation. Preference is therefore given to horizontal accumulation. It consists in multiplying small-scale businesses by entrusting them to family members. This *modus operandi* is in line with the habitus of ensuring social reproduction.

In family-owned businesses, power relations mirror the hierarchical order of the domestic unit. There is a clear divide between elders and cadets, protectors and "obligés", men and women, thus hindering the empowerment of those who are dominated. "Patrons" are frequently unwilling to let their apprentices leave in order to start their own business or look for wage work. Similarly, big companies may give the illusion that a poorly paid or free internship will result in a permanent job, thus prolonging the intern's dependency.

Gerontocracy and unequal gender relations are undoubtedly the most prevalent underpinnings of the Senegalese social contract. Most of the employment-creating "development projects" specifically address women and young people, in point of fact three quarters of the Senegalese active population. Indebted to the political decision-makers, the beneficiaries may be considered a political "adjustment factor" enabling the unequal labour landscape to function.

Economic mainstream theory stipulates that the self-regulated market should not be impeded by social and political processes. This condition was far from being fulfilled as regards Senegal in the 1980s and 1990s. Impediments were numerous, due to deeply rooted power relations. In this logic, the fictitious character of labour as a commodity is the "Achilles' heel in [the] *laissez faire* logic" (Paton, 2010:78).

7 Conclusion

The above developments have emphasised the specificity of the Senegalese labour landscape, highlighting the lack of reliable information on labour supply and demand and the ubiquity of power relations with social, economic, political and religious elements being intrinsically intertwined. These characteristics are detrimental to the smooth match between labour supply and demand. In line with Karl Polanyi's perception of labour as a fictitious commodity, there is evidence that labour does not follow the rules of a conventional market, which also hampers active labour policy and may lead to instrumentalising labour for politicking.

The Structural adjustment programmes have led to far-reaching changes in the Senegalese labour landscape. Massive lay-offs in the public and private sectors hastened the proliferation of small-scale businesses. This led to new perceptions of labour: self-employment was going to acquire its credentials, an evolution which increasingly concerned female entrepreneurship; wage labour was no longer the ultimate dream, independently of the job seekers' education level.

Experience has shown that the shift to market economy needs more than recommendations of Washington-based agencies. Indeed, national decision-makers and the population tried to avoid and postpone the reforms which, to a large extent, contradicted the Senegalese social contract. However, as soon as the Senegalese perceived the economic return of the reforms, their attitude became increasingly market-friendly (Coussy, 2006). The graft of neoliberal ideas seems to have taken hold particularly in the field of trade, IT services, consultancy, health and education. Therefore, it comes as no surprise that at 9.1 years, school life expectancy in 2023 is twice as high as in 1992 (data.uis.unesco.org); in 2022, nearly 300,000 young Senegalese enrolled in higher education, among them one-third in a private university.

Currently, the labour landscape is undergoing in-depth modifications: wage labour concerns one in three occupied workers (MEPC, 2023); salaried staff is increasingly used in the flourishing horticultural sector (Girard et al., 2022). In 2021, there are 500,000 wage workers. Since 1997, their number has increased at an annual rate of 6%, which is pretty high, compared to the population growth rate of 2.5%.

However, increased salarisation does not rule out persisting inequalities: one wage worker in three does not receive a pay slip, working for free is still widespread, and one in ten Senegalese is living under the poverty line of 1.90 USD per day. Social, religious and political considerations continue to exert pressure on economic decisions such as recruitment and dismissal. Nevertheless, as the 2024 presidential election have shown, there is a call for a profound break with the elites, a call for more democracy and a sound distance from the patronage system.

Conflicts of Interest The author has no conflicts of interest to declare that are relevant to the content of this chapter.

References

Amin, S. (1969). *Le monde des affaires sénégalais*. Editions de Minuit.

Baumann, E. (2016). *Sénégal: Le travail dans tous ses états*. Presses universitaires de Rennes.

Baumann, E., & Fall, M. A. (2013). Représentation de la dette et microcrédit au Sénégal. In B. Hours & P. Ould-Ahmed (Eds.), *Dette de qui, dette de quoi? Une économie anthropologique de la dette* (pp. 263–284). L'Harmattan.

Baumann, E., Fall, M. A., & Godfroid, C. (2015). Malaise in the Senegalese Microfinance Landscape. In I. Guérin, M. Labie, & J.-M. Servet (Eds.), *The Crises of Microcredit* (pp. 133–151). ZedBook.

Berg, Elliot Associates. (1990). *Adjustment Postponed. Economic Policy Reform in Senegal in the 1980s*. Report Prepared for USAID/Dakar, Alexandria.

Bourdieu, P. (1963). Travail et travailleurs en Algérie. Etude sociologique. In A. Darbel et al. (Eds.), *Travail et travailleurs en Algérie* (pp. 251–562). Mouton & Co..

Collignon, R. (1984). La lutte des pouvoirs publics contre les 'encombrements humains' à Dakar. *Canadian Journal of African Studies, 18*(3), 573–582. https://doi.org/10.1080/00083968.1984.10804080

Conseil économique et social. (1968). *Les problèmes de l'emploi des diplômés de l'université*. République du Sénégal.

Copans, J. (1988). *Les marabouts de l'arachide*. L'Harmattan.

Copans, J. (Ed.). (1990). Ouvrier, emploi et entreprises au Sénégal. *Pratiques sociales et travail en milieu urbain. Les Cahiers*, n° 12.

Coussy, J. (2006). Etats africains, programmes d'ajustement et consensus de Washington. *L'Economie politique, 32*, 29–40. https://doi.org/10.3917/leco.032.0029

Cruise O'Brien, D. B. (2008). *Saints and Politicians. Essays in the Organisation of a Senegalese Peasant Society*. Cambridge University Press. (First published 1975).

Cruise O'Brien, D., Diop, M.-C., & Diouf, M. (2002). *La construction de l'Etat au Sénégal*. Karthala.

Diop, M. C. (1984). L'État, la confrérie mouride et les paysans sénégalais. *Labour, Capital and Society/Travail, capital et société, 7*(1), 44–64. https://www.jstor.org/stable/43158456

Diop, M. C., & Diouf, M. (1990). *Le Sénégal sous Abdou Diouf*. Karthala.

Duruflé, G. (1994). *Le Sénégal peut-il sortir de la crise?* Karthala.

Fall, B. (1992). Evolution et configuration actuelle du marché de l'emploi au Sénégal. In E. Lee et al. (Eds.), *Ajustement, emploi et développement au Sénégal* (pp. 63–82). Bureau International du Travail.

Fall, B. (Ed.). (1997). *Ajustement structurel et emploi au Sénégal*. Codesria/Karthala.

Fall, B. (2011). *Le travail au Sénégal au XXe siècle*. Karthala.

Fassin, D. (1990). Je t'aide, moi non plus. Handicap physique et rapports sociaux au Sénégal. In J. Copans (Ed.), *Pratiques sociales et travail en milieu urbain. Les Cahiers* (Vol. 12, pp. 139–149).

Fatton, R. (1986). Gramsci and the Legitimization of the State: The Case of the Senegalese Passive Revolution. *Canadian Journal of Political Science, 19*(4), 729–750. https://www.jstor.org/stable/3227798

Gazier, B. (1992). *Economie du travail et de l'emploi*. Dalloz.

Girard, P., et al. (2022). Une agriculture familiale de plus en plus dépendante du salariat? Les travailleurs saisonniers dans l'agriculture familiale sénégalaise (régions des Niayes et du Delta). *Cahiers d'études africaines, 245–246*, 207–239. https://doi.org/10.4000/etudesafricaines.36355

Granovetter, M. (1985). Economic Action and the Social Structure: The Problem of Embeddedness. *The American Journal of Sociology, 91*(3), 481–510. http://www.jstor.org/stable/2780199

Leimdorfer, F., & Marie, A. (Eds.). (2003). *L'Afrique des citadins. Sociétés civiles en chantier: Abidjan, Dakar*. Karthala.

Maertens, E. (2008). Double Movement. A Critical Appraisal. *Social Thought and Research, 29*, 129–153. https://doi.org/10.17161/STR.1808.5694

Mbodji, M. (1991). The Politics of Independence: 1960–1986. In C. L. Delgado & S. Jammeh (Eds.), *The Political Economy of Senegal under Structural Adjustment* (pp. 21–30). Praeger.

MEF. (1982). *Méthodologie et principaux résultats de l'enquête main-d'œuvre et migration au Sénégal, 1979–1980.* Ministère de l'économie et des finances, République du Sénégal.

MEFP. (1993). *Enquête emploi, sous-emploi, chômage en milieu urbain, avril-mai 1991, région de Dakar. Rapport définitif.* Ministère de l'économie, des finances et du plan, République du Sénégal.

MEPC. (2023). *Enquête nationale sur l'emploi au Sénégal. 3ème trimestre 2023. Note d'information.* Ministère de l'économie, du plan et de la coopération, République du Sénégal.

Morice, A. (1987). Ceux qui travaillent gratuitement: Un salaire confisqué. In M. Agier, J. Copans, & A. Morice (Eds.), *Classes ouvrières d'Afrique noire* (pp. 45–76). Karthala.

Munck, R. (2006). Globalization and Contestation: A Polanyian Problematic. *Globalizations, 3*(2), 175–186. https://doi.org/10.1080/14747730600702956

Ndaw, M. D. (1984). Rapport à Monsieur le Président de la République du Sénégal sur les possibilités d'emploi pour les diplômés de l'enseignement supérieur.

Ndiaye, L. (1990). *Le secteur informel "moderne" du Sénégal.* USAID.

Paton, J. (2010). Labour as a (Fictitious) Commodity: Polanyi and the Capitalist 'Market Economy'. *The Economic and Labour Relations Review, 21*(1), 77–88. https://doi.org/10.1177/103530461002100107

Polanyi, K. (1947). Our Obsolete Market Economy: Civilisation Must Find a New Thought Pattern. *Commentary, 4*(1), 109–117.

Polanyi, K. (2001). *The Great Transformation. The Political and Economic Origins of Our Time.* Beacon Press (First edition 1944, New York: Farrar & Rinehart).

Sarr, A. (1989). *La création d'entreprises au Sénégal: L'exemple de l'Opération "Maîtrisards".* Mémoire de fin d'études, UCAD, ENSUT.

Secrétariat à l'emploi. (1985). *L'insertion des diplômés d'études supérieures dans la vie active (1980–1984). Bilan descriptif.* République du Sénégal.

Servet, J.-M., Maucourant, J., & Tiran, A. (Eds.). (1998). *La modernité de Karl Polanyi.* L'Harmattan.

Thioub, I., Diop, M.-C., & Boone, C. (1998). Economic Liberalization in Senegal. *African Studies Review, 41*(2), 63–89. https://www.jstor.org/stable/524827

Van Dijk, M. P. (1986). *Sénégal. Le secteur informel de Dakar.* L'Harmattan.

Villalón, L. A. (1994). Sufi Rituals as Rallies: Religious Ceremonies in the Politics of State-Society Relations. *Comparative Politics, 26*(4), 415–437. https://www.jstor.org/stable/422024

World Bank. (1981). *Accelerated Development in Sub-Saharan Africa, An Agenda for Action.* World Bank.

World Bank. (1989). *Sub-Saharan Africa. From Crisis to Sustainable Growth.* World Bank.

World Bank. (2007). *Senegal. Looking for Work. The Road to Prosperity.* World Bank.

Youm, P. (1991). The Economy since Independence. In C. L. Delgado & S. Jammeh (Eds.), *The Political Economy of Senegal under Structural Adjustment* (pp. 21–30). Praeger.

Zarour, C. (1989). *Etude du secteur informel de Dakar et de ses environs.* USAID.

CHAPTER 10

The Effect of Higher Learning on Graduates' Salary in Tunisia

Emna Zamel and Mahdi Barouni

1 Introduction

According to human capital theory, investment in education is justified by the positive effects it has on the individual and society (Becker, 1962). Several empirical studies estimate that higher education return on the market is higher in countries depending on knowledge-based economy (Carnoy, 1995). However, the results are mixed for middle-income countries (Colclough et al., 2010). Focusing on the quantitative aspects rather than the qualitative ones could be the cause. In the past few years, several studies had increasingly focused on the qualitative aspects of education.

In Tunisia, the transition from an elitist education to mass education was due to the increasing demand for schooling and hence the sharp rise of number of graduates, 85,000 in 2010 (MESRS, 2015). Moreover, the unemployment rate among graduates also rose, about 20% (INS, 2014). This phenomenon is characterized by a wide disparity through higher

E. Zamel (✉)
University of Carthage, Nabeul, Tunisia
e-mail: zamelemna@gmail.com

M. Barouni
University of Bourgogne, Dijon, France

M.-P. Chelini et al. (eds.), *Wage Dynamics in Africa*, African Histories and Modernities,
https://doi.org/10.1007/978-3-031-99800-3_10

education institutions. Indeed, in 2011, about 80% of graduates from several universities faced unemployment problem according to data released from the National Employment Agency and Self Employment (ANETI).

In addition, to face the increasing education demand, higher education supply has increased and was accompanied by a diversification of paths, types of institutions, curricula and duration of studies. Due to the backdrop of education supply, considering the number of schooling years to measure education can be a useful estimate in practice but is conceptually questionable if no quality education is provided.

Accordingly, assuming the quality of education provided determines the efficiency of the educational investment in the labour market, it is crucial to study the link between school characteristics and education private return.

The task is nonetheless arduous because education outputs result from the combination of a large number of factors. It is difficult to distinguish between what pertains to the individual sphere such as school performance or the individual choice and those that fall under institutions' quality.

This raises questions: can we identify additional characteristics other than the individual ones that would influence graduates' careers? Is there an institutional factor that could be related to a quality effect? Could such an effect be explained by variables related to the characteristics of institutions such as those dealing with allocated resources or selectivity? One might think that in the case of higher education, the teacher-student ratios affect the quality of education and subsequently the wages of graduates (Belfield & Fielding, 2001). Other features such as the selectivity of institutions during the university orientation or its reputation in terms of labour market performance can function as a "signal" to employers (Spence, 1973) and affect the salary of graduates.

This chapter analyses the links between individual characteristics, the characteristics of universities and the wages of graduates in Tunisia. We create a dataset by matching several databases from the Ministry of Higher Education (MESR), the Ministry of Vocational Training and Employment (MFPE) and the Social Security National Fund (CNSS).

Our final database includes 12,524 graduates (150 higher education institutions) in 2010. To provide answers to the above raised questions, we have dealt with individual variables (i.e., gender, specialities, etc.) and with variables related to the educational institutions (i.e., number of permanent teachers, alumni unemployment rate, etc.). We use a multilevel model more suited to the hierarchical structure of our data.

We start by a brief literature review before discussing Tunisia's higher education system. We then present our data and econometric methodology. Finally, we conclude with a discussion of the main results.

2 Literature Review

Since the 1960s, several economists have shown interest in the educational returns and studied the connection between the number of schooling years and wages (Becker, 1964; Mincer, 1974). Following the United States' early works, several studies have been carried out in developed countries. The results of empirical studies suggest that the returns of an additional year of study vary from 5 to 15%.

According to human capital theory, it is reasonable to expect that the quality of education improves returns in specific tracks. In fact, the links between quality and returns of education can only become significant starting from higher education (Giret & Goudard, 2007).

In the 1990s, the literature on educational outputs, and especially that focusing on the impact of the quality of education on the individual's income, has proliferated in a significant manner. Several economists, such as Brewer et al. (1996) and Harmon et al. (2001), have shown interest in the impact of university education's quality on student income. We note that the quality of education is a multidimensional concept. The resources invested by the institutions, the quality of school infrastructure, the class size, the total number of teachers, the number of experimented teachers, their know-how and competencies are usually considered as factors that impact the quality of education. It is a crucial issue of efficiency and setting priorities of any public policy aiming at improving students' performance and hence allowing them to integrate the labour market.

Some economists examine the link between the resources invested by educational institutions and the returns to education. Estimates provided by Card and Krueger (1992) based on US data suggest that the resources invested by educational institutions have a significantly positive effect on education returns. However, when they use data derived from French universities, Giret and Goudard (2007) do not show a relationship between human or financial resources invested by university institutions and earnings. Furthermore, they suggest that other factors linked to the quality of education or to a signalling effect have a positive impact on earnings. Similarly, Bourdon et al. (2012) suggest that the selectivity level at the admission to engineering schools in France and the teacher ratios in the

University Institutes of Technology (IUT) impact graduates' wage. Di Pietro and Cutillo (2006) have examined the connection between the characteristics of the Italian universities and obtaining a non-graduate job. They suggest that students graduating from universities focusing on research are more likely to perform better on the labour market. They show that the age of university can explain the network or reputation effect, and has a positive impact on the graduates' jobs quality.

Despite the increasing number of studies on the quality of education, very few have been conducted on middle-income countries and even less on African countries. To our knowledge, Case and Yogo (1999) is the only African research conducted. Based on the 1996 South African Census, they studied the impact of the educational institution on the returns to education for the black community. Unlike many studies conducted in developed countries, the research suggests that student-teacher ratio has a crucial impact on the probability of finding jobs especially for women. This brings up the question of the quality of education in the context of middle-income countries, where disparities between schools are generally different from developed countries.

The outcome of studies on the effects of the educational institution also varies according to the empirical methodology used. Conventional methods are often based on logistic estimates or on the ordinary least squares. However, the outcomes of these methods show several limitations in that they do not take into account behaviour patterns heterogeneity within a population. Various improvements have been made to this research since the mid-1980s and have mainly helped in overcoming some conventional methods' limitation. They used new procedures such as multilevel modelling (Rumberger & Thomas, 1993), which allows taking into account the correlation between observations and institutional variables. Hence, taking into account the hierarchical structure of data.

3 Tunisian Higher Education Context

3.1 Major Shifts in Tunisian Higher Education

The Tunisian higher education faced a significant geographic expansion in the 1980s (Zghal, 1986). Moreover, the massification of secondary education fed through higher education (from 6.5% enrolment in 1984 to 34.6% in 2007). This has been accompanied by a decline in quality of education (PISA[1] 2006 survey ranked Tunisian students 55th among 57 countries).

Against this backdrop, it is worth explaining the loosening admission requirements. The Ministry of Education (ME) decree (JORT, N°090, 2001, p. 3387 and following) sets the conditions to pass, retake or "redemption"[2] for the 2011 baccalaureate exam (79,466 admitted).

To be admitted in higher education, the student must mainly meet the following requirements:

$$\frac{(\text{average baccalaureate exam} \times 3) + \text{average during the year}}{4}$$

$$\text{pass if} \geq \frac{10}{20}; \text{retake if} \geq \frac{7}{20};$$

$$\text{redemption if} \geq \frac{9}{20} \text{and average during the year} \geq 10 / 20.$$

Prior to 2001, the 1992 ME decree (JORT, 1992, N°041, p. 819 and following) has implemented less lax requirements:

$$\text{pass if baccalaureate average} \geq \frac{10}{20};$$

$$\text{retake if baccalaureate average} \geq \frac{8}{20} \text{or} \geq \frac{7}{20} \text{and average graduation year} \geq 10 / 20;$$

$$\text{redemption if baccalaureate average} \geq \frac{9}{20} \text{and average graduation year} \geq 10 / 20.$$

We run a simulation on 2011 baccalaureate results using the 1992 conditions above. In this, 20% did not pass compared to 2001 requirements.

[1] Programme International pour le Suivi des Acquis.

[2] The possibility to redeem the student who has a grade that is slightly lower than the pass grade.

These quantitative and qualitative changes created major challenges when it comes to training quality and graduates' competitiveness (Zghal, 2007).

3.2 *Attractiveness Gap Between Institutions*

Successful baccalaureate candidates are allocated a higher education spot following a four-step process (Ben Sédrine, 1998). First, the preferences and school grades are ranked.[3] Admission requirements and students' capacity are also entered into the IT System. The computer matches then students to institutions according to their preferences and grades. The results are reached following a four-iteration process.

Overflow resulting from predetermined institutions' capacity is allocated to low-budget institutions offering more general studies. This harms the effectiveness of teaching and the result quality. This is further worsened by the delay in specialization (Damoiselet & Lévy-Garboua, 2000 on OECD countries). Hence, the most successful baccalaureate holders tend to be attracted to engineering, medical and business schools.

The above adverse selection process highlights the hierarchical organization of the system. Students with low grades are pushed towards academic training. This should lead to education and research jobs and hence requires excellence. On the other hand, students with high grades are over-represented in professional courses that require less intellectual capacity.

Unlike the university, schools and institutes are marked by the logic of a system which is more tied to the real economy (internships, professional guest speakers and lecturers). This focus on employable skills leads to higher demand and increased selectivity at enrolment.

3.3 *The Labour Market for Graduates*

Counter-intuitively these graduates are the ones struggling to find employment (Zamel, 2011). Unemployment amongst graduates increase to 23% in 2009 (1.4% in 1994 and 8.5% in 2004, INS). This rate is particularly high among new graduates. In addition, the unemployment rate reaches

[3] Admission criterion is handed out to baccalaureate holders, together with the past three years' intake scores. The latter as well as one's social circle help candidates feel their four to ten institutions' choices.

32% three years and a half after graduation (MFPE, 2008). Furthermore graduates are more severally hit by unemployment than unskilled workers, another proof of mismatch between the skills acquired and the economy needs. Moreover, the unemployment phenomenon spares no type of graduates even if it particularly affects people graduating from management, law or newer universities.

Apart from the above-mentioned points, labour market weaknesses are inherent to the market structure. SMEs which are the main drivers of job creation in other countries represent a small share (1.7%) in the Tunisian economy (INS, 2009). Additionally, they are more concentrated in the low added value secondary and tertiary sector (INS, 2009). The 1986 structural reforms have also shrunk the public sector absorption capacity.

In addition, the quality of graduate jobs has worsened to the extent that they do not match their qualifications. This results in an increasing number of graduates in a precarious situation. Graduates turn to internships or fixed-term employment contract thus earning lower wages. In 2010, more than 78,000 graduates have finished their higher education curriculum. They believed in the social mobility their university degree would offer them. Nevertheless, around 47% of them have not succeeded in finding their first job one year after leaving school and enrolled in the so-called AMAL programme, i.e. Active Job Research Programme (MFPE, 2012). This programme was implemented in March 2011 for first-time jobseekers who left higher education no later than 2010. In this programme, 188,500 young people benefited from developing their personal skills for active job search (MFPE, 2012).

Against this backdrop, the debate on the quality and performance of higher education is urgently required. Disparities in terms of graduate employability among regions and institutions prompt us to wonder about the existence of an institutional effect on the business integration and the graduate's salary. We seek to estimate this effect using data from administrative files relating to graduates' integration in 2010.

4 Data and Methodology

4.1 Data

In order to conduct the present study thoroughly, two types of data are required: data related to graduates and that related to higher education institutions. This study is based on original data derived exclusively from administrative files. Our data were developed by pairing multiple databases from the MESR, the MFPE and the CNSS.

The primary source of data is the registry of the university graduates. In 2010, 86,000 students were graduated from the 194 higher education institutions belonging to the 13 Tunisian public universities. Our analysis will focus on the initial training diploma and will not consider all post-graduates (i.e., PhD) and the foreign graduates as well. In addition, students graduating from the primary teacher training institutions are all recruited by the ME. Hence, they have the same career path and generally the same salary. Since we don't expect any variability among primary school teachers, we will not consider this population. Then, among the 2010 graduates we focus on nearly 75,000 Tunisians who obtained an initial training diploma (bachelor degree, master degree, engineering degree, etc.). This list is matched with the social security files from the CNSS, to identify graduates who have a job in the private sector.[4] We have performed the pairing between the two administrative files based on the ID number which is available in both information systems. We have also used several control variables available in both databases to ensure compliance of pairing as, for instance the date of birth and gender. The use of administrative registries allows us to perform the efficient and low-cost analysis on the profile of the graduates, and not on a sample as is the case in statistical surveys. This allows us to have a significant number of observations regarding each institution. However, data from the CNSS do not include individuals working in the informal sector and thus don't have any social protection. Our study therefore focuses on higher education graduates who are employed in the formal sector. The information from the CNSS files cover declared income for four years (2011–2014). First, we have selected individuals who worked at least a quarter during 2014. Then, for statistical significance issues, we have also excluded from our analysis graduates from universities for which we do not have at least ten observations. In the end, we have selected 12,524 graduates from 150 universities for our analysis.

To analyse the effect of educational institutions on graduates' income, we have supplemented these data with information on academic institutions resulting from pairing of various registries and administrative files from MESR.

[4] The CNSS is in charge of collecting the national insurance contribution for those working in the private sector.

4.1.1 *Individual Variables*

The individual variables are derived from the MESR registry of 2010 graduates and from the CNSS files. We introduce at the individual level the number of years of education according to the degree obtained. The coefficient for this variable will help in assessing the returns to education. On the individual level, we also have information on gender and on the marital status of the graduate in 2014 (single 76% and married 23%). In order to study the effect of school performance, we added educational underachievement by using information concerning the age of graduates. We use a series of dichotomous variables to describe the corresponding sector to the degree obtained in 2010: information and communication technology (18%); the health sciences (7%); economics and management (26%); law (3%); social sciences (4%); languages and literature (9%); fine arts (4%); the exact sciences (7%); and applied sciences and technology (22%). We integrate the unemployment differential variable to consider the high regional disparities on the labour market in Tunisia. It was created by comparing the national unemployment rate of university graduates (20.17%) and regional unemployment rate of university graduates in 2014 based on the 2014 population census.

We analyse the graduates' career path based on the number of quarters of work estimated through the contribution declared to the CNSS. The job seniority is assessed via the number of years declared by the last employer. Regarding the professional experience, it is determined by the number of years declared since graduation, regardless of the quarters declared during the last position. We also use the square of these variables to reflect the concavity of the income profiles. Within our database, we also have information on the type of job: employees (93%) or self-employed (7%) as well as on the company size. Finally, in order to master the seasonal effect, we use as a variable interest in the income function, the average monthly income declared in 2014. Note that the number of years of study in higher education is not correlated with gender. This result is expected to the extent that for so many years women outnumber men in most disciplines and even at the level of postgraduates' studies. Furthermore, we notice a low but positive correlation (0.1) between the number of years of education and the experience in the labour market. This can be explained by the fact that graduates who have followed relatively longer studies may fit more quickly into the labour market (MFPE, 2009).

4.1.2 *University Variables*

We also used data on the characteristics and quality of higher education institutions. The database we created provides information on the inputs in the production function of the higher education institutions. We have detailed information that characterize quantitatively and qualitatively the human resources in each university (experience, full- or part-time lecturer). Professors and associate professors represent only 13% of the total of the teaching staff. This ratio may reach 75% in some institutions. However, many institutions suffer from the total absence of experienced teaching staff (40 institutions). We use the baccalaureate score of the new students to characterize the institutions' selectivity. In addition, to characterize the academic performance of students attending a higher education institution, we used the percentage of 2011 baccalaureate graduates not meeting the university entry conditions if we refer to the parameters in the 1992 decree (see Sect. 3.1, Chap. 8). This variable is created at the institutions level from a simulation based on individual data on grades obtained during the baccalaureate exam. We have noticed a significant disparity between institutions. Indeed, in some higher institutions, about 80% of new students should not get the access to the university based on parameters of the 1992 decree. However, for other institutions, 100% of new students have the skills to enter university regardless of the rules adopted.

Furthermore, we use the MFPE database to provide information on the performance of each institution in the labour market. In fact, for each institution, we have the share of former graduates enrolled in an Active Labour Market Program (ALMP) for first-time job seekers. Thus, we consider the number of beneficiaries as a proxy of the unemployment rate for each institution. Moreover, even if this information is not available, employers have developed, through their experience, knowledge on graduate profiles from each institution. This generally leads to filter candidates during interview process according to their institution. Thus, the performance and skills of former graduates may provide an idea about the reputation of an institution. In addition, we have created a variable for the seat-occupancy rate for each institution. It allows to capture if the university has the required resources and infrastructure for the enrolled students. We have finally collected a set of variables that characterize the dominant track in each university (legal studies and humanities, economics and management, technologies and health studies, sciences, etc.).

We have noticed a strong and positive correlation (0.48) between the baccalaureate score of the last new student enrolled and the pressure

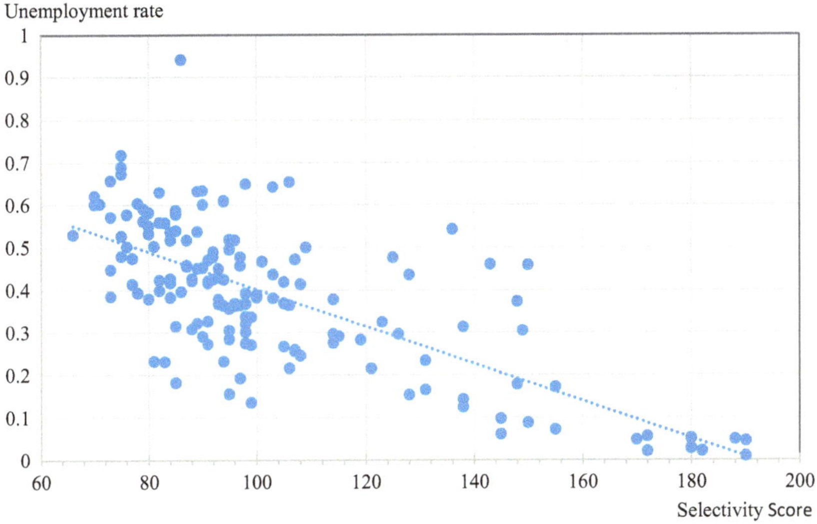

Fig. 10.1 Relationship between selectivity and the rate of unemployed. Source: Authors' calculation based administrative registries and database

during the enrolment (the number of applicants to be enrolled/the seat--capacity of the institution). This confirms the selectivity among institutions which is generated by a strong demand from new students during the orientation against a limited number of seats. The analysis also confirms that the least selective institutions are those which attract new students with low academic performance (0.61).

Figure 10.1 illustrates the relationship between the performance of the institution in the labour market through the proxy of the unemployment rate and the selectivity of each institution. We also observe a strong negative correlation between these two variables (−0.71). This statement of fact is the same for the correlation between the performance of the institution in the labour market and the rate of professors and associate professors (−0.5).

4.2 *Methodology*

We have opted for a multilevel modelling to assess the effect of the characteristics of academic institutions on graduates' income. Besides, this method is the most appropriate for the hierarchical structure of our data (Singer, 1998). We therefore undertook a two-level breakdown: a first level consisting of micro-units composed of graduates and a second level composed of the institutions of these graduates, which represent macro--units (Bressoux, 2010). We note Y_{ij} the logarithm of the average monthly income, which was declared to the CNSS in 2014 by the graduates from the university j.

The first stage consists in developing a variance components model. Before introducing any individual or institutional variable, we develop a simplified Mincer income equation.

Model 1:

$$Y_{ij} = \mu_0 + e_{ij} + \alpha_{0j} \tag{10.1}$$

μ_0 represents model's constant and provides an estimate of the overall average salary.

α_{0j}represents the error associated with each institution j. Each average relating to an institution deviates away from μ_0 by α_{0j}.

In this first stage, we seek to estimate the coefficient of the inter-class correlation. It measures the inter-institutional variance in the total variance of graduates' income.

The second stage consists in introducing into level 1 equation variables characterizing individuals. *NETU* represents the number of years of university studies. X is the matrix of k individual variables and X_{ij} is the vector related to individual i of institution j.

Level 1:

$$Y_{ij} = \pi_{0j} + \pi_{1j} NETU_{ij} + \pi_{2j} X_{ij} + e_{ij} \tag{10.2}$$

The introduction of these variables helps identify possible effects of composition. That is to say, some salary variations may be due to differences in composition of the students' population.

Level 2:

$$\begin{gathered} \pi_{0j} = \mu_0 + \alpha_{0j} \text{ with} \alpha_{0j} \sim N\left(0, \sigma_0^2\right) \\ \pi_{1j} = \mu_1 \\ \pi_{2j} = \mu_2 \end{gathered} \tag{10.3}$$

Model 2:

$$Y_{ij} = \mu_0 + \mu_1 NETU_{ij} + \mu_2 X_{ij} + e_{ij} + \alpha_{0j}$$

where μ_1 represents the estimate of the output of one year spent in higher education. μ_2 represents the effect of individual variables on salaries.

The last stage of this method consists in introducing simultaneously individual variables in the level 1 model and institutional variables in the level 2 model. First of all, we consider a multilevel model to measure only the direct effect of educational institutional variables on graduates' salary. In this case, we assume that institutional variables affect only the constant term π_{0j}. In this model, the matrix E corresponds to institutional variables and E_j the m variables' vector relating to the institution j.

Level 2:

$$\begin{aligned} \pi_{0j} &= \mu_0 + \gamma E_j + \alpha_{0j} \text{ with} \alpha_{0j} \sim N\left(0, \sigma_0^2\right) \\ \pi_{1j} &= \mu_1 \\ \pi_{2j} &= \mu_2 \end{aligned} \tag{10.4}$$

Model 3:

$$Y_{ij} = \mu_0 + \mu_1 NETU_{ij} + \mu_2 X_{ij} + \gamma E_j + e_{ij} + \alpha_{0j} \tag{10.5}$$

As a second step, we also seek to determine the indirect effect of institutional variables on salaries. We assume then that these variables act on the salary via the years of university studies (NE). The coefficient π_{1j} for the number of years of study varies thus from one institution to another.

Level 2:

$$\begin{aligned} \pi_{0j} &= \mu_0 + \gamma_0 E_j + \alpha_{0j} \\ \pi_{1j} &= \mu_1 + \gamma_1 E_j + \alpha_{1j} \quad \text{with} \begin{bmatrix} \alpha_{0j} \\ \alpha_{1j} \end{bmatrix} \sim N\left(\begin{bmatrix} 0 \\ 0 \end{bmatrix}, \begin{bmatrix} \sigma_0^2 & \sigma_{01} \\ \sigma_{10} & \sigma_1^2 \end{bmatrix}\right) \\ \pi_{2j} &= \mu_2 \end{aligned} \tag{10.6}$$

Model 4:

$$Y_{ij} = \mu_0 + \mu_1 NETU + \mu_2 X_{ij} + \gamma_0 E_j + \gamma_1 E_j NETU + \left[\alpha_{0j} + \alpha_{1j} NETU\right] + e_{ij} \quad (10.7)$$

$\mu_1 NETU + \mu_2 X_{ij}$: μ_1 and μ_2 coefficients of this term refer to the direct effects of individual variables on salaries;

$\gamma_0 E_j$: γ_0 coefficient provides an estimate of the direct effects of the characteristics of the institution on the graduate's salary;

$\gamma_1 E_j NETU$: γ_1 coefficient evaluates the indirect effects related to institutional variables on graduates' integration.

5 Findings

The inter-class correlation ratio is 23.3%. This value reflects a high variability of graduates' salary through academic institutions. These estimates are higher than the 11.7% average in Giret and Goudard (2007). We begin the process of building the model with the introduction of individual variables. The variance estimates suggest a decline in the share of variance assigned to institutions, ρ at 8.83%. This result confirms the existence of an effect of the institutions' characteristics on graduates' salaries.

5.1 *Effects of Individual Variables on Salaries*

Additional year of schooling increases wages by 14.9%. This is comparable to those obtained in other research studies investigating the outputs of education, which vary between 5 and 15% (Maguain, 2007). We also find a 20.4% gender salary gap. This is anticipated given the higher downgrade (MFPE, 2008) and discrimination (Gouider, 2009) affecting women. Young people who repeated some schooling years are subject to 9.7%/ year salary penalty. Moreover, graduate unemployment rate in 2014 was 20.17% (INS, 2014). Living in a region with one point less in the unemployment rate compared to the national average increases the graduate's salary by 0.7%. The degree's speciality such as Information and Communication Technologies (ICT) has also a significant positive impact on salaries (comparatively 12.2% lower for fine arts, 18.1% humanities, 22.8% economics). The coefficient associated with the number of years of seniority with the most recent employer is 14.3% higher than for other studies. This coefficient is 3.8% for experience. Indeed 75% of our sample has not changed jobs since entering the labour market. "Self-employed graduates" earn 57.8% less than large company' employees. This gap is reduced compared to micro enterprises (−7.5%). For small firm employees, salaries are 9.1% higher. Indeed, large companies' by-laws make salary negotiations difficult. A study (CRES, 2012) confirms this observation. We find that the marital status variable is not significant. Whilst we do not have parents' social status data, study suggests that they have no effect in Tunisia (Ben Halima et al., 2012).

5.2 *Effects of Institutions on Salaries*

We notice that the presence of professors and associate professors per 100 students leads to an increase in graduates' income equal to 4.9%. Others conclude that no such effect exists (Giret & Goudard, 2007). We also confirmed the existence of the relationship between the number of experienced teaching staff lecturers and the salary when considering the institutions' affiliation.

The overall supervision rate however does not affect the salary. Moreover, thanks to the 1992 decree, graduates witnessed 0.5% increase in salaries. The simulation also reveals that laureates who come from high pass rate institutions signal educational quality to employers.

In another variant of the comprehensive direct effect model, we introduce a variable relating to the share of the estimated unemployed using the rate of those enrolled in "AMAL". It is negatively correlated with wages (−0.8%). In fact, as in 3.3, graduates from institutions with low performance in terms of job market integration during the previous generations suffer from salary penalties. This negative effect concurs with Spence's signalling theory (1973). The latter "signals" include (education level, type of institution, institutional reputation, professional experience, etc.) "clues" (gender, age, etc.). The fact that there are many former students graduating from an institution and enrolled in "AMAL" should send a signal of weak performance and inadequate skills in the labour market to employers. We note that the institution's age is not part of these "signals". Probably due to under-developed alumni networks. Finally, we note that neither the seat-capacity nor the competitive admission process has an effect on wages.

5.3 *Indirect Effects of the Institutional Variables on Salaries*

In this final step, we integrate individual variables, institutional variables and a random variable (the number of schooling years). This model allows us to eliminate the constraint previously imposed and which establishes the same relationship between the number of schooling years and graduates' salaries in all higher education institutions. We note that the covariance between the constant and the number of schooling years is significantly negative. This result confirms that the return to education varies between institutions. Thus, the impact of an educational year is positive, but it is less important for institutions where the average salary is already high. This is also the case for institutions where the number of study years is regulated such as legal studies. Furthermore, we fail to highlight other indirect effects of the characteristics of the institutions on salaries. The results suggest that there is no link between the output of one year of education and the institution's age or the human resources deployed.

6 Conclusion

The relationship between the quality of education and the graduates' salary generated an extensive literature in the 1990s. However, Case and Yogo (1999) was the only African study so far. This work focuses on studying the quality drivers of education in the Tunisian context.

This study aims at questioning the links between the individual's characteristics, the characteristics of higher education institutions and the graduates' salaries in Tunisia. To do this, we relied on data derived from various administrative records of the Ministry of Higher Education (MESR), the Ministry of Vocational Training and Employment (MFPE) and the CNSS. In addition, we have opted for a multilevel modelling that is more suited to the hierarchical structure of data.

The key findings presented in this study are the existence of an institutional effect on the graduates' wages: the inter-institution variance represents 23.3% of the total variance. Individual variables (i.e., the number of schooling years, the speciality, gender, educational delay, the unemployment differential in 2014, experience in the labour market, etc.) have an impact on the salary. However, our research does not reveal a relation between marital status and outputs of education.

Furthermore, we explain that the effects of institutions are mainly due to three characteristics of higher education institutions in Tunisia. The first is the availability of full-time professors and associate professors, which has an impact on the quality of teaching and research at universities. The second significant feature is graduates' success rate in the baccalaureate exam according to stricter 1992 decree. This result shows that institutions that have attracted new students with good academic performance are doing better. The opening of higher education to "unready" new students can lead to an inflation of degrees, which like any inflation tends to reduce their market value. This is exacerbated by the strategy to prolong the years of education adopted by the youth to avoid joblessness. Barouni and Broecke (2014) noted that Tunisia has both a relatively high number of graduates among the working-age population and a lowest return to higher education in the 12 countries studied. The third is unemployment proxy of graduates. That can be interpreted as a signal for employers.

The output of one year of education is lower for regulated fields such as legal studies. The results of this study do not reveal an indirect influence of other institutional variables on the outputs of education in Tunisia.

Conflicts of Interest The authors have no conflicts of interest to declare that are relevant to the content of this chapter.

References

Barouni, M., & Broecke, S. (2014). The Returns to Education in Africa: Some New Estimates. *The Journal of Development Studies, 50*(12), 1593–1613. https://doi.org/10.1080/00220388.2014.9366394

Becker, G. S. (1962). Investment in Human Capital: A Theoritical Analysis. *Journal of Political Economy, 70*(5), Part 2: Investment in Human Beings, 9–49. http://www.nber.org/books/univ62-3

Becker, G. S. (1964). *Human Capital: A Theoretical and Empirical Analysis with Special Reference to Education* (3rd ed., 1994). The University of Chicago Press. https://doi.org/10.1177/000271626536000153

Belfield, C. R., & Fielding, A. (2001). Measuring the Relationship Between Resources and Outcomes in Higher Education in the UK. *Economics of Education Review, 20*, 589–602. https://doi.org/10.1016/S0272-7757(00)00037-6

Ben Halima, M. A., Kocoglu, Y., & Ben Halima, B. (2012). Le problème de l'insertion professionnelle des diplômés universitaires en Tunisie: Le rôle de l'accès aux emplois publics et privés. *Maghreb-Machrek, 211*, 39–54.

Ben Sédrine, S. (1998). Rendement interne de l'enseignement supérieur et mécanismes d'orientation universitaire. In J. M. Plassard & S. Ben Sédrine

(Eds.), *Enseignement supérieur et insertion professionnelle en Tunisie* (pp. 91–104). Presses de l'Université des Sciences Sociales de Toulouse. ISBN-13: 978-2909628417.

Bourdon, J., Giret, J. F., & Goudard, M. (2012). Peut-on classer les universités à l'aune de leur performance d'insertion? *Formation Emploi, 117*, 89–110. https://doi.org/10.4000/formationemploi.3541

Bressoux, P. (2010). *Modélisation statistique appliquée aux sciences sociales*. De Boeck. https://hal.science/hal-04106446

Brewer, D. J., Eide, E., & Ehrenberg, R. J. (1996). *Does It Pay to Attend an Elite Private College? Cross Cohort Evidence on the Effects of College Quality on Earnings* (pp. 104–123). Working Paper, 5613, National Bureau of Economic Research. https://doi.org/10.3386/w5613

Card, D., & Krueger, A. (1992). Does School Quality Matters? Returns to Education and the Characteristics of Public Schools in the United States. *Journal of Political Economy, 100*(1), 1–40. https://doi.org/10.1086/261805

Carnoy, M. (1995). Rates of Return to Education. In M. Carnoy (Ed.), *The International Encyclopedia of the Economics of Education*. Pergamon. ISBN: 0-08-042303-5.

Case, A., & Yogo, M. (1999). *Does School Quality Matter? Returns to Education and the Characteristics of Schools in South Africa*. NBER Working Paper, 7399. https://doi.org/10.3386/w7399

Colclough, C., Kingdon, G., & Patrinos, H. (2010). The Changing Pattern of Wage Returns to Education and its Implications. *Development Policy Review, 28*(6), 733–747. https://doi.org/10.1111/j.1467-7679.2010.00507.x

CRES. (2012). *Rapport de l'Enquête sur la structure des salaires en Tunisie de 2011*. République Tunisienne. Centre de Recherches et d'Etudes Sociales et Bureau International du Travail.

Damoiselet, N., & Lévy-Garboua, L. (2000). L'efficacité de la différenciation et de la sélection scolaire: Une comparaison économique des systèmes éducatifs. *Economie publique, 2*(6), 17–39. https://doi.org/10.4000/economiepublique.1613

Di Pietro, G., & Cutillo, A. (2006). University Quality and Market Outcomes in Italy. *Labour, 20*(1), 37–62. https://doi.org/10.1111/j.1467-9914.2006.00333.x

Giret, J. F., & Goudard, M. (2007). Effets établissement et salaries des diplômés des universités françaises. *Economie Publique, 21*(2), 125–153. https://doi.org/10.4000/economiepublique.8042

Gouider, A. (2009). *La discrimination par genre sur le marché du travail: Fondements théoriques et application au marché du travail tunisien* (PhD dissertation, Department of Economics). University of Paris 13 and Faculty of Economic Sciences and Management of Sfax.

Harmon, C., Walker, I., & Westergaard-Nielsen, N. (2001). *Education and Earnings in Europe: A Cross-Country Analysis of the Returns to Education*. Edward Elgar Publishing. https://econpapers.repec.org/RePEc:ucn:oapubs:10197/757

INS. (2009). *Répertoire National des Entreprises*. Institut National de la Statistique. République Tunisienne.

INS. (2014). *Recensement général de la population et de l'habitat*. Institut National de la Statistique. République Tunisienne.

JORT. (1992). N°041(819). *Journal Officiel de la République Tunisienne*.

JORT. (2001). N°090 (3387). *Journal Officiel de la République Tunisienne*.

Maguain, D. (2007). Les rendements de l'éducation en comparaison internationale. *Économie et Prévision, 180–181*(4–5), 87–106. https://doi.org/10.3406/ecop.2007.7673

MESRS. (2015). *L'enseignement supérieur, la recherche scientifique et la Technologie en chiffres*. République Tunisienne, Bureau des Etudes, de la Planification et de la Programmation, Ministère de l'Enseignement Supérieur et de la Recherche Scientifique.

MFPE. (2008). *Dynamique de l'emploi et adéquation de la formation parmi les diplômés universitaires; Volume 1: Rapport sur l'insertion des diplômés de l'année 2004*. République tunisienne et Banque mondiale, Ministère de la Formation Professionnelle et de l'Emploi.

MFPE. (2009). *Dynamique de l'emploi et adéquation de la formation parmi les diplômés universitaires; Volume 2: L'insertion des jeunes diplômés de l'enseignement supérieur, promotion 2004, analyse comparative des résultats de deux enquêtes (2005 et 2007)*. République tunisienne et Banque mondiale, Ministère de la Formation Professionnelle et de l'Emploi.

MFPE. (2012). *Rapport d'évaluation du programme de recherche active d'emploi "AMAL"*. République Tunisienne, Ministère de la Formation Professionnelle et de l'Emploi.

Mincer, J. (1974). *Schooling, Experience and Earnings*. Columbia University Press. ISBN: 0-87014-265-8.

Rumberger, R. W., & Thomas, S. L. (1993). The Economic Return to College Major, Quality and Performance: A multilevel Analysis of Recent Graduates. *Economics of Education Review, 12*(1), 1–19. https://doi.org/10.1016/0272-7757(93)90040-N

Singer, J. D. (1998). Using SAS PROC MIXED to Fit Multilevel Models, Hierarchical Models, and Individual Growth Models. *Journal of Educational and Behavioral Statistics, 23*, 323–355. https://doi.org/10.3102/10769986023004323

Spence, M. (1973). Job Market Signaling. *Quarterly Journal of Economics, 87*, 355–374. https://doi.org/10.2307/1882010

Zamel, E. (2011). *L'insertion professionnelle des diplômés de l'enseignement supérieur en Tunisie: Analyse théorique et étude microéconomique* (PhD dissertation, Department of Economics). University of Toulouse 1 Capitole and Faculty of Economic Sciences and Management of Sfax.

Zghal, M. (1986). L'orientation universitaire et le marché de l'emploi. *Revue Tunisienne des Sciences du Travail*, 17–43.

Zghal, R. (2007). Un équilibre instable entre le quantitatif et le qualitatif: L'enseignement supérieur en Tunisie. *Revue internationale d'éducation de Sèvres*, *45*, 51–62. https://doi.org/10.4000/ries.197

CHAPTER 11

The Perception of Wages in Contemporary Mauritania: Between Craze and Social Positioning

Ousmane Wague

1 Introduction

Wage labour appeared in Mauritanian society mainly during the colonial era when France imposed its political control at the end of the nineteenth century. At that time, the wages received were initially seen as a supplement to the traditional family economic resources derived from agriculture, livestock, and trade. Under the colonial regime, this monthly income entailed hard work, since prior to 1945–1950, the Mauritanian population was employed under the *indigénat* system (native status), which did not guarantee many rights to African employees. However, the regularity of wages, their amount, and the status attached to a public or private salary appealed to the Mauritanian workforce. Until the end of colonization, these wages aroused a certain amount of envy among the citizens, but they also exerted a form of social pressure on the employees who had to

O. Wague (✉)
University of Nouakchott, Nouakchott, Mauritania
e-mail: wousmane@yahoo.fr

M.-P. Chelini et al. (eds.), *Wage Dynamics in Africa*, African Histories and Modernities,
https://doi.org/10.1007/978-3-031-99800-3_11

perform rather difficult or unrewarding tasks without much power to negotiate the organization of their work.

While these rare salaried incomes were the subject of a particular craze in Mauritanian society in the past, the perception of wage employment in contemporary Mauritanian society has evolved from independence in 1960 to the present day. In 60 years, the country's population has grown from 840,000 inhabitants in 1960, multiplied by 5.5 to reach 4.7 million inhabitants today, with an increase of around 3% per year although the current rate is closer to 2.5% per year. The city of Nouakchott, founded in 1957 as the new capital with 3000 inhabitants in 1960, had 420,000 inhabitants in 1990 and now counts 1.5 million inhabitants, or one in three Mauritanians.

Over the course of two generations, Mauritanian society has undergone profound changes. The active population has grown from 200,000 in 1960 to 500,000 in 1990 to 1.1 million today, a stable ratio of one active person for every four people (youthfulness of the population, current median age of 21 years). Proportionally, the salaried population has increased significantly. Still very low in 1960, around 2 to 3% of the total active population, it rose to 40% of active people in the years 1990–2010, before various crises such as Islamic terrorism, drought in 2019, COVID, and the Ukrainian War in 2022 reduced it to 27% in 2022 (World Bank).

In all cases, salary has become an instrument of social positioning over the years.

This chapter raises questions about the sociological and sociocultural status of employee compensation and its evolution. What were the perceptions of wages and salaried work among Mauritanians during the colonial period? What role does salary play in independent Mauritania? Why does salary continue to be valued even though it results from dependent work?

We will present salaries in Mauritania from the colonial period to independence, from the 1970s to the 1990s, and from the 1990s to the 2020s to show the changing and differentiated perceptions of wage employment among the Mauritanian population.

2 Salaries in Mauritania from Colonization to Independence, Few Salaried Employees

Around 1900, Mauritanian society, composed mainly of nomads, was not really aware of wage labour as it existed in the industrialized countries of the time. The towns and cities of the new territory, which were sparsely populated—225,000 in 1911, 400,000 in 1937, and 840,000 in 1960 (Statistique Générale de la France, INSEE, *Annuaires statistiques de la France*, 1914–1960)—were inhabited mainly by traders, craftsmen, religious people, and the first employees of the colony. It has been suggested that at the time of independence, employees did not represent more than 3% of the active population (Francis de Chassey, 1979). This section will first present the methodology used to collect the data. Second, it will present the salary perceptions during the colonial period and end with a presentation of the transition under independent Mauritania.

The collection of data for this chapter required a literature review, which allowed us to collect qualitative and quantitative data on salaried work and labour during and in the years following colonization from technical reports by public institutions (reports from the French then Mauritanian Statistical Office, ILO, UNDP, French Ministry of Cooperation, 1963, the Société Nationale Industrielle et Minière, etc.). The literature on Mauritania is predominantly published in French in the fields of general (*Introduction to Mauritania*, 1979), geographical (Toupet & Pitte, 1977), anthropological (Adams, 1977), and economic (theses in particular: Pujos, 1964, Mouknass, 1968) studies. There are some studies published in English in the fields of economics (Westebbe, 1971; Seddon, 1996) and anthropology (Bennoune, 1978), as well as some official reports (World Bank, 2020).

In addition to these data, we also collected the perceptions of several employees and retirees who experienced different periods of work and retirement in Mauritania. First-hand data on the perceptions of these actors before and after independence and on their past living conditions were also collected through semi-structured interviews, specifically with several employees or retirees who had been active in the late 1970s and 1980s and though focus groups. However, this methodological approach is not without its limitations. Apart from quantitative documentary data, we found that written and quantified sources were scarce or non-existent. Furthermore, documents and statistics focusing specifically on wages during the colonial period were quite rare.

During the colonial period (1903–1960), there was no clear distinction between salary and occasional casual work among the indigenous population, regardless of whether the work was done in the north, south, east, or west of the country. Indeed, in the past, any work or paid task for the settlers, regardless of its nature, was assimilated and perceived as paid work because it brought income to the family, regardless of whether the workers were in urbanized, rural, transhumant, or nomadic areas.

In this context, the first indigenous employees were considered the most well-off and thus the "new bourgeois", "tubabaabu ngolnyagnaano" ("tubab": "white") dependent on cash and above any commercial or craftsman activities. As a result, Mauritania, like other parts of French West Africa (AOF), developed a culture of cash and salaried work during the colonial period.

In the focus groups with the elderly, several concepts and expressions were identified: "Sarwice" alluding to "service", work of "boy", or "foctionnaire", distortion of the French "fonctionnaire" meaning "civil servant". We found some ethnic variations: "Tubabu Ngollu" as a Soninké expression, "cheghle nasraani" in Hassaniya, a Mauritanian Arabic variant, or "liguéye tubakoobe" in Poular, the language of the Peul-Fulani. These meanings dominated the world of professional employment during the colonial period. These terms are still currently used which have remained relevant several decades after independence.

In sociological terms, Mauritania has three population groups, more or less divided from north to south. The Beidanes ("the whites", in Arabic) or white Moors (30% of the population) are from successive waves of Arab settlement that are more or less mixed with the pre-existing Berber and black populations. They speak a dialect of Arabic called Hassaniya. The Haratins (40%), former black slaves, partially mixed with white Moors, with whom they share the same language and culture. Black Africans (30%) made up of several ethnic groups, including the Poulars (Peuls in French and Fulani in English), the Soninkés, the Wolofs, and the Bambaras. It should also be noted that Mauritanian society is very segmented and hierarchical; mixed marriages are still rare. The Beidanes, or white Moors, dominate and hold almost all economic and political power, even if they themselves are divided between the descendants of the great families of the marabouts or warriors and those of the castes of the blacksmiths or griots. Then come the black Africans at the bottom of the psychological social ladder and the Haratine (or black Moors), former slaves.

Immediately after independence in 1960, and because of a combination of several socio-economic and environmental factors, Mauritania began to experience a renewed enthusiasm for salaried work in both the informal and formal sectors. The official end of *indigénat* in 1945–1946, with its delayed implementation on the ground and the promulgation of the colonial labour code in December 1952, prepared the ground for legal and social liberalization of the labour market. Our focus groups and semi-structured interviews revealed several trends relating to salaried work that were either convergent or divergent. Our results show that in the 1960s, salary was considered as: "a means of enrichment allowing one to collect a certain amount for the acquisition of livestock or to open shops to later become independent".

After the drought of the 1970s, a rural exodus began that confirmed this trend. Thousands of people moved to large urban centres, mainly to Nouakchott, the capital, Naouadibhou, the economic capital, and the mining towns (Zoueirat, Akjoujt, etc.). Indeed, because of their lack of resources or the fact that their agricultural activity had been severely affected and their livestock decimated, the rural population began to rush into paid work, which became a real refuge for those without work. As a result, the dependency on salaries became noticeable.

Mauritania is experiencing a double movement involving the sedentarization of the nomads who were the majority until then, and the urbanization of the rural population. In 1965, rural nomads made up 57% of the population, sedentary rural people 34%, and city dwellers 9%. In 1975, there was a sharp decline in rural nomads, whose percentage dropped to 29%, an increase in sedentary rural residents to 48%, and 23% of the population were urban dwellers.

In 1960, de Chassey (1979) summarized the sociological description as follows: 1) nomadic breeders are Moors occupying 8/10 of the territory with an average density of 0.5 to 1 inhabitant per km^2, 2) sedentary farmers are black Africans occupying 2/10 of the territory (River and south-east) with an average density of 15–17 inhabitants/km^2 and up to 35 on the Senegal River. The truly urbanized population within the territory was negligible: a few traditional Ksourians, notable or servile, and a few families of civil servants, artisans, traders, i.e., 38,000 out of 960,000. Ksourians are inhabitants of a Ksar, meaning fortified "village" or "small city" with a sedentary population.

These phenomena of sedentarization and urbanization intensified after four years of drought (1969–1973). The south was once again overwhelmed by a density of sedentary rural and urban residents who now included a high proportion of Moors. Nomadism remained predominant only in the most isolated regions of the centre and the east-southeast (9th and 11th regions). In the first region (Zouérat), the proportion of urban dwellers rose from 40% in 1965 to 79% in 1975; in the eighth region (Naouadibhou), from 66 to 78%; and in the sixth, roughly the former emirate of Trarza and including Nouakchott, from 11% to 50%. The modernization of infrastructure (Nema-Nouakchott road, industrialization of Naouadibhou, Zouérat and Akjoujt, "development" of the Senegal river) helped to attract the population. Surveys carried out by the Institute of Statistics among urban immigrants show that the majority of them want to stay in urban areas and never return to rural regions.

In the same context of trends, and still based on our interviews, several sources said that in the large urban centres of Nouakchott, Naouadibhou, and Zoueirat, and in the inland towns, paid work had become a real refuge for people or families without work who no longer had other sources of income. In other urban centres and agricultural areas, wage labour was seen as a "complement" to other income from agriculture and livestock. Thus, the typologies of salaried work presented in the focus groups are reduced to "teaching", "administration", and qualified workers such as "welders" or "scrap workers" in the Société Nationale d'Industrie Minière (SNIM) which extracts and processes iron ore. Furthermore, minor jobs for servants, waiters, guards, etc., are listed as new salaried jobs and have become the subject of new enthusiasm among the unemployed.

3 The 1970s–1990s, a Contrasting Phase in the Perception of Salary

The 1970s, 1980s, and 1990s began with a rather positive vision of wages, reinforced by the development of employment in public firms. Wage employment appeared to take on a real economic and sociological dimension, promoting a growing enthusiasm for salaried work. In the 1980s–2000s, however, wages stagnated, creating a kind of disaffection with wage employment.

According to the ONS, Mauritania's population grew from nearly 15% urban and 85% rural and nomadic in the 1960s to more than 90% urban and 10% rural in 2013, the date of the last general and nomadic population census until 2024 (RGP).

Thus, by the end of the 1970s, the urban or sedentary village environment was home to virtually the majority of the Mauritanian population. Urban wage employment had become a lifeline for many families. As a result of the drought, the collapse of traditional social structures, marked by the widespread conversion of farmers and breeders to other so-called salaried professions, led to the development of salaried employment in urban, suburban, and peri-urban areas.

In the long term, the added value of agriculture to GDP decreased from 46% in 1960 to 22% in 1990, but remained stable in 2022 around 18% (World Bank). Industry, for its part, rose from 18% of AV in 1960 to 28% in 1990 and 30% in 2022, with a more irregular development cycle than this series seems to indicate. Services started at 32% in 1960, rose to 39% in 1990, and remain at 43% in 2022, also following a fairly regular development curve. Thus, in the long run, at least one third of workers were employed in the service sector, while agriculture declined in favour of mining and industrial activities.

In order to alleviate the pressure associated with the demand for salaried employment, large public companies were called upon at the time to provide salaried employment for a large number of Mauritanians. As early as the 1970s, the Société Nationale Industrielle et Minière, formerly Miferma, employed 5000 people. According to its data (SNIM, 1974) workers accounted for 90% of the declared private employees in 1970. Two-thirds of these workers were labourers or specialized helpers. A total of 50% were employed by Miferma, 25% in the construction sector, and 20% in the tertiary sector (commerce, transport, handling services, SNIM, 1975).

Similarly, Somaco-TP (Audebert, 1965; Laurent, 1972), the first national private company, had more than 700 permanent employees in 1975 (including 10 foreign executives) and a turnover of 300 million UM (or 1.5 billion CFA francs. In 1975: 100 CFA franc = 0.47 $). The Mauritanian Ouguiya (UM, (Arabic "awqiya": ounce)) has been the official currency of Mauritania since 1973, alongside the CFA franc. It was replaced in 2018 by the second Ouguiya (rate of 10 to 1). In 1975, Nouakchott had a working population of between 20,000 and 30,000 made up of Mauritanian and foreign civil servants, a few employees in the tertiary sector, and their families. In the years following independence, the emergence and growth of a salaried sub-proletariat led, among other things, to the following evolution of the volume of salaried employment: in 1962, out of 35,000 city dwellers in Nouakchott, 18,200 were employed. In 1969, out of a population of 95,000, there were almost 17,900 employees, and in 1975, out of a population of 206,300, there were 30,000 employees (de Chassey, 1979).

It should be noted that despite the increase in the number of employees, the impact and sociological dimension of wage employment have always been visible across the different ethno-national communities and workers in general. After its deployment in Mauritania in the 1970s and 1980s, there began a real craze for this type of employment in all communities. The salary was then generally seen as a form of "survival insurance" and a means "of protecting oneself from immediate needs" (interviews, focus groups). Over the years, it has taken on a symbolic dimension, giving it a vocation for rapid or certain social advancement.

During the colonial period, a certain interest was attached to the salary, regardless of its amount. In the 1940s, poorly paid salaried work, especially of "boys", was particularly valued in comparison to a difficult and unequally remunerative life as a peasant or nomad; this would continue until the 1960s. For employees, the general opinion was: "the amount of the salary does not matter, the important thing is to have it".

The minimum wage, which was very low at the time, was not enough to support a family. The purchasing power of all workers began to decline in relative value in 1960 and has continued to do so ever since. Following the French model of an interprofessional minimum wage (SMIG) created in 1950, Mauritania has officially granted its workers an interprofessional minimum wage since independence, although this wage was extremely low. From 1962 to 1969, the SMIG (Julienne, 1963) remained fixed at around 6000 CFA francs (35.9 per hour), while imported basic necessities (tea, sugar, fabric, rice) had increased by 46%. A worker earned approximately 6000 CFA francs, specialized workers and assistants around 10,000 CFA francs, and skilled workers (one in four) between 20,000 and 25,000 CFA francs (In 1975, 25,000 CFA francs were equal to $116 and 6000 CFA francs to $ 28), although low salaries were still considered attractive (World Bank Mission, 1975).

The sociological perception of the salary means that it has evolved over the decades to become an element on which several tens of thousands of poor inhabitants depend, hence its attractiveness. It has remained quite popular. For more than three decades (1970–2000) social pressure and trade union demands led to wages being subject to the logic of the economic situation, as part of the Mauritanian economy now depended on the price of iron, gold, and other minerals.

Numerous focus group interviews revealed the continued popularity of the salary in traditional rural society and its positive social image: “He took a mandate”, “He is now paid by the state”, “Yezber Khlesse and Buuru” are all expressions present in the popular jargon of the world of work, testifying to the difference between those who are employed and those who are not. The first is a frequent expression among the Soninké to say that from now on he has a salaried job, the second is a frequent expression in the Halpoulaaren community (or Toucouleur in French), the third assimilates employees to civil servants who are paid by “Buuru”, which symbolizes the state. The word “buuru” may also be understood as a distortion of the word “bureau” (office). However, the enthusiasm for salaries diminished over time, depending on the economic situation and circumstances. We note that for three decades (1990–2020) with the rise of formal and informal entrepreneurship and the rush to markets, wages have lost their former glory, although salaried employment continues to be viewed positively by the unemployed.

Over the years, sociocultural perceptions have shown that salaried employment, even if it is no longer synonymous with enrichment, continues to attract citizens to urban areas. Indeed, low salaries, both in the private and public sectors, have continued to attract a social stratum in search of social positioning, despite low incomes. In the 1970s, the world of work represented 90% of the declared national private sector employees, and the overwhelming majority managed to maintain stable housing and remain integrated into society. These workers represented nearly three-fifths of the civil service personnel: labourers, caregivers, guards, and domestics, most of whom were contract workers and had relatively similar pay (Pujos, 1964; Vergara, 1979).

The iron mines employed 4600 workers. In 1976, direct royalties from the iron mines represented 14% of the state’s operating budget. If we take into account the taxes on the salaries of the employees of the iron mines and the companies that work for them, the taxes on imports generated by this income, and all the other taxable activities generated by this expenditure, this could represent approximately 50% of the central public revenue. In the 1970s, however, the position and proportion of employees in the strictly productive sector, dominated or managed by foreigners, remained predominant. Miferma, and today Cominor, Somina, Imapec, and a few others, still employ more than half of the workforce. Mauritanians and foreigners work in the private sector, and a quarter of the entire “modern sector", pay more than 60% of private salaries and 40% of the total wage bill (SNIM, 1975).

4 From the 1990s: Differentiation in Wage Perceptions

With the general economic and social developments, the perception of salaries became more differentiated, especially in terms of the level of remuneration. The image of the salary evolved in different ways: useful support for the poorest, acceptable for the middle classes, too modest for the richest or those seeking wealth.

Far from enabling employees to achieve their goal of caring for loved ones and other family members, the attractiveness of wage employment began to decline in the 1980s and 1990s. For many employees, salary income could support a small or nuclear family, but not a wide range of people within extended or patriarchal families. One of the main reasons is that wages remained very low in the decades following independence. The gap between salaries in Mauritania and in the West-African sub-region reflects decades of wage stagnation.

In reality, this phenomenon dates back to the end of the 1960s, when the salaries of most civil servants remained lower than those of other sectors (150,000 to 250,000 CFA francs per month in 1969) (de Chassey, 1979). Thus, disaffection with salaries began around this time. The focus groups allowed us to collect views and expressions that described employees and revealed the difficulties they encountered. Judgements such as "employee overburdened with children", "employee in debt", "poor employee", "employee facing difficult months", "employee applying for a visa at the bank at the end of the month" are all qualifiers and descriptions that recur and testify to the level of disaffection towards wage employment.

One of the key factors that has contributed to the downgrading of the salary is its low level and the burdens it places on the employee. Even in the mid-1960s, the salary did not allow employees to meet the minimum annual expenses of a married worker with two children who were reduced to the strict minimum of traditional consumption ("boubous", sugar, liquid butter, tea, millet, rice), empirically estimated in 1967 at 98,250 CFA francs. At that time, most employees were paid the minimum wage. In 1969, the SMIG was finally increased by 15% then by 10% in 1973, to 9000 CFA francs per month, but the cost of basic products had at least doubled for Mauritanian small traders because of the years of drought. This subordinate workforce, made up of minimum-wage workers and other employees in the formal and informal private sectors, was struggling to overcome its difficulties. This workforce, especially the "boys", was particularly underpaid. However, the purchasing power of all workers has continued to erode in relative terms since 1960.

The trend of wage stagnation is related to the small gap between the very decent economic growth (4% per year for 60 years) and the population growth (3%), which has been rapid for a long time. GDP increased from 667 million constant dollars (2010) in 1960 to 7.6 billion in 2022 (current GDP converted into current US dollars, 1960: 92 million, 1990: 1.5 billion, 2022: 9.8 billion), i.e., a multiplication of 11.5 (World Bank). It follows that GDP per capita in constant 2010 dollars increased from $800 in 1960 to $1600 in 2022, but its value was $1800 in 1970. This value has stagnated or declined over the past 50 years. In constant 2011 PPP dollars, the situation seems to be better: $4600 in 1990, $5300 in 2022. However, Mauritanians do not consume excessively in relation to the national product, and the balance of trade and household final consumption, which represented 90% of GDP in 1960 and 93% in 1990, fell to 71% in 2022.

The perception of wages in Mauritanian society has thus changed since independence. In particular, its image was associated with a "fixed income" on which the survival of the rural population and many extended families in urban areas depended, today as in the past. This salary has continued to evolve according to the professional opportunities offered by the labour market and the health of the Mauritanian economy.

It is therefore considered a "bulwark" against poverty in the most remote rural areas which lack resources or remain on the margins of the modern economy. However, given the performance of the national economy in recent decades and the inability of the state to provide a decent wage to all those who request it, paid work has over the years been assimilated to "poverty" or a "chore". This is because many young or middle-class employees are no longer able to satisfy even some of their most basic needs. Today, this view still prevails in the world of work in general.

Wage employment, however, has somehow remained quite popular to this day. This explains why, for more than three decades, it has been subject to the logic imposed by the economic situation under social pressure and the pressure of trade union demands. The salary has been subject to adjustments and readjustments, with ups and downs, depending on the situation, the evolution of demand, the increase in the cost of living, the multiplication of demands, and sometimes the whims of Mauritanian citizens. It has therefore become the barometer of the standard of living and has opened the door to a new social positioning of the employee. Despite their low level, employees have therefore been able to design social projects and escape from a state of unemployment to that of an employee with fewer concerns.

More than six decades after independence, the same trend in wages persists. Indeed, the comparative analysis of the minimum wage in the different French-speaking countries of West Africa developed by "mays-mouissi.com", the economic and financial analysis site focused on Africa, shows that Mauritania is one of the countries with the lowest minimum wage at 46 euros (UM 16,000). Indeed, other countries have higher salaries. In Mali, statistics going back a decade show that salaries hovered around 48 Euros or 18,000 UM. In Niger, they were around 46 euros/16,000 UM. In West and Northwest Africa, Morocco is among the highest with a minimum wage of 209 euros or 70,000 UM. It is followed closely by Equatorial Guinea and Algeria, with minimum salaries of 195 euros (UM 65,000) and 171 euros (UM 60,000) respectively.

Despite a remuneration considered to be one of the lowest in the sub-region, salaries, which are constantly evolving according to the standard of living and different economic conditions, continue to be the subject of real social enthusiasm. Many interviewees see them as a "temporary guarantee", "a fixed income that can be counted on", or "a monthly hope that temporarily protects against needs" (Interviews, focus groups). These descriptions have not evolved and are still valid today; they therefore show a real attraction for salaried employment.

However, both young and older new employees, whose qualifications are constantly increasing, are now better positioned compared to the self-employed and workers in the informal sector. Salaries are seen as a gateway to securing one's family and guaranteeing that they have the minimum to meet their needs. Wage employment increases employees' confidence in the face of their close and distant families as well as in the rest of the community.

There are two views of the salary today: at the bottom of Mauritanian society, it is viewed as a social security tool, but at the top, it loses its good image because the best-paid employees receive bonuses and benefits that are significantly higher, and successful entrepreneurs receive remuneration that is significantly higher than even the highest salaries. This trend has also been observed in countries richer than Mauritania, such as Morocco and Côte d'Ivoire.

At the current prices and without PPP correction, the IMF (2024) notes that GDP per capita is $2100 in Africa and $1800 in sub-Saharan Africa; in Mauritania, it will be a little higher at $2400, far behind Morocco (4200) but above Nigeria (1700); the world average is $13,900. In PPP, Mauritania reaches almost $8000, compared to $5000 in sub-Saharan Africa, $6500 for the African average, $11,000 in Morocco, and $4600 in Senegal.

Since 1990, when it was around $900, GDP per capita has progressed correctly. Although Mauritania is still an LDC, its indices continue to rise; its HDI (Human Development Indicator) is around 0.55 compared to 0.40 in 1990, which is the average for countries in the region. Life expectancy is now 65 years, the country has been more stable since 2011, its external debt has become moderate again, and the business climate has become less complicated by bureaucracy and corruption (Mauritania is the 130th least corrupt country out of 180 countries, according to the 2024 Corruption Perceptions Index reported by Transparency International, NGO Berlin).

With the usual precautions (formal/informal economy, RMO exchange rate, etc.), the monthly salary in Africa in 2023 is around $770, with $1700 in South Africa, $925 in Gabon, and $660 in Mauritania (with large variations depending on city, profession, gender, etc.). Internal NGO-type data (https://www.salaryexplorer.com/) consider that the average salary is about US$500 (20,000 UM), the median salary $425 (17,000 UM), with low salaries being approximately $125 (5000 UM), and high ones approximately $2265 (90,000 UM). The distribution is an ace of spades classic: 25% earn less than $280 (11,000 UM), 65% between $280 and $730 (11,000/29,000 UM), 10% between $730 and $930 (29,000–37,000 UM), and 5% above $930.

5 Conclusion

Combining in-depth field surveys and a critical review of economic reports and documents and academic and institutional literature, this chapter has attempted to explain the relationship between Mauritanians and wage employment. The perceptions of salaries made it possible to identify the multiple conceptions of salaried work and wages that Mauritanian society has developed over time.

A means to combat unemployment, poverty, social positioning, income supplement, "temporary guarantee", "fixed income to count on", "a monthly expectation that temporarily protects against needs", the benefits of a salary are associated with all these qualifiers, becoming the cornerstone of all forms of income and social and family economies.

During the twentieth century, the image of wages continued to become more positive and was seen as an element of general security for households. However, the evolution of Mauritania's growth, its urbanization, and the transition to a more industrial and tertiary economy have led to a considerable increase in the number of employees and their differentiation, from the least qualified or least autonomous workers to engineers, highly qualified directors, or medical doctors. Salaries are also perceived differently depending on social position: hope for stability for the most modest, rural, or nomadic individuals, as a guarantee of social progression for the middle classes, and as a "poor relative" situation for the upper-class categories.

Between the 1990s and 2000s, the spirit of the times and the cultural atmosphere that transcended borders, cultures, and generations led to the emergence of new sociocultural attitudes: the labour market has been liberalized; the sociological opening beyond the family to social and professional networks has gained importance; there has been a controversial but real deployment of the consumer society; cultural globalization, to which very urban dwellers, young generations, and wealthy households show a strong sensitivity, has taken precedence; and contemporary references (mobility, innovation, spending, efficiency) now influence more classical habits (stability, tradition, savings, balance). In this bustling whole, large budgets are increasingly valued regardless of the source of income and the sector of activity. Salaries and employee status, especially if they are average or precarious, are losing their prestige even in the public sector where remuneration lags far behind.

Conflicts of Interest The author has no conflicts of interest to declare that are relevant to the content of this chapter.

References

Adams, A. (1977). *Le long voyage des gens du Fleuve*. Maspero.

de Chassey, F. (1979). L'évolution des structures sociales en Mauritanie de la colonisation à nos jours. In *IREMAM* (pp. 235–277).

Julienne, R. (1963). *Economie et Plan de Développement de la République Islamique de Mauritanie*. Ministère de la Coopération, France.

Laurent, H. (1972). *Mines de Fer de Mauritanie*. Industrie Minérale.

Mouknass, H. O. (1968). *L'organisation administrative de la Mauritanie*. Thèse de doctorat, Paris, Faculté de Droit.

Pujos, J. (1964). *Impulsion externe et croissance économique*. Paris: PUF. Thèse de doctorat en économie, préface du président Ould Daddah.

Seddon, D. (1996). The Political Economy of Mauritania: An Introduction. *Review of African Political Economy, 23*(68), 197–214. https://www.jstor.org/stable/4006248

SNIM. (1974). *FERMA information*. Société Nationale Industrielle et Minière, juillet.

SNIM. (1975). *Rapport du Directeur Général*, et *Comptes Spéciaux*. Société Nationale Industrielle et Minière [Minerai de fer].

Toupet, C., & Pitte, J.-R. (1977). *La Mauritanie*. PUF, Que-sais-je?.

Vergara, F. (1979). L'économie de la Mauritanie et son développement. In *IREMAM* (pp. 177–234).

Westebbe, R. M. (1971). *The Economy of Mauritania*. Praeger.

CHAPTER 12

Cultivating Youth Economic Resilience: Diverse Income Strategies

Everlyne Ngare

1 Introduction

The Constitution of Kenya (2010) defines youth as individuals aged between 18 and 34 years, although sociocultural factors such as marital status also influence categorisation. Policy frameworks often rely on biological age for various determinations, including educational requirements, voting eligibility, and legal rights (Hansen, 2008). Additionally, Honnwana (2011) emphasises the complexities surrounding youth categorisation, particularly in contexts where sociocultural norms intersect with legal definitions.

Youth transition, conventionally perceived as an approximative linear psycho-social progression encompassing milestones like leaving home, educational attainment, relationship formation, and workforce entry (United Nations, 2007), faces challenges due to exclusionary policies that curtail economic engagement and impose regulatory constraints, thereby impeding developmental trajectories (Barry, 2005). Furthermore, the traditional linear model of transition is evolving, notably in the transition

E. Ngare (✉)
Moi University and CAP-Youth Empowerment Institute, Kesses, Kenya

M.-P. Chelini et al. (eds.), *Wage Dynamics in Africa*, African Histories and Modernities,
https://doi.org/10.1007/978-3-031-99800-3_12

from home to work, which has become less rigid and more nuanced (Leccardi, 2005).

Kenya's demographic landscape is characterised by a substantial youth population, with 75% falling within the 18–30 age range (GoK, 2006). However, despite constituting a significant portion of the labour force, youth unemployment rates are distressingly high, with 65% of youth lacking gainful employment (GoK, 2006). Moreover, only a quarter of tertiary institution graduates manage to secure employment, underscoring the formidable challenges within the labour market (GoK, 2006). In response, governmental and non-governmental initiatives such as the CAP-Youth Empowerment Institute (CAP-YEI) and the Kenya Youth Empowerment Project (KYEP) have been launched to tackle youth unemployment and promote self-employment opportunities (Kimando et al., 2012). Notably, KYEP, managed by the Kenya Private Sector Alliance (KEPSA), has facilitated training and internship opportunities for over 13,000 youth, resulting in 78% of participants securing employment subsequently (EG Review Team; IEG Review Team, 2017).

Similarly, the CAP-Youth Empowerment Institute (CAP-YEI) has rolled out programmes aimed at empowering youth and addressing unemployment challenges. These initiatives reflect the ongoing commitment within Kenya to address the critical issue of youth unemployment and foster sustainable pathways to economic empowerment and inclusion.

2 The Inclusion OG Programme

Kenya, situated in East Africa, spans an area of 580,000 km^2 and had a population of 54 million as of 2022. Over the decades, its population has undergone rapid growth, increasing seven-fold from 7.7 million in 1960 (World Bank). While the growth rate peaked at 3.1% annually in the 1960s, it has since decelerated to around 2.2% since 2005–2010. Despite this slowdown, the country still faces a significant demographic force, with a considerable number of young people requiring education, employment, and integration into the labour market. Presently, nearly 1.5 million youth necessitate these services, compared to approximately 400,000 in the 1960s. With a median age of approximately 20 years, Kenya's population aged 18–30 comprises a total of 14 million individuals, presenting substantial social, economic, cultural, and political challenges.

The workforce in Kenya has witnessed substantial growth over time, escalating from around 9 million individuals in 1990 (representing 37% of the active population) to 24 million in 2022 (equivalent to 46% of the potential active population). Noteworthy is Kenya's distinguished commitment to education within the African context, with annual public education spending amounting to 4–5% of GDP, slightly surpassing the global average (Durham, 2000).

Despite achieving an economic growth rate of approximately 4.5% per year since 1960 (at constant prices), Kenya's per capita standard of living has only experienced a moderate increase of 1.2% annually over the same period. Presently, without Purchasing Power Parity (PPP) correction, Kenya's nominal GDP per capita stands at $2100 in current dollars, slightly exceeding the sub-Saharan African average of $1800 (IMF).

According to a report by *The Star*, Nairobi Media dated March 20, 2024, Kenya's business climate is deemed favourable despite its rank of 135th out of 176 countries in the 2023 Economic Freedom Index. With a colonial history under British rule, Kenya has honed its ability to promote businesses and attract foreign investors. Currently, the total stock of direct foreign investments represents 10% of the country's GDP, with annual flows estimated at around 1%. Kenya has made notable progress towards democracy, notably transitioning to a multi-party system and enacting a new constitution in 2010. However, the country still grapples with corruption, as evidenced by its score of 31 out of 100 in the Transparency International 2023 Corruption Perceptions Index, ranking 126th out of 180 countries. Despite this, there is a perception of honesty within the public sector in Kenya.

Introduced in 2011, the CAP-Youth Empowerment Institute (CAP-YEI) is a Kenyan NGO originally hailing from India, established with the aim of training 10,000 vulnerable youth in Kenya. The institute's flagship programme, the Basic Employability Skills Training (BEST) model, is structured around a nine-step framework designed to achieve specific objectives. These objectives include equipping disadvantaged youth with life skills, job market-relevant expertise, savings education, and small business development training. Additionally, the model seeks to facilitate access to internships and job opportunities for these individuals, while also providing crucial pre- and post-job placement counselling support. Successful implementation of the nine activities outlined within the framework—ranging from market scans and curriculum development to placements and programme reviews—has been instrumental in realising the programme's objectives.

Market scans identify job market skills demanded in particular area and are likely to lead to large rates of employment. In addition, it identifies the specific skills demanded by potential employers. Furthermore, market scans help in designing appropriate curricula. Curriculum development gears towards developing the training guidelines and content vis-à-vis skills needed in the job market. The curriculum developed not only demands relevance, but it also ensures better training of much-needed skills among the trainees for their potential employers.

Student recruitment for the programme is very deliberate; it targets those individuals from very vulnerable backgrounds and who may not have any chance of further education. These individuals are identified in road shows—involving community, youth, religious leaders, and local administrators and village elders. Students are taken through induction process and life skills training. This allows students to rediscover their potential and build a sense of self-identity and to believe in themselves through self-confidence building.

Skills training is contextual; students are trained in hospitality, floriculture, electrical and electronic, automobile skills, customer relations and sales, air conditioning and refrigeration, clearing and forwarding, security and guarding, hair dressing and beauty, building and construction, and industrial garment manufacturing. This takes three months of rigorous training before students are sent out on sector industry exposure and field visits, where they meet and experience the realities of work.

After exposure and field visits, a work preparedness process is conducted in which students are trained to prepare their resumes, conduct mock interviews, and practise work ethics. Later, students are linked to internship or job placement. Programme review is conducted after batch training to identify strong and weak areas for adaptations before a new batch of training. This process has seen such great success in youth employment and entrepreneurship that CAP-YEI decided to transfer some of these programme aspects through capacity building to youth polytechnics, currently re-branded to Vocational Training Centres (VTCs). VTCs in Kenya have suffered significant effects from negative perception as centres of training for people who failed in the mainstream education system and also have poor transition from training to employment.

3 Main Results of the Programme

This section demonstrates how multiple earning strategies for youth are facilitated and sustained through programme factors. The idea is to broaden the possibilities for youth to benefit from social capital, broad skill capacities, and take advantage of every available income opportunity. It is through the access of entry income earning opportunities that set up the youth for advanced opportunities, whether through further education from savings they make from the entry level jobs or through on-the-job training. This research identified programme factors that played a critical role in preparing youth for multiple earning strategies. These include partnerships, life skills training, work preparedness, employers' demand-driven curricula, peer networking, and support for entrepreneurship startups.

3.1 *Partnership with Industry Stakeholders*

The model engages stakeholders, especially employers, in a direct and purposeful manner during various steps. During the market scan research, potential employers are asked to contribute data on employment possibilities and relevant skills set required for each job. As the curriculum is being developed or revised, they are consulted to ensure relevant skills are included in the instructional content.

Some employers and local institutional representatives, including those from financial institutions, become mentors during the training. The instructors keep in touch with employers, mentors, and financial institution representatives with an aim of having them mentor trainees, provide exposure and internship experiences, and to confirm job opportunities. This direct and purposeful engagement leads to a form of social capital for CAP-YEI trainees and later as graduates of the programme. Partnership with employers favours their access to opportunities against their competitors from other institutions without this privilege. Our study indicates that these partnerships are critical contributors to short- and midterm-term outcomes. The intra- and inter-personal characteristics of the youth that enhance their interaction with partners are nurtured in life skills training.

3.2 *Life Skills Training*

Introducing a foundational set of life skills at the beginning of training is essential for enhancing self-esteem, confidence, and a sense of personal worth. These skills not only prepare individuals for acquiring technical expertise but also serve to foster confidence by instilling belief in one's abilities, equip learners with the resilience to confront challenges, cultivate a positive mindset, introduce collaborative learning dynamics, and shape behaviour in accordance with professional ethics and standards.

When asked what aspects of the programme are related to their ability to earn income, youth highlighted aspects of life skills as critical. Specifically, they attributed their ability to communicate with people of diverse backgrounds, increased self-confidence, and an improved perspective on their potential for the future to the training at CAP-YEI. One youth described the change in how he viewed himself by saying:

> It is not only being trustworthy, but also believing in yourself. One thing that I got from the CAP-YEI program was how to be me—how to make sure that I have achieved the best out of me. Before I came to CAP, I was just like any other youth out there. I used to think I had to wait for someone to get me the opportunity—not doing it myself. But I realised that when I came to CAP it opened my mind, I knew I had so much potential that was in me. One thing that captured me is to be the best that I can be. It is trust that's a virtue—that is earned, by doing things right, but waking up early, making sure that you are groomed well, dress-up well, people can see a good picture.

Affirming the youth quoted above, stakeholders also indicated that youth who trained at CAP-YEI were trustworthy and possessed personal attributes that made them desirable employees, even though they did not have all the technical skills that youth from other programmes had.

3.3 *Ensuring the Curriculum is grounded in the Local Needs of Employers*

CAP-YEI is providing youth with relevant and in-demand skills in specific industry sectors, and it is equipping youth with cross-cutting skills. These skills include intra-personal and inter-personal work attitudes, work etiquette, as well as self-confidence and hard skills to enhance competency in the areas they train to work in.

The step-by-step summary of the BEST model curriculum demonstrates its holistic nature. It is embedded in the local context and builds social capital through successive interactions with employers, local leadership, and community-based organisations. The social capital built is reflected in how employers and financial organisation representatives become mentors and contribute to in-class training and internships.

The effort to provide a curriculum that responds to the local employment needs provides a service to both employers and graduates. The curriculum takes an approach that connects, responds, and delivers the skills demanded as well as the capacities that enable youth to succeed. Towards the end of training the curriculum provides specific guidelines to help to link youth to internships, gainful job opportunities, small business start-ups, and financial inclusion of youth through opening of bank accounts and saving money. This approach decreased the vulnerability of youth after they secured jobs and earned money. It also increased the respect they received from friends, family, leaders, and communities. This progress in turn meant a decrease in the burden to parents and elder siblings in providing for poor youth in their families.

3.4 Offering Course Duration that meets the Needs of Many Disadvantaged Youth

CAP-YEI precisely targets the most vulnerable youth in their communities—those from very poor families, neighbourhoods, and that have been out of school for at least one year. The youth demonstrated they had no chance to access higher education or work skills training. They are part of the 2009 Census Report for Kenya indicating that out of about 11 million youth, only 39% are absorbed in the job market, leaving 61% jobless and under extreme poverty. Several research data indicate about 92% of these youth lacked the vocational or professional skills demanded by the economy. They need quick and effective intervention to get them out of poverty and vulnerabilities by engaging them in economic activities that can provide for their needs.

3.5 Managing Students' Expectations

Through exposure and field visits, mentorship, as well as through internships (or attachments), trainees can get a direct feel of the real work in their respective career lines, understand the requirements for each job, meet and interact with experienced workforce, meet with mentors and potential employers, and sometimes shadow or get on-the-job training opportunities. These opportunities demystify the often 'mythical' conversations and advice that orient youth to work as easy experiences. By the time that youth complete the training, they already know what they would like to do with their careers as employees or small business owners. This managing of youth expectations does not exclude the process of getting the actual jobs through work readiness.

Work readiness is done a week prior to the end of the batch training and is used to get the trainees ready to apply for job opportunities, to participate in job interviews, and to work in normal work environments where there is interaction between them and employers as well as other employees. It includes practising of CVs/resumes writing, conducting mock interviews, training in safety precautions while at work, external assessment of students, and practising professional grooming. Assessment of this aspect is done by both an external resource person and the respective course facilitator. It ensures youth also have the knowledge of expected income in a whole range of job positions or from businesses once they start those jobs or businesses.

3.6 Work Preparedness Modules

To make sure the trainees succeed in transitioning to work, considering the tough competition for jobs from other trained youth from elsewhere, there is need to prepare them with extra skills other than the technical work skills. The need for work readiness comes from the understanding that many young people graduate or drop out from college or from high school without basic job search skills, doing job interviews, and working with other people. Some of the issues addressed during work readiness module include, for example, (1) preparing CV and cover letters, (2) subjecting trainees to external assessment by industry experts, (3) conducting real job application the last week of the training, (4) an opportunity to practise Internet job searching, and (5) preparing personal case studies (with specific questions: Who am I? Where am I now? Where do I want to go/be, and how do I get there?)

3.7 Providing Advice and Support as Young Entrepreneurs take the Leap Towards Starting Their Own Businesses

CAP-YEI increased its emphasis on entrepreneurship in a manner that is comparable to job placement for two primary reasons. First, in urban areas this was implemented because of the post-programme movement of many

CAP-YEI youth towards self-employment strategies, as well as a broader economic context in which many individuals pursue self-employment or multiple earning strategies. Second, as CAP-YEI expanded into new rural areas, jobs were harder to come by and entrepreneurial training, particularly in the agri-business chain sector, was seen as necessary for success in these areas.

To address these emerging contexts, CAP-YEI endeavoured to strengthen the entrepreneurship training component by introducing a common curriculum across all 16 sites for all youth since 2012. CAP-YEI also hired an entrepreneurship coordinator, whose responsibilities include helping site coordinators identify youth who are interested in pursuing self-employment, facilitating youth acquisition of startup capital, and highlighting successful alumni.

Additionally, CAP-YEI determined to select youth identified through aptitude/interest testing at the beginning of the programme to follow a 'vocational track'. As a result, all programme participants learn basic entrepreneurship skills, while those youth who choose the entrepreneurship track receive more in-depth training.

3.8 Peer Connections/Networking

Under the CAP-YEI programme, peer networking and group formations are encouraged during the course training. They begin as savings groups which allow youth to pull resources to start small income generation activities while in the training. Savings groups grow into entrepreneurship groups with their groups getting registered with the department of social services. These connections build up into future connections post training and were reported to be useful in terms of alerting peers of employment opportunities, further training, and partnership in businesses.

Youth reported that there were changes in their peer relationships during the course of the programme—over the course of the CAP-YEI programme, youth saw significant and meaningful increases in the availability of peer support when they had problems. Furthermore, youth also reported significant increases in the availability of practical adult support, helping them by loaning money, meals, or clothes.

4 Unwritten 'Non-Negotiable' Factors: Social Life Skills

This section discusses aspects that we call 'unwritten non-negotiable factors' because, however they are not part of the training curriculum, these factors are very important in determining the success or failure of the youth in securing opportunities. Both the written programme elements discussed above and unwritten non-negotiable factors described below are inseparable.

These factors have a significant impact on the attitude a person brings to interactions with clients, customers, colleagues, supervisors, and other stakeholders in and around training spaces or workplaces. From the longitudinal study of the programme alumni, we found that the more positive someone's attitude is, the better that person's relationships with other people is and helps enhance performance at work, in businesses, or in social interactions and networking. These are discussed in detail below and include communication, teamwork and collaboration, problem solving, and critical observation.

4.1 *Communication*

It played a pivotal role in the success of the programme, proving valuable from the initial engagement with various stakeholders in the community to mobilising youth to enrol in the training, engaging different individuals to mentor youth or deliver guest lectures, and facilitating the process of securing on-the-job training, internships, and job placements.

4.2 *Teamwork and Collaboration*

This begins from the time the youth are in the training programme—they collaborate to make learning charts, doing classroom activities, engaging in small income generation activities, forming savings groups, and participating in exposure and field visits. At the end of the training, trainees are encouraged to enrol into CAP-YEI alumni to serve as a network and platform to help them to connect to one another to opportunities. Teamwork and collaboration are very useful in solving problems including job searches, accessing government youth fund and contracts, and starting business partnerships.

4.3 *Problem Solving*

While life skills training provides a lot on which to build self-confidence and how to cope with challenges, the full-scale training on problem solving is not structured in the training. There is evidence from evaluation showing not only the complexity of challenges at workplaces, but also in their homes and in their life. The youth apply multiple strategies and tools to solve these problems. For example, sexual harassment issues at workplaces by patrons, customers, and from supervisors in the hospitality sector were reported to be rampant. Youth were able to deal with these problems without yielding into such advances or quitting their jobs. Others demonstrated a great deal of resilience in overcoming challenges relating to balancing work, studies, and their small businesses popularly known as 'side hustles'. The youth reported they are able to deal with these challenges by constantly seeking advice and support from their trainers who maintain open communication and willingness to help the youth to succeed.

4.4 *Critical Observation*

This is often discussed when trainees bring in scenarios of the places they visit in their exposure and field visits as well as on-the-job training experiences. It attracts a wealth of insights on how to deal with these scenarios when in the real world post their training. It was reported that the environment in which youth work requires them to multi-task and coordinate separate activities.

Our research found that the youth apply both the written non-negotiable (life skills and technical skills) and the 'unwritten non-negotiable factors' to succeed in securing job opportunities, initiating self-employment engagements, and other side 'hustles'. The majority of the youth who went through the CAP-YEI training practise what we call mixed livelihoods in which they earn money through multiple strategies.

5 Multiple Earning Strategies

5.1 *Employees*

A longitudinal study done by University of Minnesota (CAP-YEI learning partner) in 2015 revealed very impressive success of the youth in accessing employment. The rate of employment among sample programme alumni for year 2 of operations was 80.2% for the Replication training centres and 80.1% for Demonstration training centres. For the other two years (Year 3 and Year 4), the employment rate at the Demonstration centres had remained consistent over the ones achieved by the Replication centres.

In this study, the analysis of youth placements across various trades underscores distinct trends influenced by both trade category and gender. Specifically, male participants show a propensity for higher placement rates in six trades—Auto, Building, Carpentry, Hospitality, Electrical, and ITES—while female participants exhibit stronger placement outcomes in three trades: IGM, Clearing & Forwarding, and Hair & Beauty.

Additionally, within the context of confidence levels regarding independent job acquisition, the findings reveal significant insights. Participants completing floriculture training emerge as the most confident cohort, with a 100% confidence level in securing employment. Following closely are participants enrolled in the customer relations and sales (CRS) course, demonstrating an 80.7% confidence level, and those engaged in security training, with an 80% confidence level. These observations shed light on the nuanced dynamics within youth placement and confidence across different vocational training domains.

5.2 *Self-Employment (Entrepreneurship)*

It is important to note that youth used a variety of methods to get job placement. These included help from the course facilitator, recommendations from friends, advertisements, etc. The majority of both males and females got their jobs as the result of referrals, often by their trainers (close to 70% of males and 80% of females). The complete breakdown of data showing the overall performance of the youth, including in entrepreneurship and further education post training in the first five years of Phase 1, is indicated in Table 12.1. Overall job placement for all the youth who completed training at CAP-YEI was 76% while those who decided to do business was 7%. This increases successful transition of youth from training to income earning at over 83%.

The primary objective of the CAP-YEI programme was to facilitate 10% to 20% of its participants in initiating businesses. The programme equips all students with skills in financial inclusion and entrepreneurship, with a focus on identifying and supporting those who express interest or demonstrate proficiency in business endeavours. Over the span of five

Table 12.1 CAP-YEI overall statistics as per September 2016: End of Phase 1

Sn no.	*BEST centre name*	*Enrolled*	*Dropouts*	*Trained*	*Placed %*	*Entrepreneurs %*	*Placed + entrepreneurs %*
1	Buru Buru	1246	22	1224	75.98	6.54	82.52
2	Athi River	860	25	835	75.33	8.98	84.31
3	Nyeri South	672	8	664	73.19	5.27	78.46
4	Naivasha	706	24	682	78.74	2.93	81.67
5	Mombasa	721	30	691	74.1	7.53	81.62
6	Thika	656	4	652	77.3	11.2	88.5
7	Eldoret	531	28	503	68.19	8.95	77.14
8	Kisumu	635	16	619	74.64	7.43	82.07
9	Nakuru	679	9	670	75.97	5.82	81.79
10	Dagoretti	542	25	517	76.6	4.45	81.04
11	Kakamega	440	10	430	76.74	6.74	83.49
12	Mikindani	540	26	514	76.85	11.28	88.13
13	Machakos	333	1	332	90.96	5.42	96.39
14	Nyahururu	200	6	194	76.29	17.53	93.81
15	Meru	150	14	136	81.62	5.15	86.76

Source: CAP-YEI

years, data from the current study reveals that 7.32% of all trained youth were fully engaged in small businesses.

An end-of-project evaluation highlights that the average proportion of entrepreneurs stood at 6.1%, with the second year of programme operation recording the lowest percentage at 4.2%. Interestingly, when queried about their intentions regarding business startups, both male and female students exhibited nearly identical responses. Notably, participants who completed floriculture training displayed the highest inclination towards future entrepreneurship, with 95.7%, followed by those in security training (2%), and customer relations and sales training (90%).

Furthermore, a longitudinal evaluation conducted by a learning partner categorised sampled youth into 'marcher', 'hoppers', or 'strugglers' (Ricardo et al., 2015). This evaluation underscores the significance of entrepreneurship as an avenue for youth empowerment. 'Marchers' denote individuals who successfully secure and sustain employment over an extended duration. Conversely, 'strugglers' face challenges in securing sustainable employment, often enduring prolonged job search periods. 'Hoppers' transition between different employment statuses, moving from struggling to successful employment or vice versa. Importantly, the study highlights that many youth engage in entrepreneurship out of necessity rather than choice, particularly when faced with limited job opportunities, viewing small businesses as a means to generate income.

In a subsequent study targeting post-programme youth, it was found that approximately one out of four males and nearly two out five females had embarked on entrepreneurship ventures within six months of graduation. Among these startups, over two out five males and almost half of females had businesses operational for less than six months. Remarkably, three-quarters of these entrepreneurs had already hired at least one staff member, with the remaining quarter demonstrating varied employment structures, most employing two individuals, others employing over three or even five staff members.

5.3 *Mixed Livelihoods*

These are multiple earning strategies youth employ to increase and sustain their economic potential in a context of challenging youth unemployment. These involve (1) having a paid job as well as running a business; (2) having a full-time job and a side, including part-time jobs, and (3) having a job, running a main business, and side temporary businesses—selling small items often or occasionally when the opportunity presents itself. For example, one youth was employed in a local electrical store to sell parts. While he worked in the shop, he secured himself a few opportunities to install electrical wiring in new buildings in the city. With income increasing for him, he saved the money with the intention of opening his own electrical shop. After saving, he had enough to enable him bid for a subcontract to supply electrical equipment and electrical wiring new buildings. This particular youth continued to maintain the job at the electrical shop, opened his own electrical shop, and employed another person to run for him from where he supplied materials to buildings, he managed to subcontract electrical installations, and also did little electrical wire installations for individuals.

Another scenario is when youth engage in several casual jobs called 'vibarua jobs' that include helping out friends and family at their businesses, and/or selling goods at the market or in less formal venues. Youth were found to engage in several of these activities even when they had a main job—working for others on a casual basis as well as selling items, and they explain that these multiple streams helped to fill income gaps when their main jobs ended or when faced by increased and unanticipated expenses.

The major impetus for mixed livelihoods is necessity and an expectation that they do what they need to do. The longitudinal as well as the summative evaluation explains youth engaging in mixed livelihoods as a matter of necessity either because they can't make enough in their jobs or because there is always additional need within their families. Programmatically, there are a couple areas that help youth do this—engage in mixed livelihood streams. One is life skills training—youth talk about developing persistence and not giving up—pushing through until they succeed.

A second one youth talked about is that the entrepreneurship training they received helped them realise that they could do or engage in small pieces of income-generating activities—even on the side when their jobs were insufficient or unpredictable. For most youth, entrepreneurial activities are not their sole source of income but help to supplement the work they do for others.

The third one is financial literacy and learning in which they learn both the importance of and mechanisms for saving. Youth realised through the programme that they would need to start saving if they wanted to start even small business activities. Finally, the fact that youth are able to get their foot in the door with employers is a first step and contributes to the multiple earning strategies. However, since youth are in entry-level jobs, it is often the low wages that lead them to needing multiple streams of income. These multiple earning strategies look a potential of widening youth livelihoods if it can be integrated and nurtured in youth empowerment sector.

Overall, youth are better off in this scenario than when they were just idling at home, leading so many of them wasted in drugs and other illicit activities. There are several indicators of improved well-being among the youth by engaging in paid jobs, running small businesses, or engaging in multiple earning streams facilitate in the CAP-YEI basic employability skills training model.

As a final test of the programme efficiency of the NGO displays 12 indicators of youth well-being as a result of earning opportunities like the following: (1) youth from impoverished background and high states of vulnerability who participated got empowered with skills for work, business, as well as higher education; (4) facilitating the financial inclusion of youth through opening of bank accounts and saving money; (8) increased earning by trained youth through employment and entrepreneurship; or

(12) decrease in the burden of parents and elder siblings to provide for poor youth in their families.

It is difficult to give a broader macro-evaluation of this training work, but the high literacy rate and the low NEET (Not in Education Employment or Training) rate express a certain success of these active strategies of NGOs and government policies, in a country which offers generally a business-friendly environment. Certainly, one in three young people (32%) is unemployed compared to 10% for the average of the active population. It is also a setback to the extensive education strategy which pours more qualified young people into the job market each year than the Kenyan economy can absorb.

On the positive side, Kenya has a particularly low percentage of young people who are neither in education, employment, nor in training, at 15%, better than the continental average of 25%. This strong employability status is attributed to a high level of literacy, even if men are more educated. Kenya's adult literacy rate reaches 82.9% in 2023 (UNESCO). Of the 11.63 million young Kenyans who are working, 89%, or 10.37 million, work in the informal sector. At least 52% of employed young Kenyans work in services.

According to the latest edition of the Africa Youth Employment Clock produced by World Data Lab and the Mastercard Foundation, the "Clock" draws on surveys and datasets made available by national statistical offices, the International Labour Organization (ILO), and the International Institute for Applied Systems Analysis (IIASA).

6 Conclusion

Introduced in 2011, CAP-YEI is a Kenyan NGO originally hailing from India, established with the aim of training 10,000 vulnerable youth in Kenya (CAP-YEI, https://capyei.org/). The institute's flagship programme, the BEST model, is structured around a nine-step framework designed to achieve specific objectives. These objectives include equipping disadvantaged youth with life skills, job market-relevant expertise, savings education, and small business development training. Additionally, the model seeks to facilitate access to internships and job opportunities for these individuals, while also providing crucial pre- and post-job placement counselling support. Successful implementation of the nine activities outlined within the framework—ranging from market scans and curriculum development to placements and programme reviews—has been instrumental in realising the programme's objectives.

Youth unemployment poses a significant challenge in Kenya, compounded by the nation's sizable youth population, high graduation rates from secondary and college education, and limited availability of white-collar jobs. Despite government and international NGO efforts, youth unemployment continues to escalate. Since 2012, CAP-YEI has trained over 100,000 young people, contributing to efforts to address this pressing issue.

While government programmes such as YEDF, KYEP, and VTCs were put in place to try to help ease unemployment among the youth, these have not been sufficient enough to cater for the huge population of youth seeking income opportunities. CAP-YEI basic employability skills training model is a unique approach to youth unemployment. Its holistic approach in developing technical and life skills among the trainees facilitated multiple earning strategies. The attitude, character, and work skills competency among the youth from the BEST model enabled them to get jobs, start business, and engage in mixed livelihoods.

The abilities and flexibility for youth to use multiple earning strategies is facilitated by both the written non-negotiable programme factors (essentially the nine steps) as well as the unwritten negotiable factors. Youth from CAP-YEI are able to earn money through employment by others (paid jobs), self-employment, and mixed livelihoods. While many youth attribute their ability to use multiple earning strategies to the programme training, there is also evidence that youth resort to these to supplement their little income from a main job or business, as well as try to get by when they don't have any job or business. This is a very important idea that can be borrowed and formally nurtured in CAP-YEI, other youth empowerment NGOs, as well as in the government TVET system.

Conflicts of Interest The author has no conflicts of interest to declare that are relevant to the content of this chapter.

References

Barry, M. (Ed.). (2005). *Youth Policy and Social Inclusion: Critical Debates with Young People*. Routledge.

Durham, D. (2000). Youth and Social Imagination in Africa: Introduction. *Anthropological Quarterly*, *73*(3), 113–120.

GoK. (2006). *Kenya National Youth Policy.* Government of Kenya Government Printer.

GoK. (2010). *The Prevention of Organized Crimes Act* (p. 13). Government of Kenya Government Printer.

Hansen, K. (2008). *Youth and the City in the Global South.* Indiana University Press.

Honnwana, A. (2011). *Child Soldiers in Africa.* University of Pennsylvania Press.

Kimando, L. N., Njogu, G. W., & Kihoro, J. M. (2012). Factors Affecting the Success of Youth Enterprise Development Funded Projects in Kenya. A Survey of Kigumo District Muranga County. *International Journal of Business and Commerce, 1*(10), 61–81.

Ricardo, G. K, Julius, N., & Dal, B. (2015). New Economy Development Group, December, Ottawa.

The Star Kenya. (2022, March 20). https://www.the-star.co.ke/business/kenya/2022-03-20-kenya-best-in-africas-youth-unemployment survey/

United Nations. (2007). *World Youths Report 2007: Transition to Adulthood: Progress and Challenges.* UN Press.

World Bank, IEG Review Team. (2017). *Kenya—KE-Youth Empowerment Project, (FY10).* World Bank Group.

PART IV

Wage Gaps: Youth, Informality and Gender

CHAPTER 13

Rising Labour Market Segmentation in Egypt over 2012–2018: Youth Informal Employment Is Prominent

Adrien Frontenaud, Oksana Nezhyvenko, and Philippe Adair

1 Introduction

Over the past decade, the labour market in Egypt has undergone significant changes, as highlighted by 2011 upheaval. Among these changes, the lack of job security and the low level of associated social protection coverage have particularly affected youth. We provide an overview of the dual labour market in Egypt.

A. Frontenaud
Paris, France
e-mail: adrien.frontenaud@gmail.com

O. Nezhyvenko
NaUKMA, Kyiv, Ukraine
e-mail: Nezhyvenkoov@ukma.edu.ua

P. Adair (✉)
Université Paris Est Créteil, Val-de-Marne, France
e-mail: adair@u-pec.fr

M.-P. Chelini et al. (eds.), *Wage Dynamics in Africa*, African Histories and Modernities,
https://doi.org/10.1007/978-3-031-99800-3_13

We decompose jobs statuses into four categories: formal jobs for employees (in the public sector and in the private sector), formal self-employment, informal wage employment and informal self-employment. We focus on the youth age group 15–34 years, split into 15–24 and 25–34 years, which faces pervasive job informality. Hereafter, we adopt a job-based concept of informality, i.e., informal employment, consisting of "all remunerative work (i.e., both self-employment and wage employment) that is not registered, regulated or protected by existing legal or regulatory frameworks, as well as non-remunerative work undertaken in an income-producing enterprise" (ILO, 2013; Charmes, 2019).

Beyond simple dualism, the formal/informal divide is segmented into six categories according to work status and earnings: formal self-employed, upper-tier informal self-employed and lower-tier informal self-employed vs. formal wage employees, upper-tier informal wage employees and lower-tier informal wage employees (Fields, 2023). In addition, Flabbi and Tejada (2023) document why informal employment should be sharply disentangled, in order to avoid conflating (informal) self-employment with (informal) wage employment.

We use microdata from the Egypt Labor Market Panel Survey (LMPS) in years 2012 and 2018 (OAMDI, 2019). Despite attrition, these surveys are nationally representative and provide information on employment according to job status (wage employees vs. self-employed and formal vs. informal sector), as well as on the individual and professional characteristics of workers: age, gender, education level, marital status and geographical location (Assaad et al., 2021).

We focus on workers' occupational mobility regarding prior job status vs. current job status, age cohort, gender, etc. Distinction between employees (wage earners) and self-employed (non-wage earners) highlights income inequality.

We exclude agriculture because over 90% jobs are informal jobs, as highlighted by international experts from the Delhi Group on Informal Sector Statistics (ILO, 2013; Charmes, 2019), and thus may conceal developments specific to non-farming informal employment.

Noteworthy is the variety of tools used to address labour market segmentation. First, the use of panel data, which has been scarcely used in order to capture labour market dualism. Second, transition matrices focus on workers' occupational mobility regarding prior job status vs. current job status, age cohort, gender, etc. Third, logistic regressions upon large size samples (over 10,000 workers) estimate the probability of being in informal employment. Fourth, we apply a Mincer wage equation, which confirms labour market segmentation: formal employees earn more than informal ones, wage differentials being due to differences in human capital endowments. Fifth, we design a multidimensional job quality index, which enlarges the perspective and confirms labour market segmentation. Last, we test the wage equation on job quality indicators and disentangle supply-side and demand-side factors with an Oaxaca-Blinder decomposition.

Section 2 addresses labour market dualism, segmentation and income gaps in Egypt. Section 3 investigates occupational status and mobility according to workers' previous job position, age cohort and gender, using transition tables applied to LMPS. Distinction between employees (wage earners) and self-employed (non-wage earners) highlights income inequality. We split jobs statuses into four categories: formal wage employment (employees in the public sector and in the private sector), formal self-employment, informal wage employment and informal self-employment. Section 4 models the probabilities of occupying formal and informal wage employment, formal and informal self-employment using a multinomial logistic regression. Section 5 applies to Egypt a Mincer wage equation, also tested on job quality, which corroborates labour market segmentation: formal employees are better off (higher wage bill, larger social insurance coverage) than informal employees are, wage differentials being due to gaps in human capital endowment. Section 6 builds a multidimensional employment quality index and examines how job quality has evolved for employees. Testing the wage equation with the job quality index demonstrates that poor job quality fits indeed informal employment. Section 7 analyses wage differentials between formal and informal employees with an Oaxaca-Blinder decomposition. It shows that the unexplained component ("discrimination") from the demand side of the employers is prominent, whereas the explained component from the supply side of the workers that is consistent with human capital theory is almost negligible.

2 Labour Market Dualism, Segmentation and Income Gaps

2.1 *Definitions and Theories of Informality: A Fuzzy Set*

Extant research over half a century points out that the concept of informal economy includes distinct theories and methodologies lacking consensus. In this respect, informality is a "fuzzy set" capturing three components: the informal sector, and informal activities within the formal sector and in households. Data sources are patchy and coverage remains deficient, not least in the MENA countries.

The informal sector (the largest component) encapsulates unincorporated (micro) enterprises run by unregistered self-employed-own-account workers and employers managing less than five permanent paid employees. Informal employment extends to all precarious jobs carried out both in the informal sector and within formal enterprises and households (including domestic workers and household members producing goods and services for their own use), wherein workers are not subject to labour regulations, income taxation or employer-provided social protection (Charmes, 2019).

A threefold spectrum of theories purports to explain informality. According to a pessimistic interpretation of dualism (Lewis, 1954), persistent informality is due to labour market segmentation—into formal versus informal jobs—whereupon entry barriers to the formal economy affect workers on the labour market supply side.

Dualism is not congruent with structuralism (Castells & Portes, 1989), because the informal economy is not separated, but rather subsumed by the formal economy under subcontracting arrangements. Institutionalism (De Soto, 1986) assumes that informality stems from inadequate regulation, and excessive bureaucracy and taxation, driving small firms to exiting or being excluded from the formal economy.

The emphasis from the World Bank on lowering barriers to entry and to business activity, and levelling the competitive field, is consistent with institutionalism together with structuralism, as they focus on the demand side of the labour market and the supply side of the goods market (i.e., businesses).

La Porta and Shleifer (2014) support segmentation theory and dismiss the other two theories, contending that the size of the informal economy, approximated by the share of self-employment in total employment, declines with rising income per capita, which does not preclude the implementation of adequate formalising policies. Noteworthy is that the informal economy is restricted to employment in the informal sector and, perhaps, in households, but it overlooks informal employment within the formal economy.

Fields (2023) address heterogeneity within informal work by applying a common conceptual framework (segmented categories) and empirical methodology (panel data). However, available data were not always granular enough to disentangle lower-tier and upper-tier informal employment. Hence, cross-sectional data must provide additional information. In addition, the panel data may lack representativeness at the national level.

2.2 *Segmentation*

There is gender segmentation of informal employment according to status and income. The vulnerability to poverty risk is uneven between genders. In a five-step classification of informal workers—as employers, regular informal employees, own-account workers, casual/irregular employees and unpaid family workers—men concentrate amongst the three upper categories, whereas women are over-represented in the two bottom categories, wherein there is higher poverty risk prevalence (Chen & Carré, 2020, 71).

A survey with an even gender distribution was conducted in 2015 over a sample of 7816 individuals aged 15–29 from four MENA countries (Algeria, Morocco, Tunisia and Egypt). Among 3027 active people, one quarter is unemployed, where females are disproportionately concerned. Two out of three vs. one out of three individuals are respectively informal workers vs. formal workers. Informality is prominent for youths and supports the segmentation theory. The income gap is slightly below 45% between formal and informal employees, whether male or female; it is larger for self-employed 55.72% for males and 54.51% for females (Gherbi & Adair, 2020).

Table 13.1 illustrates the income gap between formal and informal employees in Egypt for 2012 and 2018. For youth (15–24), both men and women in informal employment earned less than their formal counterparts did in 2012. The wage gap for youth men decreased slightly by 2018, while for youth women, it reversed.

In 2012, youth men in informal jobs earned significantly less than their formal counterparts and the gap increased by 2018. For adults aged 35–44

Table 13.1 Formal/informal workers: real monthly wage and wage gap in Egypt (2012–2018)

	Informal employees		*Formal employees*		*Formal/informal wage gap (%)*	
	2012	*2018*	*2012*	*2018*	*2012*	*2018*
Youth men, 15–24	1973.53	1974.21	2801.75	2759.46	29.56%	28.46%
Youth women, 15–24	1268.06	1519.77	1967.59	3043	35.55%	50.06%
Youth men, 25–34	2490.87	2256.12	3154.03	3837.42	21.03%	41.21%
Youth women, 25–34	1287.64	1561.22	2256.47	2052.54	42.94%	23.94%
Adult men, 35–44	2551.73	2783.33	3639.45	6318.97	29.89%	55.95%
Adult women, 35–44	1101.12	1910.15	2678.56	2400.68	58.89%	20.43%
Adult men, 45–59	2606.77	2619.12	3755.83	3584.30	30.59%	26.93%
Adult women, 45–59	1689.31	2170.24	3157.94	3066.25	46.51%	29.22%
Total	2278.12	2304.94	3253.95	4040.08	29.99%	42.95%

Notes: Outside agriculture. All wages are in 2018 EGP currency, deflated with the Consumer Price Index. Wage gap in percentage

Source: Authors from Egypt LMPS in 2012 and 2018, hereafter, ELMPS12 and ELMPS18 (OAMDI, 2019)

and 45–59, the wage gap was substantial in both 2012 and 2018. Adult men in informal jobs earned considerably less than those in formal jobs did in both age groups, and this gap increased for the 35–44 age group by 2018. Adult women also faced a substantial wage gap, with those in informal jobs earning significantly less than their counterparts in formal jobs. On average, informal employees earned approximately 25.2% less than their formal counterparts did in 2012, and this gap increased to 48.3% by 2018. Across all age groups, women generally earned less than men did, regardless their job was formal or informal. Gender disparities prove persistent in both formal and informal employment.

3 Transitions in and from Job Segments and Occupational Mobility

We analyse transitions between different types of employment, unemployment and inactivity using transition matrices separately for men and women for different periods: 2012–2018 (Egypt). The issues of sample attrition, related to the establishment of longitudinal data, have been addressed to ensure national representativeness of the panel.

We split jobs into four categories: formal wage employment, informal wage employment, formal self-employment and informal self-employment. Employed population aged 15–34 is engaged in economic market activities.

Following the guidelines established in 2003 during the seventeenth International Conference of Labour Statisticians (ILO, 2013; Charmes, 2019) to define informal employment, informal jobs are identified according to the characteristics of the occupied jobs. The lack of affiliation with social security together with the absence of employment contract is defining features of informal employment. However, we dropped employment contracts and defined informal jobs according only to non-affiliation with social security. In Egypt, social security affiliation covers various situations. Although all workers are required to be affiliated, except for temporary, occasional, or foreign workers, the obligations and guarantees vary depending on their employment status or the size of the company wherein they work. For instance, self-employed workers must contribute to retirement at their discretion but not to health insurance (Selwaness, 2012). Small- and medium-sized enterprises (SMEs) are also not obliged to contribute to employees' health insurance. Although larger companies are required to contribute, they can restrict to 1% of their payroll and join in alternative insurance plans. Hence, some workers may not be covered by health insurance, although they are affiliated with social security.

As emphasised by the Delhi Group on Informal Sector Statistics (ILO, 2013; Charmes, 2019), we exclude agriculture because over 90% jobs are informal jobs, and thus may conceal developments in non-farming informal employment.

The transitions between different segments of the labour market are calculated from the two Egyptian LMPS. The weights used are those that cover the two years and ensure, for each year, the maintenance of national representativeness despite attrition (Assaad et al., 2021).

For 2012 and 2018 in Egypt, individuals aged 15–34 years in 2018 were selected. The analysis of transitions addresses all job statuses (formal wage employment, informal wage employment, formal self-employment or informal self-employment), unemployment, and inactivity over 2012–2018 in Egypt. Table 13.2 reports that around 61% of individuals initially in formal or informal wage employment remained in those categories. For women, 45.2% in informal wage employment in 2012 exited the

Table 13.2 Youth transitions between jobs, unemployment and inactivity: Egypt (in %)

2012 ↓ 2018→	*Formal wage employee*	*Informal wage employee*	*Formal self-employed*	*Informal self-employed*	*Unemployment*	*Out of the labour force*	*Total*
Formal wage employee	*60.5*	29.8	0.2	2.9	0.8	5.8	100
Informal wage employee	14.8	*61.1*	1.2	9.4	4.4	9.1	100
Formal self-employed	12.5	37.5	*12.5*	28.1	0	9.4	100
Informal self-employed	7.1	41.1	2.8	*34*	3.7	11.3	100
Unemployment	7.4	25.8	0.6	4.9	*16.4*	44.9	100
Out of the labour force	3	13.8	0.2	3.1	*7.7*	*72.2*	100
Total	7.8	21.8	0.5	5.0	7.2	57.7	100
2012 ↓ men 2018→	Formal wage employee	Informal wage employee	Formal self-employed	Informal self-employed	Unemployment	Out of the labour force	Total
Formal wage employee	*56.6*	37.6	0.3	4.4	0.3	0.8	100
Informal wage employee	13.8	*65.1*	1.3	10.2	3.8	5.8	100
Formal self-employed	12.5	37.5	*12.5*	28.1	0	9.4	100
Informal self-employed	7.3	46.7	3	*36.1*	3.6	3.3	100
Unemployment	15.2	52.9	1	11	*9.4*	10.5	100
Out of the labour force	4.9	27.6	0.4	4.9	6.2	*56*	100

Total	10.9	38.4	0.8	8.0	5.3	36.6	100
2012 ↓ women 2018→	Formal wage employee	Informal wage employee	Formal self-employed	Informal self-employed	Unemployment	Out of the labour force	Total
Formal wage employee	*67.8*	15.2	0	0	1.9	15.1	100
Informal wage employee	26.1	*17.4*	0	0.9	10.4	45.2	100
Formal self-employed	0	0	*0*	0	0	0	100
Informal self-employed	5.9	7.8	2	*21.6*	3.9	58.8	100
Unemployment	2.8	9.7	0.4	1.2	*20.6*	65.3	100
Out of the labour force	1.6	3.8	0.1	1.9	8.7	*83.9*	100
Total	4.7	4.9	0.1	1.9	9.2	79.2	100

Notes: We selected 11,133 individuals aged 15–34 in 2018 and we excluded agricultural employment. The sample comprises 22,266 observations

Sources: Authors' calculations using the Egypt Labor Market Panel Survey (ELMPS12 & ELMPS18)

labour force by 2018. More women than men remained in formal wage employment, offering better security. Notably, no women are in formal self-employment among individuals aged 15–34.

Over 53% of men aged 15–34 unemployed in 2012 transitioned to informal wage employment in 2018, showing a lack of secure employment paths whereas most women who were respectively unemployed and out of the labour force in 2012 remain in these situations in 2018.

These findings underscore the complex dynamics of youth employment in Egypt. Informal jobs persist, but shifts to formal jobs, self-employment, unemployment, and inactivity highlight a changing job landscape.

4 Modelling the Probability of Occupational Status: Logistic Regressions

A multidimensional approach complements the transition matrices by accounting for compositional effects: the probabilities of occupying formal wage, informal wage, formal and informal self-employment are modelled to identify, holding everything else constant, the effects of each individual or occupational characteristic. These correspond to age, education level and gender for individual characteristics and industry for occupational characteristics. The estimations are conducted as cross-sections for each of the years 2012 and 2018 as for Egypt. The probabilities are modelled using a logistic distribution cumulative function. The logistic regression model is multinomial, as the dependent variable includes four categories (See Table 13.3).

Thus, for both years (2012 and 2018 in Egypt), the probability of engaging in informal employment (as employees and self-employed) is higher for 15–24-year-old youths and individuals with little education (primary school). When working in industries such as mining, manufacturing and utilities, the probability of engaging in informal wage employment is notably higher than working in services (commerce, services, transport & communication, finance & business services, public administration and other services).

Regarding the estimations of the probability of having a formal wage employment, the results show that for all years in Egypt, the likelihood of holding a formal wage employment increases with age; it is higher for those who have completed at least secondary education compared to those with limited education. It is also stronger for individuals engaged in

Table 13.3 Probability of formal and informal wage, formal and informal self-employment: average marginal effects in Egypt (2012 and 2018)

	2012				*2018*			
	Formal wage employee	*Informal wage employee*	*Formal self-employed*	*Informal self-employed*	*Formal wage employee*	*Informal wage employee*	*Formal self-employed*	*Informal self-employed*
Age (ref.: 25–34 years)15–24	−0.186***	0.196***	−0.017***	0.008	−0.177***	0.193***	−0.011**	−0.005
Sex (ref.: Male) female	0.154***	−0.117***	−0.038***	0.001	0.110***	−0.137***	−0.012**	0.041***
Education (ref.: Illiterate)								
Primary education	0.081**	−0.059**	0.018*	−0.041**	0.057*	−0.028	0.002	−0.030**
Secondary education	0.271**	−0.180***	0.01	−0.101***	0.208***	−0.127***	0.001	−0.082***
Tertiary education	0.431***	−0.278***	0.012	−0.166***	0.334***	−0.175***	0.005	−0.164***
Urban (ref.: Rural)	0.036***	−0.016	0.002	−0.022**	0.017*	0.027**	−0.003	−0.041***
Industry (ref.: Manufacturing)								
Services	0.026**	−0.185***	0.032***	0.127***	0.012	−0.186***	0.023***	0.150***
Observations	**5812**				**6037**			

Notes: Outside agriculture *** ($p < 0.01$), ** ($p < 0.05$), * ($p < 0.1$)

Source: Authors' calculations

services compared with manufacturing industry. We observe a similar trend for formal self-employment, except that men have a higher probability of being in this category.

Logistic regressions display two salient patterns. First, persistent labour market segmentation and low mobility affect formal vs. informal workers. The former segment does not give up its favourable status, whereas the latter does not easily overcome barriers to entry into formal employment. Second, young male workers prove less mobile than females are, the latter eventually exiting the labour force.

5 A Mincer Wage Equation for Egypt in 2012 and 2018

We use the wage equation developed by Mincer (1974) in order to investigate wage determinants for employees. This model is a widely used framework in labour economics to analyse the relationship between education, work experience and earnings. It seeks to explain wage differentials across individuals based on their human capital attributes. It is written as follows:

$$\ln \text{Income}_{it} = \sum_{r} \beta_{rit} x_{rit} + \gamma \text{Education}_{it} + \delta \text{Experience}_{it} + u_{it} \qquad (13.1)$$

Where $\ln\text{Income}_{it}$ represents the natural logarithm of the income of worker i in year t (2012 or 2018). Income is the monthly wage of the primary job (in $ Purchasing Power Parity Adjusted).

x_{rit} is the vector of individual characteristics (age, gender, household size, marital status, etc.) in the year t;

β_{rit} are the coefficients associated with individual characteristics in the year t;

γ is the coefficient associated with education level for worker i in the year t;

δ is the coefficient associated with work experience for worker i in the year t;

μ_i represents a random disturbance and measurement error.

Table 13.4 reports the coefficients of the Mincer wage equation obtained from OLS regressions for full-time employees aged 15–34 in Egypt, as of 2012 and 2018. As of 2012, all selected variables show

Table 13.4 Mincer model of wage determination: full-time employees aged 15–34 in Egypt

	2012	*2018*
Dependent variable	*lnIncome*	*lnIncome*
Sex: Male **(Ref.: Female)**	0.443*** [0.038]	0.401*** [0.049]
Age	0.068** [0.027]	0.052* [0.030]
Age^2	−0.001** [0.001]	−0.001 [0.001]
Marital status: Married **(Ref.: Single)**	0.064** [0.028]	0.030 [0.033]
Household size	−0.014** [0.006]	−0.017** [0.008]
Education: Read and write & basic education **(Ref.: Illiterate)**	−0.003 [0.041]	0.129** [0.055]
Secondary education	−0.019 [0.040]	0.123** [0.054]
Tertiary education: Post-secondary, university & post-graduate	0.224*** [0.046]	0.255*** [0.058]
Experience	0.033*** [0.007]	0.037*** [0.007]
$Experience^2$	−0.001*** [0.000]	−0.001*** [0.000]
Formal employment **(Ref.: Informal employment)**	0.058** [0.027]	0.183*** [0.035]
Constant	4.730*** [0.350]	4.840*** [0.396]
Number of observations	4102	3543
R^2	0.116	0.118

Notes: Outside agriculture. Robust standard errors in brackets. *** ($p < 0.01$), ** ($p < 0.05$), * ($p < 0.1$). Dependent variable—log monthly wage in 2012 (monthly wage of the primary job, in constant 2018 PPP terms)

Source: Authors' calculation using ELMPS12 and ELMPS18

statistical significance in determining wages, and they demonstrate the expected influence (positive or negative). In our model, being a man increases wages compared to being a woman. "Age" is significant and positive for full-time employees, indicating that the older one is, between 15 and 34 years, the higher wage increases. Married individuals earn more than "single, divorced or widened". In contrast, household size is negative: the larger the household size, the fewer the incomes. We look at two most important variables in the Mincer model: education and experience. We divided "education" variable into several categories with "Illiterate" as a control group. The highest education level ("post-secondary, University & Post-graduate") is significant and positive for full-time employees. "Experience" shows the same relationship with income as "education", being highly significant and positive for employees, becoming slightly negative with the quadratic variable that suggests a non-linear relationship. Noteworthy is that formally employed individuals earn a higher income than informally employed individuals do.

As of 2018, coefficients go in the same direction as in 2012. In addition, "read and write & basic education" and also "secondary education" prove positive and statistically significant.

6 Job Quality Measurement: A Multidimensional Index

In countries where informal employment prevails, conventional labour market indicators, such as unemployment rates, labour force participation rates and wages, may not fully capture the complexity of the labour market. The classification of jobs as either formal or informal can oversimplify the nuances of job quality, which the job quality index provides by integrating various dimensions of employment. It helps to assess not only whether a job is formal or informal, but also its quality across multiple facets, such as health, social security, paid leave and job security. Understanding the relationships and correlations between different job quality indicators enables policymakers to design better targeted and effective interventions. The job quality index can serve as a robustness check to evaluate the impact of policies and programmes over time.

6.1 Dimensions of Job Quality: Building the Multidimensional Wage Index

Due to limited data availability on the quality of employment for self-employed workers in LMPS, the focus was directed towards wage employment. The job quality index encapsulates a standardised set of ten indicators, with equal weight assigned to each indicator (Table 13.5).

Hereafter, it is distinct from the deprivation weighted index *à la* Alkire and Foster (2011) designed in Adair et al. (2024) and from the positive weighted index designed by the World Bank (Hovhannisyan et al., 2022).

Table 13.5 The multidimensional employment quality index in Egypt

	Indicator	*Suffering from deprivations if:*
1	Poverty	Total wages are below the international extreme poverty line of US$1.90/day per capita (2011 PPP), multiplied by the dependency ratio of (4.0/1.5)
2	Health insurance	Job does not provide health insurance
3	Social security	Job is not associated with any type of social security
4	Annual paid leave	Job does not offer paid holiday leave
5	Paid sick leave	Job does not offer paid sick leave
6	Tenure	The wage employee aged 15–24 has been in his/her job for less than a year The wage employee aged 25–34 has been in his/her job for less than three years
7	Written contract	Job is not bound by written contract
8	Permanent employment	Job is temporary, not permanent
9	Excessive working hours	Wage employee exceeds more than 48 weekly hours in his/her main job
10	Second paid job	Individual works a second paid job

Source: Authors' design

Although some deprivations display slight changes, the overall trends remain stable, indicating persistent issues with respect to certain dimensions of job quality. In both 2012 and 2018, the indicators of health, social security, paid leave and sick leave are strongly correlated, whereas poverty, tenure and second job indicators are not.

According to Fig. 13.1, the share of workers with no deprivations declines from nearly 15% in 2012 to approximately 9% in 2018. This trend suggests that pure formal employment is shrinking, which may reflect deteriorating job quality or increased informalisation of the labour market. The share of workers with one to four deprivations also dropped. This trend suggests that some workers may have transitioned to categories facing more severe deprivations, namely worsening employment conditions. The most significant change is the increase in the share of workers experiencing moderate to severe (five to seven) deprivations, which highlights a deteriorating labour market. In addition, a slight increase in the share of workers experiencing eight to ten deprivations suggests a rise in the most vulnerable segment of the labour market, namely the most informal workers.

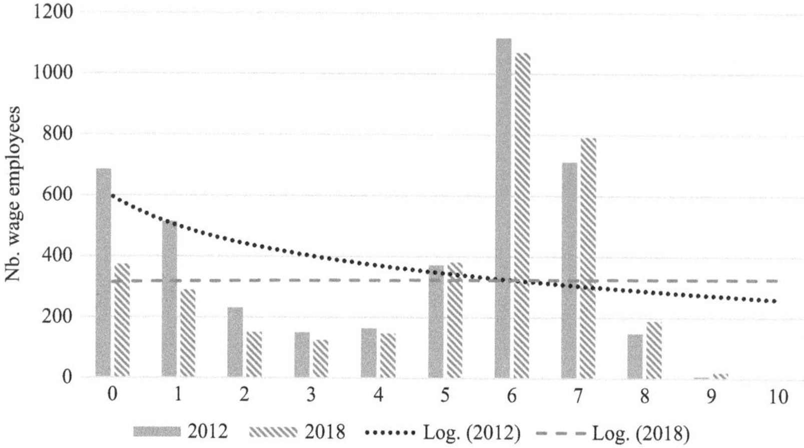

Fig. 13.1 Distribution of the job quality index in Egypt in 2012 and 2018. *Notes:* Outside agriculture. The sample includes 7645 individuals (4102 in 2012 and 3543 in 2018). *Source:* Authors, from ELMPS12 and ELMPS18

6.2 Testing the Wage Equation with the Job Quality Index

In order to test the wage equation with the job quality index, we simplify this index into four categories. Category 1 (no deprivation), category 2 (moderate deprivations one to four), category 3 (strong deprivations five to seven) and category 4 (very severe deprivations eight to ten). The rationale is that formal versus informal wage employment includes good versus poor job quality. The significant increase in workers in categories 3 and 4 suggests deteriorating employment conditions. The decline in category 1 indicates fewer wage employees in high-quality, formal jobs, reflecting a trend towards greater informality and multiple deprivations.

Table 13.6 displays the Mincer wage equation with the job quality index in 2012 and 2018. Coefficients are consistent with those in Table 13.4 reporting the wage equation.

The negative coefficients for job quality index categories 2, 3, and 4 in Table 13.6 indicate that income decreases as job quality deteriorates, from no deprivation to moderate, strong, or very severe deprivations.

Table 13.6 Model of wage determination with job quality: full-time employees aged 15–34 in Egypt

	2012	*2018*
Dependent variable	lnIncome	lnIncome
Sex: Male (Ref.: Female)	0.486*** [0.038]	0.416*** [0.050]
Age	0.088*** [0.026]	0.057* [0.030]
Age^2	−0.001*** [0.000]	−0.001* [0.001]
Marital status: Married (Ref.: Single)	0.056** [0.028]	0.030 [0.033]
Household size	−0.012** [0.005]	−0.016** [0.008]
Education: Read and write & Basic education (Ref.: Illiterate)	−0.004 [0.040]	0.129** [0.055]
Education: Secondary education	−0.003 [0.039]	0.118** [0.054]
Education: Post-secondary, university & post-graduate	0.178*** [0.046]	0.239*** [0.059]
Experience	0.018** [0.007]	0.032*** [0.007]
Experience^2	−0.001 [0.000]	−0.001*** [0.000]
Formal employment (Ref.: Informal employment)	−0.126** [0.057]	0.054 [0.059]
Job quality index category 2 (moderate deprivations) (Ref.: Job quality category 1 (no deprivation))	−0.218*** [0.037]	−0.038 [0.056]
Job quality index category 3 (strong deprivations)	−0.351*** [0.064]	−0.189** [0.074]
Job quality index category 4 (very severe deprivations)	−0.550*** [0.103]	−0.255** [0.105]
Constant	4.832*** [0.347]	4.967*** [0.400]
Number of observations	4102	3543
R^2	0.134	0.123

Notes: Outside agriculture. Robust standard errors in brackets. Outside agriculture. *** ($p < 0.01$), ** ($p < 0.05$), * ($p < 0.1$). Dependent variable—log monthly wage in 2012 and 2018 (monthly wage of the primary job, in constant 2018 PPP terms)

Source: Authors from ELMPS12 and ELMPS18

7 An Oaxaca-Blinder Decomposition

In order to analyse wage differentials between the categories of formal and informal employees, we decompose this difference into explained and unexplained components, according to the model designed by Oaxaca (1973) and Blinder (1973). The model includes two components: (1) the explained component, including endowments and characteristics, is attributable to the observable characteristics of these categories; (2) whereas the unexplained component, such as coefficients and discrimination, may reflect factors related to discrimination or unobserved factors. Noteworthy is that the explained component is rather endogenous and comes mostly from the labour supply side of the workers, which is consistent with human capital theory founding the Mincer wage equation. In contrast, the unexplained component is rather exogenous and may come from the labour demand side of the employers.

Table 13.7 reports that variables contributing the most to the explained wage differentials, in both 2012 and 2018, are age (30–34 years old), higher learning (tertiary education), years of experience, and high qualification levels (professionals).

Obviously, overall results do not align with human capital theory, in as much as wage differentials between the categories of formal and informal employees are predominantly driven by the unexplained component: 0.117 out of 0.131 of the gap in 2012 and 0.212 out of 0.230 in 2018. The explained component of the wage difference proves almost negligible and statistically non-significant in both years. Hence, our results suggest the presence of discrimination on the demand side of the labour market.

8 Conclusions and Policy Implications

The chapter highlights the prevalence and persistence of informal employment affecting youth (15–34 years old) in Egypt, using panel data surveys spanning over 2012–2018.

Transitions throughout labour market segments, formal/informal wage employment, formal/informal self-employment, unemployment and inactivity display evolving patterns. Over 50% of unemployed Egyptian men transitioned to informal wage jobs by 2018. In contrast, most jobless or inactive women in 2012 remained in the same situation by 2018.

Multinomial logistic regressions mirror transition matrices: Individuals aged 15–24 and those with low educational attainment are more likely to engage in informal employment, as both employees and self-employed individuals.

A Mincer wage equation applied to 2012 and 2018 confirms that formal employees earn more than informal ones, wage differentials being due to differences in human capital endowments.

Job quality analysis reveals that better job quality strongly associates with higher wages (i.e., formal jobs), in both 2012 and 2018. It demonstrates that as job quality worsens—from no deprivation to moderate, strong and very severe deprivations—income tends to decline.

Table 13.7 Decomposition model of full-time employees aged 15–34 in Egypt (2012–2018)

	2012			*2018*		
Variables	*(1) Overall*	*(2) Explained*	*(3) Unexplained*	*(1) Overall*	*(2) Explained*	*(3) Unexplained*
Male		−0.051***	−0.212***		−0.044***	−0.129
Age_20–24		−0.020***	−0.013		−0.011	−0.020
Age_25–29		0.011**	−0.033		0.005	−0.108*
Age_30–34		0.045***	−0.017		0.020	−0.179**
Primary education		−0.003	0.013		−0.028**	0.010
Secondary education		−0.000	0.053		−0.010**	0.060
Tertiary (University) education		0.074***	0.091**		0.108***	0.128
Experience		−0.019***	0.194**		−0.001	0.100
Experience^2		0.019***	−0.044		0.013**	0.009
Marital status not single		0.014**	−0.028		0.009	−0.067*
Household size		0.011***	−0.169***		0.005*	−0.009
Private sector		−0.018	0.040		−0.034	0.018
Managers		0.009***	0.004**		0.001	0.003
Professionals		0.036**	0.056**		0.026*	−0.010
Technicians		0.017**	0.031**		0.008	0.008
Clerical		−0.001	0.012**		−0.000	−0.016
Service_sales		0.002	0.060***		0.000	−0.029
Plant		−0.000	0.019		−0.001	−0.030*
Elementary occupation		−0.003	0.010		−0.002	0.001
Mining_activity		0.001	−0.001		0.000	−0.001
Manufacturing_activity		0.000	−0.033		0.000	−0.056
Electricity_Water		0.002	0.000		0.003	−0.004

(*continued*)

Table 13.7 (continued)

	2012			*2018*		
Variables	*(1) Overall*	*(2) Explained*	*(3) Unexplained*	*(1) Overall*	*(2) Explained*	*(3) Unexplained*
Construction_activity		−0.040**	−0.040		−0.043***	−0.076**
Wholesale_activity		−0.013	−0.059		−0.002	−0.041
Transportation_activity		0.000	−0.028		−0.006	−0.014
Accommodation_activity		−0.000	−0.017		−0.005	−0.015
Information_Financial_Real Estate		0.008*	0.002		0.006	−0.014**
Technical_activity		−0.002	−0.001		0.000	−0.013**
Administrative_activity		0.000	−0.002		0.000	−0.009**
Public_administration		−0.039***	−0.010		0.012	−0.026**
Education_Human Health		−0.086***	−0.014		−0.029	−0.026
Arts_Other_Household		0.003	−0.017*		0.000	−0.017**
Formal	6.396***			6.372***		
Informal	6.283***			6.144***		
Difference	0.113***			0.228***		
Explained	−0.013			0.004		
Unexplained	0.126***			0.224***		
Constant			0.278			0.800**
Observations	4102	4102	4102	3543	3543	3543

Notes: Outside agriculture. Standard errors are omitted due to lack of space. The full table is available upon request

*** $p < 0.01$, ** $p < 0.05$, * $p < 0.1$. Variables contributing the most to the explained wage differentials in italics

Source: Authors' calculations from ELMPS12 and ELMPS18

According to an Oaxaca-Blinder decomposition of wage differentials, the unexplained component related to discrimination on the demand side is most important and does not confirm the role of human capital on the supply side that is insignificant.

Four policy options are relevant with regard to the process of formalisation, and outcomes may take time to show up. First, economic growth through enhancing education and training, creating more formal jobs, raising the earnings of the self-employed lower tier, formalising the informal upper tier and increasing the enforcement of labour protections. Data collection is a pre-requisite for designing, monitoring and assessing policies that address the formalisation of informality. Females, being typically disadvantaged compared to their male counterparts as regards workforce participation and more prone to abide by the rules, should be given positive discrimination to enter the labour market (Adair et al., 2022, 2024).

Informality is a hot issue as regards its scope and trend in MENA (Middle East and North Africa) countries, calling upon its formalisation. Informality requires both ongoing thorough investigation as well as taking stock of evolving stylised facts.

Formalisation policies should be gauged with regard to improving employment and welfare, and promoting job creation should take place within formal sustainable organisations. In this respect, for-profit cooperatives and not-for-profit entities of the Social and Solidarity Economy (SSEs), including microfinance institutions (MFIs), could play a key role (Adair et al., 2022, 2024).

Conflicts of Interest The authors have no conflicts of interest to declare that are relevant to the content of this chapter.

References

Adair, P., Hlasny, V., Omrani, M., & Sharabi-Rosshandler, K. (2022, November). Fostering the Social and Solidarity Economy and Formalising Informality in MENA Countries. *ERF Working Paper Series* 1604. Cairo: Economic Research Forum. https://erf.org.eg/app/uploads/2022/11/1669485442_916_903601_1604.pdf

Adair, P., Berguiga, I., & Frontenaud, A. (2024, August). Enhancing Decent Jobs Creation and Access to Funding for Youth: Employment Formalisation and Financial Inclusion Foster Growth in MENA Countries. FEMISE 2023 Annual Conference Barcelona *FEM-ConfPaper2-2024*. https://www.femise.

org/en/slideshow-en/femise-conference-paper-no2-enhancing-decent-jobs-creation-and-access-to-funding-for-youth-employment-formalisation-and-financial-inclusion-foster-growth-in-mena-countries/

Alkire, S., & Foster, J. E. (2011). Counting and Multidimensional Poverty Measurement. *Journal of Public Economics, 95*(7–8), 476–487. https://doi.org/10.1016/j.jpubeco.2010.11.006

Assaad, R., Krafft, C. G., & Rahman, K. W. (2021). Introducing the Egypt Labour Market Panel Survey 2018. *IZA Journal of Development and Migration, 12*(1). https://doi.org/10.2478/izajodm-2021-0012

Castells, M., & Portes, A. (1989). World Underneath: The Origins, Dynamics, and Effects of the Informal Economy. In A. Portes, M. Castells, & L. A. Benton (Eds.), *The Informal Economy: Studies in Advanced and Less Developed Countries.* Johns Hopkins University Press.

Charmes, J. (2019). *Dimensions of Resilience in Developing Countries: Informality, Solidarities and Carework.* Springer. https://doi.org/10.1007/978-3-030-04076-5

Chen, M., & Carré, F. (Eds.). (2020). *The Informal Economy Revisited Examining the Past, Envisioning the Future.* Routledge. www.wiego.org › research-library-publications

De Soto, H. (1986). *The Other Path: The Invisible Revolution in the Third World.* Harper and Row, English translation, 1989.

Fields, G. S. (2023). Informality and Work Status. In G. S. Fields, T. H. Gindling, K. Sen, M. Danquah, & S. Schotte (Eds.), *The Job Ladder. Transforming Informal Work and Livelihoods in Developing Countries* (pp. 16–32). Oxford University Press.

Flabbi, L., & Tejada, M. (2023, June). Are Informal Self-Employment and Informal Employment as Employee Behaviorally Distinct Labor Force States? *IZA DP* No. 16225. https://doi.org/10.2139/ssrn.4479167

Gherbi, H., & Adair, P. (2020). The Youth Gender Gap in North Africa: Income Differentials and Informal Employment, *Erudite Working Paper* Series 06-2020. RePEc. https://ideas.repec.org/p/eru/erudwp/wp20-06.html

Hovhannisyan, S., Montalva-Talledo, V., Remick, T., Rodríguez-Castelán, C., & Stamm, K. (2022). Global Job Quality—Evidence from Wage Employment across Developing Countries. *Policy Research Working Paper 10134.* Washington DC, The World Bank.

ILO. (2013). *Measuring Informality: A Statistical Manual on the Informal Sector and Informal.* International Labour Office. https://www.ilo.org/publications/measuring-informality-statistical-manual-informal-sector-and-informal

La Porta, R., & Shleifer, A. (2014). Informality and Development. *Journal of Economic Perspectives, 28*(3), 109–126. https://doi.org/10.1257/jep.28.3.109

Lewis, A. (1954). Economic Development with Unlimited Supplies of Labour. *Manchester School of Economic and Social Studies, 22*(2), 139–191. https://doi.org/10.1111/j.1467-9957.1954.tb00021.x

Mincer, J. (1974). Schooling, Experience, and Earnings. NBER Books. National Bureau of Economic Research.

OAMDI. (2019). Version 2.0 of Licensed Data Files; *Labour Market Panel Surveys (LMPS)*, ELMPS 1998, 2006, 2012, 2018 Panel v.2.0; Open Access Micro Data Initiative, Economic Research Forum (ERF).

Selwaness, I. (2012). Rethinking Social Insurance in Egypt: An Empirical Study. *ERF Working Paper* 717. https://erf.org.eg/publications/rethinking-social-insurance-egypt-empirical-study/

CHAPTER 14

Dynamics of Wage Disparities in Senegal: Differences in Productive Characteristics or Discrimination?

Mamaye Thiongane and Abou Kane

1 Introduction

Gender mainstreaming is of fundamental importance in international development policies. As part of the Sustainable Development Goals (SDGs), a particular interest is attached to gender equality (SDG5) and reducing inequalities (SDG10). Unlike "sex", which is biological (male or female) and therefore does not change over time, "gender" refers more to social considerations regarding the roles assigned to men and women in their society (Petrongolo, 2019; Blau & Kahn, 2017). At the global level, there is still an average of 32% of the gender gap to be closed, and closing this overall gap will require 131 years (WEF, 2023). Out of 146 countries, listed according to calculation of the global gender inequality gap, Senegal ranks 104th with a score of 0.680 (score between 0 and 1). It is in the

M. Thiongane (✉) • A. Kane
Cheikh Anta Diop University, Dakar, Senegal
e-mail: mamaye.thiongane@ucad.edu.sn; abou.kane@ucad.edu.sn

M.-P. Chelini et al. (eds.), *Wage Dynamics in Africa*, African Histories and Modernities,
https://doi.org/10.1007/978-3-031-99800-3_14

sub-dimension "political power" that Senegal achieves its highest ranking in the world, 37th, with a score of 0.353. On the other hand, for the sub-dimensions of "health and survival", "educational attainment" and "economic participation and opportunity", Senegal ranks 97th, 125th and 137th respectively (WEF, 2023).

In addition to the principle of equality between men and women set out in the 2001 Constitution, Senegal adopted a law on equal access to elected office in 2007. To this end, absolute parity between men and women in fully or partially elected bodies was adopted in 2010. Senegal has also been implementing the national strategy for gender equity and equality (SNEEG) since 2015. All these initiatives for gender equality and equity and the efforts of women's movements in Senegal come up against socio-cultural realities. In fact, the family is the preferred setting for the construction of masculinity and social power in the patriarchal system. In Senegal, the social construct is fostered by a collective consensus on roles that legitimate men's power over women (Tøraasen, 2019; Kane & Kane, 2018; Fongang, 2014; Camara, 2012). Analysis of disparities in the labour market provides a better understanding of economic inequalities by gender.

In the fourth quarter of 2022, the national employment survey (ENES, Q4-2022) revealed that men's level of activity dominates that of women, whatever the age group considered. For a national activity rate of 60.2%, the rate for men is 69.9% and for women 50.9%. There are still differences between men and women in terms of those in paid employment. The rate of salaried employment for men (43.7%) differs significantly from that for women (30.5%). At national level, 77.2% of workers in the formal sector are men. What's more, whatever the segment observed, women have more difficulty in gaining access to stable employment. Indeed, the proportion of women is higher in small businesses (30.1%) than in medium-sized (21.9%) and large businesses (20.7%).

There is also a disparity in weekly workloads. On average, men work 42.5 hours/week compared with 40.5 hours/week for women in the formal sector (EERH, 2018).

The literature suggests that human capital, in addition to its major influence on participation in economic activity or choice of sector of employment (Kane, 2014; Kuépié et al., 2013), has an impact on wage levels. Indeed, human capital as a means of improving or signalling individual productivity should play a key role in labour allocation, but also in explaining wage levels. In Senegal, there are gender-based wage disparities. According to national employment survey for the fourth quarter of

2017 (ENES, Q4-2017), the average wage is 96,206 FCFA (or €147) per month in Senegal. Depending on gender, there is a monthly wage gap of FCFA 38,996 (around €60). The average monthly salary is 107,074 FCFA (€163) for men, compared with 68,078 FCFA (€104) for women. The Harmonised Survey of Household Living Conditions (EHCVM, 2021) shows that, in Senegal, the average salary of an employee is 112,123 FCFA (€186.17) per month. According to gender, men earn, on average, 130,667 FCFA (€199.20) per month against 104,408 FCFA (€159.168) for women, i.e. a wage gap of 26,259 FCFA (€40.03).

Human capital theory explains gender pay differentials in terms of the labour market participation decisions of household members. According to Becker (1985), responsibility for childcare and household tasks prevents women's wage income from rising faster.

These responsibilities, based on social considerations of the roles of men and women, affect employment opportunities and help to discourage the investment in human capital that the labour market requires (Becker, 1985; Mincer & Polachek, 1974).

However, depending on gender, wage differentials are not systematically explained by a difference in investment in human capital. In fact, analyses of gender disparities attribute a possible role to discrimination on the labour market in addition to these differences linked to productive capacities (Petrongolo, 2019). Studies on the decomposition of wage differentials show, in addition to the role of differences in characteristics linked to worker productivity (education, experience), the existence of a difference in valuation for similar characteristics. In the Oaxaca-Blinder decomposition of the sources of gender disparity, and its extensions such as that of Fortin-Firpo-Lemieux, there are two components. A component linked to differences in individual characteristics, known as the "explained" part, and a component linked to differences in the performance of characteristics, known as the "unexplained" part and which is considered to be evidence of possible discrimination (Petrongolo, 2019; Ahmed & Macgillivray, 2015).

In the labour market, economic discrimination by gender is suspected when equal productive capacities are rewarded differently on the basis of membership of a particular group (Ntsama, 2014; Havet, 2004).

In the Senegalese context, studies have focused on analysing gender inequalities in the labour market in terms of participation and salaries. Indeed, some authors have addressed the issue of disparities in access and revenues in different segments of the labour market (Sall & Thiaw, 2019;

Sall, 2018; Kuépié, 2016). Other authors combine microeconomic and macroeconomic information to understand the role of human capital in wage disparities or in mitigating discrimination (Malta et al., 2019). However, there is still a knowledge gap when it comes to analysing distributional wage inequalities. The existing literature only takes into account average wage differentials, neglecting the rest of the distribution. Such a narrow approach is only justified if the pay gap and the share of the gap attributable to productivity differences are uniform across the distribution. It is within this framework that we ask the following question: what are the sources of the pay gap between men and women at the average level and at different levels of the wage distribution in Senegal?

The aim of this chapter is therefore to examine the sources of gender-based wage disparities in the Senegalese labour market. The originality of this chapter lies in the fact that we proceed to a decomposition beyond the average wage by gender. Using data from the Senegalese national employment survey (ENES, 2015) and the harmonized survey on living conditions (EHCVM, 2021), the Oaxaca-Blinder decomposition method and the unconditional quantile regression method of Firpo et al. (2009) are used. In addition, this chapter provides an opportunity to strengthen the economic literature on the sources of gender disparities in the Senegalese labour market.

The first part presents the literature review on gender pay gaps. The second provides the methodology for the decomposition at the level of the average wage and at different levels of the wage distribution. The third section presents the results of the econometric estimation.

2 Gender Wage Gap, a Review of the Literature

From a theoretical perspective, several factors have been identified as sources of the gender pay gap in the labour market. Primarily, human capital theory explains it in terms of differences in qualifications. Indeed, human capital refers to a set of abilities and skills acquired and accumulated by individuals through education, training or experience that can affect their well-being through economic and non-economic spillovers (Psacharopoulos & Patrinos, 2018). So if you have less education or less work experience, it makes sense to be paid less. Disparities are also justified by differences in time allocation (Magnusson, 2010; Becker, 1985) and compensation for more arduous working conditions (Deleire & Levy, 2001; Rosen, 1986; England, 1982).

However, all these theories are not sufficient to justify the extent of persistent pay inequalities between men and women. It is within this framework that an unexplained difference in pay gives rise to a presumption of the presence of discriminatory practices in models of discrimination in the labour market. In a perfectly competitive market, discrimination is considered to be rooted in employers' prejudices. In this case, as a result of preconceptions and stereotypes, even with similar productive skills, pay inequalities are likely to persist as long as employers reward employees differently solely on the basis of their gender (Havet, 2004; Havet & Sofer, 2002; Becker, 1985).

Empirically, studies show that differences in individual characteristics related to productive capacities, such as education, play an important role in explaining wage differentials in the labour market (Kuépié et al., 2013; Livanos & Nunez, 2012). However, these factors do not fully explain wage differences between men and women. Indeed, the use of procedures to decompose the sources of the pay gap suggests that there is often a proportion that remains unexplained (Zhou & Nelson, 2017). This component of the decomposition is considered, in most cases, to be evidence of discriminatory practices in the labour market.

The Oaxaca-Blinder decomposition method (Oaxaca, 1973; Blinder, 1973) is the most common standard method for analysing the gender pay gap. This method applies a decomposition analysis limited to the mean of the wage distribution. Ntsama (2014) analysed gender pay gaps in Cameroon using the Oaxaca-Blinder decomposition following Heckman's two-stage approach to correct for selection bias. The results show that 49.4% of pay inequalities result from differences in individual characteristics between men and women. As a result, the share attributed to discrimination on the Cameroonian labour market is 50.6%. On the other hand, using the same methodological approach in the context of Madagascar, Nordman et al. (2010) find that gender differences in characteristics mainly explain pay disparities. In fact, they conclude that the best observed characteristics explain more than 60% of the wage gap in favour of men.

In the same vein, Comblon et al. (2017) show that in Cameroon and Mali differences in levels of education partly justify differences in participation and hourly wages in the labour market. Other studies in sub-Saharan Africa also demonstrate the importance of social considerations, which manifest themselves in a certain wage penalty for married women. This is particularly true for women with children, who spend much more time on unpaid domestic work (Comblon et al., 2017; Nwaka et al., 2016).

In addition to studies that have focused on analysing the sources of the wage gap on average, other authors have analysed the evolution of the wage gap at different levels of the distribution. Overall, the results suggest that the differences between men and women are marginal when they enter the labour market, but it is when they have to choose between work and family life that the differences become more pronounced.

In fact, the analyses indicate that the differences in pay stem from differences in reward for the same productive characteristics according to gender. And this result is all the more significant for the lowest and highest levels of wage distribution where the gender pay gap is widest. Ahmed and Macgillivray (2015) use the Oaxaca-Blinder decomposition and the Firpo et al. (2009) decomposition to examine the sources of the gender wage gap on average and at different levels of the wage distribution in Bangladesh. The decomposition at different quantile levels shows that the gender pay gap is highest at the lower distribution level and decreases significantly at the upper distribution level. For the sources of the pay gap, the decomposition highlights the fact that the share of discrimination is lower for the upper distribution. This is because, at the upper end of the pay distribution, men have better educational human capital endowments, which justifies their advantage in terms of pay.

This finding of a wage gap justified by better characteristics observed for men at the top of the wage distribution confirms the results previously obtained by Gardeazabal and Ugidos (2005) in Spain. Conversely, in studies of developed countries, Atencio and Posadas (2015) and Garcia et al. (2001) find that the unexplained component (discrimination) of this gap is higher at higher levels of the wage distribution. In this way, their analyses demonstrate the importance of observable characteristics linked to human capital in explaining wage differentials along the wage distribution.

In Senegal, the analysis of wage inequalities by gender focuses mainly on the disparity factors from the perspective of decomposing them at the level of the average wage distribution. Studies show that discrimination plays a major role in explaining gender pay inequalities.

Sall and Thiaw (2019) analysed the factors of wage inequality between men and women in Senegal, focusing on a segmentation based on qualification level. Using Heckman's approach, the results of the Oaxaca-Blinder decomposition show that, irrespective of the labour market segment considered, discrimination remains the main reason for wage differences between men and women. In fact, the proportion linked to discrimination against women is 94% for skilled workers, compared with 110% for unskilled workers. It is important to emphasize that in the latter segment, the fact that the female workforce has better characteristics should make it possible to reduce the wage differential by 10%. These results also confirm those previously obtained by Sall (2018), who carried out the same study with a segmentation of the Senegalese labour market by sector of activity. He found that 94% of the wage gap in the private sector is explained by discrimination, while in the public sector more than a third of the gap is explained by better characteristics for men.

Using a combination of microeconomic and macroeconomic data, Malta et al. (2019) analyse the impact of improved education on the labour market in Senegal. They show that between 2006 and 2011, the increase in the number of years of study of the working population and the reduction in the gender gap in education explain 44% of the growth in the employment ratio of women compared with men. On the other hand, 56% of the improvement in women's employment levels can be explained by a reduction in gender discrimination on the labour market. In addition, the reduction in gender discrimination should also lead to an improvement in women's wage gains and productivity levels of 4.7 percentage points.

As part of the decomposition of the sources of disparities in access to the best jobs in Cameroon, Mali and Senegal, Kuépié (2016), using an extension of the Oaxaca-Blinder method, focused on the role of these two characteristics: education and fertility. Breaking down the sources of the access gap indicates that, of these individual characteristics, education is the one that contributes most to explaining disparities. However, it is important to emphasize the major role of fertility in explaining inequalities. Following the decomposition, the comparative analysis between countries reveals that discrimination is the main source of disparities on the labour market, but this is more accentuated in Cameroon and Mali. In relative terms, differences in human capital endowment by gender account for almost 20% and 25% of the total gap in Cameroon and Mali respectively. In Senegal, differences in human capital endowment account for almost 40% of the gap. In Senegal, the two components are relatively better balanced than in the other two countries.

A fundamental common aspect that emerges from these studies in Senegal is that, beyond the significant role of differences in the human capital of women and men, social norms merit closer examination in order to understand other gender-based differences. Indeed, marital status is a key determinant of wage differentials through its potential impact on working hours and occupational choices in the labour market. In fact, social considerations mean that married women may be forced to devote more time to domestic work and, consequently, reduce their participation in the labour market. This could contribute to widening gender gaps in terms of working hours and monthly wages.

Despite these various studies in Senegal, there is still a knowledge gap, as analysis at different levels of the wage distribution remains unexploited. Indeed, the empirical evidence from the above studies focuses on analysis at the average level without taking account of the disparities that exist when we look at different quantiles.

3 Methodology

3.1 *Decomposition of Average Wage Gap Taking Account of Selection Bias*

The Oaxaca-Blinder decomposition based on non-random sample selection or on a sample reduced to workers runs the risk of being biased. One way of taking this selection bias problem into account is proposed by the two-stage procedure of Heckman (1979). This author considers that this sample selection problem could be understood as a specification error where a variable is omitted when establishing the wage equation. Heckman's procedure requires the estimation of a logistic regression in the first stage, to determine whether a person participates in the labour market, and then to calculate the "Mills ratio" for each individual.

In fact, the first step in Heckman's approach is to determine the probability of a person participating in labour market activities. The fact of being occupied or not in the labour market is expressed by:

$$y_g = \alpha_g Z_g + \varepsilon_g \{ \begin{matrix} = 1 \text{active} \\ = 0 \text{if not} \end{matrix}$$

With Z the individual and family characteristic factors of individuals i in group g = (male, female), the probability of participating in the labour market is written as follows:

$$\Pr\left(y_g > 0\right) = \Pr\left(\alpha_g Z_{ig} + \varepsilon_g > 0\right) = \Phi\left(\alpha_g Z_{ig}\right)$$

The inverse of the Mills ratio is given by:

$$\lambda_i = {\phi(Z_i)} \Big/ {(1-\Phi(Z_i))} \tag{14.1}$$

Where $\phi(.)$ is the normal density function; $\Phi(.)$ is the normal distribution function. It is this inverse of the Mills ratio (λ_i) that is added as an estimator to the wage equation, and subsequently the parameters can be estimated by ordinary least squares.

For the Heckman procedure, the inverse of the Mills ratio is introduced from the wage equations. Consequently, Mincer's payoff equations (Mincer, 1974) with correction for selection bias are expressed as follows:

$$W_h = \beta_h X_h + \rho_h \lambda_m + \varepsilon_m \tag{14.2}$$

$$W_f = \beta_f X_f + \rho_f \lambda_f + \varepsilon_f \tag{14.3}$$

With β the wage returns of the associated factor X, λ the inverse of the Mill ratio and ρ the associated coefficients which allow us to assess the existence or not of selection bias.

From Eqs. (14.2) and (14.3), the standard Oaxaca-Blinder decomposition with correction for selectivity can be written in the following form:

$$\overline{W_h} - \overline{W_f} = \underbrace{\left(\overline{X_h} - \overline{X_f}\right)\beta_h}_{\text{effect of productive characteristics}} + \underbrace{\left(\beta_h - \beta_f\right)\overline{X_f}}_{\text{effect of discrimination}} + \underbrace{\left(\widehat{\rho_h}\widehat{\lambda_h} - \widehat{\rho_f}\widehat{\lambda_f}\right)}_{\text{selectivity effect}} \tag{14.4}$$

With this equation, the wage structure for men is taken as the benchmark for the absence of discrimination.

3.2 *Breakdown of Wage Gap by Gender at Different Quantile Levels*

The use of average wage decomposition is fairly widespread, but it provides only partial information on gender pay differentials. In addition to an average decomposition, we can extend the study of pay differentials to the pay distribution. In fact, it is important to take into account different levels of the pay scale, as an analysis limited to the average does not allow us to assume that the situation between men and women is comparable. Another extension of the Oaxaca-Blinder approach is the use of the distributional approach based on quantile regressions. This approach allows an analysis of the gender pay gap adjusted for different points in the pay distribution. This is what is proposed by the unconditional quantile regression method of Firpo et al. (2009) or the RIF approach. The essential contribution of this method is that it allows us to breakdown pay differentials, making it possible to judge the situation at the bottom, middle and top of the gender pay distribution.

When we consider the qth percentile of the distribution, the gap between men and women is:

$$D(q) = c_h(q) - c_f(q) \tag{14.5}$$

With $c_h(q)$ and $c_f(q)$ the qth percentile in the sample for men and women (f) respectively.

As a first step, the Firpo et al. (2009, 2011) approach calculates the recentred influence function defined as:

$$RIF_{ji} = c(q) + \left[1(W)_i \geq c(q) - (1-q)\right] / f(c(q) \tag{14.6}$$

where $c(q)$ the qth percentile of the sample grouping men and women at this given level, $1(.)$ being a binary variable which takes the value 1 when the wage (in log) of individual i is greater than or equal to $c(q)$ and the value 0 otherwise, $f(c(q))$ corresponds to the density of the wage at the qth centile.

In a second step, OLS is used to estimate wage equations of the type:

$$W_h = \beta_h X_h + \varepsilon_h \text{and} W_f = \beta_f X_f + \varepsilon_f$$

We replace the dependent variable by its transformation into a recentred influence function and proceed with the Oaxaca–Blinder decomposition. The decomposition equation at different quantile levels (q) is written in the following form:

$$\underbrace{D(q)}_{\text{wage gap}} = \underbrace{\left(\overline{X_h} - \overline{X_f}\right)\widehat{\beta_h}(q)}_{\substack{\text{effect of the productive characteristics at} \\ q^{\text{th}} \text{ quantile}}} + \underbrace{\left(\widehat{\beta_h}(q) - \widehat{\beta_f}(q)\right)\overline{X_f}}_{\substack{\text{discrimination effect at} \\ \text{at } q^{\text{th}} \text{ quantile}}} \quad (14.7)$$

We present the decompositions at the 10th (lower distribution), 50th (intermediate level) and 90th (upper distribution) quantiles. Indeed, decomposing pay differentials at well-chosen quantiles could allow an overall appreciation of differences in the pay distribution (Boudarbat & Lemieux, 2014). In our study, we correct for selection bias at each quantile level considered. In addition, the choice of these quantile levels better meets the need for comparability between men and women, particularly at the lower and upper levels of their common distribution.

4 Data Sources and Descriptive Statistics

For econometric estimation purposes we use two surveys (2015 and 2021). The first one is the Senegal National Employment Survey (ENES, 2015) and the second is the harmonized survey on living conditions (EHCVM, 2021). We have 6000 individuals for the first and 4205 for the second. For the purposes of this chapter, the sample includes the population aged 15–59 engaged in any activity aimed at producing goods or services in exchange for remuneration. It is important to emphasize that the salaried employment to which the chapter refers concerns individuals who carry out an economic activity in return for payment of a wage. For this reason, in terms of wage aspects, we have excluded the category of self-employed individuals, employers and family workers. In fact, the self-employed and employers are in the "non-salaried employment" category, while family workers are unpaid.

The descriptive statistics provide information on the differences in characteristics and wages between men and women in our sample. For example, if we consider the 2015 survey that is specially dedicated to employment, we can notice that there are more women in urban areas, but men are more likely to be heads of household. In terms of education, the gap in favour of men widens from secondary level onwards. Men invest more in training to improve their human capital. It should also be noted that men have more stable jobs (permanent contracts) than women. In addition to higher participation in the labour market, men are, on average, better paid than women, FCFA 244,634 (€373) compared with FCFA

202,666 (€309). Salaries increase with the level of education for both men and women. It should also be noted that according to level of education, the smallest gender pay gap is observed among those with a university degree. Overall, the exploratory analysis of pay levels reveals a pay gap in favour of men, whatever the characteristic selected.

5 Results

As part of the wage decomposition, we carry out an analysis at the average level and according to different wage quantiles. These different approaches will make it possible to account for the role of differences in productive characteristics and/or differences in treatment based on gender in explaining the gender pay gap.

5.1 *Decomposition at the Average Level*

Analysis of wage levels at the average level reveals a gap (in logarithm) of 0.3983 in favour of men in 2015 and a gap of 0.254 in 2021. This means that men earned almost 39% more than women in paid employment in 2015 and 25% more in 2021.

In 2015, differences linked to productive characteristics account for 0.1786, while differences in valuation for similar characteristics account for 0.2197. In relative terms, the wage gap that can be attributed to differences in individual characteristics is equivalent to 45% (i.e. (0.1786/0.3983)*100) of the wage differences between men and women on the labour market. On the other hand, 55% (i.e. (0.2197/0.3983)*100) of this wage difference remains linked to differences in rewards or valuation for same characteristics (Table 14.1).

In 2021, the component explained by differences in individual characteristics (*Explained*) (0.153 out of the 0.254) represents 60.24% of the overall wage gap while the discrimination represents 39.76% (Table 14.2).

It is this last component that points to the existence of gender-based wage discrimination on the labour market. These results show that equal treatment for similar characteristics should make it possible to eliminate 55% of the gender pay gap on the labour market in 2015 and 40% in 2021. Conversely, 45% of this gap is simply a reflection of better productive characteristics for men (in 2015) and 60% in 2021.

When we look at the analysis by explanatory variable, the results of the estimates carried out with correction for selection bias reveal a variety of

Table 14.1 Oaxaca-Blinder decomposition of wage gap, 2015

	Wage decomposition		
Variables	*Total*	*Explained*	*Unexplained*
Prediction_1 [men]	10.733***(0.0128)		
Prediction _2 [women]	10.335***(0.0174)		
Difference	**0.3983***(0.0216)**	**0.1786***(0.01578)**	**0.2197***(0.01606)**
Residence		−0.024***(0.00586)	0.009***(0.00276)
Head of household		0.042***(0.00613)	0.018(0.09938)
Married		−0.018***(0.00241)	0.058***(0.01156)
Age		0.058*(0.02976)	0.047***(0.01684)
Age2		0.008(0.00530)	−0.035**(0.01534)
Education		0.018***(0.00241)	0.051***(0.01321)
Training		0.025***(0.00554)	−0.013(0.01306)
Handicap		−0.0009*(0.000469)	0.008***(0.00217)
Trade union membership		0.017**(0.00364)	0.018*(0.00978)
Open-ended contract		0.045***(0.00477)	−0.034(0.06313)
Selectivity		0.008***(0.00257)	0.021***(0.00442)
Constant			0.071**(0.03248)

Note: Standard errors in parentheses. * $p < 0.1$, ** $p < 0.05$, and *** $p < 0.01$

Source: Authors' calculation using ENES (2015)

roles for both the "explained or justified" and "unexplained or unjustified" components. "Explained" refers to the possibility that part of the gap can be justified by differences in characteristics, whereas "unexplained" refers to the existence of different, and therefore unjustified, rewards for the same characteristic. Given that we are talking about a difference in pay gain for a characteristic, all other things being equal, we can speak of an advantage or disadvantage of one group over another.

In terms of people's place of residence, the fact that there are more women in urban areas should give them a certain advantage. However, the relatively low level of discrimination favours men. The discrimination against women could be explained, in part, by the fact that in urban areas the female workforce is still confined to low-wage activities.

The results show that the fact that men are more often 'heads of household' helps to justify their advantage. Since the discrimination component

Table 14.2 Oaxaca-Blinder decomposition of wage gap, 2021

	(1)	*(2)*
Variables	*Differential*	*Decomposition*
Prediction_1	6.430***(0.0224)	
Prediction_2	6.177***(0.0354)	
Difference	0.254***(0.0419)	
Explained		0.153*** (0.0477)
Unexplained_1		0 (0.000536)
Unexplained_2		0.101*(0.0555)
Observations	4.205	4.205

Note: Standard errors in parentheses. * $p < 0.1$, ** $p < 0.05$, and *** $p < 0.01$

Source: Authors' calculation using EHCVM (2021)

is insignificant for the status of head of household, only the component of differences in characteristics justifies a higher wage level for men.

For the marital status of individuals with identical "married" status, discrimination in favour of men strongly explains their pay advantage. These results reflect the fact that women continue to face discriminatory practices when it comes to the social role factors associated with marriage. Indeed, the theories of statistical discrimination (Cain, 1986) help to justify this result in that women may be confronted with a priori judgements or stereotypes. A priori judgements and stereotypes can take the form of considerations linked to their attachment to the labour market or their exposure to interruptions in their activity. These considerations can lead to married women being undervalued in terms of pay, unlike men who benefit from better prejudices.

In relation to age, the proxy for potential experience, the results indicate that an advantage for men can be attributed to the fact that they are more experienced. But even at similar levels of experience, men are better rewarded. On the other hand, if we analyse age and its quadratic form together, we see that women are discriminated against for the first few years of experience, but as they accumulate more, they become progressively better rewarded. This situation can be explained by the fact that the more experience they acquire, the more unfavourable prejudices against them fade. As a result, they are able to obtain jobs previously reserved for men, and therefore better salaries.

As far as education is concerned, we can see that the gap attributable to differences in levels of education is to men's advantage. What's more, for the same level of education, men earn more than women. So, even if there is a proportion of the gap that can be justified by education levels that are more favourable to men, it is the difference in rewards for education based on gender that is more important. Such results pointing to discrimination confirm the findings of Ahmed and Macgillivray (2015).

With regard to vocational training, only the component of the pay gap that can be explained by differences in training is significant. The results show that the predominance of men who have completed vocational training mainly justifies their pay advantage. On the other hand, for individuals with disabilities, the slight advantage for men is due more to differences in salary treatment based on gender.

In terms of trade union membership, men should have an advantage because they are more represented in union activism. In addition, there is discrimination, which can be explained by the higher salaries paid to male union leaders in order to prevent workers from going on strike.

As far as individuals with permanent contracts are concerned, the pay gap is mainly explained by the fact that men are more likely to have this type of contract. Given that the discrimination component is insignificant, we cannot consider the existence of unequal treatment for men and women with permanent contracts.

It can be seen that correcting for selection bias increases both the proportion of the pay gap due to differences in individual characteristics and the proportion due to discrimination in favour of men.

The wage gap (in log) is 0.254. The explained difference is 60.24%. For the unexplained component (potentially linked to discrimination), the results show two aspects: discrimination in favour of men (unexplained_1) statistically insignificant and coefficient = 0 and discrimination against women (unexplained_2) of 0.101, which represents 39.76%.

Comparing Table 14.1 to Table 14.2 allows us to conclude that wage discrimination against women has decreased between 2015 to 2021.

5.2 *Decomposition at the Level of the Wage Distribution*

The decomposition of Firpo et al. (2009) has the advantage of providing wage differentials at different levels of the wage distribution. We will focus on the bottom 10% of wages (Q10), the median (Q50) and the top 10%

Table 14.3 Decomposition of the wage distribution at different levels

	Decomposition by quantile (q)		
Variables	*q = 0.10*	*q = 0.50*	*q = 0.90*
Total gap	**0.194*****(0.01684)	**0.401*****(0.03473)	**0.102*****(0.00913)
Explained	**0.069****(0.026168)	**0.184*****(0.04149)	**0.063*****(0.0155)
Unexplained	**0.125*****(0.01211)	**0.217*****(0.01739)	**0.039*****(0.00387)

Note: Standard errors in parentheses. * $p < 0.1$, ** $p < 0.05$, and *** $p < 0.01$

Source: Authors' calculation

of wages (Q90). Since the 2015 survey is more complete, the analysis focused on this survey for the wage distribution.

For the bottom 10% of salary levels, differences in gender characteristics explain 36% (i.e. (0.069/0.196)) of the salary gap. Discrimination in favour of men accounts for 64% (i.e. (0.125/0.194)) of the total gender pay gap. For the median of the pay distribution, 46% of this gap is due to differences in characteristics, compared with 54% due to discrimination. At the top 10% of the salary distribution, 62% of this gap is explained by differences in characteristics between men and women. Differences in valuation for similar characteristics account for 38% of the gender wage gap.

By following the evolution of the total wage gap, we see that from the level below to the median of the pay distribution, the gap increases before decreasing at the level of the upper distribution. In fact, we go from a wage gap of 21.4% in favour of men for the lower distribution to a gap of 49.3% for the median, then to a gap of 10.7% for the upper distribution. These results show that it is in the intermediate pay categories that pay disparities are most marked. The other aspect is that the gender pay gap becomes less pronounced when we focus on individuals in the top wage distribution. As for the component of the gap relating to differences in characteristics, this increases along the wage distributions considered (Table 14.3).

6 Conclusion

Gender mainstreaming in the labour market remains an ongoing issue. In Senegal, despite several labour market studies, there is still a knowledge gap regarding the role of gender differences in terms of wage disparities. The aim of this chapter was to examine the sources of gender-based wage disparities in the Senegalese labour market. We conducted a linear decomposition of the wage gaps on average and at different levels of the wage quantile using data from the 2015 Senegal National Employment Survey.

The gender wage gap decomposition was performed at the average level (Oaxaca-Blinder approach) and at different levels of the wage distribution (Firpo-Fortin-Lemieux approach). At the average level, the results indicate that wage discrimination against women has decreased between 2015 and 2021. In fact, in 2015, 45% of the wage gap is due to differences in individual characteristics and 55% to discrimination while in 2021, 60.24% of the wage gap can be explained by differences in productive characteristics and 39.76% by gender-based pay disparities (discrimination).

In other words, with equal pay in the labour market, 55% of the gender pay gap in 2015 should disappear and in 2021, 39.76% of this gap should disappear. On the other hand, a justifiable pay gap of 45% in favour of men should persist in 2015 and a proportion of 60.24% should persist in 2021. This is because men have better productive characteristics in terms of experience, education and training, which should give them a certain pay advantage. At the same time, the results show that for an identical level of human capital, men are better valued in terms of pay.

Given that an average analysis can hide disparities, we conducted the analysis at different levels of distribution for the more complete dataset, the national survey on employment (2015). It reveals the gender pay gap at the bottom 10% of salaries, the median and the top 10% of salaries. For the lowest salary levels, differences in gender characteristics account for 36% and potential discrimination for 64% of the total gender pay gap. For the median of the distribution, 46% of the gap results from differences in characteristics and 54% from discrimination. At the upper end of the pay distribution, 62% of the gap is explained by differences in characteristics and discrimination accounts for 38%. These results show that discriminatory practices diminish along the wage distribution, while the share of differences in characteristics in explaining the wage gap gradually increases.

In addition, it is also found that beyond the fact that men have an overall advantage in terms of human capital endowments, women are disadvantaged in terms of wage gains. Following on from these results, some economic policy implications can be formulated.

Firstly, better regulation of the labour market to combat stereotyping of women would make it possible to demand equal pay for similar productive capacities. These policies are more likely to be implemented in jobs offering wages at the lower and intermediate levels of the distribution. Secondly, better use of collective agreements with trade unions and the promotion of workers with permanent contracts for a certain period could eradicate gender pay gaps not linked to differences in productive characteristics.

Taking other aspects into account, such as the evolution of gender disparities over several survey periods, could make it possible to analyse the evolution of discriminatory practices in Senegal.

Conflicts of Interest The authors have no conflicts of interest to declare that are relevant to the content of this chapter.

References

Ahmed, S., & Macgillivray, M. (2015). Human Capital, Discrimination, and the Gender Wage Gap in Bangladesh. *World Development, 67*, 506–524. https://doi.org/10.1016/j.worlddev.2014.10.017

Atencio, A., & Posadas, J. (2015). *Gender Gap in Pay in the Russian Federation: Twenty Years Later, Still a Concern.* World Bank Policy Research Paper n° 7407. https://ssrn.com/abstract=2652545

Becker, G. S. (1985). Human Capital, Effort and Sexual Division of Labor. *Journal of Labor Economics*, 3, 33–58. http://links.jstor.org/sici?sici=0734-306X%2819850 ... O%3B2-E&origin=repec

Blau, F. D., & Kahn, L. M. (2017). The Gender Wage Gap: Extent, Trends, and Explanations. *Journal of Economic Literature, 55*(3), 789–865. https://doi.org/10.1257/jel.20160995

Blinder, A. S. (1973). Wage Discrimination, Reduced Form and Structural Estimates. *The Journal of Human Resources, 8*(4), 436–455. http://www.jstor.org/stable/144855

Boudarbat, B., & Lemieux, T. (2014). Why Are the Relative Wages of Immigrants Declining? A Distributional Approach. *International Labour Review, 67*(4), 1127–1165. https://doi.org/10.1177/0019793914546298

Cain, G. G. (1986). The Economic Analysis of Labor Market Discrimination: A Survey. In O. C. Ashenfelter & R. Layard (Éds.), *Handbook of Labor Economics* (Vol. 1, pp. 693–785). Elsevier/North Holland. https://doi.org/10.1016/S1573-4463(86)01016-7

Camara, F. K. (2012). Quelles sont les vraies raisons de l'exclusion des femmes. In F. Sarr (Ed.), *La Parité: Enjeux et défis dans le contexte sénégalais* (pp. 13–22). IFAN.

Comblon, V., Robilliard, A.-S., & Roubaud, F. (2017). Gender Analysis of Labour Market Outcomes in Sub-Saharan African: Recent Evidence from Cameroon and Mali. *UN Women Discussion Paper, 16*, 1–46. https://www.unwomen.org/sites/default/files/Headquarters/Attachments/Sections/Library/Publications/2017/Gender-analysis-of-labour-market-outcomes-in-sub-Saharan-Africa-en.pdf

Deleire, T., & Levy, H. (2001). Gender, Occupation Choice and the Risk of Death at Work. *NBER Working Papers, 8574*, 1–32. https://doi.org/10.3386/w8574. https://www.nber.org/papers/w8574

England, P. (1982). The Failure of Human Capital Theory to Explain Occupational Sex Segregation. *Journal of Human Resources, 17*(3), 358–370. http://www.jstor.org/stable/pdfplus/145585

Enquête nationale sur l'emploi au Sénégal / ENES. (2015). Rapport Définitif, ANSD, Dakar/Sénégal, 114 p. https://anads.ansd.sn/index.php/catalog/92/download/1255

Enquête nationale sur l'emploi au Sénégal, 4 trimestre 2017. (ENES Q4-2017). Note d'informations, ANSD, Dakar/Sénégal, 6 p. https://anads.ansd.sn/index.php/catalog/211/download/1798

Enquête sur l'emploi, a la rémunération et les heures de travail / EERH. (2018). ANSD, Rapport annuel, 8 p. https://www.ansd.sn/sites/default/files/2022-11/Rapport%20EERH_2018_VF.pdf

Enquête harmonisée sur les conditions de vie des ménages au Sénégal / EHCVM. (2021). ANSD. Final report, July 2024, WAEMU, World Bank. https://www.ansd.sn/sites/default/files/2024-07/Rapport_Final_EHCVM_2021-2022_VF.pdf

Enquête nationale sur l'emploi au Sénégal, 4e trimestre 2022. (ENES Q4-2022). Note d'informations. ANSD, Dakar/Sénégal, 9 p. https://anads.ansd.sn/index.php/catalog/281/download/2463

Firpo, S., Fortin, N., & Lemieux, T. (2009). Unconditional Quantile Regressions. *Econometrica, 77*(3), 953–973. https://www.jstor.org/stable/40263848

Firpo, S., Fortin, N. & Lemieux, T. (2011). Decomposition Methods in Economics. In O. Ashenfelter & D. Card (Eds), *Handbook of Labor Economics* (Vol. 4; Part A, pp. 1-102). Elsevier. https://doi.org/10.1016/S0169-7218(11)00407-2

Fongang, D. (2014). Narrating Fatherhood and Masculinities in Senegal: The Case of Naffissatou Diallo in A Dakar Childhood. *Spectrum: A Journal on Black Men, 3*(1), 25–48. https://www.jstor.org/stable/10.2979/spectrum.3.1.25

Garcia, J., Hernandez, P. J., & Lopez-Nicolas, A. (2001). How Wide Is the Gap? An Investigation of Gender Wage Differences Using Quantile Regression. *Empirical Economics, 26*(1), 149–167. https://doi.org/10.1007/s001810000050

Gardeazabal, J., & Ugidos, A. (2005). Gender Wage Discrimination at Quantiles. *Journal of Population Economics, 18*, 165–179. https://www.jstor.org/stable/20007949

Havet, N. (2004). Écarts salariaux et disparités professionnelles entre sexes: Développements théoriques et validité empirique. *L'Actualité économique, 80*(1), 5–39. https://doi.org/10.7202/010752ar

Havet, N., & Sofer, C. (2002). Les nouvelles théories économiques de la discrimination. *Travail, Genre et Sociétés, 7*, 83–115. https://doi.org/10.3917/tgs.007.0083

Heckman, J. (1979). Sample Selection Bias as a Specification Error. *Econometrica, 47*(1), 153–161. https://doi.org/10.2307/1912352

Kane, A. (2014). Dynamique de l'emploi au Sénégal: Un suivi de cohortes sur la période 1992–2011. *Revue d'économie du développement, 22*, 75–105. https://shs.cairn.info/revue-d-economie-du-developpement-2014-1-page-75?lang=fr&tab=texte-integral

Kane, O., & Kane, H. (2018). The Origins of the Feminist Movement in Senegal: A Social History of the Pioneering Yewwu-Yewwi. *African Sociological Review, 22*(1), 18–30. https://www.ajol.info/index.php/asr/article/view/175837/165260

Kuépié, M. (2016). Determinants of Labour Market Gender Inequalities in Cameroon, Senegal and Mali: The Role of Human Capital and Fertility Burden. *Canadian Journal of Development Studies/Revue canadienne d'études du développement, 37*(1), 66–82. https://doi.org/10.1080/02255189.2016.1122580

Kuépié, M., Nordman, C., & Roubaud F. (2013). Éducation et marché du travail. In P. De Vreyer & F. Roubaud (Éds.), *Les marchés urbains du travail en Afrique subsaharienne* (pp. 177–200). IRD, AFD. ISBN 978-2-7099-1736-0. https://horizon.documentation.ird.fr/exl-doc/pleins_textes/divers16-08/010059080.pdf

Livanos, I., & Nunez, I. (2012). The Effect of Higher Education on the Gender Wage Gap. *International Journal Education Economics and Development, 3*(1), 33–47. https://doi.org/10.1504/IJEED.2012.044952

Magnusson, C. (2010). Why Is There a Gender Wage Gap According to Occupational Prestige?: An Analysis of the Gender Wage Gap by Occupational Prestige and Family obligation in Sweden. *Acta Sociologica, 53*(2), 99–117. https://www.jstor.org/stable/20743776

Malta, V., Leyva, A. M., & Tavares, M. (2019). *A Quantitative Analysis of Female Employment in Senegal*. IMF Working Paper WP/10/241, 1–29. https://ssrn.com/abstract=3496717

Mincer, J. A. (1974). *The Human Capital Earnings Function* (pp. 41–63). National Bureau of Economic Research. https://www.nber.org/system/files/chapters/c1767/c1767.pdf

Mincer, J., & Polachek, S. (1974). Family Investments in Human Capital: Earnings of Women. *Journal of Political Economy, 82*(2), 76–108. https://doi.org/10.1086/260293

Nordman, C. J., Rakotomanana, F., & Robilliard, A. S. (2010). Gender Disparities in the Malagasy Labor Market. In J. S. Arbache, A. Kolev, & E. Filipiak (Éds.), *Gender Disparities in Africa's Labor Market* (pp. 87–154). AFD and World Bank, Africa Development Forum. https://openknowledge.worldbank.org/bitstream/handle/10986/2520/9780821380666.pdf

Ntsama, E. S. (2014). Les écarts salariaux de genre au Cameroun. *Revue multidisciplinaire sur l'emploi, le syndicalisme et le travail, 9*(2), 124–146. https://doi.org/10.7202/1036261ar

Nwaka, I. D., Guven-Lisaniler, F., & Tuna, G. (2016). Gender Wage Differences in Nigerian Self and Paid Employment: Do Marriage and Children Matter? *The Economic and Labour Relations Review, 27*(4), 490–510. https://doi.org/10.1177/1035304616677655

Oaxaca, R. (1973). Male-Female Wage Differentials in Urban Labor Markets. *International Economic Review, 14*(3), 693–709. https://www.jstor.org/stable/2525981

Petrongolo, B. (2019). The Gender Gap in Employment and Wages. *Nature Human Behaviour, 3*(1), 316–318. https://doi.org/10.1038/s41562-019-0558-x

Psacharopoulos, G., & Patrinos, H. A. (2018). Returns to Investment in Education: A Decennial Review of the Global Literature. *Education Economics, 6*(5), 445–458. https://doi.org/10.1080/09645292.2018.1484426

Rosen, S. (1986). The Theory of Equalizing Differences. In O. Ashenfelter & R. Layard (Eds.), *Handbook of Labor Economics* (Vol. 1, pp. 641–692). Elsevier. https://doi.org/10.1016/S1573-4463(86)01015-5

Sall, M. C. A. (2018). Disparités salariales et genre sur le marché du travail au Sénégal. *Revue d'Économie et de Gestion, 2*(2), 1–19. https://asjp.cerist.dz/en/article/77854

Sall, M. C. A., & Thiaw, M. (2019). Human Capital, Gender and Labor Market in Senegal. *TIJRP-Research Journal of Economics & Business Studies, 8*(9), 1–11. https://typeset.io/papers/human-capital-gender-and-the-labor-market-in-senegal-1n8rx3ycf3

Tøraasen, M. (2019). Gender Parity and the Symbolic Representation of Women in Senegal. *The Journal of Modern African Studies, 57*(3), 459–481. https://doi.org/10.1017/S0022278X19000272

World Economic Forum. (2023). The Global Gender Gap Report. Insight Report, Geneva/Switzerland, June 2023. https://www3.weforum.org/docs/WEF_GGGR_2023.pdf

Zhou, M., & Nelson, R. G. (2017). Gender Wage Gap and Discrimination in Developing Countries. *Southern Agricultural Economics, 49*(4), 1–27. https://doi.org/10.22004/ag.econ.252727

CHAPTER 15

The Evolution of the Gender Pay Gap in Cameroon

Sabine Nadine Ekamena Ntsama

1 Introduction

Labour-market challenges are becoming an important issue for development policies. The extent of unemployment, the prevalence of precarious and low-productivity jobs, the size of the informal sector, and the high number of working poor, as well as questions related to higher gender disparities, are the most striking of the labour-market characteristics in the developing countries. In addition to the negative effects of the COVID-19 pandemic since 2020 on the national economy, the security challenges imposed by the Islamist sect Boko-Haram since 2014 and the secessionist aspirations in the North-West and South-West regions since 2016 have weighed heavily on employment. Cameroon has an unemployment rate of 3.3%. The informal sector employs the largest number of workers. With a low rate of salaried employment (6 workers out of 100), this sector employs more women (85.1%) than men (70.6%). The average income of

S. N. Ekamena Ntsama (✉)
University of Maroua, Maroua, Cameroon
e-mail: nadia_ekamena@yahoo.fr

M.-P. Chelini et al. (eds.), *Wage Dynamics in Africa*, African Histories and Modernities,
https://doi.org/10.1007/978-3-031-99800-3_15

workers in the informal sector is €126.69 per month, higher than the Guaranteed Interprofessional Minimum Wage set at €66.78 (NSI, 2022).

The wage gap is the difference in pay between individuals in the labour market. The literature on this subject focuses on the empirical validity of the theories and, in particular, on their relevance to the stylised facts characterising current labour markets. This difference may be due to endogenous factors such as human capital, place of residence, and marital status and exogenous factors from the demand side (Becker's tastes-driven theory or Phelps statistical discrimination theory) all of which may differentially influence the labour-force participation of women and men and/or the discrimination against them (Anker, 1997; Baye et al., 2016; Blau & Kahn, 2017; Doumbia & Meurs, 2003; Ekamena, 2014). These differentials can be observed, for example, between rural and urban workers, between those in the primary and secondary sectors, or between the formal and informal sectors. They may also exist within the primary sector between employees of two different branches.

Women are increasingly present in the labour market all over the world. However, they are still generally disadvantaged compared with men: in most countries, they are still in the majority among unpaid workers, those in precarious jobs, and those who have given up looking for work. According to the International Labour Organisation (ILO) (2019), women will continue to be paid, on average, 20% less than men all over the world. In Africa, the gender pay gap is narrowing (Namibia, Cabo-Verde), while in other countries it is staying the same or increasing (Sierra Leone, the Gambia, Egypt, South Africa). In Cameroon, labour-market indicators show significant disparities (NSI, 2012a, 2012b, 2012c). Women tend to be over-represented in low-wage jobs and especially in the informal agricultural sector where returns and farm incomes are lower. Indeed, in 2010, 93.8% of women worked in the informal sector,[1] compared with 87.5% of men (NSI, 2010, 2012a, 2012b, 2012c; ILO, 2017).

The female population is the majority in the tertiary sector (services and trade) compared with the secondary and primary sectors. In general, women are poorly represented in the liberal professions, particularly in the

[1] "The informal sector can be broadly described as a set of units producing goods or services with the primary aim of creating jobs and income for the people concerned. These units have a low level of organisation, operate on a small scale and in a specific way, with little or no division between labour and capital as factors of production. Employment relationships—where they exist—are based mainly on casual employment, kinship ties or personal and social relationships rather than on contractual agreements with proper guarantees." (ILO, 2013)

professions of lawyer, bailiff, doctor, or chartered accountant (Ministry of Women Empowerment and the Family, 2012). In Cameroon, it should be noted that the representation of women in construction and public works, or transport and repair, does not reach 4% of the workforce. They are largely represented in garment manufacturing (84.4%), catering (75.1%), food processing (70.6%), and retail trade (54.8%) (NSI, 2012a, 2012b, 2012c). Yet, according to the ILO (2017), informal employment is heavily concentrated in the service sector.

Progress in occupational equality in the labour market is reflected in the proportion of women in higher professional positions. In 2020, there were 8 women ministers and 3 women secretaries of state in the government out of 70, 7 women out of 60 in 2012. It should be noted that these women are not heads of strategic ministries such as finance, justice, economy, or defence. Today, 61 out of 180 members of parliament are women, compared with 25 out of 180 in 2002, and are under-represented in senior positions (NSI, 2012a, 2012b, 2012c). Despite this progress over the years, the place of women in senior positions of responsibility remains limited and the gender pay gap is still felt. With regard to gender inequality in the labour market, the World Economic Forum report (2017) ranks Cameroon 87th out of the 144 countries considered. This position is justified on the one hand by the fact that 88% of all women are active on the labour market and, in similar jobs, a woman earns on average 67% of a man's salary on the other.

In rural areas, gender inequalities are widespread in the labour market, with men and women often working in different combinations of employment, as self-employed farmers, seasonal workers, or unpaid family labourers. Rural women continue to face a penalty due to the invisibility of their work in the home economy. They are heavily involved in domestic and reproductive functions, which are crucial to the upkeep of households, families, parents, and communities, but this is seen as an extension of family duties, which explains why this important part is economically invisible. In Cameroon, women are among the population's vulnerable groups. As such, the government and the international community pay particular attention to their situation, including ensuring protection of their rights. However, according to Cameroonian data, there is still limited access of women to certain jobs, leading to the persistence of gender wage gaps.

The aim of this study is to characterise the evolution of the pay gap between men and women in the labour market from 2001 to 2014. The issue is to determine in which way the gaps reflect discrimination and how this phenomenon evolved in prior years. The model we use in this study is an extension of the Oaxaca-Blinder decomposition, developed by Neuman and Oaxaca (1998). This model corrects the selection of bias problem due to the fact that only employed individuals have a wage. The database we will use to develop our work is drawn from the second, third, and fourth Cameroon Household Surveys (ECAM). These surveys were conducted in Cameroon by the National Institute of Statistics (NSI) in 2001, 2007, and 2014. This study will have four sections. Following the introduction, the second section will survey the theoretical contributions, the third section will be devoted to the methodology, and the fourth section will present the results.

2 Review of the Literature

Following the human capital theory, wage differences reflect differences in the productivity of individuals, which itself reflects differences in investment in human capital (Becker, 1964). This theoretical framework predicts that women, anticipating that their family responsibilities will not allow them to offer as many hours of work as men, invest less than men in their training; the resulting gap would thus explain the wage inequality (Mincer & Polachek, 1974). Occupational choice theory, linked to human capital theory, states that women tend to "choose" jobs and sectors which require less human capital investment and where career breaks are penalised less. This theory thus explains the differences in the labour-market position of men and women by the traditional division of household tasks. Women are likely not only to work for shorter periods, but also to move into different, lower-productivity jobs and sectors.

On the other hand, a given level of human capital will not yield the same return regardless of the job held. Furthermore, the "quantitative" education gap is expected to reduce the wage gap as women's education levels catch up with those of men. Nevertheless, a more qualitative view of training would take into account the specialities of educational courses and diplomas; from this point of view, the differences remain significant (Meurs & Ponthieux, 2006).

The gender pay gaps also depend on the wage structure of the country concerned. According to human capital theory, men and women have different endowments in terms of education and experience and are in different jobs in different sectors. Ceteris paribus, when the returns to human capital increase, the gender wage gap enlarges. The wage structure is determined by many factors, of which the wage bargaining structure is the most important. Centralised bargaining allows for the reduction of gender pay gaps (Blau & Kahn, 1999).

The theory of compensating wage differentials also makes it possible to explain wage differences. This is part of the neo-classical approach and states the preferences of workers and the type of job they do, taking into account the monetary or non-monetary compensations offered (Anker, 1997). Rosen (1986) considers atypical working hours, which should theoretically lead to compensating differences, as difficult working conditions. Atypical working hours include staggered hours, alternating groups, night work, and long days, including weekend work. The results of his study suggest that workers do not choose non-standard hours for reasons of preference. On the contrary, they all seem to want normal hours, but there is a compensating wage difference that positively influences the acceptance of non-standard hours. In the labour market, women tend to choose jobs in safe and pleasant environments. Compared with men, there are fewer women in manual work, in jobs performed outdoors, or in jobs that require considerable physical effort. According to the theory of compensating differences, wage differentials between men and women arise because of gender differences in terms of preferences for working conditions. The feared risks include accidents at work or death. It is assumed that women are more risk averse than men are and therefore prefer jobs with less risk of injury, accident, or death (Hersch, 2006).

Discriminatory behaviours also influence the labour market to a large extent and often contribute to wage differentials. Becker (1957/1971) designs a specific theoretical framework in which the wage is fixed by the conditions of competition and by measures of productivity. Productivity, on the other hand, is determined by the set of human capital variables of individuals (preferences, abilities, training, work experience, age, etc.). In the absence of any discrimination, wage differences measure differences in productivity or in individual characteristics related to production. In this framework, two individuals who differ at the level of characteristics unrelated to production (skin colour, gender), but who are perfectly substitutable in the production process, should receive identical wages since they have the same productivity. A discriminatory attitude towards one of them may result in a wage differential. Hence the definition of discrimination (equal productivity, unequal pay) and its measurement—the difference between the ratio of observed male to female wages is that which would prevail in the absence of discrimination (Becker, 1957/1971).

The statistical discrimination hypothesis also helps to explain the persistence of discrimination in the labour market. Statistical discrimination against individuals in a group on the labour market occurs when they are disadvantaged because they possess characteristics that tend to be statistically correlated with economic characteristics that are devalued by employers. Phelps (1972) shows that each employee's basic pay is that of the average employee, with a supplement or reduction depending on whether his or her productivity is assumed to be above or below average. The more reliable the signal, the more employers take it into account when setting wages, and the more they individualise their remuneration by deviating from the basic figure. As errors in measuring productivity are more common among women than men, employers take less account of the individual productivity signal when determining women's salaries. As a result, men and women will receive different pay for equivalent productivity signals.

3 Methodology

To explain the observed wage differentials according to gender, we use an extension of Oaxaca-Blinder decomposition methods (Blinder, 1973; Oaxaca, 1973). These wage difference methods allow us to neutralise those factors resulting from the socio-economic differences between employees and to distinguish them from what is due to discrimination. However, we face the problem of a possible selection bias due to the fact that only employed individuals have a wage. The wage equation will be estimated by the Heckman (1979) method in two steps. This method is based on the estimation of a selection equation by a probit model determining a correction term known as the inverse of the Mills ratio. This term is introduced into the wage equation, which is then estimated by Ordinary Least Squares (OLS).

The model we use is an extension of the Oaxaca-Blinder decomposition developed by Neuman and Oaxaca (1998, 2004). It consists of a system of two equations—the labour-market participation equation and the wage equation—as follows:

$$\begin{aligned} V_{ij} &= \alpha_j Z_{ij} + \varepsilon_{ij} \\ W_{ij} &= \beta_j X_{ij} + \mu_{ij} \end{aligned} \tag{15.1}$$

Z_{ij} is the vector of explanatory variables of the labour-market participation of an individual i of group j with $j = h, f$, W_{ij} is the log wage in the labour market of individual i of group j, V_{ij} is the variable of the labour-market participation of individual i of sex j; it is a dummy variable as follows:

$$V_{ij} = \begin{cases} 1 \text{ } if \text{ } V_{ij} = \alpha_i Z_{ij} + \varepsilon_{ij} > 0 \\ 0 \quad \text{otherwise} \end{cases}. \tag{15.2}$$

X_{ij} is the vector of labour-market wage determiners, α_j and β_j are the vectors of the associated parameters, ε_{ij} and μ_{ij} are independently identically distributed error terms (i.i.d.) following a bivariate normal distribution.

The probability of having a job is expressed as follows:

$$P_{ij} = \text{prob}\left(V_{ij} > 0\right) \tag{15.3}$$

Wages are observed for those whose $V_{ij} > 0$. The expected wage of the working individual is therefore written:

$$E\left(W_{ij} / V_{ij} > 0\right) = \beta_j X_{ij} + E\left(\mu_{ij} / \varepsilon_{ij} > -\alpha_j Z_{ij}\right) \Leftrightarrow E\left(W_{ij} / V_{ij} > 0\right) = \beta_j X_{ij} + \theta_j \lambda_{ij} \tag{15.4}$$

Where $\theta_j = \rho_j \sigma_{\varepsilon_j}$, $\phi(.)$ is the density function of a normal distribution and $\lambda_{ij} = \phi(\beta_j X_{ij}) / \Phi(\beta_j X_{ij})$ is the inverse of the Mills ratio.

The equation to be estimated for individuals who are employed becomes:

$$W_{ij} / V_{ij} > 0 = \beta_j X_{ij} + \theta_j \lambda_{ij} + \text{error} \tag{15.5}$$

The Eq. (15.5) is estimated by the Heckman procedure for women and men. Correcting for selection bias requires the decomposition of wages as follows:

$$\overline{W}_h - \overline{W}_f = \overline{X}_h \beta_h - \overline{X}_f \beta_f + \left(\hat{\theta}_h \hat{\lambda}_h - \hat{\theta}_f \hat{\lambda}_f\right) \tag{15.6}$$

If we subtract and add $\bar{X}_h\beta^*$ and $\bar{X}_f\beta^*$ in Eq. (15.6), rearranging, we get:

$$\bar{W}_h - \bar{W}_f = \bar{X}_h\left(\hat{\beta}_h - \hat{\beta}^*\right) + \bar{X}_f\left(\hat{\beta}^* - \hat{\beta}_f\right) + \left(\bar{X}_h - \bar{X}_f\right)\hat{\beta}^* + \left(\hat{\theta}_h\hat{\lambda}_h - \hat{\theta}_f\hat{\lambda}_f\right) \quad (15.7)$$

With $\bar{W}_h$ and $\bar{W}_f$ the means of the log expected wage of men and women respectively, $\bar{X}$ is the vector of the mean of the wage explanatory variables, $\hat{\beta}$ is the vector of the estimated returns to the wage determinants, $\hat{\beta}^*$ is the estimated non-discriminatory wage structure, $\hat{\theta}$ is an estimator of $\rho\sigma_\mu$, and $\hat{\lambda}$ is an estimator of the mean of the inverse Mills ratio.

The wage decomposition expression (Eq. 15.7) consists of four terms: the first two represent the part of the wage gap, in terms of performance, that is generally attributed to discrimination by the employer (the first term represents the estimated male wage advantage, while the second represents the estimated female wage disadvantage). The third term is the estimate of the justified part of the pay gap, explained by differences in the productive characteristics of individuals. The fourth term represents the selectivity effect. Selectivity is treated as a separate component, which is the simplest approach in that it does not require any a priori assumption as to whether selectivity plays a role in individual characteristics or in their performance. This selectivity effect is decomposed and introduced into other terms. After this decomposition, we obtain:

$$\begin{aligned}\bar{W}_h - \bar{W}_f = {} & \bar{X}_h\left(\hat{\beta}_h - \hat{\beta}^*\right) + \bar{X}_f\left(\hat{\beta}^* - \hat{\beta}_f\right) + \left(\bar{X}_h - \bar{X}_f\right)\hat{\beta}^* + \\ & \hat{\theta}_0\left(\hat{\lambda}_h - \hat{\lambda}_f^0\right) + \hat{\theta}_0\left(\hat{\lambda}_f^0 - \hat{\lambda}_f\right) + \left(\hat{\theta}_h - \hat{\theta}_0\right)\hat{\lambda}_h + \left(\hat{\theta}_0 - \hat{\theta}_f\right)\hat{\lambda}_f \\ \bar{W}_h - \bar{W}_f = {} & \underbrace{\bar{X}_h\left(\hat{\beta}_h - \hat{\beta}^*\right) + \bar{X}_f\left(\hat{\beta}^* - \hat{\beta}_f\right) + \hat{\theta}_0\left(\hat{\lambda}_f^0 - \hat{\lambda}_f\right) + \left(\hat{\theta}_h - \hat{\theta}_0\right)\hat{\lambda}_h + \left(\hat{\theta}_0 - \hat{\theta}_f\right)\hat{\lambda}_f}_{\text{discrimination}} \\ & \underbrace{+\left(\bar{X}_h - \bar{X}_f\right)\hat{\beta}^* + \hat{\theta}_0\left(\hat{\lambda}_h - \hat{\lambda}_f^0\right)}_{\text{endowment}}\end{aligned} \quad (15.8)$$

The terms contained in discrimination can be interpreted as unjustified pay differentials, while the endowment is the justified part of the pay differential explained by differences in the productive characteristics of individuals (Dupray & Moullet, 2004).

In Cameroon, the data sources that gather information to quantify the more recent evolution of wage discrimination are the ECAM II, ECAM III, and ECAM IV databases, which are respectively the second, third, and fourth Cameroon Household Consumption Surveys conducted in 2001, 2007, and 2014. These surveys covered the whole of the country. The operation concerned all ordinary households residing throughout the country. The various sections of the survey questionnaires covered the following areas, among others: health of household members, education, employment and income, domestic work and child labour, household standing and equipment, assets, household environment, residential mobility and migration, accessibility to basic infrastructure, agriculture and rural activities, governance and corruption, domestic tourism, household expenditure, and final consumption. A sample of 10,992 households (ECAM 2), 12,609 households (ECAM 3), and 13,000 households (ECAM 4) at national level was planned, with a margin of 5–10% for non-responses. According to studies carried out previously and elsewhere, this size was sufficient to obtain key indicators on poverty and household living standards with a satisfactory degree of precision at stratum level (NSI, 2012b, 2012c, 2017).

We restrict our analyses to individuals aged from 15 to 60, who declare themselves to be employed and receive a salary. The wage variable is the logarithm of the declared monthly income, either as an amount or as an interval. It includes wages, salaries, and other earnings in cash arising from the activity. For the self-employed, it also corresponds to the net business income, i.e., the profit, or to the mixed income for the Informal Production Units, as the profit is difficult to calculate in their case. The variables selected to explain income are age, age squared, gender, level of education, experience, experience squared, institutional sector, socio-professional category, professional training, place of residence, and marital status.

4 The Results

The results can be found in the tables below. Table 15.1 presents the results of the decomposition in a global way, while Table 15.2 gives the detailed effects of the variables.

The wage-earning population considered is that aged between 15 and 60. The estimated average monthly wage for men is higher than for

Table 15.1 Decomposition of the gender wage differentials

	2001 coefficients	*2007 coefficients*	*2014 coefficients*
Men	10.3983	10.4791	10.4493
Women	9.6752	9.9555	9.7695
Total difference	0.7230 (100%)	0.5236 (100%)	0.6798 (100%)
Explained	0.3014 (41.68%)	0.2586 (49.4%)	0.2736 (40.24%)
Non-explained	0.4216 (58.32%)	0.2650 (50.6%)	0.4062 (59.76%)

Notes: Neuman-Oaxaca decomposition. Group 1 (men): sex = 0; Group 2 (women): sex = 1; the group "sex = 1" is the reference group

Sources: Author

women. Indeed, the estimated average log wage for men is 10.39 in 2001, while that of women is 9.67; i.e., there is a gender wage gap of 0.72 in 2001; it is 10.47 for men and 9.95 for women in 2007, i.e., a gender wage gap of 0.52; in 2014, it is 10.45 for men and 9.76 for women, i.e., a gender wage gap of 0.67.

The decomposition of this gap shows that the explained share related to differences in individual characteristics is 41.68% of the total gap in 2001, 44.84% in 2007, and 40.24% in 2014. The unexplained proportion associated with differences in returns to individual characteristics and attributed to wage discrimination is 58.32% in 2001, 55.16% in 2007, and 59.76% in 2014. Our decomposition results thus support the hypothesis of discrimination against women in the labour market. The wage gap decreased from 2001 to 2007 and increased between 2007 and 2014. This can be explained by the fact that the situation of women in the labour market has not improved despite all the policies implemented. These results corroborate the World Economic Forum's finding that it takes 202 years for the average wage of men to equal to that of women (ILO, 2019).

Looking at the decomposition of the different variables in Table 15.2, those variables that contribute most to the wage gap are age, followed by experience, socio-professional category, sector of activity, and place of living. We see that there is a clear effect of human capital variables on wage differentials. Indeed, the wage gap in terms of year of study is negative, i.e., −11.85%, −8.71%, and −14.72% in 2001, 2007, and 2014 respectively. This means that the more educated women receive, on average, a higher salary than men matching the same characteristics. In this case, it is

Table 15.2 Decomposition of the wage gap variables

	2001			2007			2014		
Decomposition of the gap	*C*	*D*	*Total difference C + D*	*C*	*D*	*Total difference C + D*	*C*	*D*	*Total difference C + D*
	0.3014 (41.68%)	**0.4216 (58.32%)**	**0.7230 (100%)**	**0.2586 (49.4%)**	**0.2650 (50.6%)**	**0.5236 (100%)**	**0.2736 (40.24%)**	**0.4062 (59.76%)**	**0.6798 (100%)**
Age	−0.2186	0.9037	0.6851 (94.75%)	−0.2489	0.7596	0.5106 (97.52%)	−0.1579	0.7329	0.575 (84.58%)
$Age^2/100$	−0.2396	−0.5972	−0.8368 (−115.73%)	0.2457	−0.4864	−0.2407 (−45.96%)	0.0511	−0.1086	−0.0575 (−8.45%)
Education	0.0220	−0.1077	−0.0857 (−11.85%)	0.0610	−0.1067	−0.0456 (−8.71%)	0.0321	−0.1322	−0.1001 (−14.72%)
Experience	−0.0279	0.3073	0.3352 (46.36%)	−0.0213	0.1356	0.1143 (21.83%)	0.0370	0.3035	0.3405 (50.08%)
$Experience^2$	0.0051	−0.0102	−0.0051 (−0.70%)	0.0230	−0.0598	−0.0368 (−7.03%)	−0.0508	0.00003	−0.0507 (−7.45%)
Single person	0.1545	−0.2103	−0.0558 (−7.71%)	0.0655	−0.1566	−0.0911 (−17.39%)	−0.0042	−0.1306	−0.1348 (−19.82)
Senior managers	0.1779	−0.2103	−0.0324 (−4.48%)	0.0806	0.0154	0.0961 (18.36%)	0.2142	−0.0244	0.1898 (27.91%)
Skilled workers	0.1595	−0.0251	0.1344 (18.59%)	0.2218	0.0276	0.2495 (47.65%)	0.4747	−0.0844	0.3903 (57.41%)
Manoeuvres	0.2008	−0.0357	−0.1651 (−22.83%)	0.05831	0.0057	0.0640 (12.23%)	0.4436	−0.0232	0.4204 (61.84%)

(*continued*)

Table 15.2 (continued)

	2001			2007			2014		
Decomposition of the gap	*C*	*D*	*Total difference C + D*	*C*	*D*	*Total difference C + D*	*C*	*D*	*Total difference C + D*
Business owner	0.0342	−0.0103	0.0239 (3.3%)	0.0670	0.0024	0.0695 (13.27%)	0.0843	−0.0394	0.0449 (6.6%)
Self-employed workers	−0.5120	−0.0241	−0.5331 (−73.73%)	−0.3530	0.1275	−0.2255 (−43.06%)	−0.6620	−0.6543	−1.3163 (−193.63%)
Formal sector	0.0967	−0.0109	0.0858 (11.86%)	0.0550	−0.0205	0.0344 (6.58%)	0.0496	−0.0146	0.035 (5.14%)
Urban milieu	−0.0307	0.2153	0.1846 (25.53%)	0.0035	0.0515	0.0550 (10.51%)	0.0605	−0.0861	−0.0256 (−3.76%)

Notes: Neuman-Oaxaca decomposition; two-step Heckman model. Values in brackets are the contributions of the variables to the total variance. Group 1 (men): sex = 0; Group 2 (women): sex = 1

The informal sector modality is the reference modality for the institutional sector, the apprentice and family helper modality is the reference modality for the socio-professional categories, the married status modality is the reference modality for marital status. C: part in the difference in individual characteristics between men and women; D: part attributed to discrimination

Source: Author

the men who are discriminated against. An additional year of study would therefore reduce the probability that a woman is discriminated against.

The gender gap, in terms of experience, is 46.36%, 21.83%, and 50.08% respectively in 2001, 2007, and 2014. The difference in income between men and women is said to be due to the fact that, increasingly, in the Cameroonian labour market, the large-scale entrance of women with a high level of human capital no longer guarantees access to a better income. Women have to acquire longer experience in the labour market before they can access employment. This keeps many of them unemployed and therefore without income, or puts them into a precarious situation with a low income.

The effect of socio-professional category on the wage gap is also observable and is in favour of men among senior managers, skilled workers, and business owners. However, in the self-employed category, the wage differential is in favour of women from 2001 to 2014. This is the variable that contributes the most to the total gender wage differential. The negative sign of the unexplained share indicates that the categories "senior managers", "manoeuvre", "skilled workers", "business owner", and "self-employed" are variables that increase wage discrimination in 2001 and 2014. However, the last category is to the disadvantage of men.

Analysed by employment sector, the average wage gap is less present in the formal sector, with a gap of 11.86%, 6.58%, and 5.14%, respectively, in 2001, 2007, and 2014 in favour of men. Moreover, the negative sign of its coefficient of the unexplained share shows that the formal sector reinforces the phenomenon of discrimination against women. As far as place of living, the wage gap in urban milieux is 25.53% in 2002 and 10.51% in 2007 in favour of men and 3.76% in 2014 in favour of women. This gap is related more to individual characteristics of men and women than to discrimination. While increasing discrimination, urbanisation favours wage discrimination against women until 2007. In 2014, this is not the case.

Our results corroborate the findings of Baye et al. (2016), who show that women are penalised in terms of wages and that gender wage gaps are explained by individual and labour-market characteristics. Overall, it turns out that wage discrimination explains more than half of the gender wage gap, while the relative contribution of the structural effects of individual attributes accounts for just over 45% of the overall gap.

5 Conclusion

The objective of this study was to determine the evolution of the gender wage gap in the Cameroonian labour market. The decomposition of the gender pay gap has made it possible to isolate a residual that cannot be explained by the traditional factors of pay inequality. This residual, attributed to gender pay discrimination, indicates the extent to which the principle of "equal pay for equal work" is not respected. The estimation of the gender pay gap has shown that wage discrimination is an entrenched phenomenon among the employed population in the urban environment. The variables that contribute most to the wage gap are age squared, followed by experience and the informal sector. The variables that reduce discrimination against women are age, years of education, experience squared, and the job category "self-employed".

This study highlights the persistence of the gender pay gap over several years. Moreover, it shows that this persistent gap is largely a consequence of the structure of the labour market and is linked to different positions of women and men in this market. Despite the government's efforts to reduce inequalities in the labour market by promoting gender equality in certain recruitments, gender equality in income is still far from being achieved and much remains to be done to reduce these gender inequalities. Emphasis should be placed not only on the education of female children, but also on access of women to higher-paid job categories.

Furthermore, in Cameroon, employment problems show themselves more in terms of underemployment. This underemployment affects women much more than men because women are represented far more in informal sector activities that are not recognised, registered, protected, or regulated by the public authorities. Hence there is a need to act to improve working conditions in the informal sector, with a view to enhancing the value of women's work and strengthening their professionalism, which is the only way to ensure that their salary conditions are revised.

Conflicts of Interest The author has no conflicts of interest to declare that are relevant to the content of this chapter.

References

Anker, R. (1997). Ségrégation professionnelle hommes—Femmes: Les théories en présence. *Revue Internationale du Travail, 136*(3), 343–370.

Baye, F., Epo, B. N., & Ndenzako, J. (2016). Wage Differentials in Cameroon: A Gendered Analysis. *African Development Review, 28*(1), 75–91. https://doi.org/10.1111/1467-8268.12168

Becker, G. S. (1957). *The Economics of Discrimination* (2nd ed., 1971). University of Chicago Press.

Becker, G. S. (1964). *Human Capital, A Theoretical and Empirical Analysis, with Special Reference to Education.* Columbia University Press.

Blau, F. D., & Kahn, L. M. (1999). Analyzing the Gender Pay Gap. *The Quarterly Review of Economics and Finance, 39*, 625–646. https://doi.org/10.1016/S1062-9769(99)00021-6

Blau, F. D., & Kahn, L. M. (2017). The Gender Wage Gap: Extent, Trends, and Explanations. *Journal of Economic Literature, 55*(3), 789–865. https://doi.org/10.1257/jel.20160995

Blinder, A. S. (1973). Wage Discrimination, Reduced Form and Structural Estimates. *The Journal of Human Resources, 8*(4), 436–455. https://doi.org/10.2307/144855

Doumbia, S., & Meurs, D. (2003). Quelle égalité professionnelle entre les hommes et les femmes dans le secteur moderne en Afrique? L'exemple du Mali. *Revue Internationale du Travail, 142*(3), 321–344.

Dupray, A., & Moullet, S. (2004). Quelles discriminations à l'encontre des jeunes d'origine maghrébine à l'entrée sur le marché du travail en France. *Brussels Economic Review*. In L. Achy (Ed.), *Marché du travail et genre: Maghreb-Europe*. ULB—Université Libre de Bruxelles.

Ekamena, N. S. N. (2014). Les Ecarts Salariaux de Genre au Cameroun. *Revue multidisciplinaire sur l'emploi, le syndicalisme et le travail, 9*(2), 124–146. https://doi.org/10.7202/1036261ar

Heckman, J. J. (1979). Sample Selection Bias as a Specification Error. *Econometrica, 47*, 153–161. https://doi.org/10.2307/1912352

Hersch, J. (2006). Sex Discrimination in the Labor Market. *Foundations and Trends in Microeconomics, 2*(4), 281–361.

ILO. (2013). *Mesurer l'informalité: Manuel statistique sur le secteur informel et l'emploi informel.* International Labour Organisation. http://www.ilo.org/global/publications/ilo-bookstore/order-online/books/WCMS_222982/lang%2D%2Dfr/index.htm

ILO. (2017). *Genre et différences salariales dans les emplois formel et informel au Cameroun.* International Labour Organisation. https://www.ilo.org/africa/countries-covered/cameroon/facet/WCMS_625015/lang%2D%2Dfr/index.htm

ILO. (2019). *Women in Business and Management: The Business Case for Change.* International Labour Organisation. https://www.ilo.org/global/publications/books/WCMS_700953/lang%2D%2Den/index.htm

Meurs, D., & Ponthieux, S. (2006). Une mesure de la discrimination dans l'écart des salaires entre hommes et femmes. *Economie et Statistique, 337–338*, 135–158. https://doi.org/10.3406/estat.2006.7119

Mincer, J., & Polachek, S. (1974). Family Investments in Human Capital, Earnings of Women. *Journal of Political Economy, 82*(2), 76–108. https://doi.org/10.1086/260293

Ministry of Women Empowerment and the Family. (2012). Femmes et hommes au Cameroun en 2012. Une analyse situationnelle de progrès en matière de genre.

Neuman, S., & Oaxaca, R. L. (1998). *Estimating Labour Market Discrimination with Selectivity Corrected Wage Equations: Methodological Considerations and an Illustration from Israel.* CEPR Discussion Paper No. 1915. CEPR Press, Paris & London. https://cepr.org/publications/dp1915

Neuman, S., & Oaxaca, R. L. (2004). Wage Decompositions with Selectivity-Corrected Wage Equations, A Methodological Note. *Journal of Economic Inequality, 2*(1), 3–10. https://doi.org/10.1023/B:JOEI.0000028395.38694.4b

NSI. (2010). *Enquête sur l'Emploi et le Secteur Informel.* National Statistics Institute. https://slmp-550-104.slc.westdc.net/~stat54/nada/index.php/catalog/1

NSI. (2012a). *Autonomiser les Femmes Rurales pour éradiquer la Faim et la Pauvreté. Que Révèlent les Indicateurs?, 27ème Journée Internationale de la Femme.* National Statistics Institute. https://ins-cameroun.cm/en/document/rapport-national-annee-2012/

NSI. (2012b). *Deuxième Enquête Camerounaise Auprès des Ménages 2001 (ECAM-II).* National Statistics Institute. https://slmp-550-104.slc.westdc.net/~stat54/nada/index.php/catalog/20

NSI. (2012c). *Troisième Enquête Camerounaise Auprès des Ménages 2007 (ECAM-III).* National Statistics Institute. https://catalog.ihsn.org/catalog/2256

NSI. (2017). *Quatrième Enquête Camerounaise Auprès des Ménages 2007 (ECAM-IV).* National Statistics Institute. http://slmp-550-104.slc.westdc.net/~stat54/nada/index.php/catalog/114

NSI. (2022). *Troisième Enquête Sur L'emploi Et Le Secteur Informel Au Cameroun (EESI3), Rapport Principal.* National Statistics Institute.

Oaxaca, R. L. (1973). Male-Female Wage Differentials in Urban Labour Markets. *International Economic Review, 14*, 693–704. https://doi.org/10.2307/2525981

Phelps, E. (1972). The Statistical Theory of Racism and Sexism. *American Economic Review, 62*, 659–661. https://www.jstor.org/stable/1806107

Rosen, S. (1986). The Theory of Equalizing Differences. In O. Ashenfelter & R. Layard (Eds.), Handbook of Labor Economics, 1(12), 641–692, North-Holland, . https://doi.org/10.1016/S1573-4463(86)01015-5

World Economic Forum. (2017). *The Global Gender Gap Report*. Cologny/Geneva. https://www3.weforum.org/docs/WEF_GGGR_2017.pdf

CHAPTER 16

Conclusion: Labour, a Highly Political Issue with Manifold Research Challenges

Eveline Baumann

1 Introduction

The authors of this book were driven by a daunting challenge: analysing wage issues not only in countries south of the Sahara, but also in the North Africa and Middle East (MENA) region. This required accounting for highly diverse contexts, including demographic dynamics, range of economic sectors, work and life conditions, and factors influencing salaried work and self-employment beyond economic criteria. First, the specificities and common features of salaried work in the countries concerned will be highlighted. This leads us, in a second place, to consider the world of labour in its entirety, with formal and informal practices being closely intertwined. Finally, the political issue of labour is questioned through demographic dynamics and the risk of political unrest.

E. Baumann (✉)
Université Paris Cité, Paris, France
e-mail: eveline.baumann@ird.fr

M.-P. Chelini et al. (eds.), *Wage Dynamics in Africa*, African Histories and Modernities,
https://doi.org/10.1007/978-3-031-99800-3_16

2 Main Findings

Addressing labour issues in such a broad range of countries turned out to be a valuable asset. It confirmed, firstly, that there is a positive correlation between the increase in wage labour and GDP and, secondly, that the boundary between formal and informal businesses and jobs can shift towards more or less formality. Thus, with all due caution, we can say that the situation in the MENA region augurs well for the development of emerging countries in sub-Saharan Africa.

Modern wage theory has a long history, dating back to the sixteenth century (Chap. 1). Little by little, a divide has been established between micro- and macroeconomic approaches. This divide poses a challenge in addressing key topics, such as subsistence, labour productivity, and the balance between labour supply and demand. Nascent urbanisation has put forward migration as a central concern (Chap. 3). Structural adjustment programmes further contributed to theoretical advancements. However, limited statistical data hamper the development of reliable time series (Chap. 2). Undoubtedly, the major theoretical and interpretative challenge consists in coming up against the high degree of disparity in sub-Saharan African and, to a lesser extent, in the MENA region.

The ubiquity of informal jobs and self-employment is the main characteristic of labour; salaried work concerns only a minority of the working-age population. What is more, wages increase very slowly. Interestingly, however, the gender pay gap aligns with the global average. Whilst some African countries may be considered as emerging countries, due to their large market, the structure of their production system, and overall growth (Chap. 5), informal activities are still widespread in these countries. From an anthropological perspective, pre-market phenomena are ubiquitous and continue to play a considerable role (Chap. 4). These dynamics contradict ambitions by national decision makers and international organisations and call for a qualitative approach that bridges the gap between micro- and macro-level methods. All things considered, we might well ask whether the wage-earning society is not more of a historical exception and at least in sub-Saharan Africa a less likely objective to be attained.

Measuring income inequality is a major focus in the field of labour studies (Part II). However, there is a lack of surveys tailored to the specificities of wage work, and accounting for the various forms of remuneration, including implicit wages, such as hosting and different kinds of "social expenses" provided by the informal employers. As a result, experts are forced to rely on household surveys and analyse inequality through expenditure. Unsurprisingly, the quality of data is likely to vary over time, due to factors such as political regime changes (Chap. 7), breaking political initiatives like the Structural adjustment programmes or major events like the Covid-19 pandemic. In addition, there is a growing demand to include other indicators, such as access to health services and social provisions. In several MENA countries, perceptions of inequality do not match the outcome of data analysis (Chap. 6). This discrepancy may be attributed to heightened awareness of inequalities following the Arab spring revolutions and social media influence. The prevalence of informal activities has exacerbated inequality, whilst urbanisation and heightened school enrolment decreased inequality, as illustrated for Morocco (Chap. 8).

Part III explores inequalities through people's strategies to escape precarity. The widespread market economy plays a decisive role in shaping perceptions of work and workers. Structural adjustment plans, in particular, have had far-reaching consequences. The repercussions of these programmes for university graduates in Senegal, for example, raise questions about the validity of the term "labour market" (Chap. 9). And, multilevel modelling with higher education graduates in Tunisia illustrates how a substantial increase in tertiary education enrolment resulted in alarming levels of unemployment among graduates; this situation challenges the idea of high private return on investment in education (Chap. 10). Graduates generally lack practical skills facilitating their access to jobs in registered companies. In this regard, the state does not always live up to its responsibilities, opening opportunities for civil society organisations (Chap. 12). Finally, societal values regarding labour status have greatly evolved over time. In Mauritania, for example, salaried work was highly valued in the 1960s and 1970s, but has currently lost its prestige (Chap. 11).

Part IV delves into the question of youth and gender dynamics. In countries like Egypt and Jordan, there is a pressing need for growing regulation of informal employment, at least as concerns the upper tier (Chap. 13). Whereas data collection is a pre-requisite in this respect, not-for-profit organisations are set to play a key role. As to gender, examined in Senegal, the wage disparity cannot solely be attributed to differences in productivity, but is undeniably influenced by deep-rooted local norms (Chap. 14). These norms are also responsible for the persistent gender pay gap in Cameroon. Indeed, women tend to be confined to lower-status and poorly paid occupations, which emphasises the urgent need for a greater focus on the education of female children (Chap. 15).

Several common threads run throughout the chapters of this book. Firstly, investigations targeting specifically labour and remuneration are rare. As a result, household surveys are often drawn on, because they provide valuable insight into wage issues. Secondly, heterogeneity of the labour landscape, both among and within countries, is vast. Wage-earners make up a minority in the examined countries, and the wage sector is growing very slowly. Thirdly, the gender pay gap is comparable to other regions of the world. It is deeply rooted in society and difficult to overcome, given the very structure of the labour market. Fourthly, education plays a significant role in increasing wage labour. However, what can be seen as a rational investment on the individual level conflicts with the limits of overall labour demand. Lastly, given the demographic dynamics, it is highly unlikely that a wage-earning society will emerge in the near future, particularly in sub-Sahara Africa. We can assume that the development of IT-driven jobs will not change this situation, at least in the near future.

Therefore, the challenges for public policy are tremendous. There is evidence that the "one model fits all" approach, which was favoured during the time of the structural adjustment programmes, has shown its limitations. As a result, it is necessary to find appropriate solutions that take into account the specificities of each local context.

This leads us to go beyond wage issues and consider the world of work as a whole.

3 From Wage to Labour Issues

Despite the increasing professionalism of national statistical offices, reliable data on labour still lags behind statistical information on other fields. There are a number of reasons for this. Firstly, in many countries data collection depends, at least partially, on the priorities of the donor community, who may prefer to fund surveys on health and education, rather than labour issues. Secondly, from a political perspective, labour data is highly sensitive, which is particularly true for unemployment. Therefore, in some political regimes, national decision makers may not necessarily be keen to disclose information that reveals the failure of public policies. Thirdly, the labour landscape in the Global South is extremely complex and intrinsically polymorphous, posing tremendous challenges for experts and researchers.

Limited availability and reliability of data concern particularly informal activities. On the one hand, these activities refer to self-employment: it can correspond to a lifetime occupation, but also to an impromptu business deal that could just as suddenly vanish overnight. The spectrum of self-employment is vast, ranging from moto-taxi drivers and online gig workers to successful traders taking liberties with the legislation. Self-employed activities can be carried out in parallel to wage labour, be it in a large company or the civil service. On the other hand, informality is also at work when wage workers in duly registered companies are denied pay slips or when domestic chores are at stake (Charmes, 2019). As a result, the analytical distinction between formal and informal labour does not hold in reality, because people may straddle both spheres simultaneously throughout their lives. This vision has given way to the idea of a continuum of situations rather than an "informal sector" (Koçer, 2016; Lautier, 1994).

Perpetual straddling goes beyond the informal/formal divide. In practical terms, informal activities constitute "a way of doing things" (ILO, 1972:6) that permeates the entire range of economic activities. This "way of doing things" goes hand in hand with a specific attitude towards insecurity and life risks, ensuring that short- and long-term perspectives are coordinated while respecting social standards. Risks are spread on the individual level, but also within the family and the kinship, which gives way to multiactivity between and within economic sectors. Insofar, multiactivity is part of the social habitus, just like mixed cropping in a hostile natural environment (Baumann, 1984; Wallace, 1973). Undoubtedly, this contributes to higher acceptability of precarious working conditions, including in the platform economy, which also dampens work-related conflicts and hampers unionisation.

Besides these manifold aspects referring to everyday practices and attitudes towards labour, data collection comes up against statistical constraints: the categories used to describe labour in the Global South are designed by and for the Global North. First of all, the opposition between work and leisure is a recent invention and does not operate in the same way everywhere. Secondly, even distinctions between employment and unemployment are not naturally given. As Karl Polanyi has pointed out, these oppositions are particularly questionable in societies where the economy continues to be largely embedded in society and high value is given to physical work (2001).

What does it mean to be unemployed if there are no unemployment benefits and a small supplier credit enables people to become street vendors, selling Kleenex tissues or cigarettes on a busy crossroads? Is a jobless person who spends hours visiting influential people to find out about job opportunities not working? And while idleness is frequently considered shameful, as many sayings and proverbs testify (Bagayoko, 1991; Baumann, 2016:22–23; Gaden, 1931:207–215), what about a jobless person who leaves home every morning, pretending he or she is "in business"?

Under-employment is without any doubt a problematic question, too. For instance, when self-employed workers feel that the number of hours they work is insufficient to guarantee an acceptable standard of living. According to ILO (International Labour Organization) definition, these people are under-employed. However, is not it worth questioning, more generally, the "global standard" for working hours? As Sahlins put it "the manner by which labor-power is withheld from production is not everywhere the same. The institutional modalities vary considerably: from marked cultural abbreviations of the individual working-life span to immoderate standards of relaxation—or, what is probably a better understanding of the latter, very moderate standards of 'sufficient work'" (2011:51–52).

These different aspects of labour are of the outmost importance from a socioeconomic and anthropological perspective. At the same time, they give the impression that quantitative analysis is a procrustean bed for in-depth understanding of labour. This contrast may give way to the mutual ignorance stressed by Philippe Adair in Chap. 1.

4 Remaining Challenges: Youthfulness, the Age Dependency Ratio, and Political Unrest

Youthfulness, prevailing precarity, and high disparities in living conditions are prominent aspects of everyday life in sub-Saharan countries and the MENA region.

Let us begin by considering demographic dynamics. Although population growth is declining, it remains relatively high in sub-Saharan Africa (2.5% <), with each woman giving birth to four or five children. Whilst the process of population ageing is just beginning, the demographic transition in the region is occurring slowly. The situation in the MENA countries is quite different. On average, women there give birth to two or three children; the fertility rate has been divided by 2.4 between 1980 and 2021.

Despite this decline, the population still grows at a rate of 1.5% per year (2022), which is more than four times higher than in the EU (0.34 in 2022). Youthfulness is reflected in the median age, which divides the population into two equal parts. In 2023, half of the population in Western Europe was either younger or older than 43.2 years. In sub-Saharan Africa, the median age was 17.8, while in the MENA region, it ranged from 18.6 in Sudan to 32.3 in Tunisia (UN Population Division, 2024).

The average income level is low, ranging from $ 4400 per year in Eastern and Southern Africa to $ 14,100 in the MENA region in 2023.[1] Given the demographic dynamics, GDP growth per capita is low. Between 2010 and 2023, GDP p.c. increased at an average of 0.95% by year in Western and Central Africa, 0.12% in Eastern and Southern Africa, and 0.38% in the MENA region. What is more, wealth is distributed unequally and precarity is ubiquitous, whether in terms of access to health services and education, transportation, or housing (World Bank, 2025).

It is not sufficient to solely examine youthfulness. Rather, it should be analysed in conjunction with the age dependency ratio, which brings us back to the questions posed in this book. The age dependency ratio measures the proportion of dependents—individuals under 15 and over 65—in relation to the working-age population. By considering this ratio, valuable insight can be gleaned into the obligations placed upon those who are employed (or unemployed). It is their responsibility to provide housing, food, education, and healthcare for their dependents. Given the extreme youthfulness of the examined countries, the dependency ratio is particularly high, compared to high-income countries. As a result, in 2023 the age dependency ratio is lower in the MENA region, with 57 dependents for 100 working-age persons, compared to 81 in Western and Central Africa, and 79 in Eastern and Southern Africa.

The higher the dependency ratio, the lower the tax income and resources allocated to education and health services. The prevalence of informal activities avoiding taxation has also a negative impact on fiscal resources. Consequently, it is not surprising that the overall quality of education and vocational training is generally poor, and out-of-pocket

[1] GDP p.c. in purchasing power parity, in current international dollars. Regarding the MENA region, data in the following paragraphs does not include high-income countries. In OECD countries the annual GDP p.c. in PPP was 55,700 USD (World Bank, 2025).

expenses for healthcare services are high.[2] Additionally, public employment policy faces powerful challenges as cohorts likely to apply for jobs continue to grow at a high speed.

On the one hand, the age dependency ratio is closely connected to both fertility and population ageing. Factors such as socially determined reproduction patterns, reproductive health, elderly care, and risk coping strategies, both private and public, play a crucial role in this matter. These factors are significantly influenced by education and urbanisation. On the other hand, the age dependency ratio also depends on job opportunities and public policies that aim to encourage both salaried work and self-employment.

Whilst public authorities have only limited control over fertility, the challenges for public policy are tremendous, because social discontent is widespread, particularly among younger generations. Since the mid-2000s, various factors have fostered social malaise and led to dramatic changes both domestically and internationally. On the one hand, political events such as the Arab Spring revolutions and military coups, for example, in Guinea, Mali, Burkina Faso, Niger, Chad, Sudan, and Gabon, have dramatically reshaped the political landscape. On the other hand, climate change, the Covid-19 pandemic, and the war in Ukraine have had a profound impact on people's life. In response to these challenges, young people have emerged as key actors, violently expressing their dissatisfaction, but also showing potential as regards change through democratic processes. This was clearly demonstrated in the 2024 Senegalese presidential elections, when frustrated young people played a pivotal role in seeking to replace older elites who were perceived as self-interested and solely motivated by personal gain.[3]

Being young may have negative consequences in terms of overall wealth but can also be a valuable asset for a country. Absorbing new knowledge is accelerated by youthfulness, resulting in faster development, regardless of how development is defined. However, certain conditions must be met in order to fully harness this potential. Firstly, there has to be the right number of schools throughout the country, not just in urban areas. Furthermore,

[2] In 2020, out-of-pocket expenditure (as a percentage of current health expenditure) varies between 15% in Eastern and South Africa and 58% in Western Africa, compared to 44% in the MENA region and 12% in OECD countries (World Bank, 2025).

[3] The political programme of the elected president illustrates this wish of an in-depth renewal. See Faye (2024).

teachers need to be well-trained, and education and vocational skills must align with the needs of the economy. Secondly, there should also be a genuine demand for education from parents, which is not always the case, as in some rural areas, where limited workforce availability may prevent parents from sending their children to school.

Nigeria is a good example of what is at stake in this regard. Indeed, leaving aside the country's specific characteristics linked to its hydrocarbon-based economy, the scale and intensity of the phenomena taking place there are likely to foreshadow what could happen in other countries, in a context of rampant insecurity and economic crises, which are, among others, an outcome of global warming.

With a population of 228 million inhabitants in 2023, Nigeria is not only Africa's most populous country; it is also one of the African partner countries of the BRICS bloc. Undoubtedly, this mirrors the country's geo-strategical importance, particularly in the light of the Chinese Belt and Road Initiative. However, given tremendous shortcomings as regards governance as well as manifold environmental problems such as desertification, erosion, and pollution, Nigeria underperforms (BTI, 2024:23), and its GDP p.c. expressed in purchasing power is only a third of that of Egypt with 110 million inhabitants (World Bank, 2025).

More than two-thirds of Nigerians are under 30, but decision makers and entrepreneurs are experiencing tremendous difficulties to capitalise on the youth of the population. By 2030, more than 40 million new jobs will be needed. Wage work is expected to concern only one worker out of ten. Five out of ten first-time jobseekers will make a living out of household agriculture, and 13 million will engage in non-farm household enterprises (Jenq et al., 2021:112–113). In general, any crisis, be it the oil price recession in 2016, Covid-19, or turmoil regarding the national currency, leads to a substantial increase of household agriculture,[4] with working youth (and early school-leavers) being over-represented.

The imbalance between jobseekers and labour demand is particularly detrimental to the growing number of Nigerians with post-secondary education. Their share of the population increased from 12% in 2010 to 18% in 2019 (Adhikari et al., 2021:27). Unsurprisingly, out-migration is a widespread answer to the scarcity of jobs corresponding to their aspirations. What is more, the share of those considering emigration is

[4] Household agriculture concerned 26% of working-age Nigerians in 2010, and 10 percentage points more in 2019 (Jenq et al., 2021:110).

increasing dramatically. In 2017, 20% of all the Nigerians considered emigrating "a lot" or "somewhat"; in 2024, the percentage was as high a 43% (Afrobarometer, 2024).

By 2100, the Nigerian working-age population is projected to increase by 140%. Regarding the European working-age population, its decline is estimated at 30%. Inevitably, this situation will not only be a powerful driver for South–North labour migration, but also a conundrum for local decision makers who will have to arbitrate between short-term and long-term priorities.

To conclude, let us return to the question of the formal-informal divide. During the 50-year-long history of the concept of informality as a specificity of labour, the focus of researchers, donors, and decision makers has shifted from its description and etymological sense, to concerns about the exodus of rural labour, unemployment, insufficient overall growth, gender relations, access to loans, lack of social security, and the call for formalisation (Breman, 2023; Charmes & Adair, 2022; Peattie, 1987; Rosaldo, 2021). Informal activities therefore serve as a container to study diverse phenomena, on the micro, meso and macro level, including demographics, accounting and planification, poverty alleviation, education and vocational training, the social question, etc.

The idea of "decent work", brought to the fore by the ILO and adopted by the UN in the Sustainable development goals, is likely to bridge the gap between formal and informal activities (Barchiesi, 2019). This also means that ethical questions are increasingly legitimate when it comes to examine and work out labour policies. Some countries in sub-Saharan Africa and the MENA region—such as Cameroon, Senegal, Egypt, and Morocco—are currently introducing universal health coverage. These initiatives can be considered as a major step forward despite numerous shortcomings. However, what happens if jobs are as good as invisible? If jobs are only created sporadically or pay poor wages? When the wage-earning society is hardly likely to be attained in the near or even the distant future, as demonstrated by several chapters in this book? When tremendous digital transformations do not only give way to promising job perspectives (AUC/OECD, 2021), but also increase the gig workers' vulnerability and precariousness (Anwar & Graham, 2020)? In this case, the introduction of a universal basic income could be considered (Marais, 2022). This, however, requires a great deal of determination on the part of decision makers and a very strong political will.

Conflicts of Interest The author has no conflicts of interest to declare that are relevant to the content of this chapter.

References

Adhikari, S., Chaudhary, S., & Ekeator, N. L. (2021). *Of Roads Less Traveled: Assessing the Potential of Economic Migration to Provide Overseas Jobs for Nigeria's Youth*. World Bank.

Afrobarometer. (2024). *Majority of Nigerians Have Considered Emigration in Search of Opportunity*. Retrieved January 20, 2025, from https://www.noi-polls.com/post/nigerians-considering-emigration-for-opportunity

Anwar, M. A., & Graham, M. (2020). Between a Rock and a Hard Place: Freedom, Flexibility, Precarity and Vulnerability in the Gig Economy in Africa. *Competition & Change, 25*(2), 1–22. https://doi.org/10.1177/1024529420914473

AUC/OECD. (2021). *Africa's Development Dynamics 2021: Digital Transformation for Quality Jobs*. Addis Ababa/OECD Publishing. https://doi.org/10.1787/0a5c9314-en

Bagayoko, Y. (1991). *Initiation à la culture bamanan à travers les proverbes*. Association Malienne de Recherche-Action pour le Développement.

Barchiesi, F. (2019). Precarious and Informal Labour. In S. Bellucci & A. Eckert (Eds.), *General Labour History of Africa. Workers, Employers and Governments 20th–21st Centuries* (pp. 45–75). James Currey/Boydell & Brewer Ltd.

Baumann, E. (1984). *Les activités informelles en milieu rural, véhicule de transformations socio-économiques. Le cas du centre rural de Saa, Centre-Sud Cameroun*. Thèse 3ème cycle en Etudes africaines, Université de Bordeaux I, Centre d'Etude d'Afrique noire. https://doi.org/10.13140/2.1.1345.5685

Baumann, E. (2016). *Sénégal: Le travail dans tous ses états*. Presses universitaires de Rennes.

Bertelsmann Stiftung. (2024). *BTI 2024 Country Report—Nigeria*. Bertelsmann Stiftung.

Breman, J. (2023). A Short History of the Informal Economy. *Global Labour Journal, 14*(1), 21–39. https://doi.org/10.15173/glj.v14i1.5277

Charmes, J. (2019). *The Unpaid Care Work and the Labour Market. An Analysis of Time Use Date Based on the Latest World Compilation of Time-Use Surveys*.

Charmes, J., & Adair, P. (2022). Après un demi-siècle, l'économie informelle reste un concept heuristique et un ensemble flou? *Mondes en développement, 50*(3–4) (199–200), 255–274. https://doi.org/10.3917/med.199.0259

Faye, B. D. D. (2024). *Diomaye Président: Le projet #PDF*. Retrieved April, 25, 2024, from https://www.enligne.sn/diomaye-president-le-projet-pdf/

Gaden, H. (1931). *Proverbes et Maximes Peuls et Toucouleurs*. Institut d'ethnologie.

ILO. (1972). *Employment, Incomes and Equality. A Strategy for Increasing Productive Employment in Kenya*. ILO.

Jenq, C., Lain, J., & Vishwanath, T. (2021). Good Jobs for a New Generation: Delivering Quality Jobs for Young Nigerians after Covid-19. In World Bank (Ed.), *Nigeria. Charting a New Course. Country Economic Memorandum Technical Notes* (pp. 110–147). World Bank.

Koçer, R. G. (2016). *How Many Shades of Grey Are There? Continuum Conceptualization of Formal/Informal Divide and Its Implications.* Swiss Programme for Research on Global Issues for Development. R4D Working Paper 2016/5. World Trade Institute, Universität Bern.

Lautier, B. (1994). *L'économie informelle dans le tiers monde.* Collection Repères n°155, La Découverte.

Marais, H. (2022). *In the Balance. The Case for a Universal Basic Income in South Arica and Beyond.* Wits University Press.

Peattie, L. (1987). An Idea in Good Currency and How it Grew: The Informal Sector. *World Development, 15*(7), 851–860. https://doi.org/10.1016/0305-750X(87)90038-6

Polanyi, K. (2001). *The Great Transformation. The Political and Economic Origins of Our Time* (1st ed. 1944). Beacon Press.

Rosaldo, M. (2021). Problematizing the "Informal Sector": 50 Years of Critique, Clarification, Qualification, and More Critique. *Sociology Compass*, e12914. https://doi.org/10.1111/soc4.12914

Sahlins, M. (2011). *Stone Age Economics* (1st ed. 1972). Aldin Atherton Inc.

UN Population Division. (2024). *Interactive Access to Global Demographic Indicators.* Retrieved May 1, 2024, from https://population.un.org/

Wallace, T. (1973). Working in Rural Buganda: A Study of the Occupational Activities of Young People in Rural Villages. *The African Review: A Journal of African Politics, Development and International Affairs, 3*(1), 133–178. https://www.jstor.org/stable/45341274

World Bank. (2025). *World Development Indicators.* Retrieved January 20, 2025, from https://databank.worldbank.org

Index[1]

[1] Note: Page numbers followed by 'n' refer to notes.

M.-P. Chelini et al. (eds.), *Wage Dynamics in Africa*, African Histories and Modernities,
https://doi.org/10.1007/978-3-031-99800-3

FSC
www.fsc.org
MIX
Papier | Fördert gute Waldnutzung
FSC® C083411

Kolibri 360 GmbH
Ferdinand-Jühlke-Straße 7
99095 Erfurt, Deutschland
produktsicherheit@kolibri360.de